A Sense of the Heart

A Sense of the Heart

Christian Religious Experience in the United States

Bill J. Leonard

Abingdon Press
Nashville

A SENSE OF THE HEART:
CHRISTIAN RELIGIOUS EXPERIENCE IN THE UNITED STATES

This book is printed on acid-free paper.

Library of Congress Cataloging-in-Publication Data

Leonard, Bill (Bill J.)
A sense of the heart : Christian religious experience in the United States / Bill J. Leonard.
pages cm
Includes bibliographical references and index.
ISBN 978-1-4267-5490-6 (pbk., trade/adhesive perfect binding : alk. paper) 1. United States—Church history. 2. Experience (Religion) 3. Christianity–United States. I. Title.
BR515.L465 2014
277.3—dc23

2014021581

14 15 16 17 18 19 20 21 22 23—10 9 8 7 6 5 4 3 2 1

MANUFACTURED IN THE UNITED STATES OF AMERICA

To E. Glenn Hinson and Roger Gottlieb, great scholars, mentors and friends. One Christian, the other Jewish, both plumb the depths of religious experience within the "spirituality of resistance." I am forever grateful.

Contents

Preface

This book explores the varied nature and forms of religious experience evident among Christian individuals and communities in the United States from the colonial period to the beginning of the twenty-first century. Such experiences encompassed a broad spectrum that included conversions and revivals, holiness codes and Holy Ghost baptisms, communes and séances, mystical fervor and spiritual exploration, theological debates and denominational schisms, slave revolts and sacramental rites.

Given the wide variety of religious encounters present throughout the nation's history, a study such as this must be representative rather than all-inclusive, surveying diverse and illustrative expressions of religious experience in varying eras and specific contexts. For one thing, it examines the nurturing sacramentalism of liturgy and ritual that often marks entry into religious community, what William James warily labeled "second-hand religious life," created "by others... communicated... by tradition, determined... by imitation, and retained by habit."[1] Protestant leaders such as Horace Bushnell affirmed the power of this "Christian nurture" in drawing young persons to faith, in order "that the child is to grow up a Christian, and never know... otherwise,"[2] while German Reformed theologian John Williamson Nevin invoked the "action generated by the system of the Catechism for the great purposes of the gospel" in teaching and extending the faith.[3] Father Isaac Hecker, founder of the Paulists, linked religious experience with the sacramental grace by which "the Church has provided the means for the salvation of the Soul of the Sinner by spiritual acts such as prayer pennance [*sic*] Eucharist and her 7 Sacraments."[4] "Once-born" individuals claim their own response to religious experience.

Yet the book also engages, in James's words, "experiences we can only find in individuals for whom religion exists not as a dull habit, but as an acute fever."[5] That spiritual fever burned in Jonathan Edwards's four-year-old parishioner Phoebe Bartlet as she shrieked from her closet, "Pray, blessed Lord, give me salvation! I pray, beg, pardon all my sins!"[6] Such feverish experiences were observed by Barton W. Stone at the 1801 camp meeting in Logan County, Kentucky: "The scene to me was new and passing strange. It baffled description. Many, very many fell down... and continued for hours together in an apparently breathless and motionless state—sometimes for a few moments reviving, and exhibiting symptoms of life by a deep groan, or piercing shriek, or by a prayer for mercy most fervently uttered."[7] If less fevered, the intensity of Ralph Waldo Emerson's transcendentalist experientialism led him to challenge the corpse-cold rationalism of Calvinist and Unitarian alike. Experiential fever burned deeply in the African American preacher Jarena Lee, even when the male-dominated pulpit tradition of her day attempted to extinguish it. Some, Millerites and Premillennialists, for example, urged immediate salvific encounters before the impending return of Jesus Christ; others—Shakers, Mormons, Oneidaites—believed that their communitarian environment anticipated the impending kingdom of God. Religious experience both galvanized and polarized Evangelicals and Pentecostals, Fundamentalists and Liberals, even as it shaped the nature of certain eclectic "Spirituality Movements" for persons purporting to be spiritual but not religious.

Chapters survey those approaches, chronologically and topically, with particular attention to cultural and theological contexts, thus reflecting Matthew Bagger's assertion that "different cultures and historical epochs can take different stances regarding the justification of certain beliefs," experiences, and practices.[8] This is particularly true, as Jeffrey Stout suggested, since "the rationality of a given person's beliefs or actions is relative to the reasons or reasoning available to that person. And the availability of reasons and reasoning varies with historical and social context."[9] Some of these historical contexts were labeled "awakenings," what William McLoughlin claimed were "results, not of depressions, wars, or epidemics, but of critical disjunctions in our self-understanding." Instead of representing "outbursts of mass emotionalism" they were "profound cultural transformations affecting all Americans and extending over a generation or more."[10] American culture mirrors the birth and the death of multiple plans, programs, and "enthusiasms" for encountering the Sacred.

Definitions abound. John Calvin called this religious experience "a conversion to the life of God,"[11] while the Great Awakener George Whitefield viewed it as "heaven brought down to the soul."[12] Philosopher Friedrich Schleiermacher referred to it as "religious feeling," "a sense, a taste, an affection";[13] and William James labeled it (among other things) "immediate luminousness."[14] Abolitionist Sojourner Truth called it "a rush of love through my soul," which enabled her to confess, "Lord, I can love even the white folks."[15] Jonathan Edwards understood it as "a sense of the heart," often evident in certain "religious affections." Edwards's conversionist idiom, "a sense of the heart," provides a unifying motif for ordering varied approaches to religious experience evident in multiple religious individuals, groups, and contexts.[16]

My own interest in American religious experience no doubt began in my childhood as I witnessed its specific expressions in what may have been the last great era of religious revival meetings in American Protestant history. Some of my earliest memories involve summer revival services conducted on the parking lot of the Fundamental Baptist Church in Decatur, Texas, where my grandmother, Francis Mowery Henton, was a member. On these occasions we both soaked in the sights, sounds, and sweat of salvation, as congregants shouted to high heaven in sorrow for sin and gratitude for grace. As I have written elsewhere, those revivals were an introduction to one way of "getting saved" in American culture. At the time I supposed it to be the only way—"the traumatic event which chronicled the day and moment from here to eternity."[17] Later, I learned that those Spirit-driven "protracted meetings" were shaped not only by scripture and conversion but by the history and culture of American and Southern religion. The preachers at those summer revivals were as much the heirs of Charles Finney, Dwight L. Moody, and Billy Sunday as they were Peter, James, and John.[18] Their call to "be saved" was but one of multiple salvific entry points.

Across the years and in several theological institutions, I have offered seminars in the history of religious experience in America, learning from students whose research shaped and reshaped my own understanding of the topic. I am indebted to those individuals who chose to use a portion of their graduate programs to investigate the many facets of American religious experience. Most of the more recent students have never attended a revival meeting.

Given those studies, I was honored when Kathy Armistead contacted me with the invitation to develop a text on religious experience for Abingdon Press. Dr. Armistead has been a patient and insightful colleague, and I am grateful to her and Abingdon for the opportunity to engage in this endeavor. I am also grateful to Wake Forest University Provost Rogan Kersh and School of Divinity Dean Gail O'Day for providing research support for this study. Master's students in both the School of Divinity and the Department of Religion at Wake Forest have assisted directly and indirectly its preparation, offering insightful research and analysis. I am particularly indebted to Abigail Pratt, my graduate assistant, for providing significant logistical and editorial support. Her father, Dr. Andrew Pratt, took the first of my seminars on this subject when he and I were both much younger. Andrew Gardner, another graduate assistant, did excellent work on the index. My pastor, Reverend Dr. Darryl Aaron, and faculty colleagues, Reverend Drs. Veronice Miles and Derek Hicks, remain valuable dialogue partners for conversations regarding religious experience, especially in African American contexts. As always my spouse, Dr. Candyce Leonard, along with our daughter Stephanie, offered profound affirmation and support, ever reminding me that "it's just a book." Whatever else, it is that.

★★ *1* ★★

A Sense of the Heart: Introducing Religious Experience

In A *Treatise on Religious Affections*, written in 1746, Jonathan Edwards wrote:

> From what has been said, therefore, we come necessarily to this conclusion, concerning that wherein spiritual understanding consists; viz. that it consists in *a sense of the heart*, of the supreme beauty and sweetness of the holiness or moral perfection of divine things, together with all that discerning and knowledge of things of religion that depends upon, and flows from such a sense.[1]

In this treatise, Edwards sought to distinguish true religious experience from false in response to controversies over the revival "enthusiasms" that descended upon individuals and churches in New England and throughout the American colonies. John E. Smith observed that although Edwards wrote extensively on the revivals and their resulting religious phenomena, *Religious Affections* was "his most acute and detailed treatment of the central task of defining the soul's relation to God."[2] Jonathan Edwards was one of the first analysts of the nature of Christian religious experience in American life, offering what Smith called his "brilliant, at times pathetic, defense of 'affectionate' religion."[3]

Edwards opened the door to the exploration of religious experience, a phenomenon present throughout Christian history, often in ways more diverse, extensive, and at times bizarre than Jonathan Edwards could ever have imagined. For Edwards, "affections" revealed that religious experience was more than the "mere speculative knowledge" of intellectual analysis. It was "the sense of the heart, wherein the mind don't only speculate and behold, but relishes and feels."[4] Those who "perceived the sweet taste of honey," knew more about that miraculous substance than those who "only looked upon and felt of it."[5] Relishing an encounter with the Divine is nothing new in Christian history; analyzing such religious experience is itself a relatively new discipline, producing innumerable studies.

Robert W. Jenson suggested that for Edwards "the sense of the heart belongs to that 'one thing' that separates human beings from 'brute creatures.'" In Edwards's words, "we are always present with ourselves, and have an immediate consciousness of our own actions." Jenson calls this "a phenomenon of immediate self-awareness." Thus, "sense transcends the difference between knowing and willing."[6] The sense of the heart involves "sweet beauty," as well as "sweetness and delight," by which "knowledge is thus mediated to inclination."[7] Religion, Edwards insisted, was "a true sense of the divine excellency of the things revealed in the word of God." Those whose religion brought genuine spiritual enlightenment did "not merely rationally believe that God is glorious." Rather, that person "has a sense of the gloriousness of God in his heart."[8] Bad religion was that religious endeavor "from which the hearts' [*sic*] sense is missing."[9] Jenson concluded that comparable theological comparisons could be made with Jonathan Edwards, Kant, and Schleiermacher.

Analyzing Religious Experiences: Multiple Approaches

This book is an effort to reflect on the nature and history of religious experience in the United States. Chapters survey specific individuals, institutions, and movements that impacted and were impacted by varieties of religious experience from the colonial period to the twenty-first century. The book's purpose is to define, describe, and analyze various elements of religious experience across a wide spectrum of religious communities where varying expressions of religious liberty and pluralism exist. It suggests that defining religious experience has been both difficult and easy, depending on one's approach to the phenomenon and its actual presence in specific individuals. Definitions reflect a variety of approaches to the topic from within academia as well as from segments of popular culture.

In the book *Religious Experience*, Wayne Proudfoot noted that religion has always reflected an experiential dimension beyond or alongside dogma, ritual, or ethical codes. Experiencing Transcendence or the Other was evident in the attitudes and actions of prehistoric and native peoples; spiritual encounters were often retold or ritually reenacted from the earliest human societies. Individuals in those cultures created their own ways of interacting with their world that included a response to the mysteries that surrounded them. They created myths, stories, and rituals that helped them come to terms with their environment and the mysterious forces they encountered. Yet, Proudfoot wrote, they "did not understand what was happening to them or what they were doing" in terms of some formal methodology or analysis. He acknowledged that both the terms "*religious* and *experience* are relatively recent concepts, whose provenance is in the modern West."[10] While encountering religion is nothing new, the effort to analyze such phenomena specifically as *religious experience* is itself an emerging discipline.

These analytical tools facilitate the quest for a definition or at least a qualification of religious experience as action, phenomenon, and subject to be studied. Ninian Smart observed that a religious "perception" couldn't appropriately be called a religious experience unless it "revealed something fundamental about God's nature." He suggested that "a religious experience involves some kind of 'perception' of the *invisible* world, or involves a perception that some visible person or thing is a manifestation of the invisible world." Smart surveyed various "dimensions" of religion including ritual, myth, doctrine, and ethics, along with its social and experiential elements. He concluded that while some practitioners hope that ritual may connect them with "the invisible world... personal religion normally involves the hope of, or realization of, experience of that world."[11]

Some believe that in its most basic sense, religious experience involves a search for or encounter of the *Sacred*, the *Holy*, *God*, or the *Other*, that mysterious presence that is beyond the human. Indeed, in *The Idea of the Holy* (*Das Heilige*), Rudolph Otto utilized the term *numinous* to describe that "fascinating and awesome mystery" that may be understood as God.[12] Michael H. Barnes contended that early peoples sometimes confronted life's mysteries through "luck, magic, or omens." Such "numinous power" could be present in individuals, spirits, objects, or everyday occurrences. Sometimes it was evident as a "nonliving power," later known to anthropologists as *mana*. Sources of that power can be dangerous or welcoming environments, always fraught with peril since they contain and perhaps arbitrate good, evil, and taboos of various kinds.[13] Persons and tribes may at times be compelled to negotiate with such forces in response to acts of nature, disease, interpersonal relationships, and other realities of life in the world. In this environment, experience with the world is experience with religion. Barnes wrote that the life experience of early peoples included "numinous elements, living and nonliving" that "blend into the everyday and ordinary aspects of that reality.... In a sense the spirits are part of the clan; the numinous powers are all part of the family's homeland."[14]

Later on, in what some have called "archaic religion," special authority may be assigned to certain gods or spirits as having particularly significant interactive power. Such entities may be benevolent or malevolent, to be adored or placated. Extensive rituals may be developed for applying "respectful persuasion" occasionally or consistently. Encounter with these gods may evolve through individual or collective rituals that bring human beings as close as possible to the often unpredictable Other, whose will may be known in acts of nature that are favorable or unfavorable to the community.[15] In these early societies individuals may claim direct knowledge of or communication with gods or spirits through dreams, visions, or other supernatural actions. At such times they may believe that they have received special revelation beneficial to the individual or tribe. Those who seem to be consistent conduits of those human/divine connections may be viewed as shamans who represent or interpret supernatural revelation.

Barnes insisted that these early religiosocial responses to the Other are not to be dismissed as "primitive" superstition. Rather, he concluded that "mystery does exist—unanswered questions, unexplained events, uncertainty about the future, confusion about how to live." Barns asserted that even if supernatural explanations were not adequate, "perhaps human beings would feel compelled to invent such powers out of their dream experiences, their imaginations, their tendency to 'projection,' their wishful thinking, their needs for psychological comfort and social stability."[16]

In his study of conversion, A. D. Nock claimed that "primitive religion" responds to "natural needs," and to "the stages by which life is marked." It also works to "ensure the proper working of the natural processes and sources of supply" required in all community life. At the same time it is "an outlet for certain emotions of humility, dependence and self-dramatization."[17] This nascent religion represents a reaction to a specific environment, offering tools for both shaping and responding to the realities of a specific cultural and environmental setting.

Nock defined the conversion phenomenon as "the reorientation of the soul of an individual, his deliberate turning from indifference or from an earlier form of piety to another, a turning which implies a consciousness that a great change is involved, that the old was wrong and the new is right."[18] He maintained that it is a "positive response" to the claims made upon the life of an individual by "the prophetic religion." In Christianity conversion reflects "two forms." The first marks a return to a traditional expression of religion in which a person may have been reared but had departed. The other involves a "turning" to a religious community with which the individual had no previous experience or perhaps from no previous religious context whatsoever.[19]

Surveying religious experience in early Christianity, Luke Timothy

Johnson differentiated a variety of "troubles" that complicate efforts to interpret specific spiritual exercises. First, the cause or causes behind the experience may no longer be "visible or available for verification." Confirming the nature or even the veracity of the experience is exceedingly problematic. Second, throughout the church's history many persons "have found it profitable to fake religious experiences." Without adequate authentication, false claims are always possible, and may be emulated or gain a following.[20] Third, there can never be a truly neutral mode for studying or analyzing religious experience. Since all scholars "have a stake in the construal of the evidence," Johnson cautions students of the phenomenon to be aware of the particular approaches or intensions of the analysts.[21] Efforts to survey religious experience within Christian communities must proceed with caution.

Religious "Feeling": Schleiermacher, *On Religion*

The modern investigation of religious experience has often been traced to German philosopher Friedrich Schleiermacher (1768–1834) whose *On Religion* has been called "the most influential statement and defense of the autonomy of religious experience."[22] Schleiermacher's work was a response to the skeptics and "cultured critics" of his day influenced by modern insights drawn from science, philosophy, and the new ethics, and exemplified in the works of Rene Descartes, David Hume, and Immanuel Kant. Their views challenged traditional theistic arguments based in metaphysics, design, and proofs for the existence of God. Schleiermacher's concern was to unite religious truth with "human experience," thereby separating its sources of authority from metaphysics and ecclesiasticism. He feared that the critics were apt to see religion as merely a "spiritual disease" destructive to the intellect and guided by a dying institutionalism vested in the church, a historical presence they seemed to view as more detrimental to humanity than even "religion itself."[23] Others, however, were less shrill but not necessarily less dismissive in their criticism of religion "more as an 'oddity' than as a mental derangement."[24]

Wayne Proudfoot observed that in both *On Religion* and *The Christian*

Faith, Schleiermacher understood religion as "an autonomous moment in human experience which ought not to be reduced to science, metaphysics, or morality." It was a phenomenon with "its own integrity." Schleiermacher's concern was to protect religious belief and action "from the possibility of conflict with the conclusions of science" or the erratic ideas that shape society's continuing "moral experience."[25]

In the introduction to his English translation of *On Religion*, Terrence Tice noted that for Schleiermacher, religion was primarily "a vital inner perspective on the whole scheme of things which is centered in the process of attaining true humanity and is sustained in deeply personal feeling." It is neither art nor a method for securing knowledge, nor a code of ethical conduct, although it may have implications for all of that. Rather, it is "communal" and "infinitely personal in its creation and sustenance," able to permeate an individual's total existence.[26] Proudfoot concluded that "for Schleiermacher, religion is a sense, a taste, an affection."[27] In its most basic sense, religious experience involves "a feeling of absolute or total dependence upon a source or power that is distinct from the world."[28] Religious doctrines and practices may change or vary from era to era, but religious experience is an enduring quality that both transcends and incorporates traditional and modern categories.

Schleiermacher perceived his task as presenting the "essence" of religion "from the inside out, not to take its outer form for its essence." Thus "piety," or religious feeling, is distinct from the analytical categories of knowledge, science, and the praxis of ethics or morality. Rather, Schleiermacher insisted that "to seek and to find this infinite and eternal factor in all that lives and moves, in all growth and change, in all action and passion, and to have and to know life itself only in immediate feeling—that is religion." Where that is present, religion is fulfilled; where it is missing, "religion experiences frustration and anguish, emptiness and death."[29] Yet he was careful to assert that he in no way intended on "divorcing knowledge and conduct from piety." Rather, he contended that the moderns of his day were wrong when they failed to include religion as a "third basic element along with knowledge and conduct."[30] He insisted that there was "no true science, ethics or art without religion," and those who ignored that reality were left with little more than "a bare concept."[31]

For Schleiermacher, the "distinctive domain" of religion was this: "Your feeling is your piety...insofar as that feeling expresses the being and life common to you and to the universe in the way described and,...insofar as the particular moments of that feeling come to you as an operation of God within you mediated through the operation of the world upon you."[32] Thus "religious affections," those external expressions of internal experiences, were central to the nature of religion itself, distinct from "both intellect and will."[33] These spiritual manifestations might involve certain "experiential concepts" that represent particular feelings and included "miracles," "inspirations," "revelations," and "supernatural experiences." While admitting that one may have "a considerable measure of piety" apart from those qualities, Schleiermacher believed that they belonged "unconditionally" to religion, even though the practitioner need not feel obligated to "qualify their applicability in the slightest."[34] Schleiermacher's recognition of the presence of those affections within the realm of religious feeling anticipated continuing discussion and debate about them across varying segments of the church, particularly among Christians in the United States. Schleiermacher concluded:

> The sum total of religion, then, is to feel all that moves us in our feeling, in the supreme unity of it all, as one and the same, and to feel all that is individual and particular as mediated only through that unity—that is, to feel our being and life as a being and life in and through God.[35]

William James: *Varieties of Religious Experience*

William James (1842–1910) is perhaps the best-known analyst of questions related to religious experience of anyone in the English-speaking world. His monumental work *The Varieties of Religious Experience* continues to shape the field of study. His father, Henry James Sr., kept the family mobile, moving them between Europe, New York, and Newport, Rhode Island. James spent much of his teens studying in Europe, and then returned to Newport to pursue painting. He graduated Harvard and began medical studies there in 1863, but that endeavor was interrupted by periods of ill health. He received the medical degree in 1870, but was immediately stricken with serious illness that kept him debilitated for several years. In 1874 he began teaching at Harvard, and in 1880 he was named assistant professor of psychology, introducing the first psychology lab in the United States. He later became a professor of philosophy, retaining that position until 1907. James's monumental work, *Principles of Psychology*, solidified his academic reputation, while *The Varieties of Religious Experience* secured his influence in both psychology and philosophy of religion.

The materials that became *Varieties of Religious Experience* were originally presented in 1902 as the Gifford Lectures on Natural Religion at the University of Edinburgh. The book begins by exploring "Religion and Neurology," as James sets the boundaries for his study. His concern is less with religious institutions than with "religious feelings and religious impulses," as identified in certain literary sources "produced by articulate and fully self-conscious" individuals who detail their religious experiences in various texts. James suggests that readers of such sacred texts should utilize "spiritual judgment" for discerning documents with "revelation-value."[36] He notes that in matters of biblical interpretation, should such "revelation-value" require a form of dictation that requires the text demonstrate "no scientific and historic errors" then "the Bible would probably fare ill at our hands." If, however, one might suppose that a text could offer revelatory insights beyond "errors and passions" to reflect the "inner experiences of great-souled persons, wrestling with the crises of their fate," then it would have great importance as a source of genuine revelation.[37]

James's interests rested less with persons whose religion is inherited or passed on through specific traditions than with "individuals for whom religion exists not as a dull habit, but as an acute fever rather." He characterized such visionaries as often "creatures of exalted emotional sensitivity" who may have demonstrated "a discordant inner life," and are given to "all sorts of peculiarities which are ordinarily classed as pathological." Such pathology, sometimes involving "trances... voices... visions" and other "peculiarities," may have contributed to the individuals' "religious authority and influence."[38] James sought to move beyond the "medical materialists" who bring "belated dogmatism," not objective analysis, to the study of religious experience, largely focused on psychologically abnormal individuals. Instead, he opts for an "empiricist criterion: By their fruits ye shall know them, not by their roots," even citing Edwards's comment in the *Treatise on Religious Affections*: "The degree in which our experience is productive of practice shows the degree in which our experience is spiritual and divine."[39]

James was not interested in exploring institutional religion, specific deities, or "the art of winning the favor of the gods."[40] His concern was with religion as "*the feelings, acts, and experiences*" of individuals "*in their solitude, so far as they apprehend themselves to stand in relation to whatever they may consider divine.*"[41] By "the divine" he meant "only such a primal reality as the individual feels impelled to respond to solemnly and gravely, and neither by a curse nor a jest."[42] World religions were wildly diverse but shared concerns for spiritual experience, feelings, and emotions often characterized by "fear, awe, hope" and perhaps even "bliss."[43] Wayne Proudfoot wrote,

> Unlike Schleiermacher, James does not couple feeling with intuition, nor does he claim any special status for feeling as an exercise of the mind which precedes and informs both knowing and doing. Rather... he regards emotions as perceptions of changes in one's bodily state. But he views religious beliefs as secondary products that would never have emerged had it not been for the prior existence of religious feeling.[44]

These experiences rested on the idea that an "unseen order" exists at the deepest level of reality, that it is essentially good, and "that our supreme good lies in harmoniously adjusting ourselves thereto." The elements of that "order," whether religious, ethical, or pragmatic, arise from "'objects' of our consciousness, the things which we believe to exist, whether really or ideally, along with ourselves."[45] Whether these objects are actually verifiable or quantifiable was a major question and source of debate. James cited Kant's assertion that while words such as "soul," "God," or "immortality" have no "sense content" and are theoretically "devoid of any significance," individuals can find meaning "*as if* [they] were to be immortal." He concluded: "So we have the strange phenomenon, as Kant assures us, of a mind believing with all its strength in the real presence of a set of things of no one of which it can form any notion whatsoever."[46] The search for religious experience may be done practically, abstractly, or internally.

James distinguished certain personality types that illustrate varying approaches to religious experience. "The religion of healthy-mindedness" promotes a sense of happiness toward the primary goal of inner peace and fulfillment. Thus one should not be surprised when individuals "regard the happiness which a religious belief affords as a proof of its truth."[47] In addressing healthy-mindedness James drew on Francis W. Newman's 1852 work, *The Soul: Its Sorrows and its Aspirations*. Newman wrote, "God has two families of children on this earth, *the once-born and the twice-born*." Once-born individuals "see God, not as a strict Judge, not as a Glorious Potentate; but as the animating Spirit of a beautiful harmonious world, Beneficent and Kind, Merciful as well as Pure."[48] James suggested that the once-born tendencies were more evident within the "Romanish" tradition of Christianity than in Protestantism, "whose fashions of feeling have been set by minds of a decidedly pessimistic order."

Within Protestantism, the once-born consciousness is generally evident in more liberal traditions or nurtured through the sacramental life of certain communions. James cited Unitarian Edward Everett Hale's recollection that

> I always knew God loved me, and I was always grateful to him for the world he placed me in. I always liked to tell him so, and was always glad to receive his suggestions to me.... A child that is early taught that he is God's child,... will take life more easily, and probably will make more of it, than one who is told that he is born the child of wrath and wholly incapable of good.[49]

For the once-born, grace seemed ever present from the moment one entered the world.

Writing in 1902, no doubt with Protestant progressivism at its height, James suggested that during the previous half century liberalism and "healthy-mindedness" had triumphed over the more "morbid" element represented in "the old hell-fire theology" of the twice-born Protestantism.[50] The strength of this new "Mind-cure" optimism James attributed to renewed concern for the four Gospels, Transcendentalism, "Berkleyan idealism," "spiritism," and "scientific evolutionism."[51]

This "healthy-mindedness" James contrasted with "the sick soul," present in persons given to "maximizing evil . . . based on the persuasion that the evil aspects of our life are of its very essence" and creating a "more morbid way" of approaching religious experience.[52] Some view evil in creation and human nature as "curable," a simple "mal-adjustment with *things*." Others, however, believe that evil lies at the heart of the human condition, "a wrongness or vice" in the "essential nature" of all humans, "which no alteration of the environment, or any superficial rearrangement of the inner self, can cure, and which requires a supernatural remedy."[53]

James understood the "sick soul" to be the subject of "twice-born" responses to evil and the human condition. He wrote that "the securest way to the rapturous sorts of happiness of which the twice-born make report has as an historic matter of fact been through a more radical pessimism than anything that we have yet considered."[54] Deliverance from evil required a radical conversion to infuse goodness and spiritual fulfillment within the life of a sin-dominated human being.

James found this internal struggle with evil and despair illustrated in the testimonies of two literary giants, Leo Tolstoy and John Bunyan. He cited Tolstoy's preconversion assertion: "But my original and inward pollution, that was my plague and my affliction. By reason of that, I was more loathsome in my own eyes than was a toad; and I thought I was so in God's eyes too."[55] James admitted that "moribund-mindedness" covered a "wider scale of [human] experience" and that even healthy-mindedness "breaks down impotently as soon as melancholy comes."[56] Thus, reflecting on the once- and twice-born approaches to religion, as well as the need to confront the world realistically, James concluded, "The completest religion would therefore seem to be those in which the pessimistic elements are best developed." He speculated that from his perspective, Buddhism and Christianity seem to be the most effective of the world's religions in addressing those inevitable inner struggles.

For James, to study the *varieties of religious experience* was to recognize the existence of "two different conceptions of the universe of our experience." Once-born persons believe that "happiness and religious peace consist in living on the plus side of the account." For the twice-born, however, "the world is a double-storied mystery" ordered around "the natural and the spiritual, and we must lose the one before we can participate in the other."[57] James suggested that the lives of Tolstoy and Bunyan illustrate this inner struggle to move beyond the natural to the spiritual. He quoted the lengthy accounts of their conversion (second-birth) experiences, along with those of St. Augustine and the Canadian evangelist Henry Alline.

Of Bunyan's spiritual/experiential pursuits, James wrote, "Bunyan became a minister of the gospel, and in spite of his neurotic constitution, and of the twelve years he lay in prison for his non-conformity, his life was turned to active use.... The Allegory [*Pilgrim's Progress*] which he wrote has brought the very spirit of religious patience home to English hearts." Yet "neither Bunyan nor Tolstoy could become what we have called healthy-minded. They had drunk too deeply of the cup of bitterness ever to forget its taste, and their redemption is into a universe two stories deep."[58] James believed that these historic examples served "to acquaint us in a general way with the phenomenon technically called 'Conversion.'"[59]

"Religious Change": William James and Conversion

Conversion, *regeneration*, *receiving grace*, *experiencing religion*, and *gaining assurance* are phrases that James listed as generally delineating "the process, gradual or sudden, by which a self hitherto divided, and consciously wrong inferior and unhappy, becomes unified... right superior and happy, in consequence of its firmer hold upon religious realities."[60] So conversion is the word used for a "religious change" that occurs at the center of an individual, "especially if it be by crisis, or sudden."[61] Citing another set of conversion narratives from a wide spectrum of persons, James noted that "there are distinct elements in conversion, and their relations to individual lives deserve to be discriminated."[62]

Yet he also confessed that there are certain individuals who "never are, and possibility never under any circumstances could be, converted," upstanding persons who have no real motivation to secure such an experience; perhaps they are "incapable of imagining the invisible," or because their lives reflect "barrenness" or "dryness." Others are more salvifically problematic because they lack "sensibility" for things religious. Though this may change later in life, due to a "thaw" in the spirit, most seem unable ever to "compass the enthusiasm and peace which those who are temperamentally qualified for faith enjoy."[63]

James acknowledged that persons do come to faith in multiple ways, referencing Edwin Diller Starbuck (1866–1947) whose work *Psychology of Religion* made him one of the early authorities in the field. Starbuck distinguished between two types of conversion, characterized by *volition* and *self-surrender*. Volitional conversion involves a more gradual nurture or an evolving recognition of the importance of inner transformation. Yet the volitional approach may also involve cathartic moments when one chooses to deepen the spiritual quest, as evidenced in the conversion narrative of famed evangelist Charles Grandison Finney, who, after a time of reflection on the need for salvation, reached a crisis point, in which he determined, "I will accept it to-day, or I will die in the attempt!"[64] James suggested that, in a sense, Finney willed himself to the decisive religious experience he desired.

These conversions, James observed, "are as a rule less interesting than those of the self-surrender type."[65] Self-surrender requires sinners to relinquish their "personal will" for a higher authority of truth and the promise of fulfillment. The process reflects a sharp contrast between the sinful nature and the possibility of redemptive transformation. Starbuck believed that in most cases of this nature conversion was "a process of struggling away from sin rather than of striving towards righteousness."[66] James concluded that Christianity in its multiple forms—Catholic/Protestant, mystical, pietistic, Transcendentalist, even "mind-cure" types—reflected varying "stages of progress towards the idea of an immediate spiritual help," a "forlornness" that bears "no essential need of doctrinal apparatus or propitiatory machinery."[67] Thus Christianity is a faith tradition with an inherent affinity for religious experience.

James distinguished certain conversion-oriented churches from Catholicism and "the more usual sects of Protestantism," for whom "Christ's blood, the sacraments, and the individual's ordinary religious duties are practically supposed to suffice to his salvation, even though no acute crisis of self-despair and surrender followed by relief should be experienced."[68] By making conversion normative, revivalistic Protestantism "codified and stereotyped religious experience" into certain evangelistic formulas and procedures that gave persons the security of a prescribed route to salvation. The proponents of revivalism insisted that their approach to religious experience could be "perfect," a decisive process that began with a time of spiritual agony and despair and ended with a miraculous deliverance from sin and spiritual strife.[69]

James asked if "an instantaneous conversion" demonstrates an extraordinary act in which God apprehends the sinner in ways unique from any other "strikingly abrupt" experience. Is it a decisive way of entering into relationship with God, or is it simply one of many signs of "a strictly natural process?"[70] He concluded that converted individuals "as a class are indistinguishable from natural" individuals, so they must admit that "there is no unmistakable class-mark distinctive of all true converts."[71] While conversion might be a life-changing event for a substantial number of persons, it was impossible to distinguish between the converted individual and the "natural" one.[72]

James noted that one of the important "feelings" involved in conversion was a "sense of higher control," in which the sinner sought union with something beyond the "self." Indeed, the self is helpless as a means of insight and deliverance from corruption. Redemption, therefore, "must be a free gift or nothing, and grace through Christ's accomplished sacrifice is such a gift."[73] Referencing Martin Luther's well-documented struggle with sin and self, and his assertion that no works of religious virtue were adequate for salvation apart from Christ's sacrifice on the cross, James observed that "nothing in Catholic theology, I imagine, has ever spoken to sick souls as straight as this message from Luther's personal experience."[74]

Once conversion is secured, there are numerous signs of "the state of assurance" evident to the regenerated. These include 1) a sense of peace and "the loss of all the worry," even if "outer conditions should remain the same"; 2) a discovery of truths that were not previously evident; 3) a new way of looking at the world; and 4) an experience of what James calls "automatisms," religio-physical expressions that have little or no "spiritual significance" but may make conversion "more memorable."[75] These outbursts of "unconsciousness, convulsions, visions, involuntary vocal utterances, and suffocation" are what Jonathan Edwards would call "religious affections."[76]

The Varieties of Religious Experience concluded with a summary of some five "characteristics of religious life." First, the "visible world" is a segment of "a more spiritual universe," which provides "its chief significance." Second, the "true end" of religious experience involves "union" with that spiritual universe. Third, prayer, contemplation, or inward encounter with the Sacred involves a "process" through which the basic work of religion is done and where "spiritual energy" is generated. Fourth, psychologically, the religionist discovers "a new zest" that adds vitality to life "and takes the form either of lyrical enchantment or of appeal to earnestness and heroism." Fifth, from another psychological perspective, individuals encounter a sense of "safety" and "peace," and "a preponderance of loving affections" in relating to others.[77]

In the end James acknowledged that he was personally unable "to accept either popular Christianity or scholastic theism" even as he affirmed the possibility and need for "communion with the Ideal."[78] He also contended that the "warring gods and formulas" of the multitude of world religions actually seemed to cancel out each other. Nonetheless, these varied religions do "appear to meet" around two important elements: "uneasiness" and its "solution." Each seems to recognize "that there is *something wrong about us*" in our natural existence but that "*we are saved from the wrongness*" through an appropriate encounter with "higher powers," something beyond ourselves.[79]

Fits, Trances, and Visions: The Work of Ann Taves

In her monumental study, *Fits, Trances, & Visions: Experiencing Religion and Explaining Experience from Wesley to James*, written almost a century after *The Varieties of Religious Experience*, Ann Taves expanded the study of religious experience through the eighteenth- and nineteenth-century "awakenings" to later expressions of "Religious Experience and the Subconscious." The latter phenomena she linked to animal magnetism, "fits, visions, clairvoyance, healing, automatic writing and mediumship," as well as "conversion, mysticism and speaking in tongues."[80] Taves surveyed the experiences of those who claim religious encounter, often with powerful outward "enthusiasms" and the efforts of certain ecclesiastical or academic "elites" who have attempted to analyze or explain those experiences. She focused on "the interplay between experiencing religion and explaining experience,"[81] examining the historical, phenomenological, psychological, and confessional aspects of religious experience with particular attention to those trances, visions, dreams, and other perceptions testified to in American religious life.

Taves delineated multiple uses of the term "religious experience" in different periods of American religious history. Late eighteenth- and early nineteenth-century Protestants used the phrase within the context of specific religious traditions, often in autobiographical accounts of individual or communal spiritual travails. These, she noted, understood religious experience as "presumptively authentic and particular."[82] William James's 1902 publication viewed religious experience much more generically as "something" widely encountered and less tied to specific traditions. It was an important "object of study" that could be divorced "from the theological contexts in which it had been embedded."[83]

Taves suggested that James represented a "mediating tradition" in his studies of religious experience, explaining it as "religion-in-general, without at the same time intending to explain it away." Such efforts had a "reconstituted" effect on "traditional Protestant supernaturalism."[84] One of her great contributions to this field of study was to include a discussion of certain nineteenth-century forms of religious experience evident in spiritualism, mesmerism, animal magnetism, and other "scientific" explorations of the subconscious. These experiential phenomena, she insisted, "were freighted with conceptions about the natural and supernatural, science and religion, and in the case of the latter, the normal and the psychopathological."[85] While she acknowledged that James was somewhat unique in his comparison of "religious and nonreligious phenomena," Taves warned that such an "interesting and fruitful question" might also contribute to the loss of "a sense of religion (or not-religion) as a substantive thing." This may also mean that religious experience serves as a potential point of departure whereby "the study of religion opens... into the study of everything."[86]

Christian Religious Experience: Transcendence and Immanence

Analysts such as Ann Taves, William James, Wayne Proudfoot, and Friedrich Schleiermacher provide important insights for defining religious experience in general and Christian religious experience in particular. At the center of Christian experience is the intricate and elusive question of how an individual or community encounters the Other, moments when the transcendent becomes immanent. Christians affirm that faith begins with an affirmation that the "only God," "immortal, invisible" (1 Tim. 1:17), was "made flesh," in Jesus Christ (John 1:14), who is "Emmanuel, God with us" (Matt. 1:23). If the God who is "high and lifted up" (Isa. 6:1) was "made in the likeness" of humanity "for our salvation," then how is that salvation actualized and retained by specific human beings? And how does that possessed individual, whether once-born or twice-born, know salvation has been secured?

Implicitly or explicitly, all Christian traditions attempt to respond to those questions, offering tangible sacraments and morphologies that link creator and creature. Many begin with biblical accounts of *hierophany*, occasions when the Sacred reveals itself in the ordinary. Those encounters abound in both testaments.[87] Indeed, Christian communities have not hesitated to understand and write themselves into certain biblical encounters as evidence of God's direct engagement with individuals. In the Hebrew Bible, God "walks" with Adam and Eve in the garden "in the cool of the day." The postmenopausal Sarah laughs in the face of "the LORD" who brings word of her pending pregnancy (Gen. 18:12-15). Jacob wrestles with the "stranger" at River Jabbok (Gen. 32:18-22). Moses hears the voice of God in the burning bush (Exod. 3:3-4), and Elijah experiences the "still small voice" in the mountain cave (1 Kgs. 19:12); each story a sign of the Sacred known in the ordinary. In the New Testament, the Virgin Mary receives word from an angel that she is to bear a son who will save God's people from their sins. Encounters with Jesus by the seashore lead some fishermen to "leave their nets" and follow him (Matt. 4:20). On the Mount of Transfiguration, three apostles observe and "enter the cloud" of mystical experience with Jesus, Moses, and Elijah (Matt. 17:2-7). Jesus himself mirrors the depth of struggle and divine encounter in the Garden of Gethsemane (Matt. 26:39-42). Disciples on the road to Emmaus testify that "our hearts burned within us" in an unexpected encounter with the risen Christ (Luke 24:13). The coming of the Holy Spirit at Pentecost is perhaps the church's greatest sign of a mass religious experience, outwardly evidenced by speech in "tongues of fire" and "unknown tongues" that descended on the apostles (Acts 2:2-4). Paul's encounter with the living Christ on the Damascus road became one of the great examples of dramatic conversion (Acts 9:2-8), paralleled across the church's history by claims of other such events. Early gnostic literature speaks of a variety of visions, dreams, and revelations that inform and enliven large segments of the Christian community, challenging a developing Christian orthodoxy. *Hierophany* abounds inside and outside the biblical canon.

External and Internal Signs: Religious Experience and Church Traditions

Within Christian tradition, one of the clearest means of addressing the links between transcendence and immanence is evident in the sacramentalism of the Roman Catholic Church. From the beginning of an individual's life to its end, the grace of God is made known in the most common elements of the physical world—water, bread, wine, and oil—and in common human experiences—birth, coming of age, vocation, repentance, reconciliation, and death. Through these outward signs the Other literally enters into the creature. In the transubstantiation of the Eucharist, human beings take into themselves the very body and blood of Jesus Christ, transformed from bread and wine through the authority of Christ passed on by means of apostolic succession.

Many Reformation-born communions rejected Catholic sacramentalism in pursuit of what Quaker mystic Rufus Jones called "vital inward religion," "an actual personal contact with the central eternal Stream of Life." In this view, the God revealed in Jesus "is an Emmanuel God and has entered the darkly colored stream of history, partakes of the sorrows and tragedies of the temporal order and... we are never alone when we are striving upward."[88] This "twice-born" approach to faith involves a conversion that overcomes a spiritual struggle, often manifesting its own outward and visible signs in what Ann Taves described as "uncontrolled bodily movements... spontaneous vocalizations... unusual sensory experiences" and "alterations of consciousness and/or memory."[89]

Luke Timothy Johnson cited Joachim Wach's "four-component description" of direct encounter with the Divine, involving 1) a "response to what is perceived as ultimate," 2) an impact on the "whole person," 3) a peculiar intensity, and 4) a call to distinct action.[90] The individual is not passive, but responds to that "something" that lies beyond the self.[91] Johnson recalled Rudolph Otto's suggestion that an experience of the Holy is so all-encompassing that "the participant can neither stay nor flee but is held in suspension between them."[92] The intensity of the experience may manifest its own intentionality, and certain actions that are "appropriate to the experience itself."[93] Rufus Jones concluded that this inner experience "heartens us with the belief that we are most completely ourselves when we are nearest in spirit and character to the pattern of life which the Christian religion presents" and most human "when we approximate most closely to the nature of the God whom we worship."[94]

This book suggests that the study of Christian religious experience, a *sense of the heart,* requires a differentiation between those churchly traditions that connect encounters with the Sacred to the nurturing grace of sacraments, and those traditions in which some form of internalized conversion is required for all who would claim salvation and membership in Christ's church.

In *Revivals, Awakenings, and Reform,* William McLoughlin noted that in spite of "the best efforts of William James, most psychologists, whether Freudian or behaviorist, have reduced religious experiences to secular terms by stressing latent versus manifest context." Many viewed the idea of religious experiences as "primitive," "culturally impoverished," or "backward." McLoughlin acknowledged that some persons claimed spiritual encounters that were really the "results of pathological problems," but agreed with James that even those extreme cases could be "cathartic." McLoughlin concluded that generally, "most religious converts move from states of anxiety and inhibition to states of functionally constructive personal and social action."[95] He suggested that these encounters with *hierophany* often led persons to "a new ideological or religious understanding of their place in the cosmos," even producing a "natural and necessary aspect of social change."[96] These experiential dynamics are particularly evident in the American religious environment. As William Clebsch observed,

> The religious experience of Americans has been emphatically more voluntary than organic, more diverse than standard, more personal than institutional, more practical than visionary or (in that sense) mystical.... It has subordinated strictly theological questions about God to more experiential ones about men and women.... Typically they construed religious experience as really saving men and women (however transitorily or permanently)

> from otherwise insoluble difficulties, symbolized perhaps by Satan, . . . spiritual mediocrity, [or] perhaps by divided selves.[97]

In their effort to blend "the head and the heart as twin seats of religious experience" Americans generally sought "to come to terms with," not retreat from their environment, seeking the Sacred in the fierce landscapes of a vast land.[98]

This book surveys the history of religious experience in the United States. Its historical narrative gives less attention to psychological or anthropological analyses, while benefitting from those diverse approaches to religious experientialism in the American context. It explores the nature and diversity of religious experience in light of such distinct religiocultural issues as pluralism, voluntarism, religious freedom, democratic idealism, and Protestant privilege in the US. This unique environment not only shaped the nature of experience with the Divine, but also provided a milieu in which multiple individuals and groups cultivated encounters with the Sacred. Indeed, the American experience offered more ways and means of facilitating *a sense of the heart* than Jonathan Edwards could ever have imagined, even as he helped to set such a dynamic in motion.

★★ 2 ★★

The Heart Prepared: Religious Experience in Early America

Colonial Catholicism

The Catholic priests and friars who came to North America in the fifteenth and sixteenth centuries brought with them a tradition that both nurtured and set boundaries for Christian religious experience. Catholic spirituality was centered in the seven sacraments—baptism, Eucharist, confirmation, penance, holy orders, marriage, and extreme unction. Yet it also mirrored a piety that stretched from the earliest cult of the martyrs, through the desert fathers and mothers, to monastics and mystics exemplifying a variety of faith-related encounters. For Catholics, the Eucharist itself was the ultimate spiritual experience, in which Christ's saving death on Calvary was literally repeated at the altar in the sacrifice of the Mass. Each of the seven sacraments became important signs of the presence of grace in the tangible elements of daily life—water, bread, wine, and oil. Saints and mystics might cultivate powerful encounters with the Divine, but all could experience that presence through the sacramental.

In the Eastern Church, worship itself was a great drama surrounded by icons, holy portraits of the saints whose lives were closest to the divine presence even while they inhabited this world. In both eastern and western contexts monasticism provided disciplined environments in which the spiritual life was cultivated through the *opus Dei*, the divine work of prayer, contemplation, and intercession. Hermit cells and monastic cloisters created space in which varying forms of mysticism flourished, often born of the classic threefold mystic "path" involving awakening, purification, and union with the Other. Few who quested after the Spirit could escape some encounter with the "dark night of the soul," when God might seem distant, hidden, or conspicuously absent. From the third-century martyrdom of Polycarp to the works of Julian of Norwich, Hildegard of Bingen, Meister Eckhart, Teresa of Avila, and John of the Cross, a diverse array of Catholic mystics produced a literary corpus that would document, define, and inform the nature and variety of religious experiences. Devotion to the saints and the Virgin became routes to dynamic spiritual encounters that often entailed visions, voices, and mysterious contact with the Divine. Francis of Assisi was said to have experienced the stigmata, in which the wounds of the crucified Christ appeared on his hands, feet, and riven side. Teresa of Avila heard voices directing her actions not only toward deeper piety but also toward the founding of a new monastic order, the Discalced Carmelites. Teresa's description of multiple encounters with a "very beautiful" (apparently male) angel is perhaps the best known of her many moments of mystic rapture.

> He was not tall, but short, and very beautiful, his face so aflame that he appeared to be one of the highest types of angel who seem to be all afire.... In his hands I saw a long golden spear and at the end of the iron tip I seemed to see a point of fire. With this he seemed to pierce my heart several times so that it penetrated to my entrails. When he drew it out, I thought he was drawing them out with it and he left me completely afire with a great love for God.[1]

Conversion, while not a normative requirement of all who would claim Catholic faith, was nonetheless a viable possibility, evidenced in no less a figure than Augustine of Hippo, whose *Confessions* became one of the great conversion memoirs of the Christian church. In it, one of the church's most formative theologians details his own quest for faith and his recognition in the end that grace had been there all along. His account of that converting moment tells of the day when he heard children's voices chanting, "Take up and read." Interpreting that to be an admonition from the Divine, Augustine recalled:

> So I hurried back to the spot where Alypius was sitting, for I had put there the volume of the apostle when I got up and left him. I snatched it up, opened it, and read in silence the chapter on which my eyes first fell: "Not in rioting and drunkenness, not in chambering and impurities, not in strife and envying; but put you on the Lord Jesus Christ and make not provision for the flesh in its concupiscences." No further wished I to read, nor was there need to do so. Instantly in truth, at the end of this sentence, as if before a peaceful light streaming into my heart, all the dark shadows of doubt fled away.[2]

A mandate to convert the native North Americans and provide pastoral care to the conquerors sent Catholic clergy to the New World, bringing sacramentalism and conversionism with them. The church's effort to make conversions and claim the land in Christ's name was itself a dangerous omen to Protestants who feared that the pope and his European minions would secure a beachhead in North and South America, creating a new kingdom on earth and extending the faith that they had so recently challenged, even overturned, in the Reformation era.

Sola Fide: Protestant Responses

At once heirs and critics of Catholic spirituality, Protestants sought to restore "a sense of the heart" that was grounded in *sola scriptura* (scripture alone) and *sola fide* (faith alone). Amid their efforts to deliver the church from the theological and ecclesiastical excesses of medieval Catholicism, Protestants were compelled to develop new approaches to religious experience that offered responses to the ceaseless longings of those who sought to know how God's grace might be received and retained. If *sola fide* was sufficient for salvation, how were believers to know that Christ had truly come to them? How was such saving faith experienced and verified? Was it a simple confession of belief in Jesus, or did it involve a direct encounter with the risen Christ like that experienced by the disciples at Pentecost, or in Paul's spiritual confrontation on the Damascus road? Was it possible to know decisively that one had passed from death to life? Were there common stages of faith that moved the individual toward a "saving knowledge" of Jesus Christ? Were there steps to justification, the process of entering into faith, and if so, how were they discerned? As Protestant conversionism became increasingly normative, how was salvation secured and retained?

The responses of the early Protestant reformers were at once parallel and contradictory.

Martin Luther (1483–1546) understood saving faith as centered in paradox. All Christians are *simul justus et peccator*, simultaneously just and sinful. Martin Marty writes that for Luther, "One benefit of faith . . . was that it united the soul with Christ as a bride is united with her bridegroom." Christ and the individual soul thus "share both good *and* evil." A saving experience meant that the sinner encounters the grace and love of Christ, while Christ encounters the sins and death present in the specific soul.[3] Marty cites Luther's statement that "what Christ has is the property of the believing soul, what the soul has becomes the property of Christ," and concludes, "In this exchange Christ changes places with sinners, something that Luther agreed the heart can grasp only in faith."[4]

For Luther, faith was necessary to validate the sacraments. Little children, he believed, have sufficient, though unseen, faith, enough to make them fit candidates for baptism. Christ's *real presence*, both spiritual and physical, can be experienced in Holy Communion, by faith. While repudiating Thomistic theology regarding transubstantiation, Luther held tenaciously the belief that Christ was both physically and spiritually present in the bread and wine, a Real Presence of direct encounter with the risen One.

For John Calvin (1509–1564), individual religious experience was inseparable from election by the sovereign God. Calvin insisted that God's grace, made possible only through Christ, would find those whom God has chosen before the foundation of the world. Of Christ's role in salvation, Calvin wrote, "When we seek salvation, love, and a blessed immortality, to him also must we betake ourselves, since he alone is the fountain of life, and the anchor of salvation, and the heir of heaven. Then what is the end of election, but just that, being adopted as sons by the heavenly Father, we may by his favour obtain salvation and immortality?" The elect were chosen, "not in themselves, but in Christ Jesus." Calvin insisted that "if we are elected in him [Christ], *we cannot find the certainty of our election in ourselves*; and not even in God the Father, if we look at him apart from the Son."[5] This led Edmund Morgan to suggest that Calvin thought it "impossible in this world to form a reliable opinion about whether or not" one was included in the elect. Instead, he did offer what Morgan called "clues by which anxious Christians could predict their chances." These included justifying faith, sanctifying growth in Christian graces, and perseverance in Christian commitment.[6]

Calvin insisted that election was the central factor in an individual's salvation. He repudiated those who, "induced by what means I know not, make election dependent on faith, as if it were doubtful and ineffectual till confirmed by faith." While he agreed that it was by faith that individuals looked for the "certainty" of election, it was "false to say that election is then only effectual after we have embraced the gospel, and that it thence derives its vigour."[7] Calvin acknowledged that there was no "greater or more perilous" temptation than the doubts by which Satan "assaulted believers" as to the validity of their election. He concluded,

> For there is scarcely a mind in which the thought does not sometimes rise, Whence your salvation but from the election of God? But what proof have you of your election? When once this thought has taken possession of any individual, it keeps him perpetually miserable, subjects him to dire torment, or throws him into a state of complete stupor.[8]

Calvin's remedy for this "fatal abyss," the desire to ascertain election, was "to begin with the calling of God and to end with it." The ultimate hope of the true believer rested, not in certain feelings, personal faith or attempts to "pry into the counsel of God," but in trusting God's action in election as revealed in "the word" (scripture).[9]

Election and calling were thus inseparable. To accept such a calling was to cast everything on Christ, receiving his "guardianship and protection." When doubts inevitably arise, Christ "obviates the doubt when he spontaneously offers himself as our Shepherd, and declares that we are of the number of his sheep if we hear his voice" (John 10:3, 6).[10] So Calvin provided no precise morphology (process) for discerning election and validating one's religious experience. True believers cast themselves on God's promise of election and the protection offered to the elect by Christ himself, his death and resurrection. The elect were given the faith to "embrace Christ" and to persevere in faithfulness, a sure sign that "there is no danger of their falling away."[11] Apparently Calvin was willing to live with the Augustinian dichotomy between the visible church on earth, composed of both "wheat and tares" (Matt 13:30), true and false Christians, and the invisible church of genuine believers, a group known only to God.

Calvin's approach was not entirely satisfying to Calvinists, however. James E. Smith noted that "evangelical Puritanism" of a later era "placed much more emphasis upon the inner life and religious experience of the isolated individual than Calvin did." While sharing Calvin's concern for such churchly issues as preaching, sacraments, and congregational discipline, Jonathan Edwards and other New Light Puritans were primarily focused on "the marks of the inner life" such as "conversion, sincerity, and humiliation." Smith concluded that "for Calvin, theology was not yet that psychology of the Spirit it was to become for his later followers."[12] Less than a century after Calvin's death in 1564, certain segments of the Reformed community were expanding on his theology, especially where religious experience was concerned, and requiring a conscious conversion of all who would claim membership in Christ's church. This new, experience-based norm for church membership was an attempt to link the visible church on earth with the eternal, invisible church known only to God. For these conversionistic Calvinists, what you see on earth is what you get in heaven.

Numerous scholars have sketched this development in Protestant communities in Britain and its American colonies. Yale historian Sydney Ahlstrom observed,

> A specific conversion experience was at first rarely regarded as normative or necessary, though for many it was by this means that assurance of election was received. Gradually, as Puritan pastors and theologians examined themselves and counseled their more earnest and troubled parishioners, a consensus as to the morphology [process] of true Christian experience began to be formulated. In due course—and with important consequences for America—these Nonconforming Puritans in the Church of England came increasingly to regard a specific experience of regeneration as an essential sign of election. In New England and elsewhere "conversion" would become a requirement for church membership.[13]

The establishmentarian Puritanism of seventeenth-century New England, particularly Massachusetts, was a case in point. C. C. Goen noted that among New England Puritans, "the authorities permitted only one form of established worship while insisting that church membership be restricted to those who could testify credibly to a conversion experience. This marked an innovation within Puritanism."[14] Edmund Morgan observed that the belief that "church membership should be limited to those who could demonstrate by a narrative of their religious experiences that they had received saving faith" did not begin with Plymouth Separatists but with Massachusetts-based "nonseparating Puritans" whose views on conversion and church membership spread throughout New England. This emphasis may be traced to certain English Puritans, especially those who chose to remain within the Church of England rather than separate from it. Morgan asserted that these Puritans attempted "to exclude from the church" all persons who were not able "to persuade them in speech or writing" that they were direct recipients of God's saving grace.[15] He concluded that many seventeenth-century Reformed

Protestants sought "to establish a morphology of conversion, in which each stage could be distinguished from the next," thus enabling individuals to evaluate their "eternal condition by a set of temporal and recognizable signs."[16] By the time those Puritans arrived in colonial America, Protestant approaches to religious experience were varied and evolving.

Calvinists and Arminians

Yet even as they emphasized the need for persons to have a valid conversion experience, many British and American evangelicals disagreed over the way salvation entered the heart and life of the individual sinner. At the beginning of the seventeenth century, many European Protestants were divided between Calvinists and Arminians, the latter group gravitating toward theological positions advocated by the Dutch Reformed scholar Jacob Arminius (1560–1609). Concerned that an extreme emphasis on the all-controlling sovereignty and providence of God would undermine divine benevolence and human freedom, Arminius set forth his views in *The Remonstrance*, a treatise published after his death in 1609. The Calvinism he resisted was itself divided between supralapsarians, who believed that God's sovereignty was so complete that the Deity caused the fall of Adam and Eve in order to elect some to salvation, and sublapsarians who believed that God had chosen to save some after Adam and Eve polluted the race by choosing sin. Seventeenth-century Calvinists generally agreed on the following elements of salvation, sometimes developed around the famous "TULIP" anagram.

1. **Total Depravity** thwarts both the ability and merit of human beings to receive salvation. Due to the curse of original sin all persons born into the world carry a depravity so devastating that there is no inherent ability for them to choose the good or the gift of God's grace in Jesus Christ.
2. **Unconditional election.** No ethical differences exist between the elect and the reprobate. God's choice of some for salvation is not

based on anything they can do to deserve such grace. It is the gracious, unmerited favor of the sovereign God.

3. **Limited atonement.** Only the elect are saved by Christ's atoning death on the cross.
4. **Irresistible grace.** The elect may turn away from grace for a time, but ultimately its gracious power will overwhelm them. The elect will experience and acquiesce to the grace of God before they leave this world. Saving grace is "infused" into the heart, enabling the sinner to obtain the free will to repent and believe. Regeneration precedes repentance and faith.
5. **Perseverance of the Saints.** The elect are sustained by God in a state of grace, despite weakness and sin. The grace that initiated salvation will keep salvation in the hearts of the elect. They are ultimately unable to turn away from God's grace.

Arminianism, as reflected in *The Remonstrance* of 1610, and condemned by the Synod of Dort, 1618–1619, offered the following response.

1. The inability of persons unaided by the Holy Spirit to come to God, exercise saving faith, or accomplish anything really good. (Hence it is not Pelagian.) Individuals have a bias toward sin but are not without free will. The human race did not inherit Adam's sin.
2. Election and condemnation are conditioned on the belief or unbelief of persons, choices known but not dictated by God. All persons are potentially elected; those actually elected come on the terms of election, repentance, and faith.
3. Christ's atonement is for all, but only believers enjoy its benefits. It made no person's salvation actual, but all persons' salvation possible. Christ died for the entire race, not simply the elect, hence the atonement is general, not limited.

4. Grace is not irresistible, though it is indispensable to religious experience and the spiritual life. Through prevenient or enabling grace, individuals may exercise their free will to choose Christ. God's saving grace "cooperates" with enabling grace, bringing salvation to the heart of those who choose to believe. Through the stimulus of grace prevenient, free will cooperates with grace efficient. Thus regeneration follows repentance and faith.
5. The doctrine of perseverance is clearly open to inquiry—though the grace of the Holy Spirit is sufficient for continued victory over evil. (Later Arminians would assert that backsliding or falling from grace was a real possibility.)

These two theological viewpoints reflected distinct approaches to the nature of salvation and the possibility of a valid religious experience in Christ. For Calvinists, even those elected to salvation were unable to move toward grace for themselves. They remained totally depraved until God's grace was infused into their hearts. By that infusion of grace they were regenerated, made new in Christ, and received the free will whereby to repent of their sins and choose, or at least recognize the grace they had received. Regeneration preceded repentance and faith as part of the biblically documented way of salvation.

For Arminians, all individuals possessed a modicum of prevenient or enabling grace whereby they were able to exercise repentance and faith, when connected with God's saving grace through Jesus Christ. Thus free will and grace "cooperated" to make salvation happen. All human beings were potentially elected, an election actualized by following the terms of salvation—repentance and faith. In this process repentance and faith preceded salvific regeneration.

Calvinists, Arminians, and the Believers' Church: A Baptist Case

As the seventeenth century got underway, a growing number of Protestants in England and America, Calvinist and Arminian alike, placed increasing emphasis on the need for all persons claiming membership in the church to acknowledge an individual experience of God's grace, a conversion made possible by faith in Jesus Christ. This concept shaped a movement that came to be known as the Believers' Church. The roots of that tradition were evident with the sixteenth century Swiss Brethren, Mennonites, Hutterites, and other groups identified with the Radical Reformation. They rejected infant baptism in favor of the baptism of believers only, a rite that followed the necessary confession of faith in Christ. The *Waterland Confession* of Dutch Mennonites, 1580, defines such spiritual regeneration as "a certain divine quality in the mind of a man truly come to himself... a renovation of the mind or soul, a true illumination of the mind... bringing with it a change of will and of carnal desires. It is... a vivification which manifests itself in an honest life.... It is a removal of the stony heart."[17] This experience of grace was necessary for baptism and church membership.

The concern for a believers' church became a hallmark of numerous Protestant communions in the United States, especially among the Baptists, a movement born in 1609 from English Puritan Separatism but with spiritual "kinship" to the Radical Reformation. By making conversion normative, Baptists defined the church itself as grounded in religious experience, evidenced by a profession of faith followed by believer's baptism. Yet the earliest Baptist groups covered a wide theological spectrum, some as General (Arminian) Baptists and others as Particular (Calvinist) Baptists. Founder Thomas Helwys wrote a confession of faith entitled *A Declaration of Faith of English People Remaining in Amsterdam in Holland, 1611*, which states,

> That the church off CHRIST is a company off faithful people 1.Cor. 1.2. Eph.1.1 separated fro[m] the world by the word & Spirit off GOD. 2 Cor. 6.17. being kint[knit] vnto the LORD, & one vnto another, by Baptisme. 1Cor. 12.13. Vpon their owne confession of the faith. Act.8.37. and sinnes. Mat. 3.6.[18]

Entry into the church required confession of sin and a profession of faith in Christ, followed by believer's baptism. The *Somerset Confession* of 1656, a statement aimed at reconciling General and Particular Baptists in England, says clearly, "THAT in admitting of members into the church of Christ, it is the duty of the church, and ministers whom it concerns, in faithfulness to God, that they be careful they receive none but such as do make forth evident demonstration of the new birth, and the work of faith with power."[19]

The *Orthodox Creed* of 1679 defined the nature of the new birth accordingly:

> Those that are united to Christ by effectual faith, are regenerated, and have a new heart and spirit created in them, through the virtue of Christ, his death, resurrection, and intercession, and by the efficacy of the holy spirit, received by faith, and are sanctified by the word and spirit of truth, dwelling in them.[20]

When it came to the actual process of salvation, seventeenth-century Baptists readily divided over Calvinist and Arminian approaches. The *Standard Confession* of British General Baptists (1660) suggested that salvation began when individuals

> assent to the truth of the Gospel, [freely] believing with all their hearts, that there is remission of sins, and eternal life to be had in Christ.... And so, shall (with godly sorrow for the sins past) [repentance] commit themselves to his grace, confidently depend upon him for that which they believe is to be had in him: such so believing are justified from all their sins, their faith shall be accounted unto them for righteousness, [regeneration] *Rom. 4:22, 23, 24. Rom. 3:25, 26.*[21]

The *London Confession* of 1644, a Particular Baptist document, explains regeneration as follows:

> That Faith is the gift of God wrought [infused] in the hearts of the elect by the Spirit of God, whereby they come to see, know, and believe the truth of the Scriptures... as they hold forth the glory of God in his attributes, the excellency of Christ in his nature and offices, and the power of the fullness of the Spirit in its workings and operations; and thereupon are inabled [*sic*] to cast the weight of their soules [*sic*] upon this truth [repent] thus beleeved [*sic*] [have faith].[22]

Baptists represented a second-generation Reformation sect that required an account of a personal religious experience as a prerequisite for baptism and church membership. They reflected a growing emphasis among certain Protestant communions that made conversion an entry point to religious community.

The Heart Prepared: Searching for Signs of Election/Salvation

As personal regeneration became more normative, questions arose as to how religious experiences were to be validated. In many Puritan settings, the specific congregation or its representative leaders were asked to authenticate the experience after hearing the testimony of the convert. Votes were taken and if the congregation did not approve, the individual was encouraged to "wait on the Lord" for the certitude of faith and again request church membership. All this placed pressure on individuals and churches to provide clearer means for understanding the nature and process of an authentic conversion. As the emphasis on conversion increased among certain Protestant groups, so did the need for understanding how to be saved and how to be certain that conversion had truly occurred.

In the seventeenth and eighteenth centuries, this need for certainty in conversion seemed particularly intense among English and American religious communions that were rooted in Reformed theology. Edmund Morgan suggested that through "a host of sermons and tracts that went far beyond Calvin," seventeenth-century Puritan preachers "broke down the operation of faith into a succession of recognizable stages."[23] Yet these efforts often served to increase the uncertainty of those desperate to know if their religious experiences were the appropriate ones. This is particularly evident in the debate over "preparation," specific signs that could portend, predict, or confirm genuine faith.

In *The Heart Prepared: Grace and Conversion in Puritan Spiritual Life*, Norman Pettit observed that "more than any other Puritan divine," Thomas

Hooker (1586–1647) "looked to the order of salvation, or the *ordo salutis*, as the central concern in Christian life." Hooker, an English Puritan preacher who arrived in Boston in 1633, was, in Pettit's view, "the master of the so-called 'steps' in the process of conversion." Hooker not only stressed the importance of preparation toward religious experience, but described various dangers faced by the seeker including issues of "pride, over introspection, and of excessive reliance on 'feeling' and 'sense.'"[24]

Hooker delineated four "means" by which persons might "obtain this blessed grace," but insisted that while such measures might be useful, they would not guarantee a genuine conversion experience in and of themselves. For that, sinners "must wait upon God in the use of the means, for it is not the means that will do it, that will work faith, but the Spirit of God in the use of the means."[25] The first step was to relinquish "all those props that the soul leans upon," all the efforts to "which a poor sinner doth repair... for succor," futile attempts to find "comfort" and quiet the conscience. Second, as the "promise" of salvation moves nearer, seekers should have their "hearts possessed thoroughly and persuaded effectually of the fullness of that good which is in the promise." This required acknowledging "in the heart," the depths of the self, and the complete sufficiency of God's promise of salvation. This divine promise held a "greater good... than the soul can see anywhere else" since "all the things in the world without the promise are not good."[26] Sinners should not outdistance God's schedule for redemption, but could "labor" to "acquaint" themselves "with the goodness of the promise before carnal reason comes" and overpowers the heart. God's ways are beyond human reason and God cannot be rushed. Thus salvation would find the elect "when it is most seasonable."[27]

Third, sinners were not to suppose that they could "bring any good" of their own, even faith, to the promise, but "go to the promise for all good," even the power "to believe the promise" itself.[28] Finally, on their way to faith, the unconverted were to "make no more conditions than God makes," since the "promise requires no more of a man than that he should come to take it." Hooker asserted that "many a poor soul is kept from coming to the promise" because they added "commodities" that were not God's. In other words, "when we are content to yield to the equal conditions of the promise, then the promise carries us quite away."[29]

Throughout the treatise, Hooker set himself on the side of "preparation," ways in which the unredeemed elect could "labor for this blessed grace of God." Yet such actions did not guarantee redemption, nor were they within the realm of God's saving work in Christ. He clearly believed, however, that the "labors" he recommended, fully documented in scripture, would move persons toward grace and ready them for an experience of salvation. Norman Pettit concluded that "in spite of rigorous and demanding introspection, there can be little doubt that Hooker was essentially concerned with hopeful anticipation.... Seldom did he turn to the regenerative process without initial concern for the 'heart prepared.'" No other New England pastor of the period wrote as extensively on the topic of preparation as Thomas Hooker.[30] But was the desire to move through such "labors" itself a sign that redemption was on its way? That question struck at the heart of what became a significant controversy over the nature of religious experience in seventeenth-century New England.

Preparing the Heart: John Cotton's Response

Hooker's views brought him into conflict with that paragon of Puritan virtues, John Cotton (1584–1652), who arrived in Massachusetts on the boat with Hooker in 1633. Cotton was no friend of "preparation" for conversion and made his views known as teacher in First Church, Boston. In fact, he associated the idea of "the heart prepared" with the dreaded Arminian heresy that individuals could actually participate with God in the salvific process.

Citing texts from both testaments, Cotton declared that the relationship between God and human beings began with a covenant set forth on God's terms. Like John Calvin before him, Cotton viewed the covenant as centered in the election of some persons to salvation, a process that was initiated and facilitated by God alone with no necessary preparation on the part of the elect. Divine grace was infused into the totally depraved soul and only then was an individual regenerated and able to exercise the free will to choose Christ and salvation. Unregenerate individuals, elected or damned, had no such freedom of the will until God's external grace was internalized. Only then was the sinner regenerated, made a spiritually new creation.[31] He wrote,

> I confess I do not discern that the Lord worketh and giveth any saving preparations in the heart till he give union with Christ. For if the Lord do give any saving qualifications before Christ, then the soul may be in the state of salvation before Christ; and that seemeth to be prejudicial unto the grace and truth of Jesus Christ... It seemeth to be that whatsoever saving work there be in the soul, it is not there before Christ be there.[32]

He concluded that "Christ is offered in a promise of free grace without any previous gracious qualification mentioned." Those who taught otherwise, i.e. preparation, were promoting salvation by "works."[33]

Cotton refused to accept Hooker's suggestion that the true believer could, through certain spiritual experiences, verify the reality of salvation and know assurance—deliverance from gnawing doubt as to whether the experience was genuine. For Cotton, the only assurance was with Christ on whom one cast oneself, trusting Christ to instigate and keep the covenant with the elect. As Pettit observed, "For Cotton the process of searching out assurance from covenant conditions forced one's attention on emotional experiences that diminished the centrality of Christ."[34]

In spite of Cotton's strenuous objections, Thomas Hooker's interpretation of the preparation of the heart gained prominence among seventeenth-century New England Puritans. Cotton, on the other hand, confronted yet another complicated theological controversy regarding the nature of sanctification as taught by his faithful pupil and supporter, Anne Hutchinson (1591–1643) who arrived in Boston from England in 1634.

Sanctification as Theology and Heresy: The Ann Hutchinson Case

Hutchinson, nurse, midwife, and mother of fifteen children, arrived from England in 1634, and soon became something of a spiritual guide for many in the Boston Puritan community. She held meetings in her home for women who wished to discuss John Cotton's Sunday sermons and other spiritual topics. These gatherings were encouraged by Cotton and others until males began to attend. Devoted to Cotton, Hutchinson insisted that she was simply echoing his own sermonic insights. She agreed with Cotton that human efforts at "preparation" were no sign of genuine justification and that God was the sole author of salvation. However, she also denied that sanctification—the works of a grace-filled life—was a sure sign of one's election to salvation. This kind of works righteousness she found to be a false hope of salvation. Controversy increased when she seemed to suggest that the presence of the Holy Spirit in the life of the truly redeemed was itself a source of continuing revelation. She insisted that "the person that the Holy Ghost dwells in is a justified person." This idea appeared to challenge the Puritan insistence that scripture alone was the source of God's revelation.[35] For Hutchinson, without the witness of the Spirit individuals were acting out of a "covenant of works," not a "covenant of grace," without Spirit-induced insight into the biblical text. Hutchinson's own claim that she had such a witness evidenced in specific revelatory insights led to charges against her for theological heresy and the promotion of Antinomianism, a belief that she was free from the law of the "old covenant."[36]

Ultimately John Cotton was forced to distance himself from his loyal student. He turned away from Hutchinson, acquiescing to her trial and expulsion from Massachusetts. In 1636 she was accused, as Governor John Winthrop suggested, of "two dangerous errors: 1. That the person of the Holy Ghost dwells in a justified person. 2. That no sanctification can help to evidence to us our justification." These ideas led to her insistence that no outward "spiritual action," "gifts," or "graces" can verify justification—a valid conversion experience—except "our union with the Holy Ghost."[37] The Puritan establishment was also scandalized by Hutchinson's spiritual egalitarianism, evident when she disseminated her theological opinions in "promiscuous gatherings" of both sexes. Her belief that the Spirit was "poured out on all flesh," (Acts 2:17) enabling all who received revelation to declare themselves was a form of religious experience that Puritan leaders found unacceptable. Excommunicated and exiled, Hutchinson and her family found safe harbor in Rhode Island, welcomed by fellow sectarians such as Roger Williams and Dr. John Clarke. They moved to Long Island in 1643, where she and seven of her children were killed in one of the conflicts that arose between colonists and Native Americans.

By the 1640s, the varied conversion morphologies suggested by Hooker, Cotton, and Hutchinson illustrated that even the Calvinists could not agree on a normative process of salvation. Each specific process challenged the theological order of the other, a reality that led to charges and countercharges of heresy. To require a religious experience centered in personal encounter with divine grace was to open the door to many individual interpretations of those experiences. Norman Pettit concluded that John Cotton's Calvinism blinded him to the experiential possibilities of a direct salvific encounter with the Savior who died on the cross and the possibility of "antinomian opinions, or to an inner assurance of being brought into right relation with God by direct revelation of his spirit."[38] Rather, it was Thomas Hooker who seemed to understand that beyond the affirmation of God's sovereignty was the ever-present possibility of a religious experience as varied as each individual who encountered grace.[39]

Arminianism: The Growing Threat

The demand that all persons experience conversion before claiming full church membership was an effort to secure a "visible church" on earth, a congregational communion composed only of those who could testify to a work of grace in their hearts. But as powerful as that idea became, it also created difficulty for those bound to a Calvinist theology of election and predestination. How then could the "believer" be assured that salvation had truly been secured? In response to that important question, many Puritans turned to Covenant, or Federal, theology, a way of protecting Divine sovereignty while opening the door to the possibility of assurance of salvation. The elect received a covenant from God who was then bound to act according to certain divine self-limitations in accomplishing salvation. All who received the covenant were candidates for salvation. If they refused that possibility, then the responsibility for their inevitable damnation was theirs alone. The elect would receive such redemptive grace, "owning" the covenant in order to keep their moral part of the bargain. Morality was not the source of salvation but the inevitable and required result. The language of election, predestination, and grace remained, but such terms were interpreted in a way that implied greater human engagement in the salvific process. Some even suggested that those who claimed God's covenant by faith were assured of the promised salvation. In time, however, the dogma of election became for many "only a formal concept, divorced from experience."[40]

Covenant theology opened the door to Arminianism, an alternative theological approach that challenged the staunch Calvinist proponents of the New England Way. This movement is not to be confused with the thought of Jacob Arminius, the seventeenth-century Dutch Calvinist, who responded to John Calvin's doctrines of election, predestination, and perseverance of the saints. Rather, Arminianism in this form reflected a more positive view of human nature, the overarching benevolence of the deity, and the role of free will in forming religious experience. It took seriously the role of reason in human activities and spirituality, yet affirmed the importance of divine revelation as discovered in scripture.[41] From the point of Puritan orthodoxy, Arminianism undermined the need for radical conversion as a defining redemptive experience, implying that persons might somehow affect their salvation through cooperation in the salvific process itself. As Conrad Wright noted in his history of the movement, the Arminians insisted that if persons "will only improve their natural abilities, and endeavor to love God and do his will, [God's] grace will not be denied them." Salvation, then, was linked primarily to the free choice of a given individual, and all individuals had that choice, not simply the elect.[42] In another sense, Arminianism was one way in which certain individuals, nurtured in Puritanism, sought to retain as much of that tradition as possible while restating its grand ideals in ways that provided possibilities for the redemption of the greatest number of people.

When Conversion and Nurture Collide: The Halfway Covenant

In their zeal to require conversion of all who claimed church membership, New England Puritans faced multiple theological and ecclesiastical difficulties. One of the most dramatic difficulties related to their retention of infant baptism as a "sign of the covenant," the New Testament equivalent of Jewish circumcision. John Calvin wrote of the practice:

> For just as circumcision, which was a kind of badge to the Jews, assuring them that they were adopted as the people and family of God, was their first entrance into the Church, while they, in their turn, professed their allegiance to God, so now we are initiated by baptism, so as to be enrolled among his people, and at the same time swear unto his name. Hence it is incontrovertible, that baptism has been substituted for circumcision, and performs the same office.[43]

Federal theology allowed the founders of the New England Way to retain infant baptism as a sign of the covenant with God, while requiring a personal experience of grace for full church membership. Since the original covenant was given to "Abraham and his seed," the converted were able to have their children baptized on the basis of the same promise. Yet as these infants entered adulthood, not all of them experienced conversion for themselves. When they produced offspring, many these baptized but unconverted citizens requested baptism for children.

Hence the theological difficulty: Could the children of baptized but unconverted parents receive baptism on the basis of their grandparents' full adherence to the covenant of grace? Could the covenant skip a generation and still remain in place? To complicate matters further, church leaders soon realized that their failure to baptize the children could produce a generation that grew up outside the spiritual and disciplinary environment of the congregation.

Perhaps the most famous response to this predicament came from the Halfway Covenant, a plan approved by the Synod of 1662. It stated,

> Church members who were admitted in minority, understanding the Doctrine of Faith, and publicly professing their assent thereto; not scandalous in life, and solemnly owning the Covenant before the Church, wherein they give up themselves and their Children to the Lord, and subject themselves to the Government of Christ in the Church, their Children are to be baptized.[44]

Baptized but unconverted parents who would "own the covenant" and agree to accept the discipline of the church could present their children for baptism. Yet neither those parents nor their children were permitted to receive Holy Communion or vote in congregational business sessions until they made the necessary profession of faith. The Halfway Covenant became a classic illustration of the difficulties of demanding a discernible conversion experience of all church members while retaining infant baptism and its accompanying nurture. Yet without it, an established, culture-dominant church faced the possibility that it might lose control of its status and moral authority with large segments of the population. Likewise, the Halfway Covenant reflected the difficulty of evaluating the individual conversion and defining its morphology in discernible ways, while maintaining dogmas of election, predestination, and the absolute sovereignty of the Divine.

Congregational implementation of the Halfway Covenant was certainly not uniform. Some followed it closely, refusing membership and communion to the unconverted while baptizing their offspring. Others went well beyond it, admitting all the baptized, even the unconverted, to communion as a "converting ordinance." This was the practice of Solomon Stoddard, Jonathan Edwards's grandfather, who spent sixty years as pastor of the church at

Northampton, Massachusetts. Still others, including Edwards, rejected the covenant, viewing it as a mistaken response to a spiritual condition that only genuine conversion could alleviate.[45]

Religious Experience in 17th-Century America: Multiple Voices

In his study of religious revivals, William McLoughlin asserted that America began "in an awakening," stimulated by Puritans and sectarians alike. He insisted that a seventeenth-century "Puritan Awakening" "gave America its own culture core, its sense of being a differently constituted people, covenanted with God on a special errand into the wilderness." At the same time, certain sectarian colonists provided "millennial hopes," "pietistic perfectionism," a concern for freedom of conscience, and a "profound sense of individual piety," all of which communicated another vision of this "holy experiment."[46]

McLoughlin observed that alongside their establishmentarianism, colonial Puritans contextualized "reason and intuition,... head and heart,... realism and idealism." He believed that Puritans exercised their own sectarian rebellion "against the formalism and sacerdotalism of the Church of England." Puritan theology, McLoughlin wrote, brought sinners "to a direct experience of the spirit and removed intermediaries between" individuals and "the deity."[47] He called attention to the paradox evident in Puritan concern for "the mystical wonder and beauty of communication with God's Spirit" and their efforts to bring reason to bear on revelation. Human reason was a gift of God that enabled Christians to combat the excesses of enthusiastical religion and "distinguish truth from hallucination."[48]

The Society of Friends (Quakers), initiated in England in the 1650s under the leadership of George Fox (1624–1691), introduced an approach to religious experience in sharp contrast to that of Calvinist and Arminian alike. Drawing on the first chapter of John's Gospel, Fox insisted that the "true light that gives light to everyone" had come into the world (John 1:9).

Dormant in every human heart, this inner light needed only to be recognized and implemented by the willing spiritual participant. The Spirit that enabled such spiritual experience was the ultimate egalitarian, beyond the hierarchical boundaries of class, gender, and economics inherent of European society. Fox's *Journal* described his own spiritual struggles, evidenced early on by depression and doubt. He wrote, "When I myself was in the deep, shut up under all, I could not believe that I should ever overcome; my troubles, my sorrows, and my temptations were so great that I thought many times I should have despaired, I was so tempted."[49] Finally, he reached a point "so that I had nothing outwardly to help me, nor could I tell what to do, then, oh, then I heard a voice which said, 'There is one, even Christ Jesus, that can speak to thy condition'; and when I heard it my heard did leap for joy."[50]

The discovery of the inner light led Fox to reject the doctrines of original sin and limited atonement, as well as the necessity for external sacraments. Believers fed on Christ in their hearts and were immersed into his life by the inner activity of the Spirit. Continuing revelation was a distinct possibility, since the same Spirit that inspired the scriptures lived and worked in the life of those who acknowledged the inner light. Fox introduced a kind of mystic activism, evident in an experientialism informed by revelatory dreams and visions, and expressed in opposition to war, military conscription, and governmental oaths, as well as a "hireling ministry" of paid clergy.[51] Quakers spurned ecclesiastical hierarchy, welcoming women and men to leadership and utilizing the "silent meeting," where members waited in silence for the Spirit to inspire commentary. Their alternative spirituality and public declaration of their views often led to severe persecution against Quakers in seventeenth-century England and America. One New England critic warned of the dangers of this revelatory faith that "cast off all attendances to ordinances, as public preaching, praying, reading the Scriptures, and attending to times of God's worship, and wait for the communication of this power [or inner light.]"[52]

In their introduction to Quakerism, the editors of *American Christianity* observed that "the original emphasis of the Friends on personal experience of the Inner Light could easily have led to a completely atomistic individualism, but this was checked by the Quaker conviction as to the oneness of the Divine Light and by their sense of community."[53] Jon Butler suggested that Quakers' many spiritual gifts were manifested in certain charismatic outbursts, revelations, and even physical healing. Butler placed Quakers among those colonial sectarians that evidenced a "non-conformist thaumaturgy," evident in various "exorcisms, raising the dead, and curing the mad."[54] They used the informal "thee" to equalize conversations regardless of class, and recognized the spiritual gifts of women in proclamation and leadership of "the meeting."

Quakers were early immigrants to the colonies, not only with a strong presence in Pennsylvania, but also in antagonistic New England. They challenged social and class decorum, fearlessly preaching even when commanded not to do so. In Massachusetts Quakers were jailed and even executed when they would not cease from their preaching of the inner light. Quaker preacher Mary Dyer (c. 1611–1660) was one of those persons, hanged in Boston in 1660 for her views and her refusal to stop preaching. Thus Carla Gardina Pestana concluded that colonial "residents who abandoned orthodoxy to join this mystical, millennialistic movement took an extreme step, arguably even more so than did their counterparts in England, where the world seemed to have been 'turned upside down.'"[55]

Other colonial sectarians included the Baptists and their concern for a believer's church, personal regeneration, and freedom of religion. On one hand Baptists were more compatible with Puritan establishmentarians, sharing common views born of Reformation Calvinism and Arminianism, making normative the Puritan concern for individual conversion. In other words, Baptists seemed radical until the Quakers appeared on the scene. Seventeenth-century Quakers debated Baptists with vigor, but also stood with them on many matters related to religious liberty and the right of all persons to believe or not believe according to the dictates of conscience. Both groups also shared a profound sense of the supernatural. Jon Butler writes that Baptist dissent was evident in the piety and practice of their spirituality and supernaturalism. He cites the "untutored eloquence of the 1655 confession of faith of the English Midlands Baptists" through which they "asserted the existence of a supernatural power ('eternall, almighty, unchaingable and incomprehensible'), identified its gender ('he'), sidestepped the problem of its material existence ('a spirit having his being of himselfe'), and acknowledged both its freedom and its power ('moveing all things according to the counsel of his own will')."[56] He notes that both English Baptists and Quakers acknowledged having participated in healing practices involving the infirm.[57] Thus the early colonies reflected their own diversity, some more than others. The concern for religious experience and supernaturalism made Quaker and Baptist sectarianism fertile ground for the pending revivals. Edmond Morgan concluded that Puritans had become "rebels" of sorts "in order to put into practice their ideas of a new society. To do so they had to restrain the rebellion of others" such as Baptists, Quakers, Arminians, and Antinomians. "The result was a long conflict between the demands of authority and the permissiveness of freedom."[58] As revivals appeared on the horizon, divisions over religious experience would be compounded.

★★ 3 ★★

Colonial Awakenings: A Surprising Work

An "Awakening" Becomes "Great"

Conversion was considered a normative requirement for the earliest New England Puritans, but as C. C. Goen noted,

> With the passing of the first generation of "experienced" [converted] church members it broke down, so that on the eve of the Great Awakening most of the parish churches in New England, like the old English churches from which they had fled, harbored a mixed company. That explains why many of the Awakening's converts were church members of one sort or another.[1]

The late seventeenth and early eighteenth centuries saw numerous regional and local awakenings in various colonies North and South, in what seemed an "episodically persistent" spiritual phenomenon.[2] As the eighteenth century got underway, conversionist ministers increased their insistence that it was not enough to "own the covenant," join a church, and attempt to live morally as a proper Christian. Such actions by the unconverted were not only hypocritical; they were theologically impossible, since even the appearance of moral living was "as filthy rags" (Isa. 64:6), predicated on impure and unrighteous motives of the damned. This included the work of unconverted ministers. Since many eighteenth-century conversionists believed that the churches were filled with unsaved laity and clergy, they reasserted the need for a visible church composed only of those who had been overtaken by saving grace. This emphasis on conversion and spiritual renewal led many to believe that a "surprising work of God" had spread throughout the colonies from Georgia to New England, a religious movement that became known as the Great Awakening.

The Great Awakening is important to a study of religious experience in the United States for numerous reasons. First, it was a time when many evangelicals asserted the need for and possibility of conversion as a mandate for claiming Christian identity. Second, it became an occasion for identifying certain morphologies (processes) leading toward genuine conversion, ways and means for discerning the often elusive actions of the Holy Spirit in bringing sinners to salvation. Third, it divided various Christian communities over the nature of conversion, the appropriate methods for encouraging personal regeneration, and the place of "enthusiasm"—physical and emotional outbursts—as evidence of genuine encounter with the Divine. Fourth, the *idea* of a Great Awakening became a mythic model for later revivalists who made spiritual renewal the goal of every Christian generation. This led some to speak of a Second Great Awakening in the early nineteenth century, a Third Great Awakening by the late 1800s, and even a Fourth Great Awakening in the mid-1900s.[3]

Fifth, this mythic approach to widespread religious awakenings became for many Americans a sure sign of the country's spiritual, often political, exceptionalism. Awakenings gave clear evidence that God would rescue the nation from the brink of moral and social collapse, not unlike God's redemptive activity with ancient Israel. A renewed religious experience could have constitutional implications.[4] Finally, for many, the idea of spiritual awakenings gave increased emphasis to the necessity for revivals, conversion, and the enduring possibility of "enthusiastical" religion. Yet even as those terms became part of the evangelical vocabulary, a theological and ecclesiastical consensus as to their meaning and application remained elusive, inside and outside communities of faith.

Students of awakenings have offered varying analyses of the awakening phenomenon. Some have seen it as the first stage of a formative, unifying national identity in the colonies that anticipated the American Revolution. Others view it as evidence of the early stages of American religious and political pluralism, while still others challenge the idea that the Great Awakening was as widespread or as culturally transforming as traditionally understood. Amid these varying views, it is clear that the religious awakening raised significant issues related to the nature and process of religious experience in Protestant America.[5]

In *Inventing the "Great Awakening,"* Frank Lambert describes certain individuals and approaches that placed the colonial revivals within the context of "salvation history," linking it to other historically acknowledged periods of spiritual and ecclesiastical renewal. He cites the work of John Gillies, whose *Historical Collections* brought together documents that illustrated or even validated "revival success" throughout the church's history from the New Testament to various Reformation communities in England and New England.[6] Lambert suggests that Gillies, a proponent of the revivals and Reformed theology, was less concerned about Christianity in general than with "experimental religion," "piety," or "practical religion." He writes that "experimental religion was that experienced firsthand by an individual through conversion, a spiritual new birth." This was in direct contrast, Gillies believed, to the more formal, detached approach to faith promoted by institutionalized ecclesial traditions and religious establishments.[7]

Gillies's work was an early indication of the revival as "culture war," a division over the impact of the Awakening on colonial religious life. Certain practitioners and later analysts judged the religious outpourings as "Great" because they were widespread, revitalizing Protestant communities that had grown complacent or spiritually indifferent. Other historians were less convinced that the awakening was such a major cultural event.

While the terms *revival* and *awakening* were sometimes used interchangeably to describe a period of religious intensity with conversionistic results, *revivalism* was simply a method used by evangelical churches and individuals as a means of shaping occasions when conversions were encouraged, anticipated, and experienced. William James insisted that "in the fully evolved Revivalism of Great Britain and America we have, so to speak, the codified and stereotyped procedure" for securing the "instantaneous conversion" that many evangelical religionists thought to be at the center of Christian religious experience.[8] Revivals became an outward and visible means to an inward and evangelical end. They were a mechanism for actualizing the need for all persons (or all elected persons) to encounter conversion.[9]

The Awakening at Northampton

The eighteenth-century awakenings began in diversity and controversy. On one hand, localized awakenings characterized various churches in the late-seventeenth and early-eighteenth centuries. For example, Solomon Stoddard (1643–1729), Jonathan Edwards's grandfather and pastor of the Northampton, Massachusetts, church for almost six decades, claimed that there were at least five spiritual "harvests" between 1680 and 1719, occasions encouraged, no doubt, by his use of communion as a "converting ordinance" offered to unsaved but baptized church members.[10] On the other hand, many churches followed Stoddard's communion practices and increasingly made a personal testimony optional for securing full membership in the congregation. In 1728, church leaders in Westfield, Massachusetts, voted that "those who enter full communion may have liberty to give an account of a work of saving conversion or not. It shall be regarded by the church as a matter of indifference."[11] Thus, Norman Pettit concluded, "Until 1748, when Stoddard's grandson Jonathan Edwards restored the requirements of experiential relations, this freedom from scrutiny made church admissions virtually automatic."[12] Conversionists were increasingly disturbed that church membership had become separated from genuine religious experience.

Jonathan Edwards joined his grandfather in Northampton in 1727, succeeding him as pastor two years later. From that vantage point he became concerned that the easy admission policies for church membership practices at Northampton and elsewhere had contributed to a "time of extraordinary dullness in religion," which he described accordingly:

> Licentiousness for some years greatly prevailed among the youth of the town; they were many of them very much addicted to night-walking; and frequenting the tavern, and lewd practices, wherein some, by their example exceedingly corrupted others. It was their manner very frequently to get together in conventions of both sexes, for mirth and jollity, which they called frolics; and they would often spend the greater part of the night in them.[13]

In response to these concerns Edwards made a concerted attempt to address the issue of conversion, insisting that all church members demonstrate the necessary experience of grace. He preached often on "justification by faith alone," a topic he called "a word spoken in season" that "was most evidently attended with a very remarkable blessing of heaven to the souls of the people in this town."[14] What Edwards would later describe as "a surprising work of God" was underway as "experimental religion" flourished and "the work of conversion was carried on in a most astonishing manner."[15]

In *A Faithful Narrative of the Surprising Work of God*, first published in 1736, Jonathan Edwards provided a variety of insights into the nature of religious experience as evidenced in the Northampton church. Originally written as a letter to Edwards's friend and Boston clergy-colleague Benjamin Colman, the document appeared in three editions between 1736 and 1738. In it Edwards described the spiritual awakening he was convinced had descended on his parish, tracing certain dramatic conversion processes that were at once individually unique and spiritually consistent. The awakening was truly a "surprising work," generated by God's provident action, utilizing but not dependent upon human engagement. Edwards described conversion as

> a great and glorious work of God's power, at once changing the heart and infusing life into the dead soul; though that grace that is then implanted

> does more gradually display itself in some than in others. But as to fixing on the precise time when they put forth the very first act of grace, there is a great deal of difference in different persons; in some it seems to be very discernible when the very time of this was; but others are more at a loss.... In some, converting light is like a glorious brightness suddenly shining in upon a person.... In many others it has been like the dawning of the day, when at first but a little light appears, and it may be is presently hit with a cloud; and then it appears again, and shines even brighter.... And many are doubtless ready to date their conversion wrong, throwing by those lesser degrees of light that appeared at first dawning, and calling some more remarkable experience that they had afterwards their conversion.[16]

While the experience could occur rather rapidly in some persons, others, perhaps the majority in Northampton, took an extended period of time. Edwards wrote, "Many continue for a long time in a course of gracious exercises and experiences, and don't think themselves to be converted, but conclude themselves to be otherwise; and none knows how long they would continue so, were they not helped by particular instruction."[17] Although all the elect were to wait on God to move on their hearts, it was possible for the ministers to be of some counsel in helping sinners interpret the process.

In the *Faithful Narrative* Edwards described several of the conversions in detail, sketching certain common features of each process. Although varied in each person, the process generally included 1) a sense of dependence on God's "sovereign Power"; 2) a deep conviction of personal sinfulness and a growing sense of helplessness in efforts to secure salvation; 3) increasing terror over one's lost condition; 4) recognition of God's righteous justice in condemning the depraved sinner; 5) a growing realization that God is gracious; and 6) ultimately, an acceptance of the presence of saving grace in the heart of those elected to salvation.[18] These components, Edwards believed, were consistently evident in each of the conversion experiences he observed.

The treatise also alluded to certain theological issues that Edwards would address in greater detail in many of his later works. For example, he suggested that Arminianism, a heresy about which the "friends of vital piety trembled for fear," was "strongly to be overruled" by the power of the awakening.[19]

He acknowledged the presence of various physical manifestations present in many conversions—weeping, bodily exercises, emotional outbursts—but Edwards defended the awakening (and himself) against the charge of "enthusiasm." He wrote, "Such persons amongst us as have been thus distinguished with the most extraordinary discoveries of God, have commonly in no wise appeared with the assuming, and self-conceited, and self-sufficient airs of enthusiasts; but exceedingly the contrary; and are eminent for a spirit of meekness, modesty, self-diffidence, and low opinion of themselves."[20]

Toward the end of the essay, Edwards provided two specific conversion case studies documenting the regeneration of two young women, Abigail Hutchinson, converted on her death bed, and Phebe Bartlet, born again at the age of four. Hutchinson's "great terror" was her sin against God. Indeed, she struggled against the inescapable taint of original sin, evident in her "sin in murmuring at God's providence," and her failure to do her "duty" toward her parents.[21] After a lengthy period of spiritual "darkness," she unexpectedly "awaked on Monday Morning, a little before day, [and] wondered within herself at the easiness and calmness she felt in her mind, which was of that kind which she never felt before." These regenerative encounters continued for several days, often with "constant sweetness in her soul," an indication that conversion came less from finding grace than in being found by it.[22] Edwards reported that Hutchinson "seemed to continue in an admirable sweet composure of soul, without any interruption, to the last, and died as a person that went to sleep, without any struggling, about noon, on Friday, June 27, 1735."[23]

Phebe Bartlet's conversion reflected a particularly important Puritan reading of Reformed theology: children are as totally depraved as adults and, if elected to salvation, may receive salvation in their kindergarten years, should providence so ordain. Born in March 1731, Bartlet's ordeal with grace began in May 1735, shortly after her fourth birthday, with a sense of her own sinfulness no less intense than that of the dying Abigail Hutchinson. Her parents often found her in her own closet, mourning her sins. On one occasion, "exceedingly crying and wreathing her body to and fro," her mother inquired if she feared that salvation would not find her, to which she replied, "Yes, I am afraid I shall go to hell!"[24] Such agonies continued for days until a particular Sabbath when, asked "whether she believed in God," Bartlet replied, "Yes. And being told that Christ was the Son of God," answered, "I know it." Edwards testified that "from this time there has appeared a very remarkable abiding change in the child," illustrated in her love of the Sabbath, her desire "to hear Mr. Edwards preach," an abiding "fear of the Lord," love of scripture, and a desire to "talk to other children about the great concern of their souls."[25] Bartlet's preschool spiritual agonies were evidence that the infused grace of God could overcome the sinful nature and the terrors of hell for child and adult alike.

Finally, Edwards acknowledged that toward the end of May, 1735, "it began to be very sensible that the Spirit of God was gradually withdrawing from us, and after this time Satan seemed to be more let loose, and raged in a dreadful manner." One terrible result was that on June 1, 1735, a well-respected member of the community, Joseph Hawley II, the Northampton town clerk, and Edwards' uncle by marriage, put "an end to his own life," by cutting his throat. Concerned about the state of his soul, Hawley ultimately came to "entertain no hope concerning his own good estate."[26] The surprising work of God ended as dramatically as it began, in part because some persons believed they would never have the necessary salvific encounter. While Edwards's sermons on the joys of salvation had claimed many, his vivid descriptions of the fate of the lost had also taken their toll. George Marsden writes,

> The shock of Hawley's suicide could hardly have been greater. Up to that moment it had seemed that nearly the whole town would join the exodus to the safe haven of God's grace. Satan had used the melancholic weakness of one man to turn the logic of the awakening against itself. The outpouring that for so many seemed a means to salvation became for Hawley a cause for despair and self-destruction.[27]

Thus evangelicals learned that the call for normative religious experience could become a double-edged sword when coupled with the doctrine of election, all with dangerous implications for those who believed themselves to be on the other side of God's love and grace.

Nonetheless, what occurred in Northampton gained momentum elsewhere as revivals flourished in segments of New England and the Middle Colonies, many influenced by the preaching of that "Grand Itinerant" George Whitefield, who seemed to embody multiple elements of colonial religious renewal. Whitefield (1714–1770) was part of the Holy Club at Oxford organized by the Wesley brothers, John and Charles. A Calvinistic Methodist, he began the practice of "field preaching" by 1739, carrying the gospel into the streets and markets throughout England, a practice that John Wesley soon appropriated. But where Wesley's stay in America was disastrous, Whitefield thrived. He made some seven trips from England to the colonies, founding an orphanage in Savannah, Georgia, and traveling throughout the colonies to raise funds for that endeavor and to awaken salvation in sinners.

Whitefield's preaching style was nothing if not dramatic, extemporaneous, spontaneous, and brisling with emotion. In the early 1740s he preached to large crowds in Boston, where conversions were not only extensive but also characterized by frequent public outbursts of "enthusiasm."[28] Soon other clergy and laity were reporting on packed preaching services, multiple conversions, and a variety of "religious affections." In a 1744 treatise, Samuel Blair, pastor in New Londonderry, Pennsylvania, described the revivalistic gatherings and their accompanying religious experiences as "vastly large" and the "number of the Awakened" greatly increased. He contended that few sermons preached in his region of the country in the summer of 1739 failed to "manifest Evidences of Impressions on the Hearers." These "impressions" included fainting, sobs, or "crying in a most dolorous Manner." On occasion individuals were also struck with "some strange unusual Bodily Motions."[29] Blair noted that at times he was forced to caution the "Distressed" to moderate their religious "passions" but in ways that would not "resist or stifle" the work of the Holy Spirit upon them.[30] He acknowledged, however, that some who observed the emotional manifestations—"weeping and fainting," "mourning" and "lamenting"—appeared to believe that conversion would follow if they engaged in those enthusiasms. Blair cautioned that such persons "appear'd to be pleasing themselves just with an imaginary Conversion of their own making," thus forcing ministers to give serious attention to the proper discernment of all religious encounters.[31] Thus the 1740s became a time for defining the nature of religious experiences, evident in multiple conversions and their accompanying exercises.

Enthusiasm: The Controversy

George Whitefield was not without his critics. His attacks on the Church of England for rejecting Reformed theology produced a strenuous response from South Carolina Anglican Alexander Garden. Garden defended Anglican theology and practice by asserting that gradual, once-born nurture was God's primary method for redeeming sinners through a sustaining religious experience that encompassed a lifetime, not a single, dramatic moment. In a sermon on regeneration, he denounced Whitefield and other enthusiasts for emphasizing regeneration as "an immediate, *instantaneous* Work of the *Holy Spirit,* wrought inwardly" on heart and soul, a singular occasion when the sinner claimed to be completely transformed, with no benefit from previous faith, or the necessity for continuing good works.[32] By contrast, Garden insisted that an "ordinary and established Method" of both scripture and church involves religious experience, "not as *absolute, sole, or instantaneous,* but the *gradual co-operative* Work of God's *Holy Spirit, for* Mankind, *in* them, and, *with* them as *moral Agents.*" This long tradition both opened their eyes through law and gospel, and solidified their faith through certain "blessed *Aids and Influences*" begun at baptism and cultivated through the "*good seed of the Word,*" until they become "*Children of God... regenerate or new born.*"[33] Gardner concluded the sermon by suggesting that the revivalistic upheavals, this "arrant *Jumble* of Contradiction and Confusion," could either be "calculated by a Romish [Catholic] EMISSARY, to distract and confound weak Minds"; or it could be produced by those Protestants "of a warm, frantick [*sic*] and *Enthusiastick* [*sic*] Brain."[34] His sermon illustrates that many of the advocates of sacramental nurture as a lifelong means of grace were not going to take "enthusiasm" lying down.

Suddenly issues of personal religious experience became a public phenomenon, as individuals expressed their conversionist orientation through emotional and highly controversial actions. Questions of religious affections ultimately divided the Congregational clergy into New Lights who defended and promoted revival message and methods, and Old Lights who essentially opposed them. Emotive outbursts became increasingly common in preaching services, often exercised while the sermon was in progress.

Charles Chauncy of First Church, Boston, became particularly critical of such affections, evidenced in his widely circulated sermon, *Enthusiasm described and caution'd against*, preached in 1742. In it he noted the appropriate and inappropriate uses of the word, the former "signifying *inspiration from God*, and the latter "as intending an *imaginary*, not a *real* inspiration." An "*Enthusiast*" in this sense was one "who has a conceit of himself as a person favoured with the extraordinary presence of the *Deity*." This negative form of religious experience could be observed in the "wildness" of their "look and air," a loosening of their tongues, certain bodily exercises that included "convulsions and distortions, into quakings and tremblings,... freakish" behavior, and an "imaginary peculiar intimacy with heaven."[35]

For Chauncy, such enthusiastical religion revealed a complete "disregard" for "the Dictates of *reason*." Thus devotees distanced themselves from any rational response to the claims they made and the emotions they invoked. Those who challenged the reasonableness and order of their actions "run the hazard of being stigmatiz'd by them as poor unconverted wretches, without the SPIRIT, under the government of carnal reason, enemies to God and religion, and in the broad way to hell."[36] Enthusiasts were in one sense to be "pitied," Chauncy asserted, influenced less by a "*bad mind*" than by a "*deluded imagination*." Yet their behavior required a response since it wreaked havoc among God's people. It set ministers against each other by giving "undue preference" to some at the expense of others, and, most importantly, by undermining the "*commandment of charity*."[37]

Chauncy was particularly concerned about the way in which enthusiasts flouted or ignored biblical and ecclesiastical traditions. Itinerant revivalists crossed parish lines to preach without seeking permission from settled pastors, and certain "*private christians*" ventured beyond "their own proper station" under "pretence" [*sic*] of the Spirit's mandate. Of "particular consideration" was the tendency of some enthusiasts to "encouraging WOMEN, yea, GIRLS to speak in the assemblies for religious worship," a clear "plain breach" of the Pauline dictum that women "keep silence in the churches."[38] For Chauncy, "enthusiasm" fostered an unhealthy egalitarianism that caused persons to go beyond their proper social or ecclesial place, even impugning the Christian profession of those who disagreed with their conversionistic methods.

Chauncy assured his hearers that enthusiasm could be avoided if persons would adhere to the "*proper work of the Spirit*," the authority and tradition set forth in scripture, the appropriate use of "*Reason* and *Understanding*," and continued prayer. He warned that Christians should resist "too great stress upon the *workings* of your *passions* and [religious] *affections*" and concluded by insisting that as dangerous as these disorderly revivalistic activities might be, "let not any think *ill* of religion, because of the *ill* representation that is made of it by *enthusiasts*. Rather, "real religion," manifested in "sobriety or reasonableness," should be pursued, with close attention given to the cautionary admonitions of the "*friends* to religion... who warn us of the danger of *enthusiasm*."[39]

Chauncy's concerns led him to suggest that there might even be times when the "civil authorities" would be compelled to take action, specifically in cases where public slander was directed against specific individuals. In an essay called "Seasonable Thoughts on the State of Religion," he defended the right of all persons to declare their religious views without harassment from the state. Yet in matters where public opinion was divided, he suggested that "each Party, without Favour or Affection [from the state], should be equally restrain'd from Out-rage and Insult." This included those who saw the revival as a "Work of GOD," and those who were "Enemies to Error and Confusion." While no one should "suffer, either for his *religious Principles*, or *Conduct* arising from them, while he is no Disturber of the *civil Peace*," when individuals, "under the Notion of appearing zealous for GOD and *his Truths*, insult their

Betters, vilify their Neighbours, and spirit People to Strife and Faction," then the governmental "Authority" may be forced to intervene. Should enthusiasts "suffer" then "'tis for their own Follies; nor can they reasonably blame any Body but themselves."[40] Chauncy apparently believed that some official state-related action might be necessary in cases of slander or liable, when revivalist preachers attacked the character or the salvation of clergy or laity who disagreed with their conversionistic views. The essay ended with Chauncy's reassertion that true Christian community would reflect an environment where children honored their parents; where parents acted in "counseling reproving, warning, restraining and commanding their *Children*; where servants worked to please their masters; and where masters provided servants 'things honest and good,' all 'within the Rules of Order and Decorum.'"[41] Good religion meant all persons knew their place in church and society.

Religious Affections: The Response of Jonathan Edwards

In response to Chauncy and other revival critics, Jonathan Edwards entered the fray, producing numerous refutations, perhaps the best known of which was *A Treatise on Religious Affections*, first published in 1746. In his introduction to Edwards's treatise, John E. Smith wrote that while the Northampton pastor had already described the individual conversions that took place in his parish and elsewhere, in this work "he was anxious to center attention on the gracious activity of the Spirit in the *individual* soul." Thus Edwards "concentrated upon the activity of the Spirit in its purity and upon the positive description of the genuine religious life." Smith suggested that Edwards viewed affections as evident in those that are "vigorous enough" to move "beyond indifference," to the point where "'the motion of the blood and animal spirits begins to be sensibly altered' and some change shows in the 'heart.'"[42]

The source of genuine religious experience, Edwards believed, was the "unmixed" love of God, the primary benefit of a relationship with the

Divine.[43] He defined religious affections as "the more vigorous and sensible exercises of the inclination and will of the soul."[44] They arise, he said, "from influences and operations of the heart, which are *spiritual*, *supernatural*, and *divine*" and were inseparable from genuine religious experience.[45] Edwards wrote, "I am bold to assert, that there never was any considerable change wrought in the mind or conversation of any one person, by anything of a religious nature, that ever he read, heard or saw, that had not his affections moved."[46] Yet he was quick to acknowledge that religious affections in themselves were not an absolute verification of genuine faith, noting that certain individuals "may seem to have love to God and Christ, yea to have very strong and violent affections of this nature, and yet have not grace."[47] Edwards sought to understand the role of religious affections in the conversion of the whole person—spiritually, psychologically, salvifically, and emotionally—while offering clues for sorting out genuine affections from false ones. He defended affections as one possible, perhaps probable, result of the movement of God's Spirit on the hearts of sinners, while insisting that no mere external signs are proof positive that persons have truly encountered saving grace. God alone was the source and agent of salvation.

Amid the debates, Edwards set himself against those who believed that there were a series of discernible and consistent stages or processes leading to genuine religious experience. While certain common traits were present in many experiences (such as he charted from his Northampton congregation), it was wrong to make them normative in discerning true religion from false. Likewise, he challenged, somewhat surprisingly, the practice of having the "godly" of the congregation vote or otherwise evaluate the validity of an individual's salvation. Faith communities might offer positive acceptance of conversion stories, but should not suppose that they could certify an experience that only God could authenticate in the hearts of the elect.[48] This was a direct criticism of the Puritan practice of having the church or its leaders approve the conversion testimony of new converts seeking church membership.

Edwards insisted that conversion experiences often produced "terrors" as sinful individuals confronted their own evil natures and their complete inability to secure grace. He declared that "God's manner of dealing with" sinners is often "to lead them into a wilderness, before he speaks comfortably to them, and so to order it, that they shall be brought into distress, and made to see their own helplessness." This divinely initiated regimen could readily create such anxiety that the "anxious" might cry out, weep, or otherwise respond to the horrors of damnation.[49] Yet, with a bit of eighteenth-century psychologizing, he acknowledged that "the terrors which some persons have, are very much owing to the particular constitution and temper they are of." Certain personalities seemed "more strongly impressed with everything they are affected with, than others." In such persons "affection and imagination act reciprocally," until their religious affections are "raised to a vast height, and the person is swallowed up, and loses all possession of himself."[50]

In making a case for religious affections, Edwards provided extensive analysis of both the experiences he observed, and the manifestations they provoked. Yet his observations were conditioned by the unpredictability of the Divine and the efforts of the Evil One to give false hope by duplicating emotional outbursts that imitate genuine spiritual experiences. He concluded that demonstrating a particular "distinctness as to steps and methods is no certain sign that a person is converted," but "being without it is no evidence that a person is not converted."[51] Likewise, while it is clear from scripture that sinners "can't be brought heartily to receive Christ as his Saviour," apart from awareness of "sin and misery," "emptiness and helplessness," and a "just desert of eternal condemnation," yet there was no evidence that each one of those spiritual insights or expressions "must be plainly and distinctly wrought in the soul." They will surely occur but may not be "plain and manifest, in all who are truly converted."[52] So the "Spirit's proceeding" on those who are truly born again "is often exceeding mysterious and unsearchable." The effect is ultimately "discernible," but no one can really "tell whence it came, or wither it went."[53]

A central element of *Religious Affections* involved Edwards's description of twelve "signs" that "take notice of some things, wherein those affections that are spiritual and gracious, do differ from those that are not so." The signs point to outward and inward expressions of the movement of the Holy Spirit on individual lives. Again Edwards conceded that the delineation of such signs in no way guaranteed "any certainly to distinguish true affection from false in others; or to determine positively which of their neighbors true professors, [of religion] are and which are hypocrites."[54] In fact, he was adamant that "it was never God's design to give us any rules by which we may certainly know, who of our fellow professors are his." Rather, "it was God's design to reserve this to himself, to his prerogative." Here Edwards distanced himself from the previous emphasis on "preparation" as a sign of election and left the matter of genuine saving religious experience with the sovereign will of God.[55] He described various signs of genuine religious affections, not to provide a check list for assuring persons that they are in the elect, but, with biblical veracity, to defend the activity of the sovereign "God and Father of our Lord Jesus Christ" in converting the whole person—mind and heart, soul and body. To fragment human beings into mere intellect or emotion obscured the intent of the creator in forming human beings in intellectual and emotional complexity, especially as they encounter God's saving grace. Edwards acknowledged that unconverted individuals may have "new and surprising... religious apprehensions and affections" whereby they glimpse God's grace, yet what they experienced could instead "be nothing like the exercises of a principle of new [Christian] nature."[56] These new experiences should not be confused with genuine "spiritual things."[57]

The "Twelve Signs" reflect Edwards's commitment to a faith grounded in scripture and Reformed theology, and a believers' church composed only of those who experienced a direct encounter with Divine grace. His theology of conversion was inseparable from his Calvinist theology. This was evident in several ways. First, Edwards insisted that conversion began with the recognition of individual depravity and separation from God, not an immediate perception of God's love. He wrote that for the unconverted to claim knowledge that God "loves 'em'" is "very absurd." Even those who have a "common knowledge of the principles of religion" understood that "it is God's manner to reveal his love" to persons only "after they have believed, and not before."[58] Total depravity prevailed until God's grace was infused into the heart of the elected sinner. Only then might one recognize and receive God's love. No one could claim the "promise of the covenant of grace" until Christ had come to them by faith.[59] Before that act of regeneration occurred depravity prevailed.

Second, Edwards anchored his approach to religious affections firmly within the depth of Christian spirituality, a particular type of piety. Such "spiritual understanding consists... in **a sense of the heart**, of the supreme beauty and sweetness of the holy or moral perfection of divine things, together with all that discerning and knowledge of things of religion that depends upon, and flows from such a sense."[60] This divinely induced "sweetness and delight" moves beyond "mere notional understanding" or rational speculation to "the sense of the heart, wherein the mind "don't [*sic*] only speculate and behold, but relishes and feels." This blessed knowledge that provided a "sensible perception of amiableness and loathsomeness, or of sweetness and nauseousness," was not the same as the knowledge of "what a triangle is or what a square is. The one was mere speculative knowledge; the other sensible knowledge, in which more than the mere intellect is concerned; the heart is the proper subject of it."[61] Thus "spiritual understanding" rested primarily in "a taste of the moral beauty of divine things," preeminently revealed in "the beauty of the way of salvation [made possible] by Christ."[62]

Third, in discussing the "Twelve Signs" Edwards did not neglect a theology of sanctification, set in the context of Puritan spirituality. The sixth sign, for example, suggests that "gracious affections are attended with evangelical humiliation." By evangelical humiliation, redeemed individuals continue to recognize and own their "utter insufficiency, despicableness, and odiousness, with an answerable frame of heart."[63] The truly redeemed understood that their redemption came, not from within themselves, but as creatures "exceedingly sinful, under a dispensation of grace." This humiliation was an essential element of "the new Covenant," to bring fallen yet redeemed persons into conformity to a new nature, that of Jesus Christ. Christian living was the outgrowth of this effort to forsake "worldly inclinations," "natural self-exaltation," and personal "dignity and glory," in order to make way for the nature of Christ in the individual soul.[64]

Finally, Edwards insisted on the inseparable link between "gracious affections" and perseverance in "Christian practice." While ultimate knowledge of genuine conversion experience is known only to God, he admitted "that when the Scripture speaks of Christian practice, as the best evidence to others, of sincerity and truth of grace, a profession of Christianity is not excluded, but supposed."[65] Perseverance in grace was a sound clue to redemption.

William Clebsch observed that Edwards's theological position was built on three important propositions: "Scripture as God's revelation, the saints' experience as lively and sensible affections of holiness, and the created orders of nature and history as images or shadows of divine things."[66] While his approach mirrored classic Reformed orthodoxy, Edwards nonetheless "developed a new psychology in which really believing these truths made a visible difference in people's affections." Thus Clebsch concluded that Edwards "made religious experience so outwardly palpable that these Christian truths and the realities for which they stood became sweet to the taste, symmetrical to the eye, harmonious to the ear, pleasant to the touch and smell." They were "lively to the senses, enlightening to the mind, and delightful to the heart."[67]

The Chauncy/Edwards Debates

The Chauncy/Edwards debates remain an important illustration of the divisions that descended on the New England Way as revivals came and went in various colonies. In his study of Chauncy, Charles Lippy contended that many analysts were so enamored with Jonathan Edwards that they neglected a deeper reading of Chauncy, his motives and reflections. Many simply labeled Chauncy "a half-hearted and hardly imaginative liberal, a forerunner of later Unitarianism, or a Deist in Puritan disguise."[68] Lippy insisted that Chauncy and Edwards were both committed to Puritan ideals, often citing the same Puritan forebears to support their conflicting opinions. He wrote, "Each simply took the main tenets and spirit of New England Puritanism and pushed them to very logical but very different extremes."[69] For Lippy,

Edwards's own understanding of religious experience was a configuration of "a new principle of life," uniting the whole person to "inclination-will-mind-heart" in contrast to a rational-mental-speculative response. Chauncy, by contrast, insisted that "the understanding was the locus of religious experience" which meant that enthusiastical religion drew the "unthinking into false religion." Like other Old Light critics, Chauncy rejected the idea that regeneration rested primarily in a dramatic conversion event, preferring a redemption evident in "the continuous orderly work of a gracious God" secured through the biblically prescribed means of grace—baptism, preaching, personal discipleship, and consistent Christian living—that guided individuals toward God in Christ.[70]

In spite of their differences over enthusiasm and the means to experience the new birth, Chauncy and Edwards both contributed to the individualism that would later become a hallmark of certain varieties of religious experience in American faith communities. As Edwards and other Calvinist revivalists saw it, grace could seek out elected individuals, whatever their social or spiritual status. Election had its own egalitarian twist. For Chauncy, every individual had the logical capacity to comprehend the gospel and respond to it through the divinely ordered means of grace.[71] Lippy concluded that both Edwards and Chauncy promoted approaches that ultimately undermined or significantly modified the covenant on which the early Puritan conversionism was built. He noted that while the revivalist-New Light contingent "exalted the individual because the Spirit could radically alter one's status," rationalist-Old Lights emphasized that "the individual had power to determine whether to take advantage of the pattern of life and conduct set forth in faithful adherence to the means."[72] Conversionism and discipleship became inseparable from the individual's engagement in the redemptive process.

Revivals and Religious Experience: Other Voices

Differences over the nature and practice of revivals and revivalists led to what might be called the conversion wars—debates that raged in print and in pulpits across the colonies. Not only was there controversy over the various forms of religious enthusiasm, but also over the signs of genuine conversion, particularly among ordained ministers. It was not uncommon for antirevivalists to charge that many conversions were simply emotional exercises that were far outside the biblical and ecclesiastical norm. Supporters of the revival often questioned the conversion of those who had not or would not testify to a clear and present work of grace in their hearts.

Perhaps the most extreme ministerial enthusiast was James Davenport (1716–1757), a Yale graduate who was much influenced by George Whitefield's visit to New England. An itinerant preacher, he traveled throughout New England, stressing the need for dramatic conversion, encouraging emotional responses, and even demanding certain cathartic actions that challenged converts to burn heretical books and worldly goods. In both Connecticut and Massachusetts, Davenport alienated many of the settled clergy by attacking certain antirevival ministers as unconverted and urging their parishioners to expel or abandon them. On one tour of Massachusetts he insisted that few Boston pastors were genuinely converted, even naming stalwarts such as Benjamin Colman, Charles Chauncy, and Joseph Sewall as outside salvation. These practices led a group of the clergy to close their pulpits to him. Reverend Ebenezer Parkman noted that most of "the wise and worthy" clergy supposed that Davenport was "touched in the head."[73] Davenport's deportment became so erratic and extreme that he was dismissed as exhibiting a complete spiritual and emotional collapse. In a 1743 letter to clergyman Eleazar Wheelock, Sarah Pierpont commented that "Mr Davenport (at Stanford)...lyes [*sic*] in the dark before God for his conduct at N. London [CT]."[74]

Davenport himself finally acknowledged his failings, issuing a letter of *Confessions and Retractions* in 1744, deploring various "*unjust Apprehensions and Misconduct*" that had produced "great Blemishes to the Work of God." These included exercising "private judgment" in naming "*in public prayer*" persons he thought unconverted; "*urging*" separation from said unconverted ministers; and "*following Impulses or impressions*" without properly consulting scripture. Davenport then expressed repentance for having given in to "the powerful influence of a *false Spirit*" that led him to such "errors."[75] Received back into the Puritan fold, Davenport became a pastor in New Jersey from 1754 to his death in 1757.

Divisions also surrounded the work of revivalist Presbyterian Gilbert Tennent (1703–1764), minister in New Brunswick, New Jersey. His father, William Tennent, was the founder of Log College, an early seedbed of revival sentiments and ministerial training. The Tennents, father and son, helped to spark a religious revival that began with and then moved beyond Scottish immigrants in the Middle Colonies. Greatly influenced by the conversionism and moralism of his Dutch Reformed neighbor Theodore Frelinghuysen (1691-1747), Tennent called Presbyterians to reassert the need for a work of grace in the lives of all church members. He urged ministers to "make it their awful, constant, and diligent care, to approve themselves to God, to their own consciences, and to their hearers," before they dared call others to faith.[76] As Frank Lambert has shown, Tennent then set forth a "revival program" aimed at encouraging awakenings. Tennent insisted that churches make "diligent use of those means necessary to obtain the sanctifying influences of the Spirit of God."[77] This program included not only preaching for conversion but extensive family and church-related instruction, congregational investigation as to the validity of conversion, and monitoring candidates for ministry as to their moral and spiritual integrity.[78]

As the divisions between New Side/Old Side Presbyterians took shape, Tennent preached what became perhaps his best-known sermon, "The Danger of an Unconverted Ministry," in 1741. Taking his text from Mark 6:34, Tennent suggested that colonial America, like first-century Palestine, was witness to a religious situation where the people were "sheep not having a shepherd." He compared unconverted clergy to the "Pharisee-Shepherds" who confronted Jesus and worked to undermine his mission and message, reflecting both the "Craft of Foxes" and "Cruelty of Wolves."[79] These "Pharisee-Teachers, having no *Experience* of a special Work of the Holy Ghost, upon their own Souls, are therefore neither inclined to, nor fitted for, Discoursing, frequently, clearly, and pathetically, upon such important Subjects."[80] Because they were unconverted, they did not understand or care for making plain the way of salvation. Thus they made religious experience too easy, comforting sinners rather than convincing them of their depravity. "They have not the Courage, or Honesty, to thrust the Nail of Terror into sleeping Souls; nay, sometimes they strive with all their Might, to fasten Terror into the Hearts of the Righteous." In other words, these "blind Guides" gave false hope to the sinful and attacked those converted persons who dared to challenge their view of the gospel.[81]

Tennent's sermon reflected serious theological divisions among the pro and antirevival clergy, what he saw as a departure from orthodox (Calvinist) doctrine. He wrote that "the Doctrines of Original Sin, Justification by Faith alone, and the other Points of Calvinism, are very cross to the Grain of unrenew'd [unconverted] Nature," and asked, "Is not the Carnality of the Ministry one great Cause of the general Spread of Arminianism, Socinianism, Arianism, and Deism, at this Day through the World?"[82] Tennent concluded by acknowledging that the "visible church" on earth was composed of both "sincere Servants of God," and "many Servants of Satan" hiding under "a religious Mask." Given that reality, he insisted that harmony in the church could not be sustained "till their [unconverted] Nature be changed."[83]

Tennent's enmity toward the antirevivalists did not endure. The revivalists organized an alternative synod 1745 but the Presbyterian factions united again in 1758. This was due in part to Gilbert Tennent's work for reconciliation, illustrated in his treatise, *Irenicum*, published in 1749.[84]

The depth of division over unconverted ministers is illustrated in the case of David Brainerd, whose missionary zeal and piety made him a spiritual guide for generations of persons impacted by his journal. Brainerd (1718–1747) was dismissed from Yale College in 1741–1742 after he was overheard to suggest that one of the tutors, Chauncey Whittelsey, had "no more grace than a chair." His refusal to retract the statement led to his expulsion. Jonathan Edwards, his friend and mentor, fretted that it was unfair to require a public repentance of Brainerd since his criticism of the tutor was a "private confession." Yet Edwards also acknowledged that "Brainerd had the unhappiness to have a tincture of that intemperate indiscreet to the habitual temper of his mind."[85] Brainerd's state of mind was clearly an important element in his own melancholy spirituality, as evidenced in his diary, itself a popular publication read by generations of evangelical Protestants.

Brainerd exiled himself into the New Jersey wilderness as a missionary to the Native Americans. Contracting consumption (tuberculosis) he died in the Edwards's home, cared for by Edwards's daughter, Jerusha. Jonathan Edwards saw to the publication of Brainerd's diary, pleased that it blended intense spiritual reflection with direct Christian action, especially as aimed at the conversion of native peoples. Norman Pettit wrote that in publishing the work, Edwards depicted Brainerd "not as an individual but as a representative figure" whose life and work illustrated Edwards's concern to determine, "What are the distinguishing qualifications of those that are in favor with God, and entitled to his eternal rewards?"[86]

Yet Edwards himself did not hesitate to acknowledge the dark cast of Brainerd's spiritual nature. In the introduction to the diary he wrote that Brainerd "was one who by his constitution and natural temper was so prone to melancholy and dejection of spirit." Edwards apparently felt the need to explain Brainerd's psychological state as it related to the nature of an awakened spiritual life all together. Thus he observed,

> There are some who think that all serious strict religion is a melancholy thing, and that what is called Christian experience is little else besides melancholy vapors disturbing the brain, and exciting enthusiastical imaginations. But that Mr. Brainerd's temper or constitution inclined him to despondency, is no just ground to suspect his extraordinary devotion, as being only the fruit of a warm imagination.[87]

Edwards was careful to note that throughout his short life, Brainerd's religious experience was generally free from "imagination," or a tendency toward "enthusiasm" in religious expression. He was intense in his religious commitments, but his "religious impressions, views and affections in their nature were vastly different from enthusiasm." The depth of his self-effacement and humility stood in sharp contrast, Edwards believed, to the type of religious enthusiasm that puffed persons up "with a high conceit of their own wisdom, holiness, eminency and sufficiency."[88]

David Brainerd's diary reflected a particular facet of Puritan postconversion piety, a combination of devotion to Christ with constant struggle against the ever-present effects of depravity, a battleground between flesh and spirit. The diary provides an account of his life, including his missionary work with the Native Americans, a content interspersed with details of his deteriorating health and ceaseless spiritual angst. An entry in his diary for January 14, 1743, illustrates something of his inner struggles:

> My spiritual conflicts today were unspeakably dreadful, heavier than the mountains and overflowing floods: I seemed enclosed, as it were, in hell itself. I was deprived of all sense of God, even of the being of God; and that was misery! I had no awful apprehensions of God as angry. This was distress, the nearest akin to the damned's torments that I ever endured.[89]

This spiritual turmoil perpetuated doubts regarding his calling to the Native Americans. The January 23, 1743 entry begins,

> Scarce ever felt myself so unfit to exist, as now: I saw I was not worthy of a place among the Indians, where I am going, if God permit: I thought I should be ashamed to look them in the face, and much more to have any respect shown me there. Indeed, I felt myself banished from the earth, as if all places were too good for such a wretch as I.[90]

The reality of his struggles, even when Christian graces prevailed, runs throughout the diary. On October 18, 1742, he wrote, "In the morning, felt some sweetness, but still pressed through some trials of soul. My life is a constant mixture of consolations and conflicts, and will be so till I arrive at the world of spirits."[91] Such a "mixture" prevailed to the bitter end, a piety that became a distinct option for certain Protestant individuals across several centuries. For Brainerd, sanctification—going on in grace—remained inseparable from the fact of total depravity, even for the elect. Conversion did not completely defeat the sinful nature, which remained a constant reminder of the spiritual warfare between good and evil, flesh and spirit, even in the hearts of the elect.

Norman Pettit contrasted the piety represented in Brainerd with that of the Moravians who came to Georgia in 1735 and later established settlements in Pennsylvania and North Carolina. He wrote that Brainerd's understanding of religious experience involved "a process of guilt and pain," while Moravians emphasized God's benevolent love for humanity. The Moravians insisted that Christ had taken away the curse of original sin, freeing Christian believers "to love God without continuous penitence." While Moravians asked those seeking salvation and church membership to make a profession of faith, they did not require a public declaration of a specific conversion experience, as did many New Light Congregational churches.[92]

The New Divinity Movement: Continuing the Awakening

Such differences reveal the way in which questions of conversion impacted both the piety and the theology of colonial congregations. On one hand, the Awakening seemed primarily a movement for spiritual renewal, less concerned with challenging the prevailing Calvinism than with ensuring the conversion of church members. As Joseph Conforti observed, "The Awakening touched the hearts of so many New Englanders because it was essentially an undogmatic, pietistic call for the regeneration of American society." Yet he also notes, "ironically," that "theological divisiveness" also accompanied the revivals.[93] Whatever else it may have meant, the Awakening created a debate, less about Calvinistic dogmas than about two important and divisive spiritual issues: the need for a conversion experience for all who would claim Christian commitment, and the nature of the religious affections that accompanied conversion. Calls for spiritual renewal had significant theological implications, ultimately provoking long-term ecclesiastical divisions. The New Light, prorevival movement is a case in point. A separatist faction among both Baptists and Congregationalists encouraged New Lights to vacate traditionalist churches (and their unconverted ministers) and form new congregations of visible saints (those who testified to a conversion experience). Others, however, called the converted to remain in the old guard churches as "leaven" that would encourage revival. Among these were the representatives of the New Divinity movement, an effort to extend both revivalism and the Calvinism represented in Jonathan Edwards as a theological and conversionistic model among American Protestants. New Divinity leader Samuel Hopkins (1721-1803) added multiple "innovations" to Edwardsean thought, while another segment of the movement led by Joseph Bellamy (1719-1790) claimed a distinctly "neo-Edwardsianism" approach to conversion altogether.[94]

The phrase "New Divinity" was a disparaging term applied in 1765 to those revival supporters (like Samuel Hopkins) who claimed that unconverted but "awakened" individuals who availed themselves of certain "means of grace" were guiltier than those who gave no thought to their salvific condition. Yet it became a movement that attracted a new generation of younger ministers, many converted in the revivals, who wanted to make conversionistic religious experience normative for individual who would claim membership in New England churches and to promote a theology of "Consistent Calvinism" over against modifications that allowed for greater individual participation in the process of salvation.[95]

Samuel Hopkins's own conversion followed a classic Calvinist pattern. As a student at Yale he was moved by the impassioned preaching of Gilbert Tennent and encouraged to consider the state of his own soul by fellow student David Brainerd. As a sense of total depravity descended upon him, Hopkins began to believe that salvation was impossible. After an extended time of spiritual agony, at last conversion found him, in September 1740. He described it accordingly:

> At length I was in my closet one evening, while I was meditating, and in my devotions, a new and wonderful scene opened to my view. I had a sense of the being and presence of God, as I never had before; it being more of a reality, and more affecting and glorious, than I had ever before perceived.... I was greatly affected, in the view of my own depravity, the sinfulness, guilt, and odiousness of my character; and tears flowed in great plenty.[96]

Hopkins apparently did not realize that he was converted at that moment, but came to accept the event as a turning point in his spiritual life.

The New Divinity movement challenged the more moderate Calvinism that suggested that experience of the divine covenant involved a degree of active participation in the process of conversion. This included Bible study, prayer, church attendance, and ethical living. Samuel Hopkins and others denied this and, in the name of Jonathan Edwards, reasserted the idea that salvation was completely the work of God through an unconditional covenant. They also stressed a belief in "disinterested benevolence" by which sinners cast themselves and their eternal fate so thoroughly on God's action that they were willing to be damned should it be so ordained before the foundation of the world.[97]

So passive was the human candidate for salvation that Hopkins contended that salvation itself involved only two basic elements. The first was the regeneration infused into the heart of an elected sinner. The second aspect was evident in the sanctified actions of the converted who at last had the free will to choose the good and participate in unselfish practices of the truly saved.[98] Hopkins extended his argument with his belief that "awakened sinners," aware of their need for salvation, were, in that state, more disgusting to God than those depraved individuals who were blind to their need for redemption. Yet he also suggested, as John Conforti writes, "that the unregenerate were still obliged to use means for although their efforts were spiritually worthless and God's grace was unconditional, He [God] was more likely to convert awakened than unawakened sinners."[99]

The Great Awakening: Many *Senses* of the Heart

The Great Awakening made religious experience—an encounter with Jesus Christ—normative and divisive in American Protestantism. It spawned multiple morphologies of conversion, offered excesses and explanations for "enthusiastical" religion born of the agonies of sin and the joys of salvation. It divided churches and contributed to the ever-burgeoning pluralism of

American denominationalism. Experientially, it opened the door to a continued quest for personal salvation, often narrowing the gap between the elect and non-elect in churches within the Reformed tradition. God was sovereign; salvation was arbitrary based only on election through God's predestined, unconditional grace. Yet the possibility of redemption evident in the conversion experiences of friends and neighbors made salvation tangible, a genuine possibility for those whose hearts could or would be "prepared."

★★ 4 ★★

New Measures: Nineteenth-Century Revivalism

New Awakenings: Religious Experience and Democratic Idealism

The religious experiences evident in what came to be called the Second Great Awakening encompassed and expanded similar phenomena present in the colonial revivals. Shaped by certain transatlantic movements such as Methodism, the Second Awakening developed features that were decidedly American. This is evident in a variety of ways. First, religious liberty contributed to the demise of state-privileged religious establishments and the expansion of denominations, those "voluntary associations" uniting "like-minded and like-hearted" individuals around shared doctrine and practice.[1] Since denominations and their member congregations were voluntary associations in which constituents chose to participate, revivals became one means of securing both conversions and members. Second, the proliferation of churches and denominations made sectarian division a distinguishing mark of American religious life. Diverse religious communions often promoted varying morphologies of conversion, justification, and sanctification alike. Thus finding a normative religious experience became increasingly complex. Much depended on which salvation message was appealing enough to "draw in the net" toward conversion. Third, the wide-open spaces of the continental United States offered sanctuary for innumerable groups that wished to put their specific experiences into practice without interference from "the world." Thus Whitney Cross could suggest that western New York was itself a "burned over district" where revival fires continuously scorched the landscapes through multiple religious movements, each offering its own form of religious encounter. This environment was fertile soil for new outbursts of religious enthusiasm involving powerful physical and emotional "exercises," trances, new revelations, and other mystical frenzies. Fourth, camp meetings and seasonal revivals provided a charismatic context where these conversionistic forces were unleashed in a concerted effort to Christianize the rough and tumble culture of the frontier. As Christopher Evans noted, camp meetings "became the primary means by which once-marginalized religious groups such as the Methodists, built powerful religious movements that impacted the subsequent development of the American revivalist tradition that extends into the twenty-first century."[2] Finally, democratic idealism and revivalist conversionism combined so as to make the will freer and the possibility of salvation open to all who would freely choose to do so.

Revivals at Yale

One of the early stages of what is known as the Second Great Awakening took shape among students and faculty at Yale College in New Haven, Connecticut, across the late eighteenth and early nineteenth centuries. Chauncey Goodrich, Yale's first professor of rhetoric, described various periods of revival and related religious experiences in an 1838 essay published in the *Journal of the American Education Society*. Goodrich traced the earlier eighteenth century awakening, and then turned to events that occurred during the presidency of Timothy Dwight (1752–1817), grandson of Jonathan Edwards. Dwight began at Yale in 1795 with strong apprehensions regarding the spiritual state of the college, offering lectures on "the nature, and danger of infidel philosophy," as a challenge to the prevailing unbelief among students and faculty. Goodrich wrote that Dwight's "commanding talents, his fervid eloquence, his powerful reasonings in behalf of Christianity, both in the lecture-room and the chapel, checked the tendency to skepticism which had begun to prevail in the college."[3] As conversions began to occur in the student body, Dwight encouraged the newly redeemed to testify to their experience of grace. Goodrich concluded that "the salvation of the soul was the great subject of thought, of conversation, [and] of absorbing interest."[4]

Goodrich offered extensive descriptions of the nature of the religious experiences evident at Yale. The process seemed to begin with a sense of sinfulness that often lasted for a period of "two or three weeks." Then came a "feeling in giving the soul to Christ," an event "marked by silent peace of conscience," rather than emotional agitation. Entry into salvation came so subtly that the newly transformed were "wholly unconscious, at least for a time," that redemption had occurred. In evaluating the veracity of conversions, Timothy Dwight raised two concerns. First, he warned students not to permit emotionalism to become the primary verification of a valid experience. Second, he suggested that conversion should go beyond piety, or "too much of an inward feeling" striving for a faith that engaged the full "intercourse of life."[5] Dwight insisted that "religion, if genuine, will possess and animate" the entire person: "It is knowledge in the understanding and purity in the heart; it is kindness, modesty and candor in our social intercourse; it is uprightness, integrity and generosity in our secular concerns; it is the regulation of our desires, the government of our passions, the harmonious union of whatever things are honest, just, lovely and of good report."[6]

Goodrich delineated as many as "twenty distinct effusions of the Holy Spirit" evident in the ninety-six years he surveyed, and concluded with the hope that the "spirit of David Brainerd" (now clearly rehabilitated after his expulsion from the college) might prevail at Yale "for ages to come."[7] From these awakenings came a new generation of evangelical clergy, many of whom would move westward in an effort to bring religious renewal to a harsh physical and moral wilderness.

Religious Experience on the American Frontier

In the late eighteenth and early nineteenth centuries the "frontier" essentially meant the land west or south of the Allegheny Mountains, a region that extended to the Carolinas, Kentucky, Ohio, Indiana, and Illinois. It was a coarse environment that religious leaders viewed as irreligious at best, barbarian at worst. Lyman Beecher's *Plea for the West* challenged Protestants to establish churches on the frontier, evangelizing the unconverted, and facilitating a new Reformation that would thwart "Romanist" efforts to claim the Ohio River Valley for the papacy.

In an 1819 edition of *The Methodist Magazine*, a writer who took the name *Theophilus Arminius* described the emigrant to the "Western Country" accordingly:

> Hope buoys him up; a rising settlement surrounds him. New scenes; in succession, strike his mind. His past sufferings are forgotten.... If he was once associated with wicked company, the spell is now broken, and he chooses the good part. If formerly associated with the religious, his attachment becomes stronger; his devotion more fervent. His humble habitation prepared for public worship, becomes a Church.[8]

The writer concluded, "In the cabins and in the woods, the praises of Immanuel are chanted, and hundreds, sometimes thousands, falling into the settlements, flow to the standard of the blessed Jesus."[9]

Frontier revivalism had a significant impact on Protestant theology. First, it continued the modification of Calvinism in Protestant churches, opening the door to the possibility of redemption for all who would choose grace through Jesus Christ. For many revivalists, particularly the Methodists, the conversion process was shortened considerably, with greater emphasis on the participation of the individual in the salvific process itself. Calvinist traditions such as the

Primitive Baptists continued to affirm election and predestination uncompromisingly, opposing revivals as a form of works righteousness, offering false security to unelected sinners. Still others modified Reformed theology, preaching as if everyone could be saved and trusting God to use their preaching to awaken the elect. Second, the frontier camp meetings reinforced the usefulness of revivals bringing persons to conversion (justification) and assuring them of salvation (sanctification). They created a variety of liturgical, ideological, and pragmatic methods for defining, charting, and verifying religious experiences.

Revival preaching became a major homiletical and theological vehicle for explaining the nature of religious experience and warning listeners of eternal judgment. John Boles called such rhetoric a "verbal Passion Play" by which "the fervent clergymen offered Jesus Christ in the most effective, least demagogic way—as the loving son of a caring and forgiving father." Boles concluded that it was the "juxtaposing of fear and anxiety with love and security that made evangelical preaching so convincingly effective."[10] The frontier camp meeting and other "protracted meetings" became a particular context in which conversion and its accompanying "enthusiasms" marked a normative entrance into divine grace.

Third, frontier revivals solidified the emphasis on conversion as essential for all who would claim membership in the church. It involved a highly individualized, direct encounter with God through the atoning work of Jesus Christ, actions that made possible the imputation of "his own unblemished righteousness" into the heart every sinner who called on him.[11] It was also the witness of dissenting sectarians against those governmental, social, or familial mandates that often seemed to compel persons into the institutional church, with or without a genuine experience of grace.[12] Finally, the normative nature of conversion extended the development of a theology of sanctification, going on in grace to a deeper life of Christian piety. Boles contended that the "pietist-perfection emphasis" carried believers well beyond church attendance or evangelization to a concern for daily Christian living that included prayer, Bible study, a strong biblically based ethical imperative, and a spirit of continued encounter with the Divine.[13]

Frontier Awakenings: Camp Meeting Enthusiasm

One of the earliest revivalists to impact the frontier was James McGready (1763–1817), a Presbyterian minister converted in 1786, after recovering from a bout with smallpox. For a time he studied theology with Presbyterian pastor James McMillan, a New Light preacher. The Pennsylvania-based Redstone Presbytery licensed him to preach in 1788, and his revival sentiments were clearly evident when he assumed Presbyterian pastorates in Guilford County, North Carolina. McGready moved his family to Kentucky in 1795, and by 1797 he was serving three small Presbyterian churches on the Red, the Muddy, and the Gasper Rivers. He preached Reformed doctrines related to "regeneration, faith and repentance," affirming but not emphasizing election and predestination, and stressing the need for a personal conversion experience.[14]

In June 1799, McGready conducted a "sacramental meeting" at his Red River church, where some of the "boldest, daring sinners" in the region "wept bitterly" over the state of their souls. The gathering continued for several days after persons under conviction of sin refused to leave the premises until salvation was secured. In August a similar gathering on the Gasper River saw numerous individuals begin to cry aloud, "powerless, groaning, praying" for salvation. This happened again at the Muddy River church a month later.

By 1800, McGready witnessed the conversion of "Sabbath-breakers," "frolickers and dancers," and children between the ages of ten and twelve. The conversions progressed slowly, often involving periods of despair over sinfulness and depravity. Many fasted, prayed, and "diligently searched the scriptures," undergoing "distresses of mind inexpressibly sore, until they had obtained a comfortable hope of salvation."[15] The extent and intensity of these conversions led Ellen Eslinger to conclude that "the sacramental occasions conducted under McGready's direction in 1800 reveal a distinct shift, with greater emphasis on regeneration."[16]

Conversions often produced numerous outward manifestations. In *The Kentucky Revival, or, a Short History*, published 1808, Richard M'Nemar described these enthusiasms as beginning with "an inward throbbing of the heart; then with weeping and trembling; from that to crying out, in apparent agony of soul; falling down and swooning away till every appearance of animal life was suspended and the person appeared to be in a trance. From this state they would recover under different sensations."[17] The services, he said, usually started with a sermon, toward the end of which "an unusual outcry" began with "some bursting forth into loud ejaculations of prayer," others "beseeching... careless friends" to turn to Christ, while others were "struck with terror,... hastening through the croud [*sic*] to make their escape, or pulling away their relations." Still others were "trembling, weeping and crying out" for mercy, and some fainted and swooned until "every appearance of life was gone" and their bodies "assumed the coldness of a dead corpse."[18] These outbursts caused immediate divisions among the Presbyterians, Baptists, and Methodists that M'Nemar identified as the primary participants in the early revivals.

The outdoor settings for these "sacramental occasions" were an early stage of what became the camp meeting movement.[19] By 1800 McGready and other Presbyterian preachers recognized the role of such meetings in the conversion of large numbers of the unchurched and extended their use as an evangelistic vehicle.[20] The spontaneous camping that accompanied the early Presbyterian revivals soon developed into an intentional, programed method for soliciting and accommodating large crowds for what became both a spiritual and social phenomenon.[21]

In late spring and early summer of 1801, Presbyterian sacramental meetings held in central Kentucky brought some eight thousand people to Stony Creek, where at least 250 people were reported to have "fallen" in physical response to conviction of sin. In June another sacramental meeting at Indian Creek claimed ten thousand in attendance, with eight hundred "slain" in the Spirit.[22]

These gatherings set the stage for the Cane Ridge camp meeting of 1801, probably the largest such gathering held on the frontier. The host was Barton Warren Stone (1772–1844), pastor of a log Presbyterian church located in a cane break near Paris, Kentucky. Stone's *Biography* includes a description of his own conversion and the theology that accompanied it. Confronted by James McGready's call for "the sinner to flee from the wrath that is to come," Stone experienced a deep conviction of sin and a need for grace. He recalled that due to "the preaching, and the experience of the pious in those days, I anticipated a long and painful struggle before I should be prepared to come to Christ...before I should get religion." He spent a year "tossed on the waves of uncertainty—laboring, praying, and striving to obtain saving faith—sometimes desponding, and almost despairing of ever getting it."[23] Finally in February 1791, at a meeting in Virginia, Stone felt that his "hope began to rise, and my sorrow-worn heart felt a gleam of joy." Although the local evangelist allowed him to receive the Lord's Supper for the first time, he remained "in this gloomy state, without one encouraging word," from any of the preachers. "Several weeks" later, at a service in Guilford County, North Carolina, he discovered a new sense of God's love, not just for sinners, but for his own sinful condition. Retiring "to the woods alone with my Bible," Stone finally broke through, confessing,

> I yielded and sunk at his feet a willing subject. I loved him—I adored him—I praised him aloud in the silent night,—in the echoing grove around. I confessed to the Lord my sin and folly in disbelieving his word so long—and in following so long the vices of men. I now saw that a poor sinner was as much authorized to believe in Jesus at first, as at last—that *now* was the accepted time, and day of salvation.[24]

Now "devoted to God," Stone soon challenged several of the prevailing dogmas and practices of the revivals, starting with the lengthy conversion process required by many revival preachers. He noted that the "publicly taught" doctrines of the day asserted that "mankind were so totally depraved, that they could not believe, repent, nor obey the gospel..... *Now* was not *then*, the accepted time—*now* was not *then*, the day of salvation; but it was God's own sovereign time, and for that time the sinner must wait."[25] He also questioned the theology of election that limited salvation to those chosen before the foundation of the world. Stone was both an author and signatory of the *Last Will and Testament of the Springfield Presbytery*, published in 1804, that promoted efforts to restore the marks of the New Testament church in ordination, congregational polity, Christian unity, and biblical (especially New Testament) authority.[26]

Richard M'Nemar (1770–1839) was one of Stone's most prominent colleagues and a signer of the *Last Will and Testament*. He contributed to a document known as *Observations on Church Government by the Presbytery of Springfield* (1808). It affirmed the need for a specific conversion for all who would claim membership in the church, noting, "From what has been said, you will easily see who are the members of this church: they are believers, and only believers; for no other can be a member." Such salvation was "freely offered to all—to every creature under heaven; no person or character is excluded, who does not through unbelief exclude himself." The document concluded, "It is impossible for men to come to Christ, who do not believe in him; nor can they seek to enter into the kingdom who do not believe there is a kingdom." In the Gospels, although many spoke of Jesus as "'good master,' yet none were considered as real members but those who believed his doctrine, and felt its sacred influence in forming their hearts anew."[27] These New Light revivalists challenged both Presbyterian polity and the doctrine of election.

Conversion was essential for entrance into Christ and his church, instilling the Holy Spirit within every believer. Those who did not possess the Spirit, M'Nemar believed, were "lawless and disobedient, filthy dreamers, that defile the flesh, despise government, presumptuous are they, self-willed, who are not afraid to speak evil of dignities; *for if any man have not the Spirit of Christ, he is none of his*."[28]

A powerful spiritual egalitarianism seems to have characterized many camp meetings, evident in the activity of "exhorters" who, once redeemed, felt compelled to call others to repentance. Writing about the Cane Ridge camp meeting, Paul K. Conkin noted that a shared religious experience gave public voice to previously silent or silenced individuals who became exhorters, sometimes spontaneously, sometimes when invited to do so. Such exhortations were often a specific, sermonic event, usually following the more formal sermons by recognized preachers. As the camp meetings reached a spiritual fever pitch,

> here and there almost anyone, including those who rose from the ground as well as child converts, might burst out with an exhortation. Women, small children, slaves, shy people, illiterate people, all exhorted with great effect. Observers marveled at their eloquence, their deep feeling, and often their seeming preternatural understanding of scripture. Some believed the newly converted enjoyed the gift of prophecy, while critics often believed them possessed by demons.[29]

Critics voiced fears that many exhorters were simply undisciplined "enthusiasts," theological illiterates who had no business pontificating to others about their spiritual estate.

Religious Affections: The Frontier

Religious affections, or what some critics called "enthusiastical religion," were no less controversial on the frontier than earlier in New England. These exercises fell on persons under conviction for their sinful nature, and on those who broke through to salvation. Methodist preacher John McGee gave the "exhortation" to conversion at one of McGready's sacramental meetings. He challenged all who were present to allow "the Lord God Omnipotent [to] reign in their hearts and submit to Him, and their souls should live." After completing his sermon McGee moved throughout the meetinghouse where "suddenly persons began to fall as he passed through the crowd—some as dead."[30]

One observer at the Cane Ridge meeting recorded a vivid description of the religious affections evident at the event:

> Sinners dropping down on every hand, shrieking, groaning, crying for mercy, convoluted, professors [of religion] praising, agonizing, fainting, falling down in distress, for sinners, or in raptures of joy! Some singing, some shouting clapping their hands, hugging and even kissing, laughing; others

> talking to the distressed, to one another, or to opposers of the work, and all this at once—no spectacle can excite a stronger sensation. And with what is doing the darkness of the night, the solemnity of the place, and of the occasion, and conscious guilt, all conspire to make terror thrill through every power of the soul, and rouse it to awful attention.[31]

In his *Biography*, Barton W. Stone described the exercises as he observed them in the early nineteenth-century camp meetings. These included the "falling exercise," the "jerks," the "dancing exercise," and the "laughing" and "singing" exercises. He wrote that the "falling exercise was very common among all classes... from the philosopher to the clown. The subject of this exercise would, generally, with a piercing scream, fall like a log on the floor, earth, or mud, and appear as dead."[32] The "jerks," Stone noted, were "not so easily described," since they might affect one segment of the body, or the entire person. Saints and sinners alike could sometimes "stand in one place, and jerk backward and forward in quick succession, their head nearly touching the floor behind and before." Stone noted that after observing such activities by the "thousands," he could not recall one person who "sustained an injury in body."[33]

The dancing exercise apparently began with the jerks, especially among the converted. After dancing began, the jerks would diminish. Dancing often continued until the participant was exhausted and then "would fall prostrate on the floor or earth, unless caught by those standing by."[34] The laughing exercise, "confined largely to the religious," reflected a "rapturously solemn" attitude from the practitioner that was "truly indescribable."[35] A "running exercise" was born, Stone speculated, by attempts of individuals to escape other bodily agitations or resist the onslaughts of the devil. One such person, Stone recalled, ran until he "fell down, and there lay till he submitted to the Lord."[36] The "singing exercise," was equally uncanny, often coming, Stone said, not from "the mouth or nose, but entirely in the breast, the sounds issuing there." This "heavenly" sound apparently "silenced every thing," at the camp meeting, with a resonance like nothing previously "known in nature."[37]

Stone dismissed accusations that these experiences included a phenomenon called the "barking exercise," an action he attributed to a bad case of the "jerks," when the individual was shaking so profusely that air passed through the lungs in a way that seemed like barking. Stone concludes, "Some wag discovered him in this position, and reported that he found him barking up a tree."[38]

These experiential manifestations were both welcomed and condemned by religious leaders of the time. Stone acknowledged that "there were many eccentricities, and much fanaticism in this excitement," but insisted that they had "good effects" especially in the early days of the revival, before they became divisive and extreme.[39]

So unique were the manifestations that some revivalists created a new vocabulary for explaining them. Newell Williams called attention to Baptist preacher John Taylor's belief that a "'discovery of sin' led to a 'running issue in the heart' of the Christian that never healed." Taylor noted that "the use of running issues, is to take down swellings and throw off mortal diseases." A confession of sin forced the newly redeemed to fight against their own arrogance before God. In the battle against sin a Christian was compelled to confess that "I have a monstrous unclean running issue."[40] For Taylor, apparently the sinful nature created a spiritual wound that was ever in danger of festering.

Peter Cartwright and the Methodists

Peter Cartwright (1785–1872) was one of the most famous Methodist itinerants of the nineteenth-century church. Born in Virginia in 1785, Cartwright was taken by his parents to Kentucky while still in his infancy. The family settled in Lincoln County, Kentucky, then moved to Logan County in 1793.[41] In 1801, his sixteenth year, Cartwright fell under conviction of sin, joining his mother in prayer for the state of his soul. He sold his racehorse, gave up his playing cards, and became "so distressed and miserable" that he was "incapable of any regular business."[42]

Cartwright apparently attended the Cane Ridge camp meeting of 1801, where he fell under intense condemnation as "a guilty, wretched sinner" who joined the "weeping multitudes, and bowed before the stand, and earnestly prayed for mercy."[43] Conversion broke through, as Cartwright described it:

> In the midst of a solemn struggle of soul, an impression was made on my mind, as though a voice said to me, "Thy sins are all forgiven thee." Divine light flashed all round me, unspeakable joy sprung up in my soul. I rose to my feet, opened my eyes, and it really seemed as if I was in heaven; the trees, the leaves on them, and everything seemed, and I really thought were, praising God.[44]

Cartwright reported that from that day forward, he had been "in many instances, unfaithful yet I have never, for one moment, doubted that the Lord did, then and there, forgive my sins and give me religion."[45] He professed faith, joined the Methodist Church, and never departed from it.

Cartwright's call to preach parallels that of his ministerial contemporaries. In 1803, at the age of eighteen, he "gave up the world," and agreed to preach at a Logan County revival. He reported that during the sermon, "the Lord gave light, liberty, and power; the congregation was melted to tears." A "professed infidel" was converted and joined the Methodist Church, an early sign that helped confirm Cartwright's call.[46]

In tracing the nature of frontier religion, Cartwright offered a classic description of frontier Methodism, contrasting it with the Methodism evident in the later nineteenth century, the time his autobiography was published. The religious experience of early Methodism carried with it a disciplined life with particular ethical behavior. Cartwright was not certain that it endured as Methodists became worldlier. He wrote,

> The Methodists in that early day dressed plain; attended their meetings faithfully, especially preaching, prayer and class meetings; they wore no jewelry, no ruffles; they would frequently walk three or four miles to class-meetings and home again, on Sundays; they would go thirty or forty miles to their quarterly meetings, and think it a glorious privilege to meet their presiding elder, and the rest of the preachers.[47]

He concluded that "if the Methodists had dressed in the same 'superfluity of naughtiness' then as they do now, there were very few even out of the Church that would have any confidence in their religion."[48]

Peter Cartwright echoed many of Stone's descriptions of the "enthusiastical" exercises. He claimed to have observed "more than five hundred persons jerking at one time in my large congregation." Although Cartwright insisted that during the "great revival the Methodists kept moderately balanced" where religious affections or emotional outbursts were concerned, he acknowledged that "some of our members ran wild, and indulged in some extravagancies that were hard to control." His autobiography details some of the outward manifestations that overtook sinners and converts alike at the camp meetings. These included the "jerks," a shaking exercise that Cartwright describes as "a convulsive jerking all over," which when it struck was irresistible and unavoidable.[49] He attributed the jerks to "a judgment sent from God" to awaken sinners of their need for repentance and to reveal to professing Christians "that God could work with or without means" (outward signs) "to the glory of his grace and the salvation of the world."[50]

Cartwright reported that the jerks as well as certain "running, jumping, barking exercise[s]" often were accompanied by trances and visions at both the meetings and in individual homes. These led persons to claim to have seen heaven and hell, "God, angels, the devil and the damned."[51] He called this a "pretense of Divine inspiration" that sometimes led individuals to predict the immediate end of the world and the new millennium. Cartwright was particularly concerned about these people whom he believed played on the "ignorance, superstition and credulity of the people." They even claimed to heal the ill and raise the dead, "just like the diabolical Mormons."[52]

Religious Experience, Theological Division

More divisive than the "exercises," however, were questions regarding the process of salvation. Peter Cartwright noted that the younger Presbyterian preachers, greatly influenced by the spirit of revival, "almost to a man, gave up these points of high Calvinism, [election, predestination, perseverance of the saints] and preached a free salvation to all."[53] Many of these revival preachers were so concerned for declaring the need for salvation that they would not take time to meet the educational prerequisites for a Presbyterian's ordination. Cartwright commented that this led to the formation of a new Christian group, the "Cumberland Presbyterian Church," a Presbyterian body that softened ordination requirements to meet the needs of church and community. He nonetheless mourned the fact that the new body retained the "absurdity" of the "unconditional perseverance of the saints," what Cartwright called the "left foot of Calvinism."[54]

Barton W. Stone was among those Presbyterians who "urged upon the sinner to believe *now*, and receive salvation." Instead of insisting that sinners wait on the Holy Spirit to provide regeneration in order to make repentance and faith possible, Stone and others advocated immediate repentance and faith as the terms of regeneration. Stone declared that God desired to save sinners "*now*,... that no previous qualification was required, or necessary in order to believe in Jesus and come to him." He insisted that "Jesus died for all, and that all things were now ready" for the salvation of all who would so believe.[55]

He recalled that at first "the sticklers for orthodoxy" held their objections, largely because of their "mighty effects on the people."[56] But this was not to last. Some, fearing loss of members to Methodist and Baptist folds, began to insist on enforcing the Westminster Confession of Faith, bringing church discipline to bear on preachers such as Richard M'Nemar. These actions led M'Nemar, Stone, and others to draft the *Last Will and Testament of the Springfield Presbytery*, making their doctrines known and separating themselves from the Presbyterians.

"Accepting the Testimony": Stone-Campbell Responses

Another important response to the religious experience evident in the camp meetings came from the Restorationist approach of the Stone-Campbell movement. Born of the revivals, Restorationism developed its own ecclesiology that rejected "denominationalism" for a church composed of "Christians only," "Disciples of Christ" committed to restoring New Testament norms for defining Christian community.[57] Barton W. Stone, pastor of the Cane Ridge Church, was among the first to repudiate sectarian divisions, distancing himself from the Presbyterian system with its emphasis on total depravity, election, predestination, and conformity to creeds such as the Westminster Confession of Faith. Stone and others articulated their views in the *Last Will and Testament of the Springfield Presbytery*, in 1804. Stone's Restorationism was echoed by another Presbyterian, Alexander Campbell (1788–1866), who with his father Thomas (1763–1854) came to America as Seceder Presbyterians, only to leave that movement for the Baptists largely over the question of baptismal immersion and congregational polity.

Stone witnessed the religious enthusiasm of the Cane Ridge camp meeting and reported on the various expressions of religious experience he observed there. Yet he saw the spiritual upheavals as signs of a unity of religious experience that, appropriately cultivated, would lead Christians away from denominational division. Of those who encountered the Spirit in the revivals, he wrote, "They spoke often one to another on the subject of religion; controverted notions were not the themes of their conversation, but the Soul-cheering doctrine of heaven, and its divine effects, as experienced by themselves and others. Here was unity indeed—not in opinions, but in spirit."[58] Stone's rationalism and appreciation for the thought of John Locke led him to conclude that "faith depends not on the will, inclination, or disposition, but on testimony." Salvation was predicated on believing the "testimony." It meant simply accepting the truth of the Bible, unencumbered by creeds, and living according to that truth.[59]

Stone challenged the Calvinist idea that sinners were bound to wait on the Spirit, helpless to move toward salvation until infused by divine grace. Rather, regeneration was the result of faith itself, an act of simply "applying the means or admitting the truth into the heart." Sinners who followed that process were "quickened, renewed and sanctified," in other words, regenerated.[60] They could simply accept the "testimony" of the Bible and move toward grace even before the power of the Spirit reached them.[61] "The testimony of the Scriptures" was the means by which persons were truly converted. God dealt with a human being "as a rational creature. The strongest motives are presented to our understandings; but they cannot move, excite, or influence us, unless we believe: in other words, they are no motives at all, without faith."[62] Faith itself was such a "simple idea" that it needed no further definition. It "*is admitting testimony upon the authority of the testifier. Or it is simply believing the testimony of God.*" Stone concluded that innumerable tomes "have been written, to explain what *faith*, or *believing* is, with no better effect than to destroy its signification."[63]

D. Newell Williams suggested that Stone's understanding of religious experience was closely tied to "the Christian's relationship to the self," a spiritual dynamic grounded in humility.[64] In an 1842 essay in *The Messenger*, Stone insisted that the follower of Christ is "well convinced of his natural poverty of divine things, as holiness, righteousness and peace—he is convinced of his spiritual weakness to withstand evil, and to do good—and of his ignorance of God, and divine glories." In recognizing this spiritual reality, the believer "is humbled in heart or spirit in the sight of God."[65] The redeemed were not interested in "controverted notions, . . . but the soul-cheering doctrine of heaven and its divine effect, as experienced by themselves and others. Here was unity indeed—not in opinions, but in spirit."[66]

Alexander Campbell agreed with Stone regarding the need for Christian unity while challenging the elaborate and often "enthusiastical" conversion experiences evident in revivalistic settings. He denied that "preaching the law" was necessary in order to convince individuals of their sin and need of grace. Religious experience did not require a lengthy struggle with sin and repentance. It was a simple recognition of the "testimony" of scripture and the faith that God's promise of salvation was available to every person who chose to accept it.[67] Campbell declared, "No testimony, no faith: for faith is only the belief of the testimony, or confidence in testimony as true. . . . Where testimony begins, faith begins; and where testimony ends, faith ends." Faith itself was the simple recognition that the "testimony" itself was completely true and sense experience was an inseparable aspect of genuine faith.[68] For Campbell, regeneration brought a change of heart and a new orientation toward Christian living, but it did not require an elaborate process confirmed by emotional enthusiasms. It was simply a rationale assent to the obvious truth of the gospel testimony. As Campbell reiterated,

> Let it be again repeated and remembered that there is no other manner of believing a fact than by receiving it as true. If it is not received as true, it is not believed; and when it is believed, it is no more than regarded as true. This being conceded, then it follows that the efficacy of faith is always in the fact believed or the object received, and not in the nature or manner of believing.[69]

Individual religious experience did not validate the scriptures; instead the scriptures were the source for authenticating genuine spirituality.[70]

Religious feelings did not verify true conversion but they could be present in the process. He wrote, "We make feelings the *effect*, not the *cause* of faith and of true religion. We begin not with feelings but with the understanding; we call upon men first to believe, then to feel, and then to act." The gospel demanded a commitment of the whole person, "the head, the heart, the head."[71] He insisted that "being born again is not *conversion*, nor a *change of views*, nor a *change of affections*, but a *change of state*." He insisted that "a Christian is, indeed, one whose views are enlightened, whose heart is renewed, whose relations to God and the moral universe are changed."[72]

Baptism by immersion was the inseparable seal of faith, "the bath of regeneration"; the "last act" of the salvific process "which completes the whole, and is, therefore, used to denote the new birth."[73] Immersion was an "action" that brought the remission of sins upon those who had believed the testimony; it was "the *means* of receiving a formal, distinct, and specific absolution, or release from guilt."[74]

Richard M. Tristano suggested Campbell's approach to religious experience combined elements of both evangelical Protestantism and traditional Roman Catholicism. The need for faith and baptism (Protestantism) was united with the concept of the "remission of sins through baptism" (Catholicism). He repudiated baptismal sacramentalism as a mysterious and unexplainable act, while denying the Protestant assertion that baptism was only "symbolic."[75]

The Restorationist colleagues sought to reshape Christianity into its original form, while delivering religious experience into the hands of the people and away from the hegemony of revivalist clergy with their elaborate experientialism. The simple belief that Jesus was the Messiah and a rational acquiescence to the New Testament "testimony" was the entry-point to genuine faith. Nothing stood between the Bible and the individual in matters of church order or eternal salvation. Nathan Hatch noted this sense of radical liberty as foundational for the Restorationist movement. He cited Campbell's early declaration that God was calling a new generation of Christians "loudly and expressly…to repentance and reformation." With such a mandate they should "resume that precious, that dear bought liberty, where with Christ has made his people free; a liberty from subjection to any authority but his own, in matters of religion. Call no man father."[76]

Hatch concluded that the Restorationists' "fresh hermeneutic…proclaimed a new ground of certainty for a generation perplexed that it could no longer hear the voice of God above the din of sectarian confusion."[77] For the Restorationists, democratic idealism, Lockean rationalism, and biblical primitivism became philosophical means to a restored ecclesiastical and salvific end. Redemption was available to all who sought it through a simple act of mind and will.

A Burned-Over District

Religious experience was central to many of the individuals and groups that appeared in the so-called Burned-Over District of western New York in the nineteenth century. This region, repeatedly swept by revival fires, was a seedbed of religious enthusiasm for multiple movements. The Burned-Over District was the scene of spiritual upheavals that included revivalist Charles

Grandison Finney and Premillennialist William Miller, abolitionists the likes of Theodore Dwight Weld and Elon Galusha, and utopian ideals evident in the Oneida, Shaker, and Mormon communities. Such religious experience reflected a diversity that would come to characterize the entire nation, shaping conversion, sanctification, premillennial eschatology, communitarianism, new revelations, and social issues from abolition to temperance. For many, the "District" seemed a nineteenth-century "psychic highway," that in Whitney Cross's assessment was "particularly devoted to crusades aimed at the perfection of mankind and the attainment of millennialism happiness. Few of the enthusiasms or eccentricities of this generation of Americans failed to find exponents here."[78]

Charles Grandison Finney: Revivals, Conversions, and New Measures

Charles Grandison Finney (1792–1875) was a New York lawyer who, after a dramatic conversion, became one of the most prominent evangelists of the nineteenth century. Born in Connecticut, Finney moved with his family to Oneida County, New York, two years later. In his autobiography, published in 1876, Finney called the western New York area "a wilderness," noting that although the early settlers had founded good schools, "they had among them very little intelligent preaching of the Gospel."[79] Since his parents were not professing Christians, Finney claimed to have had limited contact with religious communities, except perhaps with the occasional itinerant preacher or in "some miserable holding forth of an ignorant preacher who would sometimes be found" in Oneida County.[80]

As a young adult he studied law in Adams, New York, and attended the Presbyterian Church, where the minister was George Gale, whom Finney identified as an Old School, "thoroughly Calvinistic" preacher. Finney recalled that Gale seemed to take "for granted that his hearers were theologians," with sermons that made his audience "more perplexed than edified."[81] Finney's conversations with Gale and his own study of the scripture convinced him that he "was by no means in a state of mind to go to heaven," should he die.[82] Concerned about his spiritual condition, he determined that by the fall of 1821 he would "settle the question of my soul's salvation at once, and if it were possible I would make my peace with God."[83] Finney's belief that he could help initiate conversion was itself a departure from traditional Calvinist insistence that sinners were passive in the initial stages of the salvific process. In his autobiography, Finney detailed the spiritual anguish of his quest for salvation, including his fear that he had committed the "unpardonable sin" by grieving the Holy Spirit. Conversion came in a religious experience that he described as follows:

> As I went in and shut the door after me, it seemed as if I met the Lord Jesus Christ face to face. It did not occur to me then, nor did it for some time afterward, that it was wholly a mental state. On the contrary it seemed to me that I saw him as I would see any other man. He said nothing, but looked at me in such a manner as to break me right down at his feet. Without any expectation of it without ever having the thought in my mind that there was any such thing for me, without any recollection that I had ever heard the thing mentioned by any person in the world, the Holy Spirit descended upon me in a manner that seemed to go through me, body and soul. I could feel the impression, like a wave of electricity, going through and through me. Indeed it seemed to come in waves and waves of liquid love.... I wept aloud with joy and love; and I do not know but I should say, I literally bellowed out the unutterable gushings of my heart.[84]

Finney's interpretation of his conversion was clearly evangelical, anchored in "the doctrine of justification by faith, as a present experience," a concept of which he was aware, but "did not know at all what it meant in the proper sense." Yet he came to view his religious experience, his justification by faith, as evident in the removal of guilt and sin. He wrote that following his conversion, "I do not think I felt any more sense of guilt than if I never had sinned."[85]

In 1822, Finney became a candidate for the ministry in his local presbytery. Although encouraged to go to Princeton, he refused, insisting that the school had "wrongly educated" its ministerial graduates, leading them away "from what a minister of Christ should be." The presbytery required him to "read theology" with his Presbyterian pastor George Gale, a common practice among nineteenth-century ministerial candidates. These sessions, Finney recalled, were "little else than controversy," given their deep disagreements over the nature of the atonement and the possibility of individual participation in conversion. Finney reported that he "could not receive" Gale's views on "atonement, regeneration, faith, repentance, the slavery of the will, or any of the kindred doctrines," differences so irreconcilable that Finney often left in "a state of great depression" after coming from Mr. Gale's study.[86] He concluded that "if" Gale had actually been converted to Christ, he had failed to experience the baptism of the Holy Spirit, "which is indispensable to ministerial success."[87] For Finney, the twin experiences of conversion and sanctification were essential to a productive ministry.

Licensed to preach by the presbytery, Finney relinquished his law practice and was appointed a missionary representative of an Oneida County female missionary society. He began preaching in two small churches, one Presbyterian, the other Baptist. During this time he came in contact with Daniel Nash (1775–1831), a well-known evangelist in the region. "Father Nash," as he was called, became a mentor to Finney as he increasingly focused on calling sinners to conversion throughout western New York. A riveting preacher with piercing eyes and dramatic, extemporaneous sermons, Finney soon gained a reputation as an evangelist who got results, promoting a variety of new approaches to religious experience.

He declared that salvation was available only through Jesus Christ, whose "vicarious death, his resurrection," enabled sinners to experience "repentance, faith [and] justification by faith." His meetings included intense public and private prayer for specific persons who had fallen under conviction of sin and desired for salvation, as well as "much personal conversation, and meetings for the instruction of earnest inquirers."[88] This latter effort was a direct challenge to the prevailing Calvinist belief that sinners should be left to themselves, waiting on God with no false assurance provided by well-meaning but salvifically helpless clergy or laity.

Nonetheless, Finney was unapologetic that genuine religion was "something for a man to do...in obeying God with and from the heart." God "induced" persons to make this decision through the work of the Holy Spirit, thus overcoming their "reluctance to obey," but sinners had a part to play as well.[89] They could take the initiative and move toward salvation of their own free will.

One important mechanism for that initiative rested in revivals as the means that God used to spread the gospel and facilitate conversion. Revivals, Finney believed, produced the "powerful excitements" necessary to lead persons to seek conversion and obey the gospel. Human beings were distracted from discovering religion by such worldly "excitements" as "desire, appetite and feeling." Revivals offered a "counter feeling and desire which will break the power of carnal and worldly desire and leave the will free to obey God."[90]

In his *Lectures on Revivals of Religion* (1868), Finney challenged the prevailing idea that "the best way to promote religion is to go along *uniformly*, and gather in the ungodly gradually, and without excitement." This approach might seem appropriate "in the abstract," but in fact it was futile. It was "absurd" to attempt to bring true religion to the world without the use of "excitements" produced by intentional efforts at provoking a revival of religion.[91]

In making his point, Finney challenged the Edwardsean idea of revival as spiritual miracle, a "surprising work of God," outside human manipulations that began and ended at the sovereign will of the Creator. Finney redefined the nature of revival and religious experience in ways that would long impact the conversion morphology of American evangelism. Revival, he insisted, "is not a miracle, or dependent on a miracle, in any sense. It is a purely philosophical result of the right use of the constituted means—as much so as any other effect produced by the application of means."[92] These "*right* means" were not concealed from or contrived by human beings. They were the divinely ordained means for eliciting religious awakenings.[93]

Awakenings began with a renewal of "backslidden" church members, who would then feel compelled to "persuade their neighbors to give [Christ] their hearts." These spiritually restored Christians urged friends and family members to be saved, and "with strong crying and tears beseech God to have mercy on them, and save their souls from endless burnings."[94] They need not wait for some mysterious divine initiative, but could simply follow a divinely ordained course to ensure that revival would occur. The Holy Spirit brought about revival in cooperation with the people of God.

As Finney's fame grew throughout the Burned-Over District, so did his implementation of certain "New Measures," ways of conducting revival meetings that opened the door to religious experience outside the bounds of traditional Calvinism. One of the first indications that something had changed was Finney's insistence that the process of conversion could be shortened considerably. God was ready to save; salvation awaited the call of the repentant soul. He wrote, "Instead of telling sinners to use the means of grace and pray for a new heart, we called on them to make themselves a new heart and a new spirit, and pressed the duty of instant surrender to God." Finney turned the Calvinistic argument around, insisting that if sinners "remained long under conviction, they were in danger of becoming self-righteous," falsely believing that they were converted through their lengthy struggles with sin and self.[95] He called for "immediate submission, as the only thing that God could accept at their hands; and that all delay, under any pretext whatever, was rebellion against God."[96]

This need for immediate conversion led him to place great emphasis on the "prayer of faith," calling on the saved to bombard heaven in behalf of specific sinners, "praying them through" to salvific victory. In doing this, Finney often called the names of the unconverted in prayer, a tactic that showed both pastoral concern or, as his critics insisted, humiliated sinners into heaven. In 1826, Ephraim Perkins, a New York layman, offered this assessment of Finney's methods:

> When he enters a place to get up a "revival" his first step is to institute meetings, styled "meetings of inquiry," nocturnal, and in various parts of the towns. These are the foundations on which he builds the superstructure of his "revivals." ... The Thunders of Sinai, the flaming curses of the broken law, the horrors of the pit, and all the epithets of lamentation and despair,

> are put in requisition by the most consummate skill, to produce consternation and dismay in the minds of those who attend the meetings.... In the latter part of these meetings, the question is put generally, "Who wishes to be prayed for tonight, or who is willing to give up his soul to God?"[97]

Undaunted, Finney continued to utilize such measures in "protracted meetings," that extended for days or weeks in one community, events that set a pattern for later conversion strategies.

One of the most controversial "New Measures" involved the practice of permitting women to pray or otherwise testify at "promiscuous gatherings" of both sexes. Finney's *Memoir* included numerous conversion accounts from women, detailing their struggles toward salvation, often against the wishes of their husbands. In Utica, Finney met "an energetic, highly cultivated, and proud young lady," a teacher who long resisted the new birth, but who sought him out after "writhing under the truth for a few days."[98] As Finney "said a few words about the place which Jesus holds,... her countenance waxed pale, in a moment after she threw up her hands and shrieked, and then fell forward upon the arm of the sofa, and let her heart break." Finney described her as "gushing out her heart before God." Once converted, she "gave up her school, offered herself as a foreign missionary, was married to a Mr. Gulick, and went out to the Sandwich Islands."[99]

Finney claimed that the 1830 Rochester revival marked his introduction of the "anxious bench," one of his most famous "New Measures," a method intended to console sinners and hasten them to faith, an outward means for impressing upon sinners "that they were expected at once to give up their hearts; something that would call them to act, and act as publicly before the world, as they had in their sins; something that would commit them publicly to the service of Christ."[100] The "anxious bench" was simply a call to "that class of persons whose convictions were so ripe that they were willing to renounce their sins and give themselves to God, to come forward to certain seats which I requested to be vacated, and offer themselves up to God, while we made them subjects of prayer."[101] The actual bench was a particular place in the church where seekers could go to receive prayers and spiritual encouragement as they struggled toward grace. Critics saw it as a crass form of works righteousness that misled sinners into thinking that there was some action they could take to accelerate conversion on their own, without waiting on the saving activity of the Spirit that alone could draw them to faith. It also implied that all who came forward could be saved, a direct challenge to the doctrine of election.

Separate "anxious meetings" were conducted "for those, who are anxious for their souls' salvation," in order "to ascertain who are anxious about their spiritual and eternal welfare, to know who have obtained hopes, and to bring hope to the convicted and distressed."[102] These gatherings were often held at night in darkened rooms, and in a "reign of universal silence" interrupted only "by now and then a dolorous groan from different parts of the room." Leaders moved from seeker to seeker with such questions as "Do you love God?" or "Have you made your peace with God?" or "Have you got a hope?"[103] "Anxious meetings" frequently produced emotional outbursts from saint and sinner alike, evident in "a burst of feeling in groans and loud weeping." Others fell down, while others continued "agonizing in prayer, till almost the breaking of day."[104]

The anxious bench was the forerunner of the "altar call" or "invitation" that became an important ritual of religious experience in many evangelical churches throughout the nineteenth and twentieth centuries. Finney's call for sinners to "come forward" to the anxious bench, a public step toward salvation, became a hallmark of later revival rituals, an outward and visible sign of an evangelical religious experience.

The New Lebanon Conference, 1827

Divisions over revival methods and emotions created significant controversy in numerous American denominations. In response, a group of Congregational and Presbyterian ministers, revival critics and supporters alike, were invited to a conference in New Lebanon, New York, July 18–25, 1827. The two coconveners were Nathaniel Beman (1785–1875), a Finney ally, and Lyman Beecher (1775–1863), a supporter of revivals who was suspicious of the New

Measures. While the ministers agreed on the need for revivals of religion, they were divided over revival practices, particularly those introduced by Finney. Their initial resolution, defining the nature of revivals, was presented after "seasons of prayer," "interspersed with singing." Approved unanimously, it stated "that revivals of true religion are the work of God's spirit, by which in comparatively short period of time, many persons are convinced of sin, and brought to the exercise of repentance towards God and faith in our Lord Jesus Christ."[105]

They affirmed that "though revivals of religion are the work of God's spirit, they are produced by means of divine truth and human instrumentality, and are liable to be advanced or hindered by measures which are adopted in conducting them. The idea that God ordinarily works independently of human instrumentality, or without any reference to the adaptation of means to ends, is unscriptural."[106] That statement marked the success of Finney's belief that revivals were less the "surprising work of God," as Jonathan Edwards had suggested, than the "right use of the duly constituted means."

They unanimously agreed that "irreverent familiarity with God" in public discourse was inappropriate, and that the use of untruths "for the purpose of awakening sinners" was unacceptable. They also rejected comments put forth by temporarily successful "uneducated and ardent young men" who made "invidious comparisons between them and settled pastors," or undermined "the value of education."[107] They concurred that "great care should be taken to distinguish between holy and unholy religious affections" and that no new measures, no matter how successful, would be acceptable without evaluation of their "biblical character."[108] In spite of these agreements, the New Lebanon Conference failed to resolve many of the deep theological divisions regarding religious experience and the use of the New Measures in converting sinners.

John Williamson Nevin Critiques *The Anxious Bench*

One of the most scathing criticisms of the New Measures came from Mercersberg theologian John Williamson Nevin (1803–1886) in a volume entitled *The Anxious Bench* (1843). For Nevin, the anxious bench was the most egregious of a highly problematic set of conversionist methods utilized by revival supporters; if it was "found wanting and unworthy of confidence" then all the new measures could be declared "unworthy of confidence at every other point."[109] A High Church Calvinist, Nevin suggested that the anxious bench produced "a false issue for the conscience," by distracting sinners from their real need to "repent and yield" their hearts to Christ, and creating "a false issue" to the "anxious soul." Such a distraction overwhelmed "the genuine religious feeling that may exist" in one seeking redemption.[110] Nevin illustrated this dilemma with the case of a young woman "sixteen or seventeen years of age, perhaps a long time under some concern" for her soul who was confronted with the demand to "come forward" and place herself on "the anxious seat." The inner debate over whether to respond publicly interrupted the necessary process of conversion, making her "farther off from God, than she was before this struggle commenced," and causing her to lose "her hold upon the inward."[111] Nevin contended that although its supporters claimed that "coming to the anxious bench is not…the same thing as coming to Christ," many persons equated the two, thereby substituting an "outward form" for an inner spiritual reality.[112]

Nevin observed that for many, the anxious bench had become "the laver of regeneration, the gate of paradise, the womb of the new Jerusalem,… represented to be far easier" at a public revival setting "than elsewhere."[113] Instead, it promoted "the delusion that the use of it serves *some* purpose in the regeneration of the soul."[114] He concluded that "no conversions are more precarious and insecure than those of the Anxious Bench."[115] Nevin chastened evangelical Protestants for relinquishing traditional processes and failing to provide proper catechetical instruction for the newly converted. Thus, "with very little instruction, and almost no examination, all who persuade themselves that they are converted, are at once hailed as brethren and sisters in Christ Jesus, and with as little delay as possible gathered into the full communion of the Church." This "wonderful infatuation," was actually "stupendous inconsistency."[116]

Normative Conversion: Nineteenth-Century Processes

By the mid-nineteenth century, conversions became increasingly normative in Protestant churches across the country, with revivals as an important mechanism for securing them. Writing in *The American National Preacher*, Philadelphia pastor Albert Barnes (1798–1870) insisted that conversion produced "a radical and permanent change" in persons' response to religion, a transformation best described by "the word regeneration, or the new birth."[117] Without that experience individuals were "entirely alienated from God," and in a "previous state" of sin. The change was dramatic and beyond words. "The exact moment may not be known," Barnes wrote, "but there *is* a moment" when the heart was transformed, a change that was "always attended by feeling" that included a "permanent peace and joy."[118] Revivals helped churches move from conversions that were "few and far between" to salvific transformations that were "numerous, rapidly occurring, and decided in their character."[119] They awakened sinners and encouraged professing Christians to become "more prayerful, more holy, and more anxious for the salvation" of others. It was "a revival in individual hearts—and nothing more."[120] Barnes acknowledged that persons might profess faith through certain conversionist rituals yet still not enter into grace. When revivals waned, the unconverted returned to their previously "worldliness and vanity... and their serious impressions vanish—perhaps to return no more."[121]

Amid a variety of controversies over New Measures, New Light/Old Light differences, and religious affections, American evangelicals shaped a somewhat normative method for experiencing and validating conversion. With the Second Great Awakening, a relatively clear process developed that formalized conversion even as it moved away from Calvinism to a more democratic, individualized process that was confirmed by certain public actions or affirmations. As Catherine Albanese wrote, "These changes were institutionalized in the new techniques that came to characterize the emotionally toned religiosity of the revivals that swept the nation in resurgent waves."[122]

Curtis D. Johnson surveyed the various revivalistic traditions and summarized the "five-step process" of conversion that became increasingly normative for those who demanded the "new birth" of all church members. It began with "conviction" of sin and recognition of their fallen nature. The second stage involved "struggle" to secure God's favor and escape damnation. Deliverance was impossible, however, if seekers tried to secure it through their own religious efforts. The spiritual frustration continued. A third step led to conversion as sinful individuals cast themselves on God's mercy to be saved or damned as Christ, the eternal judge, might decide. Fourth, this abandonment brought the realization that they were indeed forgiven and "born-again." The outward results varied. Some reported a sense of peace, while others testified to visions or other divine visitations. Some received the revelation quietly, while others were emotionally responsive at the deepest level, evidenced in tears, cries, shouts, or other forms of emotional catharsis. A fifth step produced the "recognition" that their lives were never to be the same, often producing dramatic moral reform or new spiritual gifts and biblical insights.[123] Johnson concluded, "Although the five-step pattern was common to formal, antiformal, and black evangelicals, the farther a group was from the center of society, the more dramatic and tumultuous were its conversion experiences."

Horace Bushnell and *Christian Nurture*

Another critique of the revivalistic conversion morphology came from Congregational minister Horace Bushnell (1802–1876). For Bushnell, the revivalists' emphasis on a singular conversion moment, while well intended, promoted a transactional understanding of Christian experience that was detrimental to the fullness of the spiritual life. His concern was for Christian living as a continuous process of grace and spiritual maturity, nurtured within Christian community from the moment one entered the world. He wrote,

> The importance of living to God, in ordinary and small things, is seen in the fact that character, which is the end of religion, is in its very nature a growth. Conversion is a great change; old things are passed away; behold

> all things are become new. This however is the language of a hope or confidence somewhat prophetic, exulting, at the beginning, in the realization of future victory.[124]

Bushnell reasserted the power of the "means of grace" and the teaching office of both home and church as vehicles for rearing children in Christian faith. While he did not repudiate the possibility of a dramatic conversion to Christ and salvation, he refused to make it the only or even the primary norm for religious experience. Born in Connecticut in 1802, Bushnell delayed church membership until 1821. He went to Yale in 1823, where he experienced serious doubts as to the meaning of personal faith. In 1831, when revivals descended on the Yale campus, Bushnell acknowledged an experience of conversion and a decision to enter the ministry. After graduating from Yale Divinity School, he accepted the pastorate of North (Congregational) Church, Hartford, Connecticut, where he remained the rest of his life.[125]

Bushnell's concerns reflected divisions that existed between rationalists represented in the Unitarians and conversionists represented in the New Light Protestants. To the rationalists, Bushnell offered a more esoteric approach to religious experience, what Conrad Cherry called "an art form, a kind of poetry of the divine and the human spirits."[126] He challenged certain orthodox tenets by asserting that Jesus Christ represented "God's last metaphor," and that Christ's atonement revealed both the objective and subjective nature of God's all-encompassing love. He suggested that Protestant revivalists had reduced experience with the Divine to a conversionist encounter that neglected the nurturing role of church and family.[127]

Bushnell's own approach to religious experience was thoroughly Christocentric. Christ is the means by which human beings encounter the transcendent God. In a sermon entitled "Christ the Form of the Soul," Bushnell asserted that to "embrace" Christ was to "embrace the divine Word" that "becomes united to us and habited within us." Christians used various terms for this experience including *faith*, *repentance*, *conversion*, and *regeneration*, but "the sublime reality is that the divine has made a junction with our nature, and Christ has begun to be formed within us—only begun." Regeneration in its fullness was inseparable from sanctification, "having Christ formed within us." Toward this spiritual goal, he wrote, "we have nothing else to seek."[128]

Bushnell's concern for both justification and sanctification led to his emphasis on the role of Christian education in spiritual formation, initiated from childhood. In his best-known work, *Christian Nurture* (1847), Bushnell conceived of a Christian society in which children were nurtured to faith so thoroughly that they never knew a time when they were unaware of God's love and grace. He insisted that

> the aim, effort, and expectation should be, not, as is commonly assumed, that the child is to grow up in sin, to be converted after he comes to a mature age; but that he is open on the world as one that is spiritually renewed, not remembering the time when he went through a technical experience, but seeming rather to have loved what is good from his earliest years.[129]

Such a program of education was central to the Christian mission. While it did not guarantee the Christianization of every child, it was an intentional effort to draw children to faith, especially since "infancy and childhood are the ages most pliant to good."[130] This program of familial and churchly preparation did not originate in the child's need for "a new heart" or toward "faith in Christ's atonement." Instead, children were imbued with "a right spirit" through proper spiritual care and instruction even before they recognized the appropriate cognitive elements of Christian belief. Even when more cathartic religious experiences occurred in adolescence or adulthood, the converts often recalled earlier recognition of God's love through parental and congregational guidance.

While acknowledging the inherent sinfulness of humanity, Bushnell questioned the dogma of infant depravity, and the "extreme individualism" of evangelical Protestantism. Christian profession, he believed, was an "organic experience," grounded in both individual and communal response.[131] While he differed with Baptists' emphasis on the necessity of a "born again" conversion experience, Bushnell agreed with their insights into "the beginning of moral agency . . . some definite moment when a child becomes a moral agent, passing out of a condition where he is a moral nullity, and where no moral agency touches his being."[132] Christian nurture prepared children for the inevitable moral crisis of adulthood.

Extending Religious Experience: Direct Evangelization

The Second Great Awakening provided impetus for a new conversionist responsibility—personal evangelism by which clergy and laity confronted sinners directly with their need for Christ and their eternal destination. A sign of genuine conversion was the desire to bring others to "a saving knowledge" of Jesus Christ. Conversion made every convert a personal evangelist, mandated to bring others to faith. Baptist evangelist Jacob Knapp documented this approach from the 1830s when he wrote that

> many thought me crazy when I urged the members of the church to go from house to house, and compel sinners to come in to the [revival] services of the sanctuary. The first persons whom I succeeded in starting out in this work, in the city of New York, went forth under the inspiration that this was God's method, and returned at night with their faces beaming with light and love, amazed at their success.[133]

Personal "witnessing" for Christ thus became a hallmark of evangelical conversionism.

In a memoir published in 1852, Andrew Norwood tells of an earlier revival in which the minister, D. D. Tappan, moved beyond simply asking the converted to pray for the unconverted, and take direct action with specific individuals. Members were asked to "promise to converse... seriously with three impenitent sinners daily for one week upon the subject of their soul's salvation." Those who pledged to do so were warned that "the all-searching eye of the Omniscient Jehovah is upon you, and will be upon you individually as you go forth, to witness whether you perform your vows, or whether Satan hath filled your heart to lie unto the Holy Ghost." Volunteers were compelled to report on the fulfillment of their pledges at the next service.[134] Norwood speculated on what might be the salvific results if an unconverted friend, neighbor, or married couple encountered multiple persons, male and female, who talked with them about the state of their souls. He then asked what might be the eternal implications of "*One hundred* church-members, under the solemnity of a pledge, scatter themselves throughout the parish, and converse seriously with *three hundred* careless sinners per day, week after week, upon the concerns of their souls, and the danger of eternal damnation."[135]

A Third Great Awakening? Converting the City

By the mid-nineteenth century evangelical leaders expressed concern that a new spiritual frontier, the city, was being neglected by the churches. Many came to believe that a revival with accompanying mass conversions was the primary means of bringing cities under the influence of the Christian gospel and its accompanying social values.[136] Albert Barnes and other Protestant leaders saw the cities as an important frontier to be confronted with the gospel message, "in order to avert the wrath of God and save them from the judgments of heaven."[137] Barnes asserted that "those who have been converted have been usually those whose minds have been most sedulously taught by the labors of the ministry; they have occurred eminently in our colleges and higher female seminaries—places far removed from mere enthusiasm, ... where God has made intellectual culture contribute to the purity and power of revivals." In smaller towns and rural settings persons were nurtured to conversion through "common-schools and in Sabbath-schools," in regions where "the Gospel has been long and faithfully preached."[138] These conversion-cultivating environments contrasted significantly with "the wretched, untaught, and degraded population of our cities!" Metropolitan revivals were essential in order to bring salvation to the "dark masses, ... the hordes of wandering and wretched children," and the urban elite who tread "flowery paths" of privilege while pursuing the "heights of honor and ambition."[139] Barnes called for "twenty thousand Christians" who in Philadelphia alone, would pray continuously, "O Lord, revive thy work," and he asked, "Would not the ear of God be open to their cry?"[140] The evangelization of the cities became a major theme of late nineteenth and early twentieth century evangelicals.

In 1832, Calvin Colton delineated two types of religious conversion with implications for the city. These included "insulated conversions" in which the individual, awakened through sermons or dialogue with Christians, experienced regeneration "but is virtually alone in this state and progress of his mind, apart from other persons in a similar state and search for grace." The second conversion framework reflected a more "social" dimension involving a community of seekers who found their way to grace together—as in a mass revival meeting. Colton wrote, "It is an admirable economy of God, in touching one heart by his spirit, to prepare the way for touching many hearts—to convert the social principles of our nature" from occasions of sin and evil "into instruments of a purifying and redeeming agency."[141] Mass meetings were a tool for directing evangelistic efforts toward large numbers of city dwellers.

Revival preachers had learned assorted methods to gain the attention of the unconverted, which included emphasis on the authority of scripture, human free will, the possibility of immediate conversion, and the use of certain "new measures" for encouraging commitments. Yet the urban environment had its own unique elements, including a transient population, immigrant and ethnic diversity, and a dearth of basic religious knowledge.[142] Richard Carwardine observed that where cities were concerned, the urban minister "and his energetic laity (especially church women) needed a more organized revivalism that would reach unchurched groups considerably larger and more inaccessible than in other sections of the country."[143] Strategies for "child evangelism," the conversion of children while their hearts were still pliable, blended conversion and Christian nurture through revival meetings and Sunday schools.[144]

Urban revival services were more orderly and decorous, less given to the public emotionalism characteristic of frontier camp meetings. In many

Protestant campaigns, conversion involved a decision to follow Christ through a simple act of faith, the entrance to eternal life, and deliverance from sin, as well as "from Catholicism, Unitarianism, and Infidelity." Many revivalists were particularly committed to the conversion of powerful economic and political leaders, who might be turned off by certain "enthusiastical" approaches.[145] D. L. Moody urged his supporters to keep emotional outbursts from "getting out of hand," advising the use of good strong hymns when it was necessary to calm things down.[146]

Urban evangelistic campaigns solidified the role of the professional evangelist, individuals without specific pastorates, who traveled from town to town holding revivals, often with a certain degree of celebrity. Across two centuries, their numbers included Dwight Lyman Moody, Reuben Archer Torrey, Billy Sunday, T. T. Martin, Oral Roberts, and Billy Graham. Carwardine concluded that the urban evangelist generally "was not concerned with long-term developments in the spiritual life of the church. His interest lay simply in promoting a revival in one expectant church after another," an intentional effort to produce religious experiences, conversions that transformed the "lost" into the "saved."[147] Robert Mapes Anderson concluded,

> Beginning with Moody conversion became little more than a simple business transaction. All that was required was the assent of the will signified by a walk to the altar, a handshake, signing a card, or simply raising a hand while the rest of the audience remained with heads bowed in prayer, lest they embarrass the "convert."[148]

H. Richard Niebuhr was even more direct, equating such cautionary evangelism with the "institutionalization of the kingdom of Christ," whereby

> regeneration, the dying to the self and the rising to new life—now apparently sudden, now so slow and painful, so confused, so real, so mixed—becomes conversion which takes place on Sunday morning during the singing of the last hymn or twice a year when the revival preacher comes to town. There is still reality in it for some converts, but following a prescribed pattern for the most part in its inception and progress, the life has gone out of it.[149]

While urban evangelism brought new members into Protestant churches, it tended to promote religious experience as salvific transaction, no muss, no fuss. Thus William McLoughlin dismissed the suggestion that such nineteenth- and twentieth-century urban revivalism sparked a "Third Great Awakening," since it revealed no significant changes in "the terms of salvation or Americans' understanding of their relationship to God's will and laws."[150]

Religious Experience/Conversion as Transaction

By the late nineteenth and early twentieth century, conversion among many evangelicals was less a transcendent experience than a salvific transaction, a simple belief that provided the forgiveness of sins and entry into eternal life. Jerald Brauer observed that as revivalism became a normative mechanism for conversion processes, there was a clear "shift away from the centrality of the covenantal community, the elite ministry, and the holy commonwealth to a clear and unambiguous emphasis on the centrality of the converted individual." The emphasis was on community participation in the salvific process, experiences that were grounded in a particular method for entering into grace.[151] Thus the conversion experience became "the central and all-pervasive" issue in determining salvation and sanctification, entering in and going on in faith. Salvation involved "the conversion experience itself, the proper preparation for it, success in achieving it, and the analysis of its authenticity."[152]

Revivalism shortened the conversion process considerably, even as it "excised conversion from a carefully constructed doctrinal context," a religious experience outside the "control of a religious elite" (clergy).[153] Likewise, the concern for mass evangelism reshaped the theology of conversion until "one must standardize and recycle both the process and the nature of salvation for each individual."[154] C. C. Goen suggested that the individualization of religious experience had implications for understanding the nature of the church. From the revivalists' perspective, conversion began with the individual who then joined the church, thus subordinating "the church to individual experience and private feeling or personal preference."[155]

Sermons from the so-called "prayer meeting revivals" of the pre–Civil War era illustrate both the theological and methodological road to salvation set forth by certain urban preachers. One specific collection of sermons, entitled *The New York Pulpit in the Revival of 1858*, contains homiletical responses to the times with emphasis on the need for and way of salvation. New York Presbyterian James W. Alexander mourned the state of evangelical religion in the United States. He declared,

> Time was, when the population of many regions of America was almost entirely religious; it is not so now. . . . The agency of the Holy Spirit has been cast into the shade; new and dangerous views of regeneration have become common; while the tendency has been away from dependence on God and towards a religion of fabrication.[156]

Alexander concluded, "Unless the means of grace can be made in some degree to keep pace with the growth of our population, our rising States must be abandoned to error, infidelity, and disorder."[157]

Baptist pastor William Ives Budington insisted that "to believe in Christ is to be saved; that is, to begin the experience of salvation at once, and be in the way to all that it imports forever hereafter." Salvation involved three elements: "An inward renewal, an outward hope before God, and the peace of a perfect love that casts out fear."[158] Faith involved a simple confession of faith in Christ, an act for which there was no prerequisite. He noted, "Nothing but the sense of sin is necessary to make salvation real and welcome."[159] Once belief was established and conversion occurred, the new believer was called to become more "Christ-like." In this ultimate religious experience, Budington asserted, "the guilt of sin shall be pardoned; the power of sin broken; and the effects of sin for ever supplanted by the grace of God."[160]

Reformed Church pastor Theodore L. Cuyler warned seekers not to "*be content with mere feeling*," noting that "tears never saved a sinner; hell is vocal with the wails of the weepers. *Faith is better than feeling*."[161] Sinners had only to exercise faith in Jesus to receive it immediately. A comparison to other conversions was futile since "the Holy Spirit deals with no two hearts precisely alike."[162] The details of the transaction might vary. Some might involve significant religious feeling, while others might not. The issue was not the external experience but the internal regeneration produced through faith in Christ.

Dwight Lyman Moody: More "New Measures"

Few American evangelists had more impact than the nineteenth-century Chicago preacher, Dwight Lyman Moody (1837–1899). Although "led to Christ" by his Sunday school teacher in 1855, Moody's salvation testimony was rejected by the voting members of the Mt. Vernon Congregational Church, Boston. Only after additional spiritual mentoring was he received into the church in 1856.[163] In 1858 Moody established a popular Sunday school aimed at children of "The Sands," a Chicago tenement project. Its success and a concern to evangelize the cities led him from the business world to full time evangelistic work in 1860. His earliest efforts involved street evangelism, directly inquiring into the eternal state of his listeners' souls.[164] Soon Moody became an evangelist for the newly formed Young Men's Christian Association (1844), from which he developed a growing reputation. By 1873 he was holding "revival campaigns" in various towns and cities.[165]

Moody adapted many of Charles Finney's New Measures to urban campaigns that involved elaborate planning, presubscribed budgets raised from businesses and wealthy patrons, along with commitments from area churches representing various denominational traditions. He eschewed use of the classic anxious bench popularized by Finney for fear that urban seekers would hesitate to be singled out as unregenerate. At the end of every service he simply invited persons in need of prayer to stand, encouraging the spiritually troubled to visit "inquiry meetings" where trained counselors aided them in their spiritual quest.[166] In those postservice gatherings inquirers were presented the "plan of salvation" and invited to confess faith in Christ on the spot.[167] William McLoughlin wrote that although revivalism had become a normative method of evangelization among certain Protestant groups by 1875, "it was not until Moody applied the techniques of corporate business enterprise to evangelism that it became possible to promote city-wide interdenominational revivals at will." In a real sense Moody modernized Finney's methods in ways that shaped urban crusade-evangelism for a century. Yet unlike Finney, whose social concerns grew out of his conversionistic piety, Moody was a theological traditionalist whose response to the poor was inseparable from his desire to bring them to salvation through Jesus Christ.[168]

Moody's services included boisterous singing, preaching, personal testimonies, and calls to conversion. Many of his meetings were held in hippodromes and other public arenas in hopes that city dwellers would be drawn to nonecclesiastical settings. Although admission to the meetings was free, tickets were often required, a practice comparable to other public events. Moody enlisted the talented musician Ira Sankey (1840–1908) as song leader, choir director, soloist, and hymn writer for his campaigns. Sankey's ability to move a crowd with popular gospel songs set to memorable hymn tunes played a major role in drawing persons to the meetings and to conversion.[169]

Moody's stress on the immediacy of salvation influenced his emphasis on a "sinner's prayer" that settled once and for all the salvific relationship between sovereign God and penitent individual. In a sermon entitled "Sinners Seeking Christ," Moody cautioned Christian counselors in the "inquiry-room" to avoid delaying conversion for those struggling with their sins. He declared, "If I read my Bible correctly, the man who preaches the gospel is not the man who tells me to seek Christ tomorrow or an hour hence, but *now*."[170] He admitted that he could not adequately "explain regeneration,... but one thing I know—that I have been regenerated.... God gave me a new heart."[171]

In "Regeneration Is Instantaneous," Moody described conversion as an immediate religious experience. He compared the sinner's situation to that of the people in Noah's day who were either inside or outside the ark. To be outside the ark, spiritually speaking, was to be "exposed to the wrath of God continually, and you cannot tell the day, nor the hour, nor the minute when you may be swept into eternity."[172]

Moody's concern for immediate conversion was predicated on the belief that judgment and eternity were ever at hand. He warned,

> If a man goes out [from the revival meeting] without salvation, it won't be my fault; it will be your own. It will not be because the ark is not open, but because you will not accept the invitation to enter; it will not be because the blessing is not there, but because you will not take it, for it's there. May God open your eyes to accept Him before you leave this building—to accept salvation as a gift.[173]

In a sermon entitled, "There Is No Difference," Moody made it clear that repentance was the entry point for an initial experience with Christ who "died *for the ungodly*." The process was simple: "If you turn to Him at this moment with an honest heart, and receive Him simply as your Savior and your God I have the authority of His Word for telling you that He will *in no wise cast you out*."[174] It was less important to know "the day and the hour" when one entered into God's grace, than that believers "really do love God above every thing else—that God has the first place in our hearts."[175] On one hand, Moody insisted that individuals had to give up "trying to save themselves" and let God "save them."[176] On the other hand, he required persons to engage the Spirit by choosing to repent and believe, exercising their free will, noting, "If we seek for this gift of the Holy Spirit we shall find it."[177]

The converted were mandated to bring others to faith. Indeed, for Moody, one of the primary results of an "experience with Christ" was to lead new believers toward leading others to a similar encounter. He insisted, "Let every young convert cry, 'O God, give me a soul.' Try to win others to Christ.... I believe there is not a young convert in this building that can not win at least one soul to Christ within thirty days, if they will.... Find a poor, lost one, and tell him of Christ and Heaven. I pity from the depths of my heart that Christian who can't help his brother to obtain salvation."[178] One sure sign of the baptism of the Holy Spirit was a desire to serve Christ, by "winning" others to the faith.[179]

R. A. Torrey: The "Sinner's Prayer"

Moody's longtime associate, Reuben Archer (R.A.) Torrey (1856–1928), exemplified the links that developed between evangelism and fundamentalism. For Torrey, conversion was necessary for all who would claim Christian faith and escape damnation to a literal and fiery hell. Salvation was primarily a transaction that could produce immediate redemption for the sinner, a simple belief in the divinity and sufficiency of Christ. To believe in Jesus was to put one's "confidence in him as what he claims to be." Jesus was the "*Sin-bearer*," "*a divinely taught and absolutely infallible Teacher*" and the agent of reconciliation between a just God and sinful humanity.[180] Sinners could put their confidence in Jesus because he delivered humanity from the power of sin, and was "the Light of the world...the One to follow wherever He leads."[181] He bore the sins of humanity and was the truest representative of God's infallible word.

Faith in Christ was the simple belief that Jesus was who he said he was, the infallible Son of God and the substitute for the sins of humanity. True believers were those who confessed Christ "*before the world, and in witnessing for him*" in the world.[182] To put one's confidence in Christ as savior was to be "saved," a simple spiritual transaction that could be accomplished "in an instant."[183] Indeed, Torrey was adamant that no special spiritual "feeling" or deep conviction of sin was necessary for this immediate salvation. In a sermon entitled "What Are You Waiting For?" he declared, "Men and women, Christ is a Saviour. God offers Him to you; you take Him and it is done. Feeling or no feeling, will you take Him to-night?"[184] Ideally, all men and women should make the confession of faith in Christ as savior, "*because it is the only way to be saved.*"[185]

In "Heroes and Cowards," Torrey sketched out the process whereby a genuine conversion could occur, bringing with it specific spiritual benefits. He confessed that he could "guarantee one thing...that if you will accept Jesus Christ with all your heart and surrender your whole life to him, and His control, and publicly confess Him before the world, God will send His Holy Spirit into your heart, filling it with a joy that you never knew before."[186] Through simple acceptance of Jesus as "Lord and Saviour" one received the Holy Spirit, a sure sign of genuine religious experience.

Torrey was one of the earliest evangelists to articulate what became the "sinner's prayer," a simple confession by which individuals invited Jesus into their hearts, the entry point to conversion and Christian experience. Seekers were asked to repeat the simple prayer that Torrey prayed in their behalf: "Oh God, I believed that Jesus died for my sins on the Cross, and I found peace through believing, and now I believe that Jesus rose again, and that He has all power in Heaven and on earth, He has got power to set me free today."[187] If they affirmed that confession of faith, then salvation was secured. The sinner's prayer became the entry point for multitudes of persons who utilized it to claim Christian faith for themselves.

Conversion was indeed an escape from hell, a literal place where the damned—those who never accepted Christ as savior—spent eternity in unending punishment. In a sermon called "Hell," Baptist evangelist T. T. Martin (1862–1939) described the particulars of that fiery realm prepared for those who refused to follow Christ. He concluded with a simple remedy for escaping that horrific eternal destiny:

> How can you avoid going to Hell? How simple and easy: "Christ died for our sins" (I Corinthians 15:3); just as one man pays another man's fine, as one man pays another man's debts to save his home for him, as one man goes to war in another's place and dies in his place.... There is no other way. Let those who think it morally wrong for the innocent to bear the penalty of the guilty go on to Hell for their own sins, and we who believe it right will accept the Saviour and go on to heaven.[188]

The various styles of "hell-fire preaching" came to be associated with popular revivalism and revivalists as a dramatic incentive for experiencing conversion and escaping damnation.

Billy Sunday: "A Contemporary Bunkshooter"?

The twentieth-century evangelist Billy Sunday (1862–1935) carried many of Moody's practices into his own brand of revivalism. Sunday, known for his flamboyant style and earthy preaching, also offered conversion through a simple confession of faith. In a sermon entitled, "Why Delay Your Real Conversion?" Sunday asked,

> What does converted mean? It means completely changed. Converted is not synonymous with reformed. Reforms are from without—conversion from within. Conversion is a complete surrender to Jesus. It's a willingness to do what he wants you to do. Unless you have made a complete surrender and are doing his will it will avail you nothing if you've reformed a thousand times and have your name on fifty church records. Believe on the Lord Jesus Christ, in your heart and confess him with your mouth and you will be saved. God is good. The plan of salvation is presented to you in two parts. Believe in your heart and confess with your mouth.[189]

Sunday's approach to religious experience included war on liquor, infidelity, and certain rationalistic assertions that cast doubt on biblical revelation. His crusades in towns and cities from the Midwest to the East were both evangelical revivals and temperance crusades, a call to salvation and an all-out offensive against local liquor traffickers.

At the same time, Sunday attempted to make the "old, old story of Jesus and his love" appealing to his modern listeners, particularly young people. Fighting Darwinism tooth and nail, he nonetheless made some attempts to accommodate modernity. William McLoughlin observed that perhaps his "most serious departure" from traditional evangelical orthodoxy was in the "apparent nonchalance with which he equated salvation with decency, patriotism, and manliness, and the way he played down the necessity for any personal crisis experience" as essential to the new birth. Conversion could come, he believed, "without any fuss."[190] While Moody gave great emphasis to the fact that conversion experience involved significant spiritual struggle, Sunday made it much easier, often with what McLoughlin called "a simple shake of the hand and a firm resolution to do better."[191] Jesus was ready to save, no muss, no fuss.

Sunday's public persona made him controversial in many segments of American culture, including the poetry of Carl Sandburg, whose composition, "To a Contemporary Bunkshooter," was supposedly directed at the revivalist, his conversionism and his motives. It begins,

> You come along... tearing your shirt... yelling about Jesus.
> Where do you get that stuff?
> What do you know about Jesus?[192]

Such criticisms of revivalists and revivalistic methods mirrored the debates about faith, dogma, and religious experience that descended on American Protestants in the early twentieth century as reflected in the so-called Fundamentalist/Modernist Controversy.

Revivalism: An Evangelical Norm

The phenomenon known as the Second Great Awakening solidified revivalism as the evangelical Protestant mechanism for conversion, religious experience, and entry into Christian faith. Revivals and camp meetings represented the early stages of later nineteenth- and twentieth-century evangelical "crusades" to bring salvation to the American multitude in outdoor stadiums, public arenas and local congregations. From Charles Finney to Billy Graham, specific "plans of salvation" charted the way to grace, opening the door to the church, Christian living, and salvation in this world and the next. Once-born Christians continued to come to faith through the nurture and sacraments of more traditional Christian communions. But even nurture presupposed a national Christian ethos by which each generation was inducted into faith by families that understood the importance of extending Christian identity, if not elaborate religious encounter, to their children. Amid the competition of American denominations and sects, clarity as to the nature of religious experience and the process for securing it remained significant if not essential. From conversionist communities of faith new movements developed, often with new salvific morphologies. Religious liberty and free will meant that "switching" from group to group became a decided possibility, as diverse and perhaps more esoteric religious experiences were made available.

Yet as effective a tool for mass conversions as revivalism might be, it highlighted the continuing division between once- and twice-born Christians.

The nurturing churches welcomed children into the world with "Christian nurture" in ways that meant those children might never know a time when they felt outside the grace of God. Evangelical churches talked the language of dramatic conversion, and many found their way to grace through such a spiritual catharsis. But they also nurtured children, some of whom also affirmed the once-born nature of their journey of faith. When doubts assailed, however, those who prayed the "sinner's prayer" might have no more or less assurance of salvation than if they had simply received a consecrated wafer on their tongues.

★★ 5 ★★

Over-Souls and Spirits: Transcendentalism and Spiritualism

The Transcendentalist Club

"Nature is made to conspire with spirit to emancipate us."[1] So Ralph Waldo Emerson (1803–1882) wrote (anonymously) in the 1836 essay *Nature*, a treatise that some believe to be the first real manifesto of American Transcendentalism.[2] *Nature* was published the same year that the Transcendentalist Club was formed in Boston, initially as a gathering place for Unitarian ministers engaged in dialogue regarding the important theological and philosophical ideas of the era. It soon became a philosophical, theological, and literary community composed of persons who offered diverse approaches to the great questions of the times.

The original group included Ralph Waldo Emerson (1803–1882), George Putnam (1814–1872), Frederick Henry Hedge (1805–1890), George Ripley (1803–1880), Orestes Brownson (1803–1876), Amos Bronson Alcott (1799–1888), William H. Furniss (1802–1896), James Freeman Clarke

(1810–1884), Convers Francis (1795–1863), Theodore Parker (1810–1860), Sophia Peabody (1809–1871), and Margaret Fuller (1810–1850). Heirs of Puritanism, Romanticism, and the Enlightenment, they offered varying analyses of New England Calvinism and Unitarianism, often suggesting that both ideologies spawned "corpse-cold" responses to issues of mind and spirit. Sydney Ahlstrom observed that these New England "romantics belong first of all to the genus of religious enthusiasts, of which Puritanism was another, earlier species. The Edwardsean New Lights were an intermediate factor no less important for the Transcendentalists than was German pietism for Schleiermacher."[3]

They were a diverse group, to be sure. Bronson Alcott founded Fruitlands, a short-lived communitarian society, with innovative educational techniques aimed at awakening the inherent innocence and insight extant in every child. Physical birth was humanity's real "new birth," the door to a spiritual culture that "lifts the body from the drowsy couch; opens the eyes upon the rising sun; tempts it forth to breathe the invigorating air; plunges it into the purifying bath, and thus whets all its functions for the duties of the day." It was the individual's daily link to the larger creation.[4]

Unlike many participants in the Transcendentalist Club, James Freeman Clarke remained a Unitarian minister, linking Christianity with revelation evident in nature and utilizing traditional Christian language to describe a new theological order. In a *Manual of Unitarian Belief*, he set forth basic principles of Unitarianism, with an emphasis on the role of conscience and the revelatory elements of both natural and revealed religion. In rejecting the "dead orthodoxy" of Calvinism, Clarke insisted that conversion was not only possible, but demanded "a radical change, not a superficial one."[5] He noted that "conversion is almost the same thing as repentance," a decision to "turn round in order to go the right way." It was not a once and for all, supernaturally imposed experience, but the simple realization that "when we are conscious that we are not obeying the truth and not doing our duty, we need to turn round and to enter at once upon a new path. This is conversion; and this act may become necessary many times in the course of our life." Clarke concluded that a converted person "is one who has determined to do right and has begun to do right." This regenerate individual "is one in whom the habit of right-doing is established, one who has come to love it, and to whom it is no effort."[6]

Clarke was foremost among those Transcendentalists who wrote appreciatively of other world religions and imported their sacred documents into the US. In a treatise on "heathen religions," he affirmed the religious experiences of other faiths, insisting that "they are not superstitions, but religions" that "instead of degenerating towards that which is worse; their movement is upward toward something better." Their truths, however, were "partial and incomplete," requiring a "universal religion . . . to fulfill and harmonize them." That religion, Clarke asserted, "can be nothing but Christianity."[7]

Orestes Brownson, also a Unitarian minister, had a limited association with the Transcendentalists, and turned to Roman Catholicism in 1844. Brownson observed of his Transcendentalist colleagues, "On many sides they expose themselves to ridicule, but at bottom there is a serious, solemn purpose, of which even they are but half conscious."[8] Margaret Fuller became founding editor of *The Dial,* a Transcendentalist journal, and used it as a vehicle for communicating her own formidable literary and feminist views. *The Dial* was published 1840–1844 as "a Magazine for Literature, Philosophy and Religion." It included essays, poems, commentary, and analysis from a variety of outstanding New England philosophes.

These highly individualistic men and women shared what Patrick W. Carey called "a common distaste for the past and a yearning for a new and fresh liberation of the human spirit," especially in their rejection of the old ideological categories promulgated by Calvinists and Unitarians.[9] Yet they also disagreed among themselves as to the nature of reality and its application to individual life; as James Freeman Clarke noted, "No two of us thought alike."[10] Octavius Brooks Frothingham, the movement's earliest historian, summed it up accordingly when he wrote that Transcendentalism "amounted merely to this, that man had a natural capacity for *receiving* supernatural truths, when presented by revelation. The *possession* of such truths, even in germ; the power to unfold them naturally, by process of mental or spiritual growth they denied. . . . The soul, according to them, was recipient, not originating or creative."[11]

Transcendentalists and their movement had numerous antecedents. Many were nurtured within Unitarianism, and its emphasis on reason in sorting out religious truth, its belief in the connections between the natural and the supernatural, and its insistence that Jesus, while subordinate to God, was the moral and spiritual model of human potential. Many concurred with the ideas elaborated in "Unitarian Christianity," a sermon preached by William Ellery Channing (1780–1842) at the 1819 ordination of Jared Sparks. The sermon delineated such Unitarian ideals as a more historical-critical approach to scripture; the unity of God; Jesus as "a being distinct from, and inferior to God"; and Jesus's death on the cross as a sign of God's sacrificial love, not a payment for divine wrath.[12] Channing's views on religious experience were also influential in shaping Transcendentalist thought, evident in yet another ordination sermon preached in 1828. In it he suggested that

> the divine attributes are first developed in ourselves, and thence transferred to our Creator. The idea of God, sublime and awful as it is, is the idea of our own spiritual nature, purified and enlarged to infinity. In ourselves are the elements of Divinity. God, then, does not sustain a figurative resemblance to man. It is the resemblance of a parent to a child, the likeness of a kindred nature. . . . That unbounded spiritual energy which we call God, is conceived by us only through consciousness, through the knowledge of ourselves.[13]

Although Channing himself generally resisted a move toward Transcendentalism, his views on divine immanence no doubt resonated with many in the movement.

In *Spiritual Freedom*, Channing insisted that real religion was not found in a controlling ecclesiastical hierarchy or a divisive sectarianism; nor was it a community in which a few elitist clergy became the primary sources of exegetical and ecclesial authority. It was not "bestowing on one a prerogative" that is not enjoyed by all persons. Rather, "It must be regarded as the revelation of a common Father, to whom all must have equal access, who invites all to the like immediate communion, who has no favorites, who has appointed no infallible expounders of his will . . . and calls upon all to follow fearlessly the best convictions of their own understanding."[14] He asserted that religion gave "life, strength, elevation to the mind, by connecting it with the Infinite Father. . . . It is religion alone, which nourishes patient, resolute hopes and efforts for our own soul."[15] "I call that mind free," Channing declared, "which escapes the bondage of matter, . . . does not content itself with a passive or hereditary faith . . . which sets no bounds to its love, which is not imprisoned in itself or in a sect, [and] which recognizes in all human beings the image of God and the rights of his children . . ."[16] For Channing, this "spiritual freedom" was exactly what "Christ came to give." He envisioned a new community that was liberated in "thought and affection, and in the unrestrained action of our best powers."[17] Channing's alternative spirituality set the scene for Transcendentalist speculation.

Transcendentalists distanced themselves from Unitarians by placing greater emphasis on Divine immanence in the world and the individual soul. They challenged the Unitarian belief that the supernatural veracity of Christianity was evidenced in the miracles of Jesus. In Theodore Parker's words, they rejected the difference between "*revealed* and *natural* religion," since "all actual religion is revealed to us, or it could not be felt, and all revealed religion is natural or it would be of no use to us."[18] In attempting to protect supernatural revelation through the external verification of miracles, Unitarians ignored the inherent presence of immediate religious experience resting in the soul of every human being. Many were intrigued by the moral and spiritual teachings of other world religions, especially Hinduism and Buddhism, often suggesting that Divine immanence, present in all human beings, inhibited attempts to project a "sharp antithesis between Christianity and the ethnic religions."[19]

Transcendentalists were the heirs of a particular strain of modern philosophy that began in Europe, associated with the idealism of Immanuel Kant, and set forth in his *Critique of Pure Reason* and other works. Kant challenged Lockean insistence on the boundaries of human reason, and contended that the mind held elements that went beyond sense experience. Transcendental ideas thus represented "those primitive or *a priori* elements of the mind that condition all knowledge."[20] Kant agreed with John Locke, David Hume, and others that the mind comprehends "objects of possible experience in space and time," but he also asserted that there are ideas that go beyond experience and become "useful notions that the mind employs to organize what it does experience in space and time." Thus reason exceeded merely "processing information" to become "an active source driven by curiosity and a rage for order, including the rage to establish its own order and unity."[21] Of this Kantian approach, Emerson wrote,

> The Idealism of the present day acquired the name Transcendental from the use of that term by Immanuel Kant . . . who replied to the skeptical philosophy of Locke, which insisted that there was nothing in the intellect which was not previously in the experience of the senses, by showing that there was a very important class of ideas or imperative forms, which did not come by experience, but through which experience was acquired; that these were intuitions of the mind itself; and he denominated them Transcendental forms.[22]

As Henry D. Gray suggested, it appears that Transcendentalism was impacted, if not formed, "by the deliberate importing of certain imperfectly understood elements of German idealism into American Unitarianism."[23] While Emerson referred to Kant as a philosophical mentor to his own transcendentalist concepts, he extended Kantian ideas considerably. For Frederick Ives Carpenter, New England Transcendentalism not only "modified" Kant's views but broadened traditional Puritan theology to new concepts and religious possibilities. They "applied this philosophic idealism and this religious enthusiasm to the practical reform of American Social institutions," contributing to a "renaissance" in literature, begun with no one other than Emerson himself.[24] Like Kant, Emerson believed that "Reason" was more than intellectualized rationalism or sense experience. It maintained a transcendental quality grounded in "the intuitions of the mind itself."[25]

In a lecture entitled *The Transcendentalist* (1842), Emerson defined the movement in various ways, noting,

> What is popularly called Transcendentalism among us, is Idealism; Idealism as it appears in 1842. As thinkers, mankind have ever divided into two sects, Materialists and Idealists; the first class founding on experience, the second on consciousness; the first class beginning to think from the data of the senses, the second class perceive that the senses are not final, and say, the senses give us representations of things, but what are the things themselves, they cannot tell.[26]

Emerson affirmed the spiritual elements of Transcendentalism, based in a particular approach to religious experience, noting,

> The Transcendentalist adopts the whole connection of spiritual doctrine. He believes in miracle, in the perpetual openness of the human mind to new influx of light and power; he believes in inspiration, and in ecstasy. He wishes that the spiritual principle should be suffered to demonstrate itself to the end, in all possible applications to the state of man, without the admission of anything unspiritual; that is, anything positive, dogmatic, personal. Thus, the spiritual measure of inspiration is the depth of the thought, and never, who said it?[27]

Thus Carpenter concluded that Emerson's style of Transcendentalism was "not philosophically pure" but involved an effort to reconcile both nature and the supernatural.[28] William Clebsch concurred, noting that "Emerson left us a vision of religion or spirituality, [but] not a full-philosophy of religion, not a developed theology."[29]

Catherine Albanese understood Transcendentalism as "an explicitly religious phenomenon" with a decidedly American character. Thus Emerson and his colleagues articulated a worldview that was ordered by the ancient idea of correspondence. This vision of reality saw the universe as "a living book in which one could read the secrets of the soul." Even language became a tool "which mirrored the natural creation."[30] Clebsch wrote that "Emerson thought of religiousness as being receptive to an experience in the full range of its meaning.... In religious experience one sensed that one was receiving a given universe whose hospitality was everywhere self-evident and thereby one was realizing truest selfhood."[31]

In terms of religious experience, Transcendentalism was a bridge between America old and new. While the early leaders scorned Unitarian rationalism, they remained rooted in the Unitarian rejection of Trinitarianism and substitutionary atonement, insisting that all persons retained the potential for direct connection to the Divine. Like their Unitarian forebears, Transcendentalists decried sectarian dogmatism wherever it appeared. They shunned the dogmas of eternal punishment and original sin. Human nature was untainted by the curse of Adam; human beings were freely capable of discovering profound spiritual experience within themselves.[32] Yet many Transcendentalists were uncomfortable with Unitarian support for Lockean philosophy, particularly its rejection of the possibility of innate ideas and its claim that sense experience was the primary means of encountering reality ("Sensationalism").

Beyond Unitarianism, Transcendentalists reasserted the power of internal encounter with the Source of all things. Writing in 1908, H. C. Goddard suggested that "first and foremost," Transcendentalism represented "a doctrine concerning the mind, its ways of acting and methods of getting knowledge. Upon this doctrine the New England transcendental philosophy as a whole was built.... This philosophy teaches the unity of the world in God and the immanence of God in the world."[33] Emerson's quest for what he called "the religious sentiment" took him outside Unitarianism and beyond traditional Christian rituals, dogmas, and biblical revelation itself.[34]

In his 1876 history of the movement, Frothingham wrote that in "the living faith of New England" the "pagan" origins of philosophy had become so thoroughly Christianized that

> the fact of immediate communication between the soul of the believer and its Christ was so earnestly insisted on, the sympathy was represented as being so kindred and organic a nature, that in reading the works of the masters of New England theology, it requires an effort to forget that the speculative basis of their faith was not the natural basis of the philosopher, but the supernatural one of the believer.[35]

Frothingham believed that the signs of this idealism were evident in such "spiritual writings" as Jonathan Edwards's *Treatise on Religious Affections*, a document revealing that when Puritan orthodoxy turned to religious experience it entered a realm in which "the human soul and the divine were in full concurrence." In moving beyond Puritan conversionism, Transcendentalists claimed for humanity "what Protestant Christianity claimed for its own elect."[36] In the heady context of American progress and democratic idealism, Transcendentalism extended direct encounter with the Other (Emerson's *Over-Soul*) to all who would discover its presence in themselves and in the world.

In *Nature*, Emerson insisted that creation is not the result of an all-sovereign power but an all-encompassing will, an energy both present in and revealed through Nature itself, and evident "in each ray of the star, in each wavelet of the pool." Everything in the universe was born of that "spirit" and "conspires with it," a reality that is the source of all true "religious sentiment." By means of such a spirit, he wrote, "the universe is made safe and habitable."[37] Emerson proclaimed that nature was so "glorious with form, color, and motion" that every "change" from chemicals to vegetation "from the sponge up to Hercules, shall hint or thunder to man the laws of right and wrong, and echo the Ten Commandments." He concluded, "Therefore is nature ever the ally of Religion: lends all her pomp and riches to the religious sentiment. Prophet and priest, David, Isaiah, Jesus, have drawn deeply from this source."[38]

Emerson's optimism about the human condition rested in the relationship he saw between Nature and the human, a correspondence that all persons could realize if they would but exercise their freedom of will. In the section on beauty, he wrote,

> Every rational creature has all nature for his dowry and estate. It is his, if he will. He may divest himself of it; he may creep into a corner, and abdicate his kingdom, as most men do, but he is entitled to the world by his constitution. In proportion to the energy of his thought and will, he takes up the world into himself.[39]

Likewise, Emerson rejected the Puritan idea that sinful human beings had lost the spark of the Divine through the curse of original sin and thus required some external infusion of grace. He declared "that behind nature, throughout nature, spirit is present; one and not compound, it does not act upon us from without, that is, in space and time, but spiritually, or through ourselves." Human beings, therefore, possessed inherently "that spirit, that is, the Supreme Being." This inner force/dynamic "does not build up nature around us, but puts it forth through us." Humanity rested "upon the bosom of God . . . nourished by unfailing fountains," and drawing, as needed, "inexhaustible power" from that inner experience of spirit. Who then could "set boundaries" on the extent of human possibilities? Once the expansive nature of these internal opportunities was recognized, it became clear "that man has access to the entire mind of the Creator [and] is himself the creator in the finite." This recognition of "where the sources of wisdom and power lie," along with the "golden key" of virtue, combined to "animate me to create my own world through the purification of my soul."[40]

Through the idea of correspondence Emerson sought to unite the external world of nature with the interior world of the soul, what he called a "radical correspondence between visible things and human thoughts."[41] Nature gave evidence of the correspondence between the entirety of the world and the inner life of the human, leading in its most complete form to wholeness realized or anticipated. For Emerson, a clear correspondence existed between spirit and nature. This "Over-Soul" was at the heart of all things. As H. C. Goddard observed, "The soul of each individual is identical with the soul of the world, and contains, latently, all which it contains."[42]

Emerson was certain that mind and nature were thoroughly related, noting, "Every natural fact is a symbol of some spiritual fact. Every appearance in nature corresponds to some state of the mind, and that state of the mind can only be described by presenting that natural appearance as its picture." He concluded, "That which, intellectually considered we call Reason, considered in relation to nature, we call Spirit"; and suggested that "the visible creation is the terminus or the circumference of the invisible world."[43] As Catherine Albanese suggested, "At the apex of the structure of correspondence in the universe which Emerson contemplated was the model which nature gave for the living of human life. Nature became the point of departure for a life-orientation system; it was 'ever the ally of Religion.'"[44] William Clebsch confirmed that as poet, Emerson saw the great realities of existence reflected in significant "correspondences" among God, nature, and human beings.[45]

Emerson's *Divinity School Address*, delivered at Harvard in 1838, soon became an important and controversial Transcendentalist manifesto against the prevailing orthodoxies of Protestant New England. Eschewing the Calvinist doctrine of election and the mediated grace of external sacraments, as well as the corpse-cold rationalism of the Unitarians, Emerson insisted that each individual could comprehend the unity of all things only through immediate experience. He declared that the great error of organized Christianity was that "it has dwelt, it dwells, with noxious exaggeration about the *person* of Jesus. The soul knows no persons. It invites every man to expand to the full circle of the universe, and will have no preferences but those of spontaneous love."[46] Emerson contended that the experience of the Other "cannot be received at second hand. Truly speaking, it is not instruction but provocation, that I can receive from another soul. What he announces, I must find true in me, or reject; and on his word, or as his second, be he who he may, I can accept nothing. On the contrary, the absence of this primary faith is the presence of delegation."[47] Thus Jesus could be an illustration of a soul's direct encounter with the Other, but could not mediate that experience to or for other individuals, each of whom must learn and receive it for themselves. Indeed, Jesus's faith "in the infinitude of man" was lost when the beliefs and experiences of the "saint" or the "poet" undermined the individual's direct experience with truth. Once seekers abandoned their "own knowledge of God," and took on a "secondary knowledge," mediated by St. Paul, or Quaker George Fox, or spiritualist Emanuel Swedenborg's knowledge, they would "get wide from God" for as long as "this secondary form" endured.[48]

Such immediate experience of reality was never static. No singular moment of conversion could settle forever the state of the soul amid the expanding forces of the universe. Rather, life at its fullest involved a process of unending experience and continued growth toward an element of oneness with all things. Emerson resisted any resource, including the life and work of Jesus, that mediated or interfered with direct encounter with the Over-Soul. Shackled by the dogmas of the past, nineteenth-century Protestant orthodoxy promoted religion centered on "the base doctrine of the majority of voices, [and] usurps the place of the doctrine of the soul."[49]

With an element of Quaker spiritual egalitarianism, Emerson repudiated his Unitarian ministerial credentials, refused to administer or receive the sacraments, and pursued that inner experience which recognized the presence of the Over-Soul within all things. This Over-Soul he described as that "Unity . . . within which every man's particular being is contained and made one with all other; that common heart of which all sincere conversation is the worship, to which all right action is submission." Within every person "is the soul of the whole: the wise silence; the universal beauty, to which every part and particle is equally related; the eternal One."[50] He claimed that "all spiritual being" resided in humanity and thus "there is no screen or ceiling between our heads and the infinite heavens . . . no bar or wall in the soul, where man, the effect, ceases, and God, the cause, begins."[51] Unity with the Divine was present from the beginning and had only to be recognized in the soul of each individual.

For Emerson, religious experience did not require an elaborate process of conversion whereby one rejected inherent sinfulness in hope of receiving some infused, external grace from God. Rather, that grace was present in all persons from their entry into the world. He wrote that the mysterious union between humanity and the Divine was "ineffable," yet even "the simplest person who in his integrity worships God, becomes God," discovering a new self deep within. Such redemption also involved direct encounter with Other, beyond the shackles of the dead past. He insisted that "when we have broken our god of tradition and ceased from our god of rhetoric, then may god fire the heart with his presence."[52]

There could be no substitute, no mediator, no "second" between the individual and the Other. "Reliance" on a secondary "authority" marked "the decline of religion, the withdrawal of the soul." He went so far as to suggest that even the intercessory prayers of others were "hurtful" until an individual "made his own." Pressing the argument to the fullest, Emerson declared, "We not only affirm that we have few great men, but, absolutely speaking, that we have none; that we have no history, no record of any character or mode of living that entirely contents us."[53]

Everything necessary for a transcendent encounter with ultimate truth was inherent in all human beings from the moment they entered the world. It reached its zenith when an individual recognized "that the Highest dwells in him." Emerson wrote eloquently, "The soul gives itself, alone, original and pure, to the Lonely, Original and Pure, who, on that condition, gladly inhabits, leads and speaks through it.... It is not called religious, but it is innocent."[54] Once this welcoming inner Spirit had been discovered, wholeness was truly possible as a "unity" no longer characterized by "a spotted life of shreds and patches." This was "that trust which carries God with it and so hath already the whole future in the bottom of the heart."[55]

Emerson and Edwards

Numerous scholars have explored the collective and contradictory insights that Emerson and Jonathan Edwards brought to the pursuit of religious experience, all with varying results.[56] In one sense, they represented distinct approaches to religious experience. Edwards, grounded in Reformed theology, envisioned a process of conversion by which sinners cast their depraved souls on God's saving grace, infused into the hearts of those elected to salvation. Emerson insisted that salvific enlightenment was inherent in all humanity, evident throughout nature and fully recognized by those who understood that they were microcosms of an all-permeating Over-Soul. Yet in separate but parallel ways, both Edwards and Emerson envisioned a new humanity in a new land. Both suggested that recognition of the Divine presence in individual lives would institute a new era in human life. Edwards, a postmillennialist, believed that the religious experience evident in the Awakening presaged a golden age of the church in anticipation of Christ's return. He wrote that

America was the scene of that preparation, adding, "This new world, is probably now discovered that the new and most glorious state of God's church on earth might commence there" and concluded that "God is about to turn the earth into a growth already but in a wilderness." America, the newest and least-anticipated environment for divine action, would become the millennial point of entry.[57] Sacvan Bercovitch suggested that in linking nature and the individual, Emerson too anticipated "a new man in a paradisiacal New World." He noted, "For both Edwards and Emerson, the image of the New World invests the regenerate perceiver with an aura of ascendant millennial splendor; and for both of them, the perceiver must prove his regeneration by transforming himself in the image of the New World." Emerson's more optimistic view of human nature nonetheless had millennial implications, evident in his assertion that "the [American] land is the appointed remedy for whatever is false and fantastic in our culture."[58] Bercovitch cited Emerson's insistence that "the Genius or Destiny of America is...a man incessantly advancing, as the shadow on the dial's face, or the heavenly body by whose light it is marked.... Let us realize that this country, the last found, is the great charity of God to the human race."[59] While Edwards and Emerson certainly differed as to the nature of and candidates for religious experience, they shared a belief that America was a divinely appropriated place where, in Emerson's words, a "new love, new faith, new sight shall restore [creation] to more than its first splendor."[60] The terms of religious experience might differ but the outcome seemed surprisingly similar.

Perry Miller observed that Edwards opposed the Antinomianism that became, in Emerson's words, "the corpse-cold Unitarianism of Harvard College and Brattle Street."[61] He characterized Edwards's conversionistic religious experience as a new dynamic, noting that while the Northampton preacher held "himself by brute will power within the forms of ancient Calvinism, he filled those forms with a new and throbbing spirit. Beneath the dogmas of the old theology he discovered a different cosmos from that of the seventeenth century, a dynamic world, filled with the presence of God, quickened with divine life, pervaded with joy and ecstasy."[62] Emerson, Miller believed, simply discarded the old Calvinist dogmas in ways that left him "free to celebrate purely and simply the presence of God in the soul and in nature, the pure metaphysical essence of the New England tradition. If he could no longer publish it as orthodoxy, he could speak it fearlessly as the very latest form of infidelity."[63] Miller recounted Emerson's response to a Calvinist-leaning friend: "I see you are speaking of something which had a meaning once, but is now grown obsolete. Those words formerly stood for something, and the world got good from them, but not now."[64] The millennium was not simply a pending occurrence; it was already present and "shines in on us at unawares."[65]

Nonetheless, Norman Pettit's assertion that Emerson promoted "what might be called militant indifference to prescribed experientialism" clearly distinguished him from the conversionism of Jonathan Edwards. Pettit cited Emerson's advice to those struggling with sin and depravity: "Do not cumber yourself with fruitless pains to mend and remedy remote effects. Let the soul be erect, and all things will go well." In fact, Pettit indicated that in many respects Emerson promoted an "innate antinomianism, or absolute assurance [of salvation] from birth." In other words, for Emerson, when it came to the "spiritual condition of the heart, ... all of life was preparation, all of life, assurance."[66]

Margaret Fuller: A Nineteenth-Century Woman

Margaret Fuller , one of the most outspoken feminists of the early nineteenth century, served with Emerson as editor of *The Dial*, and her views on the liberation of women were first published in that periodical. Her Transcendentalist sentiments were sometimes questioned, however, by those who claimed she was less romanticist than mystic. Octavius Frothingham wrote that "strictly speaking, she was not a Transcendentalist, though Mr. Channing declares her to have been 'in spirit and thought pre-eminently a transcendentalist.'" Bronson Alcott suggested that she adopted "the spiritual philosophy, and had the subtlest perception of its bearings." Others have concluded that "she was enthusiastic rather than philosophical, and poetic more than systematic."[67] Emerson wrote of Fuller,

> Left to herself, and in her correspondence, she was much the victim of Lord Bacon's *idols of the cave*, or self-deceived by her own phantasms.... Her letters are tainted with a mysticism which, to me, appears so much an affair of constitution, that it claims no more respect than the charity or patriotism of a man who has dined well and feels better for it. In our noble Margaret, her personal feeling colors all her judgment of persons, of books, of pictures, and even of the laws of the world.... In short, Margaret often loses herself in sentimentalism; that dangerous vertigo nature, in her case, adopted, and was to make respectable.... Her integrity was perfect, and she was led and followed by love; and was really bent on truth, but too indulgent to the meteors of her fancy.[68]

Fuller's feminist views were apparent in an article entitled "The Great Lawsuit: Man *versus* Men; Woman *versus* Women," published in the July 1843 edition of *The Dial*. It represented the first installment of what became her best-known book, *Woman in the Nineteenth Century*, published in 1845. The book signaled Fuller's own inner quest, of which Transcendentalism was certainly a part. It also represented what Bernard Rosenthal called "the first American extended polemical statement defining and advocating women's rights." In his introduction to Fuller's book, Rosenthal posited that it demonstrated her mystical approach to religious experience as well as her own "awareness of the worldly injustices confronting women."[69]

Woman in the Nineteenth Century traces women's actions and the resulting cultural responses across Western civilization. It demonstrates Fuller's own understanding of and approach to religious experience. Fuller called mysticism "the brooding soul of the world," and insisted that it "cannot fail of its oracular promise as to Woman." Thus mysticism became a vehicle by which she challenged the prevailing views of women and their role in the society. She wrote,

> Whenever a mystical whisper was heard, from Behmen [Jacob Boehme] down to St. Simon [Claude Henri de Rouvroy], spring up the thought,

> that, if it be true, as the legend says, that Humanity withers through a fault committed by and a curse laid upon Woman, through her pure child, or influence, shall the new Adam, redemption, arise. Innocence is to be replaced by virtue, dependence by a willing submission, in the heart of the Virgin-Mother of the new race.[70]

Fuller believed that the "especial genius of Woman" included three distinct elements: "Electrical in movement, intuitive in function, spiritual in tendency." Male and female genders represented "two sides of the radical dualism," yet she maintained that "there is no wholly masculine man, no purely feminine woman."[71] This leads Cynthia J. Davis to conclude that for Fuller, "gender no longer seems to matter (that is, to be materialized) either at the level of content or of form." Rather, her "true woman... is both spiritually exalted and physically attenuated." Fuller's vision was for a society in which both men and women reflected "a purified intelligence, an enfranchised soul—no less."[72] Fuller even utilized the word *Exaltadas* to describe what Davis called the "radiant, spiritual femininity" that personified her ideal.[73]

While warning that women had frequently been led astray by representatives of "priestcraft," Fuller acknowledged several specific individuals whose spirituality demonstrated respect for and insight into woman's spiritual and intellectual abilities. She praised her mentor William Ellery Channing for regarding women "as souls, each of which had a destiny of its own, incalculable to other minds, and whose leading it must follow, guided by the light of private conscience." She called Channing "dear and reverend," especially for the "unbroken respect" he gave to women.[74] Fuller also extolled the spiritual insight of Emanuel Swedenborg for its "harmony between the scientific and poetic lives of the mind." Swedenborg, she believed, promoted an "idea of Woman" that was "sufficiently large and noble to interpose no obstacle to her progress."[75] She concluded that Swedenborg's spiritual creativity "allows room for aesthetic culture and the free expression of energy," all qualities of the spirit that were offered to women as well as men.[76] Fuller praised the spiritual insights of Quakerism for its openness to "Woman on a sufficient equality with Man" and concluded that while Quakerism's original vision was "pure, its scope is too narrow" and needed to be "merged in one of a wider range."[77]

Fuller's mysticism was not unique to members of the Transcendentalist Club. Catherine Albanese contended that "Emerson's prescriptions for each individual were summed up in his mystical theory and spelled out in his notion of self-culture. His remedies for society arose from a discussion of the collective existence of selves in the flow of history."[78] In Albanese's view, Emerson's mysticism revealed similarities with the classic "mystic way" including awakening, purification, and union with the Divine. Yet "he differed from them concerning the means as well as the outcome of the experience." For Emerson, "God was in the universe" and nature was God's "projection; and God was in each human being."[79]

The idea of divine immanence was at the center of Transcendentalist approaches to religious experience. Religion, as Theodore Parker noted, was not regeneration or "a change of nature," but the continued cultivation of the inherent presence of the Over-Soul, "a life-germ inborn in the heart." Jesus's life and death was not the atonement for humanity's sins or the source of regeneration, but the example of how each person could actualize the natural divinity inherent in the race. Jesus's own divinity could be discovered by all who had eyes to see and ears to hear; it "reveals itself as that inspiration which visits all who are pure in heart."[80] In its most basic sense, Transcendentalist spirituality was concerned for divine immanence, "intuitive perception," a "rejection of external authority," and "a radical social ethic."[81] Transcendentalism narrowed the distance between the Divine, creation, and humanity, an emphasis short-lived in nineteenth-century America, but revisited in the twentieth- and twenty-first-century pursuit of a more generic spirituality.

Spiritualism: Experiencing the Beyond

Margaret Fuller's positive response to the work of Emanuel Swedenborg was not the only appreciative evaluation of the popular spiritualist among members of the Transcendental Club. In *Nature*, when Emerson observed that questions of "mind over matter" had "exercised the wonder and the study of every fine genius since the world began," he included the name of Emanuel Swedenborg along with that of Egyptians, Brahmins, Pythagoras, Plato, Francis Bacon, and Gottfried Leibnitz.[82] Spiritualism had implications for Christian and non-Christian alike.

Beliefs and practices related to the occult were present in the American colonies from the beginning. The Christian-oriented Europeans who arrived in the fifteenth and sixteenth centuries found that Native Americans were well schooled in shamanic practices that included spirit possession, revelatory visions, and dreams, and communication with spirits, animals, natural forces, and other expressions of the sacred. Catherine Albanese observed that "the distinction between natural and supernatural worlds, an easy shorthand for describing Euro-American religions, is forced and strained when applied to the traditional religions of Native Americans. Indians have seen awesome and mysterious power at work seemingly everywhere."[83] Shamanic individuals in every tribal context served as sources for channeling, interacting with, and interpreting varying elements of the experience of the sacred in the world. Such a response to the supernatural, experienced in a particular time and space, was inseparable from "the ancient idea of correspondence," connections by which Native Americans understood their specific communities to be microcosms of "a larger reality that surrounded them."[84] They connected themselves and their environment to the scheme of things in the broader world—forests, mountains, rivers, and prairies—and the universe of sun, moon, stars, and sky. Interaction with spirits was part of that sense of correspondence. This might include links to the spirits of deceased relatives or other tribal members, often thought to remain nearby for a period of time after death. It might involve messages sent through particular spirit vehicles, as in the Oglala Sioux stories of the "White Buffalo Calf Woman," who could bring life instructions to specific individuals. Or it could provide a "vision quest" in which "guardian spirits would reveal their relationship to the seeker and bestow the knowledge/power desired."[85]

The early English colonists were not ignorant of the occult or immune from certain of its practices. Jon Butler documented the presence of colonial occultism evident in experiences entailing magic, witchcraft, astrology, amulets, potions, and quests for healing that even involved negotiations with certain demonic spirits, practices pursued by certain Christians even when condemned by the clergy. Such actions were not limited to the superstition-prone lower classes, but included many well-born and educated persons who investigated a "more learned occultism."[86] Butler concluded, for example, that by the late seventeenth century, "Virginia's learned occult milieu was reflected in the books owned by the colony's emerging aristocratic elite."[87]

Butler theorized that the "evangelical conversion ritual also paralleled occult exercises in eighteenth-century America." In fact, clergy may have shaped conversion morphologies in ways that offered a response to the deep and enduring questions addressed by certain occult practices, evident in concerns about birth, death, finances, interpersonal relations, and other realities of life. He wrote that in the early days of colonial revivalism, "at least for a while, colonists went to hear revival ministers in large numbers and enacted rituals of doubt, inquiry, and resolution that paralleled encounters between wise men and clients of an older, now folklorized, occultism."[88]

Occult pursuits continued in spite of revivalist attempts to wipe them out through conversion, sermons, and witch hunts. Stories detailing the supernatural activities of witches and other "familiars" in the occult firmament extended from the colonial into the postconstitutional eras of national life. Divining rods were used by many to seek out water or treasure; and astrological speculations, often perpetuated in the *Farmer's Almanac*, were widely pursued. Death, an ever-present reality from the cradle to old age, was a frequent visitor in every family, often leading to elaborate rituals for dying and perpetuating memorials to the deceased.[89]

The rise of spiritualism in popular American culture was not unrelated to earlier occult practices: the desire to communicate with dead family or friends, especially those who died too soon, and a growing interest in metaphysical speculation inside and beyond traditional religious communions. Spiritualism is an implicit element of metaphysics, a philosophical approach to life's perpetual questions, often condemned or distanced from traditional religious viewpoints, and engaging various supernatural or intellectual approaches to issues of human existence. Indeed, some view the life of the mind itself as a "metaphysical religious focus."[90]

Albanese suggested that such metaphysical expressions are evident in at least four areas of religious life in the United States. These include 1) an "elite esoteric religion" present in colonial England and America; 2) certain occult practices involving herbs and magic brought by immigrants to the "Atlantic colonies"; 3) a nineteenth-century form of metaphysics that became evident in middle-class, educated persons, often with particular attention to spiritualism; and 4) a more public expression of metaphysical beliefs and practices of New Thought, offering methods for dealing with illness and certain "spiritual energy."[91] Transcendentalism, mesmerism, and spiritualism were evidence of this latter quest.

Many of these movements have been linked to Hermeticism, a highly eclectic religious philosophy often related to Hellenism, and attributed to the writings of Hermes Trismegistus, a priestly figure thought to have lived in ancient Egypt. These sources promoted magic, mysticism, and pagan religious views. The term *Hermeticism* later was used to describe a variety of Hellenistic-oriented mystical approaches including Neoplatonism, gnosticism, alchemy, and certain types of magic.[92]

Mesmerism

Mesmerism was in many respects a bridge between traditional concerns for human transformation through conversion and the possibility of human self-improvement through new "scientific" discoveries that unlocked the inner and outer worlds. In his *Reflections on the Discovery of Animal Magnetism*, published in 1779, Austrian Franz Anton Mesmer (1734?–1815) distinguished twenty-seven guidelines for explaining his scientific discoveries that could facilitate physical and spiritual healing. Animal magnetism, so-called, was a powerful internal force or energy that could unlock recuperative properties for every form of disease. Should a body's animal magnetism become disordered, Mesmer believed that it could be restored by passing magnets over unwell individuals in order "to supercharge their nervous systems with this mysterious, yet life-giving, energy."[93] "Mesmerism," as it came to be called, had a great impact on certain intellectual and populist subgroups in Europe in the late eighteenth and early nineteenth century. Mesmer himself claimed to have accomplished cures for multiple maladies. Early on this was achieved by swinging magnets above the bodies of the infirm; later, the magnets were replaced by the *baquet,* connecting patients to a particular type of magnetized water running through iron pipes to a large tub of water in which patients reclined. Official studies commissioned to investigate the veracity of such practices and the existence of animal magnetism as a genuine physiological presence led to documentation of a variety of cures, as well as the condemnation of Mesmer's practices and philosophy.[94]

In his study of Mesmerism and its impact on American religious and popular life, Robert C. Fuller contended that the movement represented the first stage of a larger phenomenon in which nineteenth-century devotees of "new science" developed alongside but distinct from Christian communities. He claimed that revivalism opened the door to self-examination and the alleviation of spiritual struggles through conversion, noting, "American Protestantism, with its obsession for saving souls through distinct conversion experiences, created a metaphysical climate which assured mesmerism of a receptive audience."[95]

By the time of the Second Great Awakening, when animal magnetism first came to the attention of Americans, revivalist Charles G. Finney was already describing revivals as the "purely philosophical result of the right use of the constituted means."[96] In other words, there were "scientific" principles set forth in scripture that when properly heeded would produce individual conversion and mass revivals. Human beings could affect their salvation by activation of their own free will. In his study *The Burned-Over District*, Whitney Cross suggested that individuals such as Franz Mesmer and Emanuel Swedenborg sought to demonstrate the way in which "new scientific discoveries" would "confirm the broad patterns of revelation as they understood them," thereby offering humanity "ever-more-revealing glimpses of the pre-ordained divine plan for humanity and the universe."[97] Mesmerism anticipated the wholistic religious concerns of many individuals who sought to harmonize revelation, dreams, health, intellect, and economics, what Sydney Ahlstrom called "harmonial" religions. Jon Butler noted that mesmerism introduced a new kind of religious experience that connected various spiritual and personal concerns confronting Americans in the Romantic period. He wrote, "Mesmerism's emphasis on reconciling individual and universal forces, on healing, and on dreams, visions, and spiritual introspection found sympathetic resonances in an increasingly romantic, impulsive, willful America. Mesmerism's attraction to those at the edges of Christianity also demonstrated the undisciplined energy of spiritual creativity in the early national period."[98]

By the time popularized approaches to animal magnetism found their way into American public life, the movement had become associated with cathartic moments in the lives of seekers concerned to redirect their existence beyond failures and mistakes—a conversion of sorts. Yet, as Fuller suggests, the mesmerist view of human nature was more positive and less traumatic than the revivalist-induced agonies over sin, guilt, and hell. It had rituals aplenty involving water, magnets, and even hypnotism, and thus offered a new option outside traditional dogmas and conversionist morphologies.[99]

Numerous individuals, many of whom were clergy, served as bridges between Christianity, animal magnetism, and spiritualism. One such clergyman was La Roy Sunderland (1802–1885), an evangelical revivalist with connections to Baptists and Methodists, and concerned with religious experience, social reform, and theological education. His abolitionist sentiments led him to edit *Zion's Watchman*, the earliest Methodist antislavery periodical, 1836–1842.[100] While links between mesmerism and revivalism were frequent topics of nineteenth-century conversation, Sunderland was the only individual to explore what Ann Taves calls "rudimentary controlled experiments on religious subjects to see if muscular rigidity and visions could be artificially induced through mesmeric means." Sunderland believed that trance-like states he observed in revival settings were evidence of the Divine presence, a close parallel to explicitly mesmeric measures. Sunderland was one of a few preachers to connect revivalistic religious experience with the phenomenon of animal magnetism, even as he challenged certain mesmerist practitioners who required clairvoyant mediums or special types of fluid.[101] His particular method he called "Pathetism," which he described accordingly: "When a relation is once established between an operator...and his patient, corresponding changes may be induced in the nervous system of the latter (awake or entranced) by suggestions addressed to either of the external senses."[102] Sunderland bridged Christian and mesmeric ministry by asserting the relationship between the "shout tradition" of Methodist revival enthusiasm with certain external outbursts present in animal magnetism healing rituals.[103]

Universalist pastor, later mesmerist John Dods (1795–1872) was another articulate defender of the relationship between animal magnetism and Christian ideals. He wrote that mesmerism's "energizing and regenerating powers" that drew on "the doctrine of psychological impressions, in connection with the gospel of Jesus Christ," was "destined to renovate the world and usher in the millennial dawn."[104] This kind of talk was readily denounced by more orthodox Protestants who saw mesmerism as a false attempt to offer another gospel to troubled individuals.

Nonetheless, mesmerism represented the first stage of a more extensive array of metaphysical movements that provided a scientific explanation for ancient quests and new methods for conquering age-old spiritual and mental struggles. Whitney Cross wrote, "Mesmerism led to Swedenborgianism, and Swedenborgianism to spiritualism, not because of the degree of intrinsic relationship between the three propositions but because of the assumptions according to which American adherents understood them."[105] The healing techniques and possibilities evident in mesmerism had significant implications for the healing revivals of the early twentieth century.

Emanuel Swedenborg: Beyond Death

It was none other than Oneida perfectionist John Humphrey Noyes who offered an early description of Emanuel Swedenborg's popularity in nineteenth-century America, noting that his ideas appeared at a time when the "Bible and revivals had made men hungry for something more than social reconstruction."[106] Noyes wrote that Swedenborg "suited all sorts," commenting,

> The scientific were charmed, because he was primarily a son of science, and seemed to reduce the universe to scientific order; the mystics, because he led them boldly into all the mysteries of intuition and the invisible worlds; the Unitarians, because, while he declared Christ to be Jehovah himself, he displaced the orthodox ideas of sonship and tri-personality; even the infidels favored him, because he discarded thirty-two of the sixty-six commonly accepted books of the Bible.[107]

Swedenborg's influence captivated not only those groups, but also impacted Transcendentalists, spiritualists, millenarians, certain advocates of mysticism, and even aspects of the "positive thinking" movement that developed in the twentieth century.[108]

Emanuel Swedenborg (1688–1772) was a mining engineer, scientist, and Swedish Lutheran layman content to speculate about varying theological categories, until he experienced a dramatic religious conversion in his late 50s. From then until his death he wrote prolifically about the nature of the Divine, religious experience, the second coming of Christ, Christian doctrine, and biblical interpretation. In describing the powerful experience that descended upon him around Easter, 1744, Swedenborg wrote,

> I had in my mind and body the feeling of an indescribable delight, so that had it been in any higher degree the whole body would have been, as it were, dissolved in pure joy. In a word I was in heaven and heard speech which no human tongue can utter, with the life that is there, with the glory and inmost delight that flows from it.[109]

Conversion brought new religious enthusiasm and a continuing series of revelations experienced through dreams, visions, and conversation with spiritual beings, some of whom he claimed were from other planets. His books were known to Americans by the late 1700s and gained increased popularity in the early nineteenth century, particularly among a certain intellectual clientele.

Swedenborg insisted that he had received special inspiration that unlocked the secrets of scripture with truths that transcended dogmatism and sectarian division. The idea of correspondence united every aspect of life—the natural world, the human and the heavenly—in one great organic configuration. "On earth, as it is in heaven," was not an ideal phrase. Life in the material and spiritual worlds was bonded intricately. The concept of correspondence runs throughout his many publications, in his insistence that "communication by correspondences is what is called influx." Thus all life, "whether man, spirit or angel," sprung directly from God. Jesus personified that correspondence, connecting both worlds inseparably.[110]

Human nature was not inherently depraved, but endowed with spiritual and intellectual potential that needed only to be unlocked through extended inner reflection and contemplation, often enhanced through interaction with heavenly beings and spirits. These spiritual encounters offered new insights into the meaning of scripture and raised the possibility of healing from disease.[111]

In his *Spiritual Diary*, published in 1758, Swedenborg wrote,

> A spiritual idea is that by which a man, while he lives as a spirit, and thus separated, as it were, from the body, acts and thinks. That ideas of this kind are, as was said before, more full and more perceptive of things, is evident from the fact, that by means of a spiritual idea it can be known and perceived to the life how the case is in regard to man's non-ability to think, much more to act of himself anything that should not be sin, even while he intends good, as, for instance, his own conversion and self-moved repentance,—how all this may be done, and yet there may be sin, not only in the general act, but in the minutest particulars,—all this, I say, may be set forth and shown most vividly to a spiritual idea.[112]

This "spiritual idea" offered the receptive individual a variety of spiritual encounters, including the possibility of direct contact with "angels and spirits." Swedenborg published numerous accounts of such experiences, which he insisted were available to all persons if they would but give themselves to spiritual exploration. Some descriptions of this receptive state sound strangely like those of a somnambulistic regimen parallel to mesmerism. The individual moves "between sleeping and waking," yet seems fully awake, the "senses being as much awake as in the most perfect state of bodily wakefulness," including sight, sound and even touch. He observes that "in this state also spirits and angels are seen to the life, and are also heard, and, what is wonderful, are touched, scarce anything of the body then intervening."

In the *Arcana Celestia*, a multivolume series explicating truths found in Genesis and Exodus, and begun soon after his conversion, Swedenborg claimed to have attained an "out of body" state at least three or four times. A deeper experience, he said, allowed him to be "carried by the spirit to another place," some "two or three times."[113] While such encounters were possible for the spiritually contemplative, Swedenborg acknowledged that on occasion he had been "granted to be in both spiritual and natural light at the same time." At such moments he was able to view "wonderful things of Heaven," and to enjoy "company with angels," just as he would with human beings. These encounters brought new revelations, insights into "truth in the light of truth," and thus to be "led by the Lord."[114]

As Swedenborg understood it, the eternal world lay near the temporal one, and, at least for a time after death, the dead close at hand. At death, he wrote, "the internal parts of the body grow cold, the vital substances are separated from the man wherever they may be, even if enclosed in a thousand labyrinthine interlacings, so that nothing vital can remain behind." Initially, departed spirits encounter angels and other benevolent spirits but soon learn to follow a pattern for living that mirrors their earthly existence. The good may inhabit one of three separate heavens, while the evil ones abide in one of three hells where sinners are gathered according to their worst desires.[115]

Such descriptions were evidence of an expanded revelation given to him directly from the Divine, encounters that informed the contents of scripture and opened the door to new truth, itself a promise of the progress of human knowledge and links to God. These truths, he asserted, were not dreams, but genuine manifestations from God given "to send me to teach those things which will be of his New Church, which is meant by the New Jerusalem in the Revelation..."[116] This "New Church" was the spiritual community that was gradually taking shape as a sign that the second coming of Christ had already occurred and would prepare the world ultimately to recognize the fullness of that apocalyptic event. Swedenborg's many revelations and writings were direct descriptions of what that "New Church" and the earthly Kingdom would represent.[117]

Andrew Jackson Davis: The Poughkeepsie Seer

Andrew Jackson Davis (1826–1910) was in many ways a bridge between mesmerism and spiritualism. Known as the "Poughkeepsie Seer," Davis gained prominence, first as a healer who would diagnose illness while in a mesmerized trance, and then as a spiritualist (or protospiritualist) who claimed to have communed with various dead spirits and traveled through trance and vision to other planets. He was a prolific writer, whose ideas were widely circulated. His autobiography, published under the title, *The Magic Staff*, begins with accounts of his earliest clairvoyant experiences beginning as early as 1829. The original vision, received by Davis when he was only three and a half, revealed his "personal littleness," and "*my desolate state*," more terrifying "because I could see nothing like myself in any direction."[118] Similar visions and dreams appeared throughout his childhood. In 1843 he met William Levingston, a prominent mesmerist who came to his father's store in Poughkeepsie. Conversations between the two led to Davis's first mesmerist experience under Levingston's guidance, an event that indicated Davis's willingness to "yield to the mystic power."[119] Thus he claimed to have entered a new dimension of spacial, mental, and spiritual consciousness, noting that from then on, "there was a mystery hanging over my path—a spell on my soul—a higher calling from the pinnacle of some unknown mountain" that constantly sent him back to Levingston "to test and demonstrate what the new power could accomplish."[120]

Within a year Davis entered multiple clairvoyant states that led to a sense of being "born again" and empowered him to envision various "*centres* of light" whereby to look within other human beings, not only to view their "physical organs," but into the depth of their being, "its form, aspect, and color also, simply by observing the peculiar emanations surrounding it."[121] These experiences he understood as evidence of a "mystic vision" by which he beheld "the penetrating senses of the spirit" that all persons experienced after death. His senses were heightened to the point that he could detect the entire universe from "every little grain of salt or sand," to the ultimate interaction of the whole of creation.[122] These visions brought ecstatic joy, wholeness, and a mission "to bestow health, to snatch from death the suffering infant, to guide the blind man into the light, to sound the voice of healing in the ear of the deaf, to be a support when disease oppressed my neighbor," all with a profound sense of personal humility.[123]

At the center of his clairvoyance was the "Magic Staff," a spiritual object that became the "mental cane" continuously present with him, by which he "examined the sick," and on which he leaned "whenever things went wrong." It was a resource in which he trusted unreservedly "at all times."[124] By 1845 Davis had joined with physician Silas Smith Lyon and Universalist pastor William Fishbough in extending his anointing to others. Lyon took Davis into a "magnetized" state while Fishbough recorded and revised (edited) Davis's trance-induced pronouncements, documenting them for future use.[125] The three founded a journal known as *The Univercoelum and Spiritual Philosopher* in 1847. It endured for two years, publishing essays from a variety of individuals who claimed enlightenment, significantly influenced by Transcendentalism, Universalism, Swedenborgianism, and the views of Andrew Jackson Davis.[126] Soon Davis was interacting with individuals and groups, often entering into a clairvoyant state, during which he diagnosed specific illnesses or pending maladies. He practiced medicine essentially by means of trances, then was paid for his diagnoses. Davis even claimed that in his quest to discover "the relation of Christianity to Civilization," he was transported back in time to the point that he was able to "fix upon the exact events which preceded and characterized the birth and life" of Jesus. From these experiences he concluded that "every other question—scientific, ethical, psychical, poetical, prophetic, literary, &c., with which I come into institutional *rapport*—is subjectionable to my voluntary investigation." The "Magic Staff" became the interpretive tool for understanding these revelations and moving them beyond mere subjectivity or personal opinion.[127] The staff sustained him through his own illnesses by summoning friends to his bedside from this world and the next.[128] In fact, in one dramatic passage in *The Magic Staff* Davis claimed to have "passed directly into the superior [spiritual] state" that enabled him to meet and "salute" "the gifted Swede" Emanuel Swedenborg himself.[129]

The magic staff was also the spiritual vehicle that led Davis to propose his "Harmonial Philosophy," the belief that God and spirits were material beings, uniting Nature inseparably with the Divine. In the first volume of his five-volume work, *Great Harmonia*, Davis wrote, "Inasmuch as God is a Fact, a Reality, a Principle, it is agreeable with science to suppose that he is Substance—is Matter."[130] Ultimately, this Harmonial Philosophy was the great intention of a life that "Father-God and Mother-Nature have in reserve for every son and daughter." While not every male or female would enter "the mystical ordeal of magnetization," nonetheless the "laws of mind" would ultimately "waft each soul into 'the superior condition'" that would create "that totality of Divine life in the soul."[131] Davis predicted that the "Harmonial Age" would eventually descend upon the world, the final great dispensation, "a period of Peace and Happiness," just ahead. The constant desire of human beings for a "New Jerusalem," or an "Era of Universal Unity," was ideas whose "primary source" rested in "Father-God and Mother-Nature."[132]

Davis's popularity on the lecture circuit and among the upper classes did not blunt criticism from those who understood his views and practices to be an attack on traditional religion, particularly Christianity. An 1853 essay in *The United States Review* called him "a guiding star" of a movement by which "skeptical minds" sought "to pursue... 'human progress,' to disprove Christianity, and to remodel society." It noted that his purported contact "with the other world," through "rappings" was the result of "mental delusion" or "ingenious imposture."[133] Davis's ideas impacted a small but intense group of people who were gaining influence across the country. As this editorial understood it, Davis's great threat came from his belief "that *nothing either in the Bible or Creation is to be received as truth, unless it can be reduced to the text of Human Reason.*" Davis and the "infidels" who adhered to his views sought to undermine Christianity through "a denial of its doctrines and mysteries" by suggesting that they are incomprehensible by reason.[134]

Davis concluded his autobiography with various speculations on the nature of religion itself, including the role of Jesus for the church and the cosmos. He insisted that Christ's incarnation was "absolutely necessary" for restoring the union "between God and the ultimates of humanity." He confessed that Jesus was "the Way, the Truth, and the Life" and that persons must surrender themselves unconditionally to him as "their exemplar and their moral and spiritual guide." Yet he acknowledged that this christocentric affirmation did not imply "that the whole infinite *quantity* of the Divine essence was shut up and comprehended in any limited space or form," including in the man Jesus.[135]

By 1867 Davis had developed an even more expansive concept regarding the incarnations of divine inspiration. In a work entitled *The Arabula, or the Divine Guest*, intended to extend his earlier autobiographical reflections, he declared that divine revelations to the human race were known in the likes of Krishna, Buddha, Osiris, Adonis, Apollo, Bacchus, Jupiter, Socrates, Plato, Confucius, and Jesus. Each of the mysteries demonstrated by and through these spiritual mentors offered "*a singular unity* of design... and a purity of doctrine as evidently proving that this common origin was not to be sought for in the popular theology of the Pagan world."[136] Once again Davis insisted that the belief that "the whole Light [of human insight] should be manifested in one person [Jesus], is conceived to be impossible." For all his brilliance, Jesus had no knowledge of "the locomotive, the steamboat, vaccination, Peruvian bark, chloroform, either, iodine" and other discoveries made by modern science, geography, or biology.[137] In his analysis of nineteenth-century spiritualism, Frank Podmore wrote that Davis challenged claims that the Hebrew and Christian scriptures were the only sources of "infallible inspiration."

Podmore noted that in Davis's later works he viewed Jesus "as a great moral reformer, but not in any special sense divine."[138]

In his final autobiographical work, Davis moved beyond spiritual speculation to action, citing Theodore Parker's belief that the quest for truth involved an evolution from emotion to thought and "abstract idea," all of which ended in action. Davis's own action was evident in his intense opposition to human slavery, especially as present in the United States. He wrote,

> False Democracy, or that which really exists in the administration of either party, denies the manhood of a black man, rejects the political individuality of woman, however refined and intelligent and exalts the ignorant, the brutal, the swindler and the drunkard, to the commanding position of "American citizens," entitled to vote at elections, and to have a voice in the enactment of laws for the government of sober, docile, intelligent Africans, and also our white mothers and daughters, who are equal, often superior, to the white fathers, sons, and brothers of the world.[139]

The *Arabula* included additional descriptions of visions and encounters with the dead, including Davis's communication with the spirit of his deceased father.[140] It concluded with a "New Collection of the Gospels," Davis's own written illustration of the eclectic possibilities available to humanity in the thought of various seers and prophets, including gospels of "St. Confucius," "the Son of Brahma," "St. Emma" (Emma Harding, a well-known British spiritualist), "St. Theodore" (abolitionist Theodore Parker), and of course, "St. Ralph" (Ralph Waldo Emerson), among others.[141] Andrew Jackson Davis placed the Christian gospel within the larger context of what Robert W. Delp called "a new cosmogony and a scheme for elevating the human estate." His "Harmonial Philosophy created a framework for what became the spiritualist phenomenon, opening the door to the more famous work of the Fox sisters."[142]

Popular Spiritualism: The Fox Sisters and Beyond

For certain nineteenth-century intellectual and economic "elites" spiritualism became a "rational" route to religious experience and the apocalyptic through new insights drawn from science and nature. As Catherine Albanese observed,

> Spiritualism...brought together the theology of materialism (one could talk easily to spirits because they were matter, albeit highly refined) with an empiricism that insisted on the tangibility of scientific "proof" of spirit visitations and a social program that would translate the experience of spiritualism into a new science of the perfect society.[143]

Spiritualism had scientific, religious, mysterious, and popular influence on numerous populations in nineteenth-century America. While many in the Christian community were highly critical of its tenets and methodologies, its claims were not lost on many practicing Christians. Ann Braude concluded that spiritualism involved "a religious response to the crisis of faith experienced by many Americans" in the mid-nineteenth century. It offered an option for remaining "religious for those disaffected from Calvinism or evangelicalism in the antebellum years," and later on for "those disillusioned by Darwinism, biblical criticism and the rise of science."[144] As a movement, spiritualism offered an alternative "that supported the individualist social and political views of antebellum radicals."[145] The spiritualist view of human nature was far more positive than that of classic Calvinism. No radical conversion experience was required of a humanity that already bore God's image by virtue of creation.[146]

In addition, spiritualism combined elements of science and spirituality that were important concerns of nineteenth-century Americans. Laurence Moore wrote,

> In the interest of science and in the service of a population excited by scientific discovery, spiritualists proposed a religious faith that depended upon seeing and touching. Transforming a concern for man's inward spiritual nature into an empirical inquiry into the nature of spirits, they built a belief in an afterlife upon such physical signs as spirits from another realm could muster.[147]

Although Emanuel Swedenborg, Andrew Jackson Davis, and even the Shakers claimed to have engaged in a variety of spiritualist, otherworldly encounters, the popular beginning of the nineteenth-century spiritualist phenomenon in the United States is usually traced to the 1848 "rappings" of Margaret (1833–1893) and Kate Fox (1833–1892) who lived in Hydesville, New York, a region of the Burned-Over District. In 1848, when Margaret Fox was fifteen years old and Kate was twelve, they lived with their parents John and Margaret Fox in a house in Hydesville. Some of the townspeople believed the house to be haunted, a conviction confirmed when strange noises, later known as "rappings," broke out on the premises. Then on March 31, 1848, Margaret and Kate claimed to have experienced visitations from a specific individual that was the source of the rappings and who was attempting to communicate from the spirit world. When these spirit sounds persisted, the sisters maintained that they had discovered a method of communicating with an entity they called "Mr. Splitfoot," and later identified as Charles Rosna, a spirit claiming to have been murdered in the house, his body buried in the cellar. Multiple excavations revealed bone fragments in the cellar floor, confirming for many the veracity of sisters' claims.[148] News of the revelations spread, causing a local Methodist minister to offer his services as an exorcist. When the rappings continued, the minister turned his criticism on the Fox family, and the sisters departed the Methodist Church.[149]

By November 1849, Margaret and Kate joined their older sister, Leah Fox (1814–1890) in conducting public séances in Rochester and New York City.[150] As their fame increased, supporters and critics began extensive efforts to validate their claims, fostering debates inside and outside Christian communities. After their 1850 visit to New York City, Horace Greely wrote that after extensive investigation, "we believe no one to this moment pretends that he has detected either of them in producing or causing the Rappings; nor do we think any of their contemners has invented a plausible theory to account for the production of these sounds, nor the singular intelligence which (certainly at times) has seemed to be manifested through them."[151] The Fox sisters thus established the basic elements of the spiritualist experience, including the following: 1) certain spirits of deceased persons sought to communicate from beyond the grave, 2) specific individuals in this world had the ability to act as "mediums" for contact with the dead, and 3) these interchanges involved a code that facilitated transmission.[152] In time, spiritualist gatherings took on religious overtones, in which mediums offered homilies on the basics of spiritualist ideology and practice as well as "readings" from the spirit world aimed at particular audience members. Todd Jay Leonard traced the development of actual "spiritualist camps" where devotees received spirit readings, where "aspiring mediums" were trained in contact techniques, and where recognized mediums were ordained "as spiritualist ministers."[153]

Other spiritualists appeared on the scene, with multiple approaches, intentions, and varied personal reputations. Controversy increased criticism from leaders in the ecclesiastical and scientific communities. Laurence Moore noted that while Andrew Jackson Davis's trance-based spiritualist experiences were impossible to verify since he was the sole witness to them, the spirits allegedly communicating through the Fox sisters engaged in dialogue (rappings) with members of the audience who put them to the test. While onlookers were permitted, the primary format of the Fox sisters' séances involved a circle of persons who had some connection to the spirits that were seeking to communicate.[154] Moore discerned a certain connection between Transcendentalism and spiritualism, asserting that the initial "attitude toward the supernatural" present among the spiritualists could be traced to various Transcendentalist ideas. Yet spiritualists' insistence that their practices were scientifically "observable" and verifiable through the five senses often separated them from the more esoteric, mystical elements of spiritual exploration as advocated by Transcendentalists.[155] Ralph Waldo Emerson ultimately dismissed the entire spiritualist enterprise, labeling it "the rat hole of revelation."[156]

The critics claimed to have been vindicated when, years after their youthful rappings began, Margaret Fox confessed that she and her sister had fabricated the entire enterprise. The action came, not from the dead, but from an uncanny ability to crack the knuckles of their toes to produce sounds they attributed to spirits. At an 1888 enclave in New York, both Margaret and Kate Fox denied the veracity of their previous claims and labeled as fraudulent the entire spiritualist enterprise. A year later Margaret recanted her recantation but her reputation was already irrevocably damaged. The three spiritualist Fox sisters—Margaret, Kate, and Leah--died within a few years of each other (1890–1893), after struggling with alcohol, depression, and poverty. Nonetheless, as Ann Braude suggested, "Whether or not Kate and Margaret controlled the raps, they did not determine the meaning attributed to them by observers. The interpretations of investigators, rather than the manifestations themselves, provided the content of the new religion."[157] Indeed, many prominent nineteenth-century Christians found themselves intrigued if not attracted by spiritualism. These included Charles and Isabella Beecher, Harriet Beecher Stowe, and even Abby Ann Judson, daughter of the well-known abolitionist, William Lloyd Garrison. Mary Todd Lincoln participated in White House séances in an effort to contact her late son, Willie.[158] As Braude and others have suggested, many American women, excluded from Protestant pulpits, found an outlet for their spiritual gifts and insights as spiritualist mediums, a legacy of leadership that had implications for early feminist and female suffrage movements.[159]

Many spiritualists remained sympathetic with Christianity, yet, as Todd Jay Leonard noted, most accepted Jesus "as one of many 'Savior Christs' who have lived on the earth plane at different times" and in a variety of cultures and locations around the world.[160] The formation of the National Spiritualist Association in 1893 (the year of Margaret Fox's death) was a small but tangible sign of the institutionalization of spiritualism in American society. Spiritualist retreat centers such as Lily Dale, New York, continued to bring together mediums and those who sought communication with spirits of the departed. Nonetheless, by the late 1800s spiritualism—that belief that "communication with the so-called dead is a fact, scientifically proven"—was in decline.[161] In her study of the Fox sisters, Barbara Weisberg attributed this decline to such modern advances as extended life expectancy, decreasing infant mortality, new employment options for women, and "spiritualists' own resistance to organization." She contended that the movement seemed less "revolutionary" as various churches promoted more positive views of human nature, distancing themselves from the idea of a literal hell and Calvinistic total depravity.[162] Yet as Ann Braude noted, in spite of spiritualism's challenge to Calvinism, "its own doctrines remained permanently outside the pale of acceptable public opinion." Of those who were intrigued by direct connection to the dead, few viewed spiritualism's revelatory insights as a replacement to Christian belief and piety.[163] Weisberg observed that increasing technology may also have had an impact on spiritualist declines simply because electricity and other discoveries had the effect of illuminating the darkness inside and outside American homes. Thus, "it became easier to exile many ghosts simply by illuminating the cause of the haunting."[164]

Alternative Spiritualities: Transcendentalism and Spiritualism

Transcendentalism and spiritualism offered alternative approaches to and interpretations of spiritual experience in a Protestant environment where the doctrine of original sin had implications for once-born and twice-born individuals alike. They offered more optimistic views of human nature and links that united human beings to the broader creation. Transcendentalists looked beyond the Unitarianism that gave them birth, exploring the aesthetic and literary implications of ideas as old as Platonic Realism, and rejecting the corpse-cold rationalism of Calvinist orthodoxy and Unitarian liberalism. Spiritualists offered nineteenth-century Americans the hope of communication with the dead, many of whom were snatched out of this world too soon in the vulnerabilities of disease, childbirth, poor health care, and warfare that plagued the times. They anticipated the possibilities of modern science in some of its most primitive forms.

★★ *6* ★★

At the Marriage Supper of the Lamb: Communitarians and Religious Experience

During the nineteenth century, religious experiences took Americans in directions orthodox and heretical, individualistic and communitarian, expanding approaches to conversion, and contributing to the formation of new societies, many based on millennial conjectures and communitarian design. The American Constitution, with its Bill of Rights, made religious liberty normative, even if granted grudgingly to those who stood outside the Protestant establishment. While Protestant revivalism continued to make conversion normative, the newly converted often kicked over the theological traces, claiming novel revelations that reshaped the nature of conversion itself. If direct encounter with God was possible, indeed necessary, for regeneration and sanctification, might that also bring spiritual insights that expanded on or ventured beyond traditional biblical interpretations?

Nowhere was the possibility of new revelations more evident than in the development of certain communitarian groups, formed around religious experience, community of goods, millennial hopes and (often) issues of sexuality. Many began with fresh approaches to sanctification, insights into Christian living that took them to the theological and sectarian margins in response to revelatory encounters with the Divine. Most anticipated the immediacy of Christ's millennial return, viewing their own communities as advanced copies of God's pending rule and reign. Many reflected decidedly utopian intentions, believing, as John McKelvie observed, "that God had revealed to them the essential nature of His Kingdom, and that it was their task to establish this Kingdom throughout the earth." This supreme, if quixotic, vision was grounded in the idea of "the existence of a distinct conception of how the new world is to be brought into being." God's New Day would be brought in, but not without the witness of those who were called to implement it for the entire world to behold.[1]

These utopian communities often claimed a new biblical hermeneutic that redefined the nature of family, sexuality, worship, personal piety, and religious experience itself. Many were at once Restorationist and futurist in outlook. They sought to replicate the practices of the early Christians, their Pentecostal experientialism, intense worship, and their willingness to "share all things in common" (Acts 2:44). Yet they also believed that the "signs of the times" pointed to the immediacy of Christ's second coming, promises long overlooked and rediscovered in their transformative communities. These new revelations brought assurance that Christ's New Day was at hand and a warning that all persons should prepare for "the wrath that is to come" (Matt. 3:7). For many who joined these endeavors, personal spirituality was inseparable from communitarian experimentation.

The United Society of Believers in Christ's Second Appearing (Shakers)

In 1758, at the age of twenty-two, Ann Lee (1736–1784) joined the group of "Shaking Quakers" led by the prophet and prophetess James and Jane Wardley, whose quest for further revelation had led to their dismissal from the Society of Friends.[2] Their religious enthusiasm was apparently influenced by the revelatory practices of a French community known as the "Camisards," or "French Prophets." Formed following the revocation of the Edict of Nantes in 1685, the act that granted religious toleration to Protestants, the Camisards were given to apocalyptic revelations, often expressed through visions, trances, and speaking in tongues. Such charismatic visitations led to prophetic assertions, including their anticipation of the collapse of the Catholic Church and its "anti-Christ pope." In the early 1700s, some Camisards even engaged in armed attacks on Catholic militias in France. When an amnesty was offered them in 1705, certain Camisard prophets moved to London, extending their criticism of religious establishments to the Anglican Church. As their millenarian speculations failed to materialize, some of their devotees departed, while others continued to evangelize in England and Scotland.[3] John Whitworth suggested that Camisard beliefs were evident in the apocalyptic views of a group organized in Manchester, England, by James and Jane Wardley, self-declared prophets who promoted "the imminence of the millennium, and the continuance of revelation, manifested in prophecies accompanied by physical seizures."[4] Members of the group claimed to have received various spiritual visions, direct messages from God; some testified to an ability to heal spiritual and physical afflictions. In the 1770s, no one anticipated that a near-illiterate woman named Ann Lee would claim a new revelation from God that would lead to a new community of faith.[5]

In his history of the Shakers, Stephen J. Stein wrote, "The religious origins of the Shaking Quakers, therefore, remain an open issue, but that uncertainty does not obscure a more significant observation. The development of the Manchester society followed a pattern typical of scores of sectarian groups in eighteenth-century England."[6] A specific worship service in the Wardley-led group might involve a period of classic Quaker silence as well as certain ecstatic moments that included

> A mighty trembling, under which they would express the indignation of God against all sin. At other times they were affected, under the power of God, with a mighty shaking; and were occasionally exercised in singing, shouting, or walking the floor, under the influence of spiritual signs, shoving each other about,—or swiftly passing and repassing each other, like clouds agitated by a mighty hand.[7]

In 1762 Ann Lee (1736–1784) married Abraham Standerin (or Stanley), a Manchester blacksmith. Within the first years of their marriage Lee endured four pregnancies, each ending with the death of the infant. Those traumas affected her deeply, producing physical exhaustion, emotional outpourings, spiritual melancholia, and a reluctance to continue sexual intercourse with her husband. Emaciated from fasting and unending stress, she experienced a conversion that she described as a moment when "My soul broke forth to God which I felt as sensibly as ever a woman did a child, when she was delivered of it." Conversion was accompanied by a revelation that sexual intercourse itself was the cause of the fall of Adam and Eve, the tangible source of original sin.[8]

After the death of her fourth child in 1766, Lee extended her participation in Wardley's congregation, and in 1772 she was arrested with three other Shaking Quakers for preaching fanatical nonconformist opinions. That initial court appearance led to other incarcerations with charges of promoting heretical doctrines, disrespect for the established clergy, fanatical preaching, and glossolalia.[9] Ann Lee herself was often set upon by angry mobs when she preached in public.

Prison was the setting for a profound revelation delivered by Jesus Christ himself, who offered comfort and what Shakers called "the grand vision of the very transgression of the first man and woman in the Garden of Eden," that singular act of sexual intercourse whereby humanity "was lost and separated from God."[10] Lee thus gained leadership among the "Wardley group," her strange revelations tolerated for a time by the magistrates as long as they were not promoted publicly.[11] Additional visionary revelations led Lee to conclude that members of her group—some eight or so in number—should migrate to America in order to find a safer place to develop their community and proclaim their views. Thus the little band arrived in New York in 1774 where members secured various jobs, Lee working as a housekeeper and laundress, until they could purchase land in Niskeyuna, New York, near Albany, and establish their first settlement.

The religious enthusiasms characteristic of the American awakenings created a ready-made constituency, at least among those in the small community drawn to the new revelations, miracles, and healings. The group apparently did not begin active proselytization until around 1780, preferring to remain cloistered on the Niskeyuna land. In that year, Ann and two Shaker men were jailed for disturbing "the publick [*sic*] peace" and advising "friends to the American cause [Revolutionary War] from taking up arms in defence of their liberties."[12] The arrest marked the beginning of Lee's public ministry, and by 1781, she joined William Lee and James Whittaker in a series of missionary "journeys" that involved travel around the Northeast, particularly Rhode Island and Massachusetts. Their preaching brought antagonism, often from mobs, like the one that dragged Lee from a building where she was speaking and flogged her in the mistaken belief that she was a British spy disguised as a female.[13]

Since their sermons were not transcribed, it is difficult to know how the earliest Shaker evangelists declared themselves. Indications are that theirs was an ecstatic spirituality, given to charismatic worship and continuing revelation, an unashamed assertion that Christian "perfection" (sanctification) could keep the redeemed from falling into sin. The peculiar quality of Shaker worship captivated friend and foe alike. One early commentary came from Separate Baptist Valentine Rathbun Sr., who joined the Shakers around 1780, only to become disillusioned with what he identified as the community's "inconsistencies and falsehoods." Yet even as critic, Rathbun provided some of the earliest descriptions of Shaker enthusiastical religious practices.[14] He noted that Shakers replaced the status quo of Protestant worship with worship based on "the dictates of the spirit that governs them." He described those practices as follows:

> When they meet together for their worship, they fall a groaning and trembling, and every one acts alone for himself; one will fall prostrate on the floor, another on his knees and his head in his hands; another will be muttering over articulate sounds, which neither they or any body else understand. Some will be singing, each one his own tune; some without words, in an Indian tune, some sing jig tunes, some tunes of their own making, in an

> unknown mutter, which they call new tongues.... Others will be shooing and hissing evil spirits out of the house, till the different tunes, groaning, jumping, dancing,... makes a perfect bedlam; this they call the worship of God.[15]

Shaker attention to "last things" also attracted considerable attention and was at the heart of their early identity. Looking particularly to the books of Daniel and Revelation, Shakers fashioned a vision of a new community, in which Jane Wardley became a John the Baptist-like voice preparing the way for Ann Lee, "a woman clothed with the sun," who, like that biblical woman, had literally "fled into the wilderness" of America.[16] Early Shaker *Testimonies* attest to the belief that Ann Lee was identified with that prophetic figure in Revelation. One 1816 *Testimony* connects her mission to God's continuing revelation:

> And this same woman, whom the world of mankind have rejected, (even as they rejected the stone which afterwards became the head of the corner,) the same, saith the Lord, hath become the Mother of the New Creation. And although the beastly powers of antichrist did arise and persecute the *woman* and her righteous seed; and although the dragon did cast forth floods out of his mouth, to swallow up and destroy her testimony, as soon as it was brought forth; yet the earth helped the woman: for I the Lord did always stir up the spirit of someone to befriend my Anointed, and rescue her from the cruel grasp of her enemies.

Likewise, the Shakers linked biblical prophecy with their own pilgrimage from England to America, a land especially prepared by the Divine as a place where a new revelation might flourish. The *Testimony* continued,

> And when my times were accomplished, and a place was prepared in the wilderness, I gave unto the woman whom I had chosen to bring forth the testimony of eternal truth, to a lost world, sufficient power to waft her troubled and persecuted spirit, with her little company, across the foaming deep, amidst perils and dangers on every side, to the place I had prepared, there to be "nourished for a time, times and half a time, from the face of the serpent." And thus did the subjects of my little kingdom find rest to

> the soles of their feet, in the wilderness, which I the Lord had prepared for them until the times were accomplished for them again to proclaim that testimony, which should arouse that serpentine nature in man, and again open its mouth to spew forth, as a flood, all manner of evil, falsely, with the intent to destroy from the earth doctrines so calculated to strike a death blow to the carnal life of the creature, and bring into contempt all which was of man's invention.[17]

The *Testimonies* suggest that early Shakers understood Mother Ann Lee to be the female counterpart to Jesus and that both were representatives of the fullness of God, an androgynous being whose nature exemplified elements both male and female. Christ's "second appearing" was made known in Mother Ann who brought in God's New Day (the kingdom of God) evidenced within the burgeoning Shaker communities. To experience the "kingdom life" was to follow a simple process that involved 1) individual confession of sin to the elders of the community, 2) acceptance of the community of goods ("they held all things in common"), and 3) to take up the "cross" of celibacy ("in the kingdom of heaven there is neither marrying nor giving in marriage").

Shaker John Dunlavy's work, *The Manifesto, Or a Declaration of the Doctrine and Practice of the Church of Christ* (1847), represents a more systematic approach to Shaker doctrinal views. The book affirmed the salvific role of Jesus as mediator between God and humanity, and the object of faith for those who would claim salvation and Christian identity. Yet it also confirmed the role of "the woman," Ann Lee, in extending the revelation begun by Jesus. Dunlavy strongly defended the Shaker view of God's dual nature, writing,

> And nothing can be more consistent and according to order, than the idea of a twofold corresponding relation in God, as exhibited in his creation, called Father and Holy Ghost, or Mother, as the source from whence Christ in his first and second appearance, or the Son and the Daughter, should spring and come forth, to be in their proper lot and corresponding relation, the joint visible parentage of the faithful family of God.[18]

Dunlavy insisted that Christ's first appearing as male was made known through the coming of the Holy Ghost as both the "Spirit of truth" and the

"Spirit of promise." "But in her corresponding relation to the Father, as a Mother having children [converts], she was never fully revealed until the present day. In this day the mystery of God is finished."[19]

A later document, *The Divine Book of Holy and Eternal Wisdom*, edited by Sister Paulina Bates and published in the 1840s, reflected the Shaker tradition that salvation began with the confession of sin and acceptance of God's full revelation made known in both male and female messengers. One document reads,

> And this is my decree, that by obedience shall man slay the enemy within; and the first step of obedience which man can perform acceptable in my sight is this: After receiving a knowledge of the way of life, and becoming convicted of his lost state, he is then required to confess unto Me, in the presence of my appointed witnesses, every known sin and transgression which he has ever committed in his life. These witnesses, in whose presence the confession is to be made, are called, appointed and anointed by my holy Anointed Ones, those whom I have anointed to stand as my agents unto man, as the mediators in likeness of my beloved Son and Daughter, who are invisible to the natural eye, and ever will remain thus invisible to man, while clothed in tenements of clay; yet they perform their work upon the earth, through their appointed agents, who will ever be the fountain and source whereunto all souls may look for Christ upon earth. Again, saith the Lord of hosts, these are the appointed agents in Christ, the emblems of the Anointing, the Christ in his first and second appearance, first in the male, and second in the female, which rendereth the power of salvation complete, and which bringeth both male and female upon an equal footing for salvation.[20]

Celibacy itself was a religious experience, or at least a religious commitment, the ultimate sign that God's New Day was at hand. Shaker communities were the earthly models of the life that the redeemed should pursue in this world and the next. Again, *The Divine Book of Holy and Eternal Wisdom* was clear in uniting celibacy and a "kingdom life," as one of the passages states:

> But "woe to them that are with child, and to them that give suck in those days!" Yea, woe, woe, woe be to them that still cleave to the works of generation, in the day wherein man hath been called to arise and come forth into

> the resurrection of life; that resurrection in which man is called to be as the Angels of God in heaven, neither marrying nor being given in marriage; but walking in the straight path of the regeneration, marked out by him who is a perfect pattern for all. And thus shall it be when my trumpet shall echo through the earth to gather my elect: "Two shall be grinding together; the one shall be taken and the other left." Those who will hear my voice and come forth at my call, shall be taken and gathered into my fold in Zion.[21]

One of the most amazing visionary and prophetic gifts that Lee passed on to members of the community, especially females, was the ability to commune with the dead. Indeed, for Shakers, the veil between this world and the next was very thin, and from the beginning of the movement there was a sense that communication with the departed was a special revelation of the new community. In fact, Shakers apparently held to the possibility that salvation might occur after death. As one early document states,

> Mother Ann, and the Elders with her, uniformly taught the doctrine of a free offer of the gospel to *all souls*, whether in this world, or in the world of spirits. That none could be deprived of the offer of salvation because they had left the world before Christ made his appearance; or because they had lived in some remote part of the earth, where the sound of the gospel had never reached their ears. Their labors in the work of regeneration were not confined to this world, but extended to the world of spirits, and their travail and sufferings for the salvation of departed souls, were often distressing, beyond description. Cornelius Thayer, of Patridgefield, came to see the Church, soon after the opening of the gospel, and embraced the testimony. After he had confessed his sins, and received the promise of eternal life, Mother Ann told him to read a chapter in the Revelations, concerning the woman clothed with the sun. Elder James read, in the Epistle of Peter, concerning the gospel being preached to those who were dead, that they might be judged according to men in the flesh, and live according to God, in the spirit. He said, "The gospel is preached to souls who have left the body." And Mother said, "I see thousands of the dead rising and coming to judgment now, in this present time." [*Cornelius Thayer.*] Not long after the opening of the gospel at Watervliet, Mother Ann was speaking to a large number of the Believers, concerning those who were called by the gospel,

> and of their bearing and travailing for other souls, and she said, "If there is but one called out of a generation, and that soul is faithful, it will have to travail and bear for all its generation; for the world will be redeemed by generations." Elder William Lee, and Elder James Whittaker often spoke in the same manner, concerning the redemption of souls. [*Hannah Cogswell*].[22]

Ann Lee died in 1784, exhausted by years of imprisonment and physical abuse from assorted mobs in England and the US. Her chosen successors, Lucy Wright and John Meacham, the latter a former Baptist preacher, solidified the organizational structure of the order and expanded communities throughout New England, creating a council of male and female elders who presided over the societies, adjudicating confessional and disciplinary procedures. Worship became more orderly, formalizing dancing and testifying while continuing to allow for the spontaneity of shouting, singing, prophecies, and messages from the dead as channeled through community members. Shaker settlements spread from Sabbathday Lake, Maine, through Massachusetts and Ohio to Pleasant Hill and South Union, Kentucky, the sect's two southernmost communities. Shaker compounds became sanctuaries for runaway slaves as well as women and children who sought safety from abusive family situations.

Almost from the beginning sanctification was a major emphasis of Shaker spiritual life. Conversion through confession of sin and deliverance from the evil of sexual relations freed and empowered believers to pursue Christian perfection. Communal outlets for the continued confession of sin and the possibility for discipline created a context for extended spiritual formation. Communal worship and personal devotion enhanced spiritual experience, purged individuals of sin, and offered opportunity for new revelations through ecstatic encounters with the Holy Spirit and revelatory spirits.

Visitors to the community were frequent, often describing what they observed regarding Shaker worship and religious experience. Baptist Andrew Broaddus traveled from Virginia to Kentucky in 1817, spending time at the South Union Shaker community in southern Kentucky. It is an intriguing vision of the way in which ordered dance steps facilitated ecstatic religious experience.

> The men formed in rows, making a solid column in one room; the women facing them in the same manner in the other; and the communication was opened. They stood in silence two or three minutes, and then broke forth in a loud and melodious manner; in singing an anthem, which might last ten minutes. Then changing their position, they stood in readiness for the sacred dance; the men in rows facing their row of singers, and the women in a similar attitude. The musick began with a lively, animating and pleasing tone, and the dance went on in complete unison with the time. Words composed for the occasion in lively rhyme, soon followed.[23]

Broaddus observed a change in the production as the "singers grew more animated, keeping time by stamping with the foot; while the dancers went on with answerable animation, traversing the room up and down, backwards and forwards, and sometimes facing about, with a simultaneous motion. At certain quick parts of the time the singers strike the time by several loud clappings." He concluded that the dancing, which manifested many different steps and hymn-tunes, offered "an appearance of solemnity and devotion as well as animation, which one would hardly expect to find, judging from common report."[24]

The Shakers linked religious experience with apocalyptic hope. In many ways they conceived of their communities as literal demonstrations of the nature of the kingdom of God, the avant-garde of the rule and reign of God in human life consummated at the end of the age. Their life was a witness to the coming kingdom. Like the early Christian communions in the book of Acts they eschewed private property for communal living. Entrance to the community was a willingness to confess one's sins and take up the "cross" of celibacy. Initial confession was not enough, however. Members were continually monitored and were required to participate in continuing confessional occasions with members of the ruling council. Female elders heard the confessions of women, while male elders heard the confessions of men.

By the 1830s as the original zeal waned, a new sense of revelation and enthusiasm descended upon the communities, bringing with it a renewed sense of immediate spiritual encounter. This phenomenon, known as "Mother Ann's Work," apparently began in 1837 in the Watervliet community, initially present in various children as the vehicles of revelations, spiritual outbursts, and occasionally seizures. The outpourings spread, perceived to be a genuine work of the Holy Spirit descending on multiple Shaker compounds.[25] The revival was thought to be evidence of Ann Lee's continuing presence with and care for her children.

Spiritual manifestations were varied. Some fell into trances that led believers to speak in tongues or present new revelations. "Instruments" were individuals who received a word for the community directly from God or specific spirits of the dead. Some were given new liturgical practices including songs, tunes, and dances. As a fulfillment of certain revelations, especially those of prophetic intent, Shaker elders were instructed to send copies to assorted world leaders. Messages from Holy Mother Wisdom were particularly strong during a period from 1842 to 1843, and included Divine disclosures that were aimed at revitalizing the identity and action of the sect in their communities and their witness to the world.[26] The renewal also extended certain spiritualist encounters with the souls of the departed, who gave specific instructions to the specific communities, creating a period of "intense involvement with spiritual phenomena unlike any other" in Shaker history.[27]

Certain psychic-related spiritual gifts were also evident in the collective worship services of each community. In his early survey of nineteenth-century Shaker life, first published in 1875, non-Shaker Charles Nordhoff cited Shaker elder Frederick Evans's comment that from the earliest days Shaker "exercises" included "singing and dancing, shaking, turning, shouting, *speaking with new tongues, and prophesying*." Evans testified to his own conversion to Shaker views in 1830 because of the "spiritual manifestations" he observed. He claimed to have experienced "visions" for some three weeks, a phenomenon he said delivered him from "materialism." Evans insisted that from 1837 to 1844, "there was an influx from the 'spirit world,' confirming the faith of many disciples who had lived among Believers for years."[28]

Nordhoff referenced Elder James S. Prescott's 1874 book *Shaker and Shakeress*, which includes an account of the initial entry of the North Union Society into encounters with the "spirit world." The phenomenon began with a group of girls on whom spiritual visitations unexpectedly descended. Elders were summoned to the room where the girls were stricken and immediately "saw that the girls were under the influence of a power not their own—they hurried round the room, back and forth as swiftly as if driven by the wind—and no one could stop them." Thrown into what seemed an unconscious state, they were carried to their beds, from which they "began holding converse with their guardian spirits and others, some of whom they once knew in the form, making graceful motions with their hands—talking audibly, so that all in the room could hear and understand, and form some idea of their whereabouts in the spiritual realms they were exploring in the land of souls."[29] This was only the first of many similar "'spirit manifestations,' the most remarkable we ever expected to witness on the earth."[30] Not all revelations brought healing.

Elkins recounted additional spiritual experiences during this seven-year period, including occasions when Shaker women received additional revelations, sometimes as mediums for a variety of spirits. In one case, a certain "female instrument, said to be employed by the spirit of Ann Lee," approached a male Shaker "and uttered in a low, distinct, and funereal accent a denunciation which severed him as a withered branch from the tree of life." The man cried out for forgiveness of his sins, so inconsolable that "his ardent vociferations now degenerated into inarticulate yells of horror and demoniacal despair." As a result, the man confessed "his blasphemous profanity" to the trustees the next morning, "prior to his leaving the society."[31] Of these phenomena Elkins concluded, "I have myself seen males, but more frequently females, in a superinduced condition, apparently unconscious of earthly things, and declaring in the name of departed spirits important and convincing revelations," often with a "foreign tongue" in a specific prophesy.[32]

For Shakers, one of the early signs of the Spirit's presence was found in the revelation of hymns or hymn tunes for the edification of the community. One such musical revelation is found in this hymn from the early 1840s,

> I mean to be obedient. And cross my ugly nature,
> And share the blessing that are sent, To every honest creature;
> With every gift I will unite, And join in sweet devotion—

To worship God is my delight, With hands and feet in motion.
Come, let us all be marching on, Into the New Jerusalem;
The call is now to ev'ry one To be alive and moving.
This precious call we will obey—We love to march the heav'nly way,
And in it we can dance and play, And feel our spirits living.[33]

Certain "vision songs," or songs "heard in vision" demonstrate the linkage between worship, religious experience, charismatic gifts, and spiritualism in Shaker communities. Members received these songs and accompanying tunes from the spirits of persons they channeled privately or in communal worship. Most were simple words and melodies, often taken down and reused in collective worship. One such song, probably given in a trance-like state, came from Clarissa Shoefelt, a Shaker in the Watervliet community who received the revelation in October 1857 during the time of "Mother Ann's Work." It reads simply, "How happy pretty little angels are, O how happy."[34]

Another source of experience and renewal came from "Holy Mother Wisdom," whose revelations were made known to various Shaker individuals, particularly women. As one of the *Testimonies* commented,

> Truly in this, and in no other way, may the purposes of God be fulfilled, and the woman arise from a state of sin and disgrace, to that honor and glory for which she was created in the beginning. And thus it is accomplished. The Wisdom of God is revealed from on high, and the image of her eternal brightness is brought forth in the female of God's own choice, endowed with sufficient power from on high, to undermine and lay low, all the crooks and windings of the subtile charmer and beguiler of the innocence of the first man and woman, and to bring forth living souls, who are able to bruise the serpent's head, and daily trample his vile and artful insinuations under their feet.[35]

The apocalyptic vision of the community remained, even as the Shaker population declined throughout the twentieth century, continuing to look to a new era in which true religious experience would prevail. In one of the *Testimonies*, the Lord would again

> return to my vineyard, and enlarge the borders thereof, to make room to gather and plant, until all souls that desire to be regenerated from a state of sin and sorrow, into a state of life and peace, by being planted in the gospel soil in the vineyard of the Lord, can have that privilege. And this is the work of the regeneration of the souls of the children of men; that they be taken in mercy from a state of the wild forest of sin, and transplanted into the gospel soil; there to take root and grow into newness of life, leaving behind the life of sin, and daily increasing in the life of righteousness.[36]

Nonetheless, demographics, celibacy, overextended land holdings, the rise of the Industrial Revolution, and new regulations regarding the care and education of orphans took their toll as communities closed one by one, leaving only the community in Sabbathday Lake, Maine to retain a modified connection to history. The Shaker witness remains as some locations have become museums to the heritage and history, and as their music and furniture have retained popular appeal. Their apocalyptic vision of the nature of God's New Day in the world and their multifaceted approach to religious experience and Christian sanctification make them powerful representatives of a particular type of Protestant monasticism.

The Oneida Community: "The Marriage Supper of the Lamb"

The Oneida Community, founded by John Humphrey Noyes (1811–1886), was, like the Shakers, a communitarian, perfectionist, apocalyptic sect. Yet the way in which Oneida members understood the pragmatic implications of those theological ideals could not have been more different. Though relatively short-lived, Oneida was a dramatic experiment in perfectionism, marriage, and sexuality, a fascinating alternative to the Protestant monasticism of the Shakers.

Noyes, the founder, came to faith through the impact of the northeastern revivals sparked by the preaching of Charles G. Finney, Lyman Beecher, and other New Measure evangelists. Converted in Putney, Vermont, in 1831 after attending one of Charles Finney's campaigns, Noyes struggled with sin and grace in ways that paralleled other revivalists of the time. While convinced of the activity of grace in his life, he was plagued by doubt, even as he believed himself to be spiritually transformed. He wrote,

> The Bible seemed a new treasure of precious thought; Christians seemed kindred spirits; the matters of God and of eternity seemed alone worth attention. When at last I was told by an experienced Christian that these were evidences of conversion, I was enabled to lay hold on the promises. Light gleamed upon my soul in a different way from what I expected. It was dim and almost imperceptible at first, but in the course of the day it attained meridian splendor. Ere the day was done I had concluded to devote myself to the service and ministry of God. It were an endless task to enumerate the thoughts which passed through my mind during several succeeding days.[37]

Noyes moved vigorously into evangelical conversations, particularly concerned for sanctification or perfectionism.

In 1831 he entered the Congregationalist-based Andover Seminary, transferring a year later to Yale Theological School, where his piety was greatly influenced by the experiential perfectionism of the New Divinity movement led by New Haven minister Nathaniel William Taylor (1786–1858). Taylor's emphasis on the possibility of a realized sinlessness in this life captivated Noyes, who soon joined the New Haven Free Church, a nondenominational community of persons concerned for postconversion sanctification.[38] He then began claiming periods of sinless perfection, an action that created controversy and criticism from students and faculty at Yale. Even Taylor, his mentor, distanced himself from Noyes's perfectionist assertions. In May 1834, a disillusioned Noyes spent three weeks in New York struggling with faith and doubt. Ultimately, he concluded that perfectionism was less a particular behavior than in a relinquishing of oneself to God's grace and forgiveness.[39] Of that revelation he wrote, "Three times in quick succession a stream of eternal love gushed through my heart and rolled back again to its source.... All fear and doubt and condemnation passed away. I knew that my heart was clean, and that the Father and the Son had come and made it their abode."[40]

Still controversial, Noyes's perfectionist declarations led to the revocation of his Congregationalist preaching license, closing the door to any Protestant-related ordination.

As his theological insights moved outside the margins of orthodoxy, Noyes came to the conclusion that a spiritual return of Christ had already occurred in 70 CE with the fall of Jerusalem. This revelation, long overlooked or unrecognized in the church, carried with it a mandate to establish a new millennial community, the initial stage of the full establishment of God's New Day. He insisted,

> Between this present time and the establishment of God's kingdom over the earth lies a chaos of confusion, tribulation and war such as must attend the destruction of the fashion of this world and the introduction of the will of God as it is done in heaven. God has set me to case up a highway across this chaos, and I am gathering out the stones and grading the track as fast as possible.[41]

The New Day (kingdom of God) would ultimately be established on earth and fully evident to all creation. Until then, Noyes and those who accepted his message were called to mirror that long-anticipated realm. This avant-garde community was the recipient of a special revelation not unlike that of the prophets of old. In a document called "Bible Communism," published in 1849, Noyes wrote that

> the men and women who are called to usher in the Kingdom of God will be guided not merely by theoretical truth, but by direct communication with the heavens, as were Abraham, Moses, David, Paul. This will be called a fanatical principle. But it is clearly a Bible principle, and we must place it on high above all others as the palladium of conservatism in the introduction of the new social order.[42]

Noyes instituted that "new social order" at Putney, Vermont, in 1838, with a group composed largely of family members, including Harriet Holton, whom he married that same year. The centerpiece of the new society was Christian perfectionism, defined as "the immediate and total cessation of sin." Yet this "salvation from sin" was "not a system of duty-doing under a code of dry laws, Scriptural or natural; but is a special phase of *religious experience*, having for its basis spiritual intercourse with God."[43] Noyes's earliest followers were convinced that the intent of all "positive" religionists was to discover a genuine relationship with God, "to give him their hearts, to live in communion with him. These exercises and the various states and changes of the inner life connected with them constitute the staple of what is commonly called *religious experience*." Such an encounter would ultimately conquer all "selfishness in the heart," and put an end to sin in the sanctified life.[44]

Perfectionism was a second blessing that provided deliverance from sin through the power of the Holy Spirit in the life of the believer. Noyes wrote, "If our theory concerning the progressive nature of spiritual experience is correct, we may expect to find in the later records of the Primitive Church evidence of the existence of two distinct classes of believers: a class that was yet in a carnal state, and a class that had attained perfect holiness. In the writings of Paul we find proof that this was actually the case."[45] Like the post-Pentecost Christians described in the book of Acts, these perfectionists believed in holding "all things in common," thereby constituting a community of goods.

For John Humphrey Noyes, perfectionist affirmations had biological implications. The coming of God's New Day required a radical response to communal living centered in a complete reorientation of the nature of marriage. In an 1839 essay published in Noyes's periodical, *The Witness*, he articulated those changes, to the consternation of most persons who read them.

> I will write all that is in my heart on one delicate subject, and you may judge for yourself whether it is expedient to show this letter to others when the will of God is done on earth, as it is in heaven, there will be no marriage. The marriage supper of the Lamb, is a feast at which every dish is free to every guest. Exclusiveness, jealousy, quarrelling, have no place there, for the same reason as that which forbids the guests at a thanksgiving dinner to claim each his separate dish, and quarrel with the rest for his rights. In a holy community, there is no more reason why sexual intercourse should be restrained by law, than why eating and drinking should be—and there is as little occasion for shame in the one case as in the other. God has placed a

> wall of partition between the male and female during the Apostacy, for good reasons, which will be broken down in the resurrection for equally good reasons. But woe to him who abolished the law of the Apostacy before he stands in the holiness of the resurrection. The guests of the marriage supper may have each his favourite dish, each a dish of his own procuring, and that without the jealousy of exclusiveness. I call a certain woman my wife—she is yours, she is Christ's, and in him she is the bride of all saints. She is dear in the hand of a stranger and according to my promise to her I rejoice. My claim upon her cuts directly across the marriage covenant of this world, and God knows the end.[46]

This understanding led him to advocate "Complex Marriage," the belief that in the community of the sanctified, there were to be no "exclusive" male/female relationships centered in marriage. Sexual intercourse could be experienced between those who freely chose to be together. In "Bible Communism," Noyes wrote, "In the Kingdom of God the intimate union that in the world is limited to the married pair extends through the whole body of communicants; without however excluding special companionships founded on special adaptability. John 17:21."[47] Perfectionists could thus engage in sexual relations as arranged within the community; all sanctified members of the apocalyptic order were potentially married to each other. As Lawrence Foster wrote, Noyes "sought to institutionalize a communal sense of 'salvation from sin' in which freedom from legalistic adherence to specific forms of behavior would nevertheless be tempered by total submission to the will of God—of which Noyes considered himself the ultimate arbiter on earth."[48] "Exclusive love" had no place in the kingdom of God.

The society at Putney instituted Complex Marriage in 1846, much to the dismay of their Vermont neighbors. Opposition was so severe that members were forced to abandon their original location in 1848 and transfer it to Oneida, New York, within the boundaries of the Burned-Over District. By 1851 there were some 205 members in a highly structured community that included "mutual criticism," a continuing exercise of self-examination carried out by the elders; "male continence," a method of male birth control; and "stirpiculture," a form of eugenics whereby the community decided which members were best suited for producing the most promising offspring. In time, more humanist elements of philosophy prevailed among the Oneidaites and the evangelical-perfectionist emphasis waned.[49]

Nonetheless, the Oneida society achieved a significant financial success through the manufacture of metal goods, particularly the production of animal traps invented by member Sewell Newhouse. These traps, used extensively in the American West, gave economic solvency to the group. Criticism of the order continued, even as a new generation of leaders appeared on the scene, including Noyes's son Theodore. Conflict inside and outside the community created considerable strife, particularly after Noyes was charged with statutory rape for his encounters with younger female members of the group. These litigations forced Noyes to seek exile in Canada in 1879. From there he declared that it was time for Oneida to abandon Complex Marriage, and the practice was ended in 1880. By 1881 the community assets had been divided among the remaining members, who constituted a corporation known as Oneida Company, Limited.[50] Noyes's perfectionist, experimental society had lasted only a few decades, but many of its efforts—birth control, eugenics, sexual freedom—anticipated later developments in modern secular society.

The Mormons: The Kingdom in the West

Religious experience was at the heart of revelations reported by Joseph Smith (1805–1844), the founder of the Church of Jesus Christ of the Latter Day Saints, the Mormons. While Mormon beliefs and practices are far too complex for this study, it is important to note the religious experiences that shaped the origins of the movement. Joseph Smith's family moved to the Canandaigua-Palmyra region of western New York in 1816. The area was part of the revival-swept, burned-over district where the call for conversion and religious enthusiasm was a steady theme. So too was the appearance of multiple denominations, each competing for members and orthodoxy. Mormon historian Richard Bushman suggested that Smith's primary religious concerns revolved around a quest for the true church and the true nature of conversion.

He cited Smith's comments that "notwithstanding the great love which the converts to these different faiths expressed at the time of their conversion, and the great zeal manifested by the respective clergy, who were active in getting up and promoting this extraordinary scene of religious feeling," the initial encouragement to join whatever church one preferred soon turned into "a scene of great confusion and bad feelings" as preachers and converts divided over which church was the true one, or at least the truest of the true.[51] Smith soon concluded that humanity "had apostatized from the true and living faith and that was no society or denomination that built upon the Gospel of Jesus Christ as recorded in the new testament and I felt to mourn for my own Sins and for the Sins of the world."[52]

Embarking on a quest for conversion and truth, Smith experienced what Mormons refer to as the First Vision in the spring of 1820 in the woods near his home. This vision, visited upon Smith when he was fourteen, became for him a moment of personal conversion as well as the initial revelation that, when informed by later visions, led to the discovery of a new revelation (the Book of Mormon) and the call to restore the Church of Jesus Christ. Recalling that vision twelve years later (1832) Smith wrote that "the Lord opened the heavens upon me and I Saw the Lord and he Spake unto me Saying Joseph my Son thy Sins are forgiven thee, go thy way walk in my statutes and keep my commandments."[53] Further reflection led him to publish additional commentary on the vision in 1835 and 1838. Bushman concluded that in the later remembrances "the promise of forgiveness through faith in Christ was dropped from the narrative, and the apostasy of Christian churches stood alone as the message of the vision."[54]

The First Vision brought Smith into contact with two heavenly "personages," God the Father and God the Son. Smith was thus introduced to the Son by the Father, and received their admonition to avoid all existing "sects" since all were false and had no connection to the true church.[55] Other visions followed. The next was on September 21, 1823, the first visitation of the spiritual being who identified himself as the angel Moroni, a survivor of the great internecine wars between primitive American tribes called the Nephites and the

Lamanites. Smith described Moroni as clad in "a loose robe of most exquisite whiteness. It was a whiteness beyond anything earthly I had ever seen; nor do I believe that any earthly thing could be made to appear so exceedingly white and brilliant.... Not only was his robe exceedingly white, but his whole person was glorious beyond description, and his countenance truly like lightning."[56]

Joseph Smith claimed that it was at this visitation that Moroni first told him of certain golden plates "giving an account of the former inhabitants of this continent, and the sources from whence they spring." With them were two stones, "called the Urim and Thummim—deposited with the plates, and the possession and use of these stones were what constituted 'seers' in ancient or former times; and that God had prepared them for the purpose of translating the book."[57] A third vision took place on the same day, when Moroni returned to reiterate the same message and to warn Smith that the plates were not to be used to secure material wealth. Thus the formation of Mormonism began with an encounter between Joseph Smith and a spiritual being (Moroni) whom he could see and hear. In one of her many works on Mormonism, Jan Shipps called attention to the fact that these visions were received by Smith while in a trance-like state that left him exhausted and unable to complete his routine farm work. This "phenomenon of visionary trance" became for Smith a cathartic moment, like those experienced by St. Paul on Damascus Road or the prophets of ancient Israel.[58]

The golden tablets described in Moroni's visitation were translated by Smith using the Urim and Thummim, magic stones that enabled him to decipher the texts and dictate to various certain amanuenses. In the region around Palmyra, New York, "seerstones," amulets thought to aid in the discovery of lost treasure or unlock other psychic secrets, were a common instrument of local "folk magic."[59] The translation of the golden tablets from what Smith believed to be "reformed hieroglyphics" became the Book of Mormon, first published in 1830. The Mormon church was born in that translation and its accompanying visions of truth, wisdom, and obedience.

Joseph Smith's religious experiences, visions, and revelations were certainly not new to nineteenth-century revivalistic America. Protestant conversionists were given to new experiences with the Divine that led them to embark on new religious endeavors, especially in the burned-over district of western New York. Millennial speculations, dramatic conversions, prophetic predictions, and direct contact with God and heavenly beings often were combined by individuals and groups who sought to restore the true church in the latter days before Christ's complete return. Smith's beliefs had all of those elements with one important addition: a series of new sacred texts—the Book of Mormon, the *Pearl of Great Price*, and *Doctrines and Covenants*—that supplemented traditional Hebrew and Christian scriptures, providing answers to specific theological questions that had long haunted the *sola scriptura* tradition of Reformation Protestantism. Like the Shaker and Oneida communities, Smith and his followers offered new definitions of the nature of marriage, family, and sexuality, evidenced not only in polygamy but in other doctrines regarding the role of men, women, and children in the restored Christian family.[60] As Lawrence Foster concluded, "In pragmatic American fashion, the Mormon religion thus combined Biblical literalism with a dispensational interpretation of history to free itself for continuing religious and social innovation, a type of innovation that Jason Briggs described as 'walking backward towards the future.'"[61]

Alexander Campbell, himself a Restorationist, wrote of the Book of Mormon, "There never was a book more evidently written by one set of fingers, nor more certainly conceived in one cranium since the first book appeared in human language, than this same book." He acknowledged that it offered responses to "every error and almost every truth discussed in N. York for the last ten years," including "infant baptism, ordination, the trinity, regeneration, repentance, justification, the fall of man, the atonement, transubstantiation, fasting, penance, church government, religious experience, the call to the ministry, the general resurrection, eternal punishment, who may baptize, and even the question of freemasonary [*sic*], republican government, and the rights of man."[62] For example, the book of Moroni, chapter 8, informs readers that the baptism of infants is not required, noting, "And their little children need no repentance, neither baptism. Behold, baptism is unto repentance to the fulfilling the commandments unto 'the remission of sins'" (Moroni 8:11).

Whitney Cross noted that while the revivalists stressed "salvation from personal sins" as a way of preparing for life in the next world, Smith's "ideas about earthly and heavenly society alike judged happiness more largely in terms of physical comfort and earthly abundance." Cross suggested that Smith re-emphasized the necessity of communal response to the needs of others "which had been long declining in the Puritan tradition of old New England."[63] The religious experiences of the first baptized Mormons often reflected revelatory, mystical encounters with God. As a Methodist, Solomon Chamberlain received visions prophesying an approaching restoration of New Testament Christianity. On receiving reports of the revelations in the Book of Mormon, Chamberlain arrived at the Smith home demanding to know if anyone there believed in "visions or revelations." Joseph Smith's brother Hyrum responded that "we are a visionary house." Chamberlin and his spouse were soon baptized by Joseph Smith in Lake Seneca, and he began a missionary journey, circulating copies of the Book of Mormon in New York and neighboring Canada.[64] Awakened to visionary encounters, many revival converts found that the teachings of the Book of Mormon answered their questions and enlivened their sense of God's eschatological timetable. Many took the formal step of confessing faith in Jesus Christ, affirming Mormon beliefs, and receiving a new baptism into the Church of Jesus Christ of the Latter Day Saints.

Restorationism was a major element of Mormon ideology. The earliest Mormon-authored histories of the church placed it in the context of creation, the final era of multiple "dispensations" that stretched from Adam and Eve through John the Baptist and the advent of Jesus Christ as "a dispensation of the meridian of time." Since innumerable false churches had ignored or rejected Jesus's true teaching, Smith's revelations in the Book of Mormon and other revelatory documents were evidence of the "dispensation of the fullness of times," the reinstitution of genuine Christian community in the latter days. Smith's mystical encounters with "the Father and the Son" had set the long-lost record straight.[65]

Nineteenth-century non-Mormons were predictably antagonistic, attributing Smith's revelations to what Shipps calls "a diseased imagination," or more likely "a gigantic fraud."[66] Shipps wrote that Mormonism's early critics insisted the movement was "'blinding' its adherents so effectively that when they heard Smith's report of his visions and his explanation of the origins of the Book of Mormon, they could not distinguish truth from falsehood."[67]

Richard Bushman contended that Smith's initial vision of 1820 "resembled a conversion experience—the forgiveness of sins and the joy and elation afterward." Yet later descriptions of that religious experience tended to minimize the conversionist aspect for a sign of a new dispensation. He also noted that "Mormon theology," at least early in the movement's history, revealed "few signs of having wrestled free of Calvinism." However, although the two theologies shared "a common biblicism," Calvinism in no way served as the basis for Smith's understanding of conversion or religious experience.[68]

More contemporary analyses view Smith's experiential approaches as closely tied to other nineteenth-century religiocultural trends. Literary critic Harold Bloom believed that Mormonism was an ultimate American religion, incorporating elements of eschatological and political idealism within the certainty of Smith's own visionary dream. Smith thus linked the "Mormon Kingdom of God" with his own prophetic revelations to create a new American spiritual identity that would ultimately break "all the sinful kingdoms of the world."[69] Bloom suggested that the two central elements of the "Saints' vision" involved the fact that "no other American religious movement is so ambitious, and no rival even remotely approaches the spiritual audacity that drives endlessly towards accomplishing a titanic design."[70] He concluded that, "Mormon history is Joseph Smith, and his continued effect upon his Saints."[71]

In an ambitious evaluation, Catherine Albanese asserted that Smith's visions were impacted by a variety of spiritualities that included Swedenborgian spiritism, "Kabalism, and Hermetic lore.... Moreover, the careful correspondences of the Swedenborgian cosmos were refracted in a Mormon light in which heaven was, indeed, an earthlike place and earth itself shone with the borrowed light of the heavenly world."[72] Smith's early use of seerstones, divining rods, treasure hunting, and various items used in the practice of magic were relatively common occult practices in the region that gave birth to early Mormonism. Albanese concludes, "The puzzle of the prophet can be solved with convincing ease if one follows Smith in the elision of material and spiritual treasure. One should dig for gold, yes, but—for a New world alchemist of the earth—the gold should be the philosopher's stone of a new religion."[73]

Communitarians: A New Experiential Norm

The three communities discussed here illustrate the way in which Protestant conversionism informed issues of justification, sanctification, and life in this world and the next. They also demonstrate the way in which conversion could take persons in new directions of theological and experiential speculation and diversity. Each—Shakers, Oneidaites, Mormons—possessed a sense of religious experience that involved new revelation, new Christology, and new ways of living in the world. Two gave novel interpretations to old texts, while one produced a completely original canon thought to complete divine revelation once and for all. Yet they were also born of the religious and cultural realities of their times—offering options for what to do after salvation is secured and rethinking the nature of family in light of the realities of nineteenth-century biology, fertility, and mortality. In anticipating Christ's return they found in America a sacred space that enabled them to solidify their views, preach their gospels, and energize their converts.

★★ 7 ★★

The Yoke of Jesus: African-American Religious Experience

He saw white spirits and black spirits contending in the skies. The sun was darkened, the thunder rolled. "And the Holy Ghost was with me, and said, 'Behold me as I stand in the heavens!' And I looked, and saw the forms of men in different attitudes. And there were lights in the sky, to which the children of darkness gave other names than what they really were; for they were the lights of the Saviour's hands, stretched forth from east to west, even as they were extended on the cross on Calvary, for the redemption of sinners. . . ." On May 12, 1828, the Holy Spirit appeared to him, and proclaimed that the yoke of Jesus must fall on him, and that he must fight against the serpent when the sign appeared.[1]

Thus nineteenth-century missionary and historian Thomas Wentworth Higginson described a religious experience that descended upon Nat Turner (1800–1831), an encounter that compelled the Virginia slave preacher to take up arms against perpetrators of the South's Peculiar Institution in August 1831. Turner, "ordained" by virtue of his ecstatic visions, was captured and executed for leading a slave rebellion that killed some fifty-five white adults in Southampton County, Virginia. The Nat Turner Rebellion struck fear into the white population, confirming the suspicion that their enslaved subjects would ultimately rise up against them. It also reflected the unruly nature of Christianization among slave populations, transforming salvation for heaven and obedience on earth into a spiritual mandate for liberation from chattel slavery itself. Spiritual experiences could have worldly implications. While God's retributive justice might set things right at the great-white-throne judgment, many slave-converts longed for liberation in the here and now, however difficult it might be.[2]

Some were less militant but no less determined than Nat Turner in their response to enslavement. In January 1807 a "complaint" was brought to the Forks of Elkhorn Baptist Church in Kentucky, "against Sister Esther Boulwares [slave] Winney,"

> 1st for saying she once thought it her duty to serve her Master & Mistress *but since the lord had converted her*, she had never believed that any Christian [should have] kept Negroes or Slaves—2nd For saying she believed there was Thousands of white people Wallowing in Hell for their treatment to Negroes—and she did not care if there was as many more.[3]

Conversion led the woman named Winney to speak boldly, even when she was "excluded" (dismissed from) from the Forks of Elkhorn Baptist Church.[4] It fostered a spiritual empowerment that she refused to conceal. As Cecil Wayne Cone observed,

> The conversion experience led to different expressions in the religious life of the slave. But underlining these varieties of expression was the experience of the presence of the Almighty Sovereign God wherein the slave was commissioned by the divine for a definite task in the world. Most of the accounts of the conversion experience conclude with God's telling the slave to return to this world.[5]

Katharine Dvorak added that "like their white counterparts, the devout [slaves] sought conversion, the grace to live faithful Christian lives, and salvation. Frequently, southern blacks felt morally superior to whites."[6] Evangelization brought forth converts, but not necessarily with the results white evangelizers intended.

African Religion—African-American Christianity: The Influences

Christianization also shaped rituals and religious experiences that many believe had African roots. Others are not so sure. In his monumental study, *Slave Religion*, Albert Raboteau explored the relationship of African religion to the evolving spirituality of those Africans who were carried off to North America as slaves. He examined a variety of African religious practices related to deities, ancestors, "drumming and dancing," initiation rites, shamanistic leaders, and other rituals, all of which shaped particular forms of religious experience in traditional tribal settings. Raboteau concluded that these varied traditions often extended

> relatively far into the past of colonial slavery; others have died out with the passage of time; and still others have developed out of more recent contact with Africa. Moreover, Afro-American cults have modified traditions and added new ones. Yet, despite discontinuity and innovation, the fundamental religious perspectives of Africa have continued to orient the lives of the descendants of slaves in the New World.[7]

The debate over African influence on slave spirituality and religious identity has long divided scholars engaged in African-American studies. One position, represented by E. Franklin Frazier, suggested that African religious traditions were torn from slaves by the very "process of enslavement."[8] Another view, evident in the work of Melvin J. Herskovits, asserted that African-American culture, religion included, was strongly impacted by multiple "Africanisms."[9] In *Slave Religion*, Raboteau generally agreed with Frazier, at least where North American slavery was concerned. He wrote, "Under British North American slavery, it seems that the African religious heritage was lost. Especially does this appear so when black religion in the United States is compared with the cults of Brazil and the Caribbean."[10] This scenario implied that Christian religious experience in slave communities was shaped more by white revivalistic conversionism and "enthusiastical" religion than by African religious practices.

By the latter twentieth century, a reevaluation of the evidence led Henry H. Mitchell to affirm "the unmistakable case for African religious survivals" in the spiritual experience of African-Americans.[11] Mitchell noted that as early as 1915, W. E. B. DuBois called attention to the role of the black "priest" on southern plantations as one who interpreted "the supernatural," providing pastoral care, and articulated "the longing and disappointment of a stolen people." When the "Negro church" took shape as "the first distinctively Negro American social institution," it was not initially "a Christian church" but a community that adapted African fetish rituals that became known as "voodoo-ism."[12] Mitchell also referenced a 2001 work in which Albert Raboteau commented, "Thousands of Africans from diverse cultures and religious traditions, forcibly transported to America as slaves, retained many African customs even as they converted to Christianity."[13] In her study of Bible Belt religion, Christine Leigh Heyrman acknowledged that given the "absence of direct testimony" from African-Americans themselves, their connections with African religions are "filled by a flurry of speculation." Nonetheless she insisted, "It is certain only that, by dint of affinities between African and Christian cosmologies and forms of revelation, the first black converts started syncretizing the two religious traditions."[14] Anthony Pinn surmised that before Christianity was introduced to slaves in the Great Awakening eras, "there was a roughly one-hundred-year period during which complex African traditions could have taken root." He concluded that "the lack of direct evidence should not prevent an acceptance of 'extra-church' practices as viable."[15]

"Black worship" was evident as early as the 1750s, and the "Invisible Institution" of secret religious gatherings evolved into a variety of Christian practices. One observance with African overtones involved the "ring shout," a tribal practice that many believe found its way into African-American Christian worship. The "ring shout" or "ring dance" was utilized in certain of the camp meetings, often on the last night of the event, when black and white alike marched around the camp, joining in a symbolic pilgrimage of song and shout. Daniel Alexander Payne (1811–1893), a bishop in the African Methodist Episcopal Church (A.M.E.), offered a less than positive assessment of the practice as he witnessed it in 1878: "After the sermon they formed a ring, and with coats off sung, clapped their hands and stamped their feet in a most ridiculous and heathenish way. I requested the pastor to go and stop their dancing." Payne reported that the group reluctantly ceased their "singing and rocking."[16]

Henry Mitchell described numerous elements of African-American religious experience that he believed reflected African roots, beginning with "the tradition of 'shouting,' or possession by the Holy Spirit." He connected the practice to African traditions in which individuals were seized by the spirit of "sub-deities" thought to affect specific personal needs. In each context, shouting and possession revealed "the height of the rite, the greatest evidence of the presence of the deity in the service."[17] Mitchell linked African religious customs to the (Negro) Spirituals evident in "tone scale as well as the... call-and-response patterns" in which the community or congregation answered or engaged the speaker orally, a tradition he observed as traditionally West African.[18]

Both Mitchell and Melville Herskovits contended that water baptism by immersion, an act intricately related to black Baptists and the theology of believer's baptism, was "a clear throwback to the powerful water rituals in African traditional life." Herskovits associated this sacramental routine with water-oriented rites evident in Nigeria and Dahomey.[19] Albert Raboteau disagreed, suggesting that implied connection "blurs important distinctions" whereby possession by a god in African "water cults" is distinct from baptism by water and Spirit in Judeo-Christian tradition.[20] The debates over African influence nonetheless give evidence of certain varieties of religious experience in African-American faith contexts through slavery time and beyond.

Some nineteenth-century Protestant observers did testify to what they understood as the African "associations" of the slaves they sought to Christianize. Presbyterian clergyman Charles Colcock Jones (1804–1863), whose book *The Religious Instruction of the Negroes* (1842) served as a handbook for both converting slaves and encouraging them to submit to their masters in Christian obedience, wrote that most slaves were "indefinite and confused" in their understanding of the rudiments of Christianity. He suggested that while "Mohammedan Africans" from the "old stock of importations," gave ear to the gospel, they often attempted to "accommodate Christianity to Mohammedanism." He insisted that in spite of Christianization efforts, many slaves continued to believe "in second sight, in apparitions, charms, witchcraft, and in a kind of irresistible Satanic influence. The superstitions brought from Africa have not been wholly set aside."[21]

Whatever the precise lineage of African and African-American spiritualities, some writers continue to lament the way in which African religious experiences and rituals were wrenched from slaves and slave society, concerted attempts by slave owners to ignore or undermine tribal rituals and identities of the enslaved. In a 2006 address in Ghana, New Testament scholar Brad Braxton offered an alternative reading to Exodus 34:11-16, "inserting different ethnic or tribal names" as evidence of the spiritual imperialism of those who dragged African peoples into American bondage:

> Observe what I the God of colonial violence and greed command you—my colonial British missionaries to the Gold Coast of Africa. As you invade the Gold Coast to enslave the people and pillage their resources, I will drive out before you the Akan, the Fante, and the Ga, and the Ewe, and the Mossi, and the Yoruba. Tear down their altars of African Traditional Religion where they have met the Great God for centuries; cut down their sacred poles where they have named and dedicated their children to the Great God and raised their families in righteousness. In the name of colonial religion, refer to their sacred traditions as "fetishes," and call those dark people "pagans." For although those indigenous Africans were the architects of religion and knew the true and living God millennia before the Christian religion was formulated, convince them that their sacred traditions are demonic rituals.[22]

African slaves brought many types of religious experience with them on the ships of the Middle Passage. Implicitly or explicitly, they carried something of that spirituality into the religious life and ritual actions that took shape among them within and beyond slavery time.

Evangelizing the Africans

In all probability the first Africans landed in the American colonies at Jamestown in 1619. Sociologist C. Eric Lincoln wrote of that arrival, "During the summer of 1619, twenty Africans held captive aboard a Dutch frigate were turned over to the English colonist at Jamestown, Virginia, in exchange for provisions for the ship's crew. This event marked the beginning of the black experience with English America and American Christianity."[23]

As the seventeenth-century slave trade expanded North and South, limited attention (if any) was given to the evangelization of the newly arriving slaves. In 1689, Puritan patriarch Cotton Mather criticized those who mistreated their black "bondsmen" while claiming that they were intellectually incapable of responding to Christian conversion. Mather denounced those who offered such excuses as a denial of the "*Master in Heaven*" by doing nothing "to bring your Servants unto the Knowledge and Service of that glorious *Master*." He was quick to add that Christianization would improve slave efficiency and obedience.[24] Nonetheless, many slaveholders resisted evangelization, fearing that baptism would imply an evangelical liberation detrimental to enslavement rationales.

Certain Anglican clergy appear to have been among the earliest advocates of slave evangelism. British Bishop William Fleetwood (1653–1723) preached a 1711 sermon assuring slaveholders that nothing of the slave's earthly state would change, noting that masters were "neither prohibited by the Laws of God, nor those of the *Land*, from keeping Christian slaves. Slaves, he insisted "are no more at Liberty after they are Baptized, than they were before.... The Liberty of Christianity is entirely spiritual."[25] Salvation was promoted; slavery preserved.

H. Shelton Smith suggested that the hesitancy to convert slaves to Christianity had less to do with the liberating power of baptism than a hesitancy to give slaves a time off for religious education, a fear that rebellion might be fomented in slave-based worship assemblies, and a suspicion that conversion made slaves worse, not better, laborers. Slave owners also expressed concern regarding "the equalitarian implications of Christian fellowship. On becoming a Christian, the slave joined a community that professed oneness in Christ." Did becoming members of white churches imply some type of spiritual equality with the dominant race?[26]

Amid these debates, certain white Christians continued to insist that the church had a gospel mandate to Christianize the slaves, "as a means of realizing God's redemptive purpose." This was particularly true of Methodists and Baptists, who by 1845 reported a combined membership of some 260,000 African-Americans.[27] Holiness bishop L. V. Stennis noted that the sermons of Methodist and Baptist preachers offered "many blacks the hope and the escape they needed from their earthly woes. The preachers also placed an emphasis upon feeling as a sign of conversion. This feeling found a ready response in black slaves who were repressed in so many ways."[28] For many, "feeling" was inseparable from conversion.

The Second Great Awakening was particularly important to the evangelization of slaves, and its revivals often evidenced powerful religious experiences among the Africans. Virginia Baptist preacher John Leland (1754–1841) commented in 1790 that slaves "commonly are more noisy in time of preaching than the whites, and are more subject to bodily exercise, and if they meet with an encouragement in these things, they grow extravagant." Georgia Methodist Jesse Lee (1758–1816) observed of the first day of an 1807 revival that "we had a gentle and comfortable moving of the spirit of the Lord among us; and at night it was much more powerful than before, and the meeting was kept up all night without intermission. However, before day the white people retired, and the meeting was continued by the black people."[29] Thomas Rankin, another Methodist divine, reported on a 1776 revival that encompassed segments of eastern Virginia, noting that during one of his sermon many participants were "on their faces crying mightily to God," and that "hundreds of Negroes were among them with tears streaming down their faces."[30]

Christine Heyrman contended that while the emotional outbursts of slaves may have closely paralleled those of Anglo-Saxon converts, they may have been more problematic "because they defied control," a challenge to the white preachers who had "dominance over the direction of worship." Likewise, the ecstatic behavior of blacks may have "somehow eluded... [the] comprehension of white religionists. Heyrman asked, "Could it be that when black worshippers wept and screamed, collapsed and sank into trancelike states, that such behavior meant something other to them than what it did to white evangelicals?" Amid their overt response to the common elements of revivalistic experience, did the Africans devise their own spiritual insights undiscerned by their masters?[31]

Conversion Experiences: *God Struck Me Dead*

The Awakenings brought Christian conversion to slaves and the slave context in ways that both mirrored and differed from similar experiences in the Caucasian population. Conversions came in revival meetings, secret "hush arbor" gatherings of slaves outside the watchful eyes of the overseers, and in private moments when the divine presence invaded the life of a specific individual. They were instances of spiritual struggle and sorrowful repentance, salvation and revelation, sometimes punctuated by the voice of God or other spiritual beings who brought visions of liberation and blessedness. In a volume entitled *God Struck Me Dead: Religious Conversion Experiences and Autobiographies of Ex-Slaves*, scholars from the Fisk University Social Science Institute published the interviews conducted with ex-slaves from 1927 to 1940, specifically involving conversion testimonies. One researcher, Andrew Polk Watson, spent three years (1927–1929) engaged in interviews with a group of ex-slaves, recording their conversion narratives, and often discovering "little or no variation from one telling to the next."[32] Another researcher, Paul Radin, noted that the conversion recollections reflected a common process that began with a "sense of sin" and ended with a new awareness of redemption, forgiveness, and cleansing from iniquity. Radin insisted, however, that within those experiences slaves sought "a status that [they] had ordained, not a fictitious one imposed from without," a perception that could only be found "in the realm of dreams, fantasies, and visions."[33] He observed that Christianity as a system of dogma held little appeal for the slave converts and concluded that antebellum Negroes were "not converted to God"; rather, they "converted God" to themselves. Conversion provided a "fixed point" in a world of contradictions and injustice, offering a renewed sense of personhood that engendered "joy and enthusiasm."[34] Radin contended that for whites conversion meant "that Christ had forgiven" their sins, while for slaves it meant "that Christ had recognized [them] and that [they] had recognized Christ." For slaves, conversion became an opportunity "to attain individuation. The sins would take care of themselves."[35] In these cases conversion was inseparable from personhood.

Many slave conversion narratives involve "a voice" from God, Jesus or an angel that captures the individual's attention and then provides instructions regarding securing salvation and comprehending the Christian's calling. One verbatim began,

> One day while in the field plowing I heard a voice. I jumped because I taught it was my master coming to scold and whip me for plowing up some more corn. I looked but saw no one. Again the voice called, "Morte! Morte!" With this I stopped, dropped the plow, and started running, but the voice kept on speaking to me saying, "Fear not, my little one, for behold! I come to bring you a message of truth."[36]

In commenting on the testimonies published in *God Struck Me Dead*, Mechal Sobel pointed out that more often than not "the seeker is called by name...signifying that God knows this name and is ready to encounter or know the soul of that person....The call by name is of ultimate significance."[37] In some testimonies, the appearance of an angel or other mysterious beings evoked both spiritual transformation and immediate danger. One ex-slave described that sensation:

> I looked and saw my old body suspended over a burning pit by a small web like a spider web. I again prayed, and there came a soft voice saying, "My little one, I have loved you with an everlasting love. You are this day made alive and freed from Hell. You are a chosen vessel unto the Lord. Be upright before me, and I will guide you unto all truth. My grace is sufficient for you. Go, and I am with you. Preach the gospel, and I will preach with you. You are henceforth the salt of the earth."[38]

Some conversions began early in life. One former slave noted,

> When I was twelve years old I professed religion. One Sunday I began trembling like a leaf, and the tears were rolling down my face. For three days I couldn't eat or drink, and the white folks that owned me whipped me twice. I thought I would die. Then Jesus came to me just as white as dripping snow, with his hair parted in the middle just as white as snow. Then I was cut off like a streak of lightening. I didn't know nothing. I had never known anything about the Bible, but it was revealed to me. I was taught how to pray by the Lord.[39]

Sobel observed that the "black visions of death and rebirth" share common qualities with those of whites, but these conversion experiences of blacks reflected four distinct elements. First, most visions demonstrate a sense of "two selves," a "little me" and a "big me" (old life/new life) throughout the encounter. Second, the salvific journey takes the soul from "Hell to Heaven"; one's eternal destination is dramatically transformed. Third, there is frequently "a little (white) man" who guides the sinner's journey from sinfulness to grace. Finally, the vision of God often involves some description of "whiteness."[40] Sobel contended that these visionary elements were particularly evident among Afro-Baptists and provided an "integration (generally not recognized) in which *a new cosmos was forged uniting African and Baptist elements in a new whole*." Thus, "aspects of African soul and spirit found an intrinsic role in the black Baptist rebirth experience, infusing the Christian Sacred Cosmos with an African one." These visions offered "firm evidence of the Afro-Christian quality of the black faith."[41] Likewise, the sense that an "irreducible spirit" was at the heart of the slave's "true nature and value" made conversion a liberating experience. Such a spirit "was not a gift of the white man." Rather, this revelatory Spirit was eternal, brought from Africa by the slaves, "not as a deity," but in their own inner selves. Sobel went so far as to suggest that white religionists themselves "did not share in the African awareness of the complexity of souls and their eternal life."[42] Increasingly, in many later Anglo-Saxon revival contexts conversion would become more transaction than encounter.

Conversion brought a fusion of the individual's mortal spirit with that of the eternal Christ, a mysterious union sometimes referred to as "the thing." It involved an assurance that no matter how difficult life's journey, or how unjust the abuse, the believer would never be forsaken by Jesus the Savior. One spiritual asserted,

> Well, I been travelin' all through this way
> Well, I take Jesus, he will be my friend
> Well, I've been travelin' through this way
> Well, I cried out
> I take Jesus to be my friend
> He will lead me, safely through
> Whiles I'm travelin', whiles I'm stumblin' all the time
> When I'm on my lonesome journey,
> I want Jesus Be with me.[43]

Hush Arbors: The Secret Prayer Gatherings

Religious experiences among slaves were frequently nurtured through secret prayer meetings (sometimes known as "hush arbors") held outside the gaze of overseers. These meetings took place in seclusion, sometimes deep in the forest or in cane breaks on the margins of the farms and plantations. The spiritual "steal away, steal away, steal away to Jesus," is thought to have been both a confession of faith and a code for confirming a clandestine gathering for prayer, preaching, and spiritual fellowship.[44] Much has been written about the tactics used by slaves to protect the secrecy of such meetings with strategies that included hanging wet quilts around the meeting area, or speaking toward the ground or into a container of water. Albert Raboteau wrote, "The most common device for preserving secrecy was an iron pot or kettle turned upside down to catch the sound." The pots might be placed at the center of the gathering place, tilted so as to muffle the sound. As one participant noted, it was to "catch" the noise so the overseer "wouldn't hear us singin' and shoutin'."[45] Sometimes there was preaching, but often the secret meeting involved occasions of group prayer, singing, and spiritual ecstasy. Peter Randolph, a freed slave and Baptist minister, described moments in which the preacher at a furtive assembly felt the Holy Spirit, grew increasingly excited, "and in a short time, there fall to the ground twenty or thirty men and women under its influence."[46] Prayers for strength and freedom were ever-present elements of these gatherings. Peter Randolph commented, "The slave forgets all his sufferings except to remind others of the trials during the past week, exclaiming: 'Thank God, I shall not live here always!'"[47] Raboteau concluded that "forbidden to pray for liberation [in master-dominated church services] slaves stole away at night and prayed inside 'cane thickets... for deliverance.'"[48] In those meetings religious experience thrived and the black church took shape.

The Preachers

The black preacher was and remains one of the most important agents of religious experience within African-American Christian communities. Concerning that early role, W.E.B. DuBois wrote,

> The black religious fervor in America is a continuation of their African heritage. The transplanted African priest became an important person in plantation life from the beginning, serving as interpreter of the supernatural, the comforter of those who were in sorrow, and the resentment of the people so far from their homeland.[49]

Early efforts to evangelize slaves led to the appearance of slave preachers who articulated the need for and meaning of conversion and its accompanying spirituality. Black preachers offered pastoral care amid the terrible suffering of slave life, and, often with powerful rhetoric, articulated the nature of Christian faith, the need for conversion, and the promise of salvation and justice to come, all under the watchful scrutiny of the slave owners. These preachers, especially those sanctioned by the white constituency, had to navigate a difficult terrain of sincere response to their own people while placating white masters who feared that they might foment insurrection or interpret Christianity beyond master-slave subordination. Raboteau observed, "Usually illiterate, the slave preacher often had native wit and unusual eloquence. Licensed or unlicensed, with or without permission, preachers held prayer meetings, preached and ministered in a very difficult situation." He cited one ex-slave who commented, "Back there they were harder on preachers than they were on anybody else. They thought preachers were ruining the colored people."[50]

Biblical literacy was one of the greatest challenges confronting the early preachers. Slaves heard the Bible read and preached, but seldom encountered the printed text; yet they harnessed the power of oral tradition and a rhetorical prowess that marked the beginning of the African-American pulpit. South Carolina plantation owner J. Motte Alston, commenting on the biblical memorization he observed in the black preachers of the 1830s, noted, "It was quite wonderful what retentive memories [the slaves] had, for few could read."[51] Peter Randolph, converted while enslaved, "became impressed that I was called of God to preach to the other slaves... but then I could not read the Bible, and I thought I could never preach unless I learned to read the Bible."[52] Many did learn to read, often through surreptitious instruction. Others testified that biblical literacy fell upon them through the miraculous work of the Spirit of God. Rebecca Cox Jackson (b. 1795), a Shaker prophetess and black freedwoman, reported that when her family refused to teach her to read she was assured in her spirit that it would come to her. Not long after, she recalled a revelation that began, "'Who learned the first man on earth?' 'Why God.' 'He is unchangeable, and if He learned the first man to read, He can learn you.'" She knelt down and "prayed earnestly to Almighty God if it was consistent with His holy will, to learn me to read His holy word. And when I looked on the word, I began to read."[53]

More "conventional means" for literacy, though difficult to secure, were sometimes provided by certain white ministers, literate black preachers, or "most often . . . older slave women" who taught reading and writing. Allan Dwight Callahan concluded that "African-American literature . . . begins with religion, the Evangelical religion of slaves who heard the text of the Bible speak to them and made of its letters a sacred quest." Thus, "for African Americans . . . religion was both opportunity and mandate to acquire letters."[54]

Luke Powery, Dean of the Chapel, Duke University, suggests that early African-American spirituals often linked preaching and religious experience. He insists that for African-Americans, both the spiritual and the pulpit reflect "a theology of divine suffering," grounded in the sense of "catastrophe and tragedy" inherent in the gospel. Such spiritual preaching exists within "an ecology of community" in which "suffering and death are a communal [religious] experience." In worship, the "call and response" that occurs between preacher and congregation "reveals the communal nature of black spirituality."[55] Powery contends that religious experience in African-American life created "a necessary response" to the vicissitudes of slavery and the reality of suffering. Both sermon and spiritual were signs of "the slaves' refusal to be stopped" in their pursuit of both spirituality and liberation.[56]

Preachers and "the Call"

The centrality of the "call" to ministry was present in African-American religious life from the beginning. Some preachers moved quickly through conversion to calling, while others were more hesitant, even resistant to the idea. In *God Struck Me Dead*, one preacher recalled,

> When God called me I had applied in hell, but my name wasn't on the roll. . . . It was from here that God delivered my soul, turned me around, and gave me my orders. . . . As I went along, a voice called out, "Oh, William!

> Oh, William! Oh, William!" When he said that he turned me around out of the big road into a little path, my face being toward the east. He spoke again and said, "Go preach my gospel to every creature and fear not, for I am with you, an everlasting prop. Amen."[57]

In his study of "the African-American call to ministry," William H. Myers detailed the process of the "call experience," including the "urge" to preach the gospel, a religious feeling that often haunted the individual early in life. Though it was frequently resisted, ultimately the "urge" was too powerful to refuse. Some found it confirmed by certain "signs" that included voices, visions, bright lights, particular physical sensations, or traumatic life events.[58] Others sensed the call through the "nurture" of particular familial or churchly mentors. Myers concluded that the "key component" of these experiences "is an irresistible urge to preach that does not abate until fulfilled. It is often validated by a variety of aural, ocular, and other sensory signs such as visions, voices, accidents, and awakenings at unusual times."[59] Ordination procedures required a statement of conversion and call as part of the necessary credentialing.

Call experiences abound in African-American religious communions. Richard Allen (1760–1831), of the African Methodist Episcopal Church (A.M.E.), was born into slavery in Philadelphia. As a child he and his family were sold to a more benevolent master with whom he lived until he was in his twenties. When that master faced financial crisis, he sold Allen's family members to buyers in various locations, decimating the family unit. Converted at age seventeen, Allen reported, "I was awakened and brought to see myself poor wretched and undone, and without the mercy of God, must be lost. Shortly after I obtained mercy through the blood of Christ, and was constrained to exhort my old companions to seek the Lord."[60]

Allen soon came to doubt this experience, fearing that hell was his inescapable "portion." He recalled, "I cried unto Him who delighted to hear the prayers of a poor sinner; and all of a sudden, my dungeon shook, my chains flew off, and 'Glory to God!' I cried. My soul was filled. I cried, 'Enough! For me the Savior died!'"[61] Sanctification was secured.

After his Methodist master permitted Allen and his brother to purchase their freedom he became a "licensed exhorter," securing certification that permitted him to preach throughout Pennsylvania. In the 1780s, at a meeting in Radford Township, Allen reported that "many were the slain of the Lord. Seldom did I experience such a time of mourning and lamentation among the people. There were but few colored people in the neighborhood—the most of my congregation white. Some said, 'This man must be a man of God. I never heard such preaching before.'"[62] Tensions between freed blacks and white members of the Methodist Episcopal Church created a sense of second-class status among the African-Americans, contributing to the decision to establish a new denomination. The African Methodist Episcopal Church was founded in Philadelphia on April 9, 1816, with Richard Allen as its first bishop, an office he maintained until his death.

Allen was less responsive to the call of females to preach, as illustrated in the life and work of Jarena Lee (1783–?), a woman who made no secret of the calling she believed God had placed upon her. Born to freed parents, Lee wrote about her religious experience, call, and ministry in an autobiographical account published in 1836. In her twenty-first year she received conversion through the preaching of Richard Allen, then pastor of Bethel Church in Philadelphia. It occurred, she recalled, at a service of worship where although

> hundreds were present, I did leap to my feet, and declare that God, for Christ's sake, had pardoned the sins of my soul. Great was the ecstasy of my mind, for I felt that not only the sin of *malice* was pardoned, but all other sins were swept away together. That day was the first when my heart had believed, and my tongue had made confession unto salvation.[63]

Not long after her conversion, Lee received "a religious visit" from "a certain coloured man, by name William Scott" who urged her to seek "entire sanctification of the soul to God." After a time of spiritual struggle with what she specifically identified as "pride, anger, self-will" that remained in her "fallen nature," she received sanctification.[64]

By 1811 Lee had sensed the call to preach, an experience initiated at the sound of "a voice which I thought I distinctly heard, and most certainly understood, which said to me, 'Go preach the Gospel!'" When she objected that "no one will believe me," the voice reiterated her call, and promised, "I will put words in your mouth, and will turn your enemies to become your friends."[65] Lee took her case to the venerable Richard Allen, who did not question her call, but advised her against attempting to fulfill it with the Methodists. Lee commented, "But as to women preaching, he [Allen] said that our [Methodist] Discipline knew nothing at all about it—that it did not call for women preachers." Of that ruling, Lee remarked, "O how careful ought we to be, lest through our by-laws of church government and discipline, we bring into disrepute even the word of life. For as unseemly as it may be now-a-days for a woman to preach, it should be remembered that nothing is impossible with God." She asked why it should be considered "heterodox, or improper" for women to preach, "seeing the Saviour died for the woman as well as the man."[66] Lee's sense of call was undeterred, an objective that in 1818 induced her to interrupt Allen's sermon at Bethel Church in an attempt to assert the power and validity of her call. Allen was impressed, not angered, by the action and endorsed her calling, advocating her work in the African Methodist Episcopal Church as a "traveling exhorter" but not a "licensed preacher."[67] The door to full ministerial recognition would remain closed.

Jarena Lee published two editions of her autobiography, the last in 1849. After that she was lost to history with no discernible record of her death available. She summarized her ministry and her spirituality accordingly:

> In my wanderings up and down among men, preaching according to my ability, I have frequently found families who told me that they had not for several years been to a meeting, and yet, while listening to hear what God would say by his poor coloured female instrument, have believed with trembling—tears rolling down their cheeks, the signs of contrition and repentance towards God. I firmly believe that I have sown seed, in the name of the Lord.[68]

Jarena Lee is one illustration of the ministerial vocation that came to many African-American women. Her spiritual experiences mirrored those of many nineteenth-century Methodist-related preachers who journeyed through conversion, sanctification, and calling. In many African-American ecclesiastical settings, preaching was not simply a theological or conversionist discourse but was itself a religious experience. One nineteenth-century "white missionary" noted that when a black preacher entered the pulpit,

> There is a wonderful sympathy between the speaker and the audience, described as rude eloquence and genuine oratory, the sermons of black preacher's excited emotions. They were orations in which exposition was not attempted. Description, exhortation, appeal formed the warp and woof. The whole being expressive of... all Negro experiences, trials, comforts, and assurances.[69]

Nonetheless, African-American preachers and preaching reflected a complexity of personalities and contexts so diverse that Harry Richardson could conclude that "the stereotype of the 'slave preacher' must be discarded."[70] Richardson insisted that African preachers should be understood as exercising their gifts in particular settings that incorporated pastoral and prophetic insights into varying personal, spiritual, and cultural realities. Cornish R. Rogers captured that complexity by noting,

> Black preaching tends to be more evocative and descriptive than didactic. Its message always stresses the awfulness of the present followed by the glory of the future. The black church operates its interior life as a family. The black preacher became a father figure—invested with power—and not a suffering servant figure, as many white ministers are expected to be. Moreover the black preacher was looked upon as a leader to be followed rather than a model to be emulated.[71]

Rogers suggested that the black preacher was also "God's holy priest... a power broker between the black community and the white structures of power."[72]

"The Religious Feeling of the Slave"

In *The Souls of the Black Folk* (1903), W. E. B. DuBois (1868–1963) summarized "the religious feeling of the slave" in terms of three discernible features: "the Preacher, the Music, and the Frenzy." DuBois called the preacher "the most unique personality developed by the Negro on American soil," an office and person who combined "a certain adroitness with deep-seated earnestness...tact with consummate ability." Music involved "that plaintive rhythmic melody, with its touching minor cadences, which, despite caricature and defilement, still remains the most original and beautiful expression of human life and longing yet born on American soil."[73] In another section of the book DuBois writes plaintively, "They that walked in darkness sang songs in the olden days—Sorrow Songs—for they were weary at heart."[74] He acknowledges that these songs "are the articulate message of the slave to the world," that may at points reflect a "joyous" quality of life. Yet he concluded,

> But not all the past South, though it rose from the dead, can gainsay the heart-touching witness of these songs. They are the music of an unhappy people, of the children of disappointment; they tell of death and suffering and unvoiced longing toward a truer world, of misty wanderings and hidden ways.[75]

"Frenzy or shouting," DuBois believed, occurred when the "Spirit of the Lord passed by," making worshipers "mad with supernatural joy," variously evident in silence, "low murmur and moan," or even "the mad abandon of physical fervor." Such physical frenzy expressed itself in "stamping, shrieking, and shouting...wild waving of arms,...weeping and laughing,...the vision and the trance."[76] This enthusiastical expression gained such a "hold" on black religionists "that many generations firmly believed that without this visible manifestation of the God there could be no true communion with the Invisible."[77] Christian religious experiences within the context of slavery had multiple expressions, captured insightfully by DuBois.

C. Eric Lincoln and Lawrence H. Mamiya surveyed what they viewed as the defining elements of "the black sacred cosmos" with decisive implications for understanding religious experience in African-American congregations. This cosmos was centered in God as revealed in Jesus of Nazareth. Indeed, they concurred with Henry Mitchell, James Cone, and Gayraud Wilmore in suggesting that "throughout Black religious history the reality of Jesus as the Son of God made flesh finds a deep response in black faith and worship." Jesus's life and teaching, his suffering, death, and resurrection reflected God's tangible, incarnational response to the human condition.[78] In the words of the spiritual, "Nobody knows the trouble I've seen; nobody knows but Jesus."

African-American Christianity also cultivated an all-important concern for the reality of freedom, as "release from bondage" in slavery time, and by the twentieth century as a means for "social, political, and economic justice." Likewise, freedom meant "the absence of any restraint that might compromise one's responsibility to God."[79] As another Spiritual asserted,

> Before I'll be a slave I'll be buried in my grave
> And go home to my Father and be free.[80]

At the same time, Lincoln and Mamiya insisted that "the core experience of the black cosmos" involved the conversion of persons to faith in Jesus Christ. They cited Mechal Sobel's contention that "black religious experiences" were viewed by white Christians (Baptists) as "particularly ecstatic," distinct from those encountered by whites. Their conclusion was that well into the twentieth century, "a qualitatively different cultural form of expressing Christianity" was present in "most black churches."[81] Such a distinction was not lost on African-Americans themselves, as one ex-slave explained it:

> I stays independent of what white folks tells me when I shouts [in religious services]. De Spirit moves me every day, dat's how I stays in. White folks don't feel sech as I does; so dey stays out.... Never does it make no difference how I's tossed about. Jesus, He comes and saves me everytime. I's had a hard time, but I's blessed now—no mo' mountains.[82]

This experience of the grace of God experienced through Jesus Christ was adapted and interpreted by blacks inside and beyond the slave experience. Henry Mitchell insisted that such an approach to grace supplied the "existential needs" of African-American Christians as well as offering a "sense of liberation" while at the same time including "a sound and deep awareness of human frailty, Black and White."[83] God's grace undergirded a sense of God's merciful providence, an emphasis that Mitchell viewed as "virtually universal among slave believers, and very common among all Blacks." This perception of providence he called "a great gift, a racial and cultural streak of genius, to be able to 'bounce back.'"[84]

African-American Religious Experience: Beyond Slavery

The African-American church began with a religious experience characterized by suffering, bondage, and injustice. Offered as a way of preparing Africans for heaven and confirming their servitude with divine sanction, Christianity became for many a way of promise of both salvation and for justice, a religious experience that involved conversion sure enough, but also took seriously the way in which God's own self, made known in Jesus, experienced suffering and death with individual and communal implications. Religious experience bounded by feeling, engaged in struggle, and coping with injustice, became a way of responding to the realities of slavery and Jim Crow, suffering and vulnerability.

W.E.B. DuBois's assessment of the power of preaching, the spiritual and "frenzy" in African-American churches, continued after Emancipation. Religious experiences known in conversion (justification) and Spirit baptism (sanctification) remain central to the spirituality of African-American Christians, who encounter the divine presence individually and collectively inside and beyond the services of the church. Would-be ministers, male and female, are still required to articulate a sense of call that, if not punctuated by an ecstatic experience, reflects the depth of the individual's life and identity.

While the calls to conversion and sanctification parallel those of white Protestants, there are decided differences. In multiple studies of the theology of black liberation, James H. Cone asserted that "Black Theology" was inseparable from "the black experience—a life of humiliation and suffering."

He insisted that "the black experience should not be identified with inwardness, as implied in Schleiermacher's description of religion as the 'feeling of absolute dependence.'" It was "not an introspection" by which individuals contemplated their egos. Cone declared, "Black people are not afforded the luxury of navel gazing."[85] While black theology did not dismiss "the importance of God's revelation in Christ," black people were compelled "to know what Christ means when they are confronted with the brutality of white racism."[86] Cone contended that a liberationist response to such racism involved a spiritual experience with "the Blackness of Jesus," the insistence that the God who entered history in Jesus of Nazareth "transformed it through his cross and resurrection." In Jesus, God identified with the poor and the oppressed. In the US, this meant "that God was on the side of oppressed Blacks in their struggle for freedom and against whites who victimized them."[87]

Womanist Spirituality: "A Lived Experience of Faith"

Womanist theology represents another facet of and approach to African-American religious experience. The term *womanist* is attributed to novelist Alice Walker in *In Search of Our Mother's Garden* (1983), and taken from the word *womanish*, often used by black women as a mature behavior, the opposite of *girlish*, meaning "frivolous, irresponsible, not serious." Mothers might address "female children, 'you acting womanish,' i.e., like a woman."[88] These womanist actions reflected behavior that is "outrageous, audacious, courageous or *willful*."[89] Toinette M. Eugene elaborates on that description, noting that

> to be a faithful womanist... is to operate out of this system of black moral value indicators that flow from biblical understanding based on justice and love.... It is precisely the womanist religious responses of endurance, resistance, and resiliency offered in the face of all attempts at personal and institutional domination that may provide a renewed theological legacy of liberation for everyone concerned.[90]

In *Introducing Womanist Theology*, Stephanie Y. Mitchem noted that the origins of the movement parallel the "development of black theology, feminist theology, and other liberation theologies," but with varying distinctions. Its approaches are "deconstructive and constructive," with varying "disciplinary tools." Mitchem observed that "womanist theology offers opportunities for black women to feel fully participative in the theological processes and dialogues." For her, womanist theology is "the systematic, faith-based exploration of the many facets of African American women's religiosity," and centered "on the complex realities of black women's lives."[91] This theological approach poses varying questions that grow out of the lives and actions of African-American women. These include, "Where is God in the experiences of black women? By what name should this God be called? What does it mean to live a life of faith? How should black women respond to God's call?"[92]

Mitchem suggested that black women initiate "religious explorations," not in theological or doctrinal speculation, but "in daily life." These theological insights and approaches represent responses to "life situations" and are often misunderstood "as superstition or dismissed as having no value." Rather, it is "the spirituality, or the magic," that sprang "from the values that life has taught black women."[93] Likewise, one important emphasis of womanist theologians requires listening to "the meanings that already exist in black women's lives... the lived theologies of individual black women" and the often communal nature of their religious experiences.[94]

Linda E. Thomas described womanist intentions to link past experiences and practices of black women with those of contemporary women. She wrote,

> The method of womanist theology validates the past lives of enslaved African women by remembering, affirming, and glorifying their contributions. After excavating analytically and reflecting critically on the life stories of our foremothers, the methodology entails a construction and creation of a novel paradigm. We who are womanists concoct something new that makes sense for how we are living in complex gender, racial, and class social configurations. We use our foremothers' rituals and survival tools to live in hostile environments.... In other words, the past, present, and future fuse

> to create a dynamic multi-vocal tapestry of black women's experience intergenerationally.[95]

Emilie Townes contended that womanist "spirituality is embodied, personal, communal as it brings together the historic force of black women's spiritual lives with the demand of the spirit to contextualize and live one's faith. It is reflection on the particularity of one's own faith journey lived and unfolded in community."[96] Again, womanist studies engage the narratives and reflections on religious experiences long known to and expressed by black women, often overlooked or undermined by slave owners, cultural and religious establishments and ecclesiastical communions, including, often especially, African-American churches. Townes offered a larger description of womanist spirituality, excerpted here:

> womanist spirituality is a
> lived experience of faith
> it is embodied in people
> and found in the concrete contexts in which people live out their faith
> it is grounded in the context of struggling for faith and justice
> it takes on antagonistic dualisms as unhealthy in many places in our faith journeys
> it is an ongoing faithfilled process—a ripening and ripening into wholeness
> living out womanist spirituality—integrating faith and life
> means that we recognize that we are made in God's image
> indeed, God's presence is the very fabric of our existence
> immanent & transcendent
> close as our breathing
> no, God is not an option or on the supplemental reading list
> for God's love for us is unconditional
> yes, God makes demands, has commands

and perhaps the simplest and hardest of these
is that we are called to live our lives out of the possibilities
not our shortcomings
answering yes to God's what if
this love moves us to grow in compassion, understanding, and acceptance of each other
it is the formation of a divine/human community based on love and hope
and pointed toward justice
we are to listen for and hear the word of God
a call for responsibility, contemplation
in the lives of others *and in our lives*
for in the personal search for spiritual understanding we are also engaged in the human struggle.[97]

As Townes indicated, womanist spirituality is concerned about religious experience that is both personal and communal, sanctifying religious communions and the society at large. Womanist scholars have not hesitated to challenge areas of injustice they believe perpetuated by church and culture at the expense of women. In *Sexuality and the Black Church: A Womanist Perspective*, Kelly Brown Douglas cited Toinette Eugene's insistence that spirituality moves beyond worship, prayer, or church attendance to include "the human capacity to be self-transcending, relational and freely committed." It engages all aspects of life, "including our human sexuality."[98] Townes concluded that womanist thought "is a paradise built on enduring faith and an outright colored stubbornness that simply will not stop until justice comes."[99]

Religious Experience and Civil Rights: A Ceaseless Calling

Religious experience was and remains inseparable from the work of liberation in overcoming racism as social and personal policy and practice.

Indeed, many leaders of the Abolition and Civil Rights Movements testified to encounters with the Divine that impelled them to public action against racism.

In *God's Long Hot Summer: Stories of Faith and Civil Rights*, Charles Marsh documented the faith and work of Mississippi civil rights activist Fannie Lou Hamer (1917–1977) in ways that reveal the power of religious experience in the battle for equal rights in the mid-twentieth century. Marsh suggested that Hamer's "piety" formed around "two interconnecting images of Christ," one that emphasized his life, death, and resurrection, and the other shaped by the radical nature of his liberating acts in the world. Hamer affirmed her own conversion from sin to new life, while insisting that more was "at stake than the fate of... [her] individual soul." She was thus empowered to declare to the racist American "pharaohs": "Let my people go."[100]

Marsh described the summer of 1963, when Hamer and other representatives of the Southern Christian Leadership Conference (SCLC) were arrested in Winona, Mississippi, for attempting to be served at a "whites only" lunch counter. Mrs. Hamer, jailed with other civil rights workers, was beaten by two black inmates on the orders of the white police. Hamer recalled, "So they had me lay down on my face, and they beat with a thick leather thing that was wide. And it had something in it heavy." Marsh suggested that "the next day something happened that slowly transformed the killing despair of the jail and dispersed the power of death." Hamer noted, "When you're in a brick cell, locked up, and haven't done anything to anybody... sometimes words just begin to come to you and you begin to sing." And sing she did:

> Paul and Silas was bound in jail, let my people go.
> Had no money for to go their bail, let my people go.
> Paul and Silas began to shout, let my people go.
> Jail doors open and they walked out, let my people go.

"Singing brings out the soul," Hamer declared, fighting Jim Crow tooth and nail.[101] Undeterred, she warned, "If them crackers in Winona thought they'd discouraged me from fighting, I guess they found out different. I'm going to stay in Mississippi and if they shoot me down, I'll be buried here."[102]

Charles Marsh cautioned that Hamer's "serious devotion to Jesus" should not be dismissed as a mere "motivational tool"; rather, her "faith was far greater and infinitely more complex than the utility it offered." It was "charged by all the literal and exquisite detail of the Gospel story." Hamer herself cited Ephesians chapter 6 and the call to "put on the whole armor of God" in order to confront the "principalities . . . powers . . . and spiritual wickedness in high places." She recalled, "This is what I think about when I think of my own work in the fight for freedom."[103] For Hamer and other black civil rights activists, religious experience was inseparable from social justice.

Perhaps there is no more poignant example of the relationship between religious experience and human liberation than that described by Martin Luther King Jr. (1929–1968) in *Stride Toward Freedom*, the story of the Montgomery Bus Boycott. In that volume King recounted the communal decision, personified in Rosa Parks, to challenge segregation on municipal transportation in Montgomery, Alabama, the first capitol of the Confederacy. King, relatively new pastor of the Dexter Avenue Baptist Church, rose to leadership of that movement and with it the larger Civil Rights Movement in the US. As controversy over the boycott led to threats of violence, King's struggle with the mantle of leadership reached a catharsis in January 1956 with a threatening, late night phone call, warning that he would soon regret moving to Montgomery.

Unable to sleep and about "to give up," King made coffee and, sitting at the kitchen table, confronted his fears. Exhausted and struggling to find courage, he took his case to God, confessing that while he knew he was standing "for what I believe is right," he was at that moment afraid for his life. Right then, King recalled, he encountered the Divine presence "as I had never experienced it before." King acknowledged that from that moment on, "my uncertainty disappeared," with the assurance of God's presence in his life and his work he "was ready to face anything."[104]

That mystical encounter solidified King's leadership in the Montgomery boycott, and its success impelled him into the larger Civil Rights Movement with demonstrations and dissenting actions across the South. He was assassinated in Memphis, Tennessee, in 1968, leading a civil demonstration in behalf of multiracial sanitation workers in that city. King's own ability to blend personal spirituality and political action contributed to a movement that broke the back of Jim Crow "separate but equal" segregation in the American South.

Yet not everyone in the African-American community during the twentieth-century struggles for civil rights found religion fulfilling its promises. In his novel *The Fire Next Time*, author James Baldwin (1924–1987) described his conversion and decision to become a "Youth Pastor" at a church in Harlem, a position he occupied for some three years.[105] Baldwin described an occasion when, during a service presided over by the church's female pastor, "everything came roaring, screaming, crying out, and I fell to the ground before the altar." He called it

> the strangest sensation I have ever had in my life—up to that time, or since. . . . And the anguish that filled me cannot be described. It moved in me like one of those floods that devastate counties, tearing everything down. . . . All I really remember is the pain, the unspeakable pain; it was as though I were yelling up to Heaven and Heaven would not hear me.[106]

Baldwin reported that he remained on the floor before the altar all night long, noting, "Over me, to bring me 'through' the saints sang and rejoiced and prayed. And in the morning when they raised me, they told me that I was saved."[107]

Baldwin ultimately relinquished his formal connections with the church as an institution, disillusioned by his belief that "there was no love in the church. It was a mask for hatred, self-hatred and despair. The transfiguring power of the Holy Ghost ended when the service ended, and salvation stopped at the church."[108] Yet as *The Fire Next Time* seems to indicate, Baldwin could not relinquish a continuing sense of the Spirit, wherever it might appear. He wrote,

> In spite of everything, there was in the life I fled a zest and a joy and a capacity for facing and surviving disaster that are very moving and very rare. Perhaps we were, all of us—pimps, whores, racketeers, church members and children—bound together by the nature of our oppression, the specific and

> peculiar complex of risks we had to run; if so, within these limits we sometimes achieved with each other a freedom that was close to love.... This is the freedom that one hears in some gospel songs, for example, and in jazz. In all jazz, and especially in the blues, there is something tart and ironic, authoritative and double-edged.[109]

Baldwin's search for freedom from racism and homophobia led him to spend much of his adult life in France, where he produced a canon of literary works that often reflected his love-hate relationship with institutional Christianity and its inability to carry the liberating message of Jesus to its broadest conclusions.

African-American Spirituality: Within and Beyond a Community

African-American religious experience reflects both internal and external expressions, evident from the camp meeting "enthusiasm" to the "call and response" of contemporary congregations. It has elements of conversionism, sanctification, and radical social action evident in the great rhetorical tradition of African-American preaching and a dissenting tradition present in abolitionism, civil rights, and enduring social activism in behalf of persons on the margins. Many of its experiential and liturgical traditions spilled over into Evangelicalism, Pentecostalism, and segments of the Charismatic Movement. It has also produced deep divisions over the work of the Holy Spirit in calling women to ministry, sexuality, ministerial authority, and the nature of the church's sociopolitical engagement. To paraphrase James Melvin Washington, at its most prophetic moments, however, African-American religious experience transformed "Puritan Tribalism" "into a particularistic expression of the human yearning for freedom." In ways both general and particular, it blended experientialism and action to "forge distinctive theologies and spiritual praxes as vehicles for psychic and material deliverance."[110]

★★ *8* ★★

Experiencing the Full Gospel: The Holiness and Pentecostal Movements

Seeking Sanctification

Religious experience was at the heart of the Holiness and Pentecostal movements that took shape in the United States in the late nineteenth and early twentieth century. Rooted in a theology of sanctification—an enduring spirituality beyond the initial grace of conversion—these sects placed particular emphasis on the baptism of the Holy Spirit as a "second blessing" evoking the "Full Gospel" victory over sin.

A concern for sanctification is evident throughout Christian history present in the sacramental, liturgical, and mystical life of Roman Catholicism, Eastern Orthodoxy, and the Protestant Reformers, but the stress on a decisive "second baptism" in the Spirit became a central element of the Holiness and Pentecostal traditions. For John Wesley (1703–1791), sanctification was a hallmark of the "order of salvation," a sustaining spiritual gift that followed justification and conversion. Sanctification was a way of ensuring perseverance, cultivating the "fruit of the Spirit" (Gal. 5:22-25), and deepening a relationship with God through the power of the Holy Spirit. Wesley preached frequently on what he called "sanctification," "Christian Perfection," or "Holiness," all of which involved the deeper life of Christian experience following the new birth.

Wesley understood salvation to include both justification and sanctification. In *The Principles of a Methodist*, he wrote that "the preventing [enabling] grace of God, which is common to all, is sufficient to *bring* us to Christ, though it is not sufficient to carry us any *further* till we are justified."[1] Justification occurred through faith in Christ by which one was "born again" but only "in the *imperfect* sense for there are two [if not more] degrees of regeneration." The second "degree" involved sanctification, "the highest state of *perfection* in this life." The sanctified individual was thus "born again in the full and perfect sense. Then they have the indwelling of the Spirit."[2]

Wesley explained that to speak of "one that is perfect" simply meant "one whom God hath 'sanctified throughout,' even in 'body, soul, and spirit'; one who 'walketh in the light, as he is in the light,' in whom 'is no darkness at all, the blood of Jesus Christ his son having cleansed him from all sin.'"[3] Sanctification involved the decision of the justified believer to deepen Christian discipleship by the power of the Holy Spirit, an experience by which "in every thought of our hearts, in every word of our tongues, in every work of our hands," one manifested the spirit and actions of Jesus himself.[4] Yet, as Donald Dayton observed, such sanctification "is not 'sinless perfection' in the strong sense if by that one means being beyond the possibility of sinning. It is a perfecting of the ability to love according to one's capacities at a given point in one's life pilgrimage—a purifying of intentions and a focusing of the will."[5] It also provided assurance of salvation and guarded against falling from grace.

In a widely published sermon on "Christian Perfection," Wesley delineated what sanctification was and was not. It was not a freedom from ignorance, mistakes, temptations, or infirmities. Perfection (sanctification) was "the glorious privilege of every Christian," even those who were new to the faith. But, Wesley insisted, "it is only of those who *are strong* in the Lord, 'and have overcome the wicked one,'... that it can be affirmed they are in such a sense perfect, as secondly, to be freed from evil thoughts and evil tempers."[6]

John Wesley and the Methodist movement he generated were not unique in emphasizing a continuing experience of grace. Evangelist Charles Finney concluded his *Lectures on Revivals of Religion* with an admonition to new converts to "grow in grace," a process involving "not a gradual giving up of sin," but relinquishing sin "instantly and wholly."[7] The sanctification process required "intense earnestness and constancy in seeking increased religious light, by the illumination of the Holy Spirit." Indeed, "no effectual religious light" was possible apart from the "inward showing" of the Spirit.[8] Sanctification was also evident in the founding of Oberlin College where Finney became Professor of Theology and later President. "Oberlin perfectionism" became an early hallmark of a school given to evangelical conversionism, abolition, women's rights, and coeducation.[9]

The Way of Holiness

By the mid-nineteenth century, many in the camp meeting–revival tradition were concerned that Methodism had forsaken its early emphasis on the sanctified life for more formal, less revivalistic approaches to gospel preaching and Christian living. In 1867 a group of Methodist clergy and laity founded the "National Camp Meeting Association for the Promotion of Holiness" (NCMA) in an attempt to renew holiness preaching and practice within the revival tradition. Its goal was to offer greater emphasis to "a profound religious experience" by which professing Christians would discover the second blessing of spiritual empowerment by the Holy Spirit.[10]

The Holiness movement was at once an extension of the Wesleyan emphasis on sanctification and a source of continuing spiritual guidance for new converts. Holiness set forth the boundaries of Christian living for those called to be "in the world but not of it," shielding them from corrupting influences and promoting spiritual and ethical behavior. It was also an attempt to expand the meaning of salvation to include life in this world and the next, not simply a transaction to get sinners into heaven. Likewise, the second blessing or baptism in the Holy Spirit provided assurance of salvation and confirmation that the believer had truly passed "from death unto life." For many revivalists, the emphasis on holiness was a response to emerging denominational bureaucracies and congregational formalism thought to minimize "heart religion" and the ethical rigors of Christian discipleship.[11]

Holiness revivals recaptured earlier conversionist enthusiasm with dramatic emotional outbursts from participants struck by the Spirit. Robert Mapes Anderson cited a five-week holiness meeting in Hartford City, Indiana (1884), when, "Men, women and children were struck down in their homes, in their places of business, on the highways, and lay as dead. They had wonderful visions, and arose converted, giving glory to God."[12] An 1886 revival of some "25,000 souls" near Alexandria, Indiana, provoked this account: "The power of God fell on the multitude.... Many fell to the ground. Others stood with their faces and hands raised to heaven. The Holy Ghost sat upon them. Others shouted, some talked, others wept aloud. Sinners were converted, and began to testify and praise God."[13]

While speaking in tongues was sometimes manifested amid the overall religious exhilaration of those events, the practice was not normative in the early holiness meetings or mandated by those who affirmed the need for a post-conversion second blessing of the Spirit.

Phoebe Palmer and "Altar Theology"

Early holiness leaders like Phoebe Palmer (1807–1874) insisted on the need for all Christians to discover a new commitment to Christ. In his introduction to a collection of Palmer's writings, Thomas Oden insisted that Palmer "is arguably the best representative figure, male or female, of the beginnings of the Holiness tradition of spirituality in America." He concluded that her theology of holiness impacted four global traditions, "Wesleyan, Holiness, Pentecostal, and Charismatic." Thus she became "the most influential woman in the largest, fastest growing religious group in mid-nineteenth-century America—Methodism."[14] Palmer's spiritual activism led her to begin the "Tuesday Meetings for the Promotion of Holiness" in her New York City home in 1836. She was instrumental in the publication of the *Guide to Christian Perfection* (later known as the *Guide to Holiness*) begun in 1839, a major resource for promulgating holiness views. She and her husband, Dr. Walter Clark Palmer (1804–1883), became editors of the journal in 1864.[15]

Charles E. White, Palmer's early biographer, summarized her concept of sanctification accordingly:

> First she followed John Fletcher [Wesley's associate] in his identification of entire sanctification with the baptism of the Holy Spirit. Second she developed Adam Clarke's suggestion and linked holiness with power. Third, like Clarke, she stressed the instantaneous elements of sanctification to the exclusion of the gradual. Fourth, again following Clarke, she taught that entire sanctification is not really the goal of the Christian life, but rather its beginning. Fifth, through her "altar theology" she reduced the attainment of sanctification to a simple three-stage process of entire consecration, faith, and testimony; and sixth, she held that one needed no evidence other than the Biblical texts to be assured of entire sanctification.[16]

Palmer viewed the second blessing as a cathartic experience that ended in emotion-laden religious enthusiasm. The old sinful nature was purged away, replaced by a Christ-like character that provided victory over sin.[17] Those seeking complete cleansing from sin could simply claim the promises of scripture and move into the experience of holiness.

Palmer defined "Gospel holiness" as a particular state in which the believer achieved sanctification through "faith in the infinite merit of the Saviour," an act that produced consecration of every aspect of life to God. Such "holiness implies salvation from sin, [and] a redemption from *all* iniquity."[18] By faith, believing individuals placed their souls on the altar of God's love and grace. This "altar terminology" was an important element of Palmer's spirituality. She wrote, "The altar, thus provided by the conjoint testimony of the Father, Son and Holy Spirit, is Christ." Christ's death on the cross became "the sinner's plea" for grace and mercy. Through the "operation" of the Holy

Spirit, believers "confess their sins," and through God's justice and faithfulness are not only forgiven but also cleansed "from all unrighteousness."[19]

Palmer's idea that all believers could and should experience the sanctifying gift of the Holy Spirit led her to maintain that the Spirit continued to be poured out on all flesh, as promised in Joel 2:28-29 and repeated in Acts 2:17. Thus women received that gift as fully as men, enabling them to participate in the "ministry of the word."[20] She wrote:

> God has, in all ages of the Church, called some of his handmaids to eminent publicity and usefulness; and when the residue of the spirit is poured out, and the millennium glory ushered in, the prophecy of Joel being fully accomplished in all its glory, then, probably, there will be such a sweet blending into one spirit,—the spirit of faith, of love, and of a sound mind, . . . that the wonder will then be, that the exertions of pious females to bring souls to Christ should ever have been opposed or obstructed.[21]

Holiness was not simply a fulfilling spiritual experience but a great equalizer over artificial divisions, a divine cleansing that produced internal and external results. It required a rigorous ethical code of life and action, manifesting spiritual gifts of patience, kindness, peace, and love, in sharp contrast to the values and lifestyles evident in the sinful world. Moral rigor was essential for holy living. The goal was to have all one's "energies concentrated in the one endeavour and *intention* of living a life of entire devotion to God." Only this intense religious commitment would enable the truly sanctified to travel "unpolluted through the world."[22]

In her 1845 essay, "Entire Devotion to God," Palmer described how one might "enter into the enjoyment of holiness," citing several case studies of persons who had given themselves completely to the cleansing power of Christ's blood and had entered into a life of holiness. Her emphasis on the individual's exercise of free will in seeking the Spirit and its sanctifying life reflects a Wesleyan/Arminian emphasis on human participation in the salvific and sanctification processes. She concluded: "Holiness is a state of soul in which all the powers of the body and mind are consciously given up to God; and the witness of holiness is that testimony which the Holy Spirit bears with our spirit that the offering is accepted through Christ. The work is accomplished the moment we lay our all upon the altar."[23]

Not long before her death in 1874, Palmer recalled a dramatic spiritual encounter thirty-four years earlier that confirmed her call to ministry. It included a period of unrelenting spiritual struggle when, like the classic mystics, her "naked soul seemed to be tending as in the more immediate presence of the All-seeing, to whom all things are naked and open. Such piercing views of my utter nothingness, and the intense spirituality of the *Word of God*, seemingly would have crushed me, but I pleaded that my spirit might not fail before Him."[24] Ultimately she received deliverance through the power of the Holy Spirit that alone "can reveal to the soul its hidden meaning" and brings a seeker to the "great fundamental truth of Christianity *Holiness to the Lord*."[25] For Palmer, holiness, like conversion, often began with a cataclysmic spiritual encounter. It was the way of Christian perfection, "experimentally proved" by faith.[26] Palmer's influence in the early Holiness movement suggested that the baptism of the Holy Spirit had implications for expanding the role of women as preachers who would address gatherings of males and females, a practice forbidden by most Protestant communions.

Hannah Whitall Smith: The Christian's Secret

Quaker writer Hannah Whitall Smith (1832–1911) was another holiness leader whose book *The Christian's Secret of a Happy Life* became a popular text for guiding laity into sanctification. Born in England to devout Quaker parents, Smith's early life was characterized by a quest for things spiritual. In an autobiographical work entitled *The Unselfishness of God*, Smith detailed her lengthy journey toward conversion and sanctification, a process that included religious experiences, doubt and apostasy, reaffirmation of Christian commitment, and finally a discovery of the way of holiness.[27] Hannah Whitall married Quaker Robert P. Smith (1827–1898) in 1851, and theirs was a relationship anchored in a shared spiritual pilgrimage. In 1865 while living in New Jersey, they were introduced to Wesleyan holiness, each experiencing the baptism of the Holy Spirit.

Smith's investigation of sanctification and its experiential implications continued. A journal entry from 1867 described her realization that she could simply trust Christ for "deliverance from the power of sin as well as from its guilt."[28] Sanctification was not easily attained since it required a dying to self in every aspect of life. Smith's Quaker sensibilities made her suspicious of Methodist theology, which she labeled "a mixture of error," but she acknowledged that "it is far better to *have* the experience, even if mixed with error, than to live without it, and be very doctrinally correct, as was my former case."[29]

Smith claimed sanctification for herself with the recognition that not only was Christ "my Saviour for the future, but He was also my all-sufficient Saviour for the present." She affirmed, "No words can express the fullness and the all-sufficiency that I saw was stored up for me in the Lord," and her "whole soul was afire" with the realization that Jesus Christ was "a far more complete Saviour than I could have ever conceived of."[30] She defined sanctification as

> both a sudden step of faith, and also a gradual process of works. It is a step as far as we are concerned; it is a process as to God's part. By a step of faith we get into Christ; by a process we are made to grow up unto Him in all things. By a step of faith we put ourselves into the hands of the Divine Potter; by a gradual process He makes us into a vessel unto His own honor, meet for His use, and prepared to every good work.[31]

Just as faith in Christ brought justification from the future "penalties of our sins," so sanctification meant recognizing that Christ offered deliverance "from the bondage of our sins." "He is to be our Life."[32]

Entrance into the "interior life" incorporated at least two important steps: "First, entire abandonment; and second, absolute faith."[33] It required the complete "surrender [of] yourself to be all the Lord's, body, soul, and spirit; and to obey Him in everything where His will is made known; according to Rom. 12:12," and was centered in the belief "that God takes possession of that which you thus abandon to Him."[34] Smith perceived the "second blessing" to be a spiritual replacement of one's human nature with the nature of Christ himself.

Robert Smith experienced the second blessing in "true Methodist fashion" at a Holiness Association camp in 1867. His wife offered this description of her husband's entry into sanctifying grace:

> Suddenly from head to foot he had been shaken by what seemed like a magnetic thrill of heavenly delight, and floods of glory seemed to pour through him, soul and body, with the inward assurance that this was the longed-for Baptism of the Holy Spirit.[35]

The Smiths began to hold preaching-missions at home and abroad, spending several years in England as speakers on the holiness circuit. They made no secret of their universalist sentiments, a fact that seems not to have diminished their popularity, although certain holiness leaders urged them to keep their universalism to themselves.[36] Eventually, Robert Smith's deteriorating physical and mental condition created great stress for the couple, and they were forced to return to the United States in 1875. Although they remained popular with the evangelical public, the Smiths minimized their holiness activities after their return to the states. Hannah Smith concluded that God intended them "to be good human beings in this world, and nothing more."[37] Her influence on the Holiness movement was considerable, offering a new morphology for continued experience of the Holy Spirit.

Representative Holiness Movements

Holiness experience led to a variety of new sects and denominations, each with their own approaches to the theological and experiential elements of entire sanctification. The Wesleyan Methodist Connection split from the Methodist Episcopal Church in 1843 in opposition to a continuing tolerance for slaveholders in the parent body. Its leaders also decried the use of alcohol and participation in "secret societies" as detriments to holy living.[38] The Free

Methodist Church was formed in 1860, supporting abolitionism and an ethical code so rigorous that its members were sometimes known as "Nazarites."[39] The group forbade the use of liquor and tobacco, theatre going, membership in secret societies, extravagant dress, and expensive jewelry—convictions that were outward signs of personal and communal holiness.[40]

In 1867 the National Camp Meeting Association for the Promotion of Holiness was formed in Vineland, New Jersey, in an effort "to glorify God in building up the church in holiness and saving sinners."[41] Post–Civil War era holiness camp meetings spread throughout the country. Melvin Dieter cited a description of the Spirit's descent at a late nineteenth century Texas holiness revival: "There is hardly a moment when from the quivering voice of holy women, grizzely *[sic]* good men and even children, the throne of [G]od is not dynamited with burning and firey *[sic]* supplications, all of one tenor and one purpose, that of the coming of the Holy Ghost."[42] In May 1885 the First General Holiness Assembly convened in Chicago, with this doctrinal affirmation:

> Entire Sanctification more commonly designated as "sanctification," "holiness," "Christian perfection," or "perfect love," represents that second definite stage in Christian experience wherein, by the baptism of the Holy Spirit, administered by Jesus Christ, and received instantaneously by faith, the justified believer is delivered from inbred sin, and consequently is saved from all unholy tempers, cleansed from all moral defilement, made perfect in love and introduced into full and abiding fellowship with God.[43]

The statement represents a concise, relatively inclusive approach to the second blessing that would be approved or improved upon by numerous holiness groups, some of which extended the baptism of the Holy Spirit into more emotional enthusiasms.

By the 1890s, one emerging faction movement involved the work of Benjamin Hardin Irwin of the Iowa Holiness Association, who labeled entire sanctification a "baptism of fire." In 1898 the Fire-Baptized Holiness Association was formed in South Carolina, drawing constituents from holiness associations in at least nine states. In central Appalachia, Baptists near Camp

Creek, North Carolina, held revivals in 1896 that produced dramatic emotional outbursts such as "weeping, shouting, trance, and ecstasy." Some even claimed to have experienced healing and glossolalia.[44] Other groups such as the South Kansas Fire Baptized Holiness Association affirmed baptism by fire as a "third work of grace," beyond baptism of the Holy Spirit.

The Church of God (Anderson, Indiana) was formed in 1881 by those who linked Wesleyan holiness with Restorationist ecclesiology in hopes of creating a church united beyond denominational divisions. They sought to restore the church to its New Testament origins within the spirituality of holiness sanctification.[45] The Church of the Nazarene (1895) became one of the largest Holiness denominations, stressing conversion, sanctification, and a rigorous ethical code. It brought together several smaller holiness sects.

Pentecostals: Spirit Baptism, Healing, and Glossolalia

By the early twentieth century, some within the Holiness movement suggested that healing and glossolalia (speaking in tongues) were definitive, outward manifestations of the work of the Holy Spirit for both sanctification and spiritual empowerment. This became the basis for Pentecostalism, a distinctive Protestant movement characterized by ecstatic religious experiences; alternative denominational groups; and new, often controversial, approaches to justification, sanctification, healing, and evangelical identity.

Defining and tracing Pentecostal religious experience is a complex endeavor. In *Theological Roots of Pentecostalism*, Donald W. Dayton observed that the Pentecostal movement did not begin *de novo* but was an elaborate expression of charismatic theology and religious exercises (glossolalia and healing, for example) evident throughout Christian and American history. Such spiritual gifts were evident among the early Shaker and Mormon movements as well as in early Holiness communities.[46] He noted that, while speaking in tongues and healings were characteristic of the Pentecostal phenomenon, the theological and doctrinal interpretations of those gifts of the Spirit were not uniform among many Pentecostal sub-groups. Dayton found "clues" to

Pentecostals' collective identity in a phrase from the "Statement of Truth" of the Pentecostal Fellowship of North America. It affirmed: "We believe that the full gospel includes holiness of heart and life, healing for the body and baptism in the Holy Spirit with the initial evidence of speaking in other tongues as the spirit gives utterance."[47]

Roberts Mapes Anderson suggested that differences over the experience of and theology for Spirit baptism divided the Holiness movement into two major and one "minor faction."[48] These included persons in the "Wesleyan wing" who believed that Spirit baptism and sanctification were singular moments of grace following conversion (justification) that offered deliverance over sinful actions evident in the lives of professing Christians. Another group, which included the British-based Keswick Movement, maintained that sanctification was an ongoing post-conversion spiritual experience, in which the baptism of the Holy Spirit served as "an enduement of [spiritual] power." A smaller segment of holiness believers, many related to the Fire-Baptized Holiness community, identified sanctification "as a second act of grace" and Spirit baptism as a third empowering spiritual experience.[49] Pentecostalism thus represents a community of diverse movements built on the possibility of conversion, sanctification, and a concern for the poor—experiences and actions often expressed in a variety of ecstatic, charismatic gifts and signs.

Grant Wacker traced three early theories of Pentecostal origins. A "compensation model" suggested that Pentecostalism appealed to persons who, unable to attain certain material accoutrements of "worldly" success, retreated into an "otherworldly" theology and mindset based in "supernatural religion." A "functional model" viewed Pentecostalism as offering strategies aimed less at escaping adversity than providing "a creative resource for dealing with it." A "mobilization model" understood Pentecostalism as shaped by the ability of its leaders to engage constituents in institution-building, an effort that "tumbled into obscurity when they failed to keep those structures intact."[50]

Wacker offered another approach, insisting that "*the genius of the Pentecostal movement lay in its ability to hold two seemingly incompatible impulses in productive tension*."[51] Those impulses combined the "primitive and the pragmatic," an intense (primitivist) desire to encounter the Divine, an encounter confirmed by certain external "signs"; and a pragmatic capacity to connect "within the social and cultural expectations of the age."[52] Pentecostals built on the revivalistic tradition of evangelical conversion, extending the process of holiness-sanctification through Spirit baptism verified through certain outward signs including speaking in tongues, healing, and Spirit-inspired visions and revelations. Over time, glossolalia became less a once-for-all experience than a continuing sign of the Spirit's power, external evidence of God's abiding presence in a willing vessel.

Early Pentecostal Experiences: Charles Fox Parham

The origins of a distinct Pentecostal movement are usually traced to Kansas and a school maintained by the holiness evangelist Charles Fox Parham (1873–1929). Parham's encounters with experiential religion began with his conversion at the age of thirteen, when he claimed to have experienced a light from heaven that "penetrated, thrilling every fibre [*sic*]" of my being; making me know by experimental knowledge what Peter knew of old, that He [Jesus] was the Christ, the Son of the Living God."[53] Later on he became convinced that he had miraculously healed himself of a heart condition, discarding medical prescriptions and obtaining a cure through the power of prayer.[54] Aided by representatives of the American Bible Society, Parham secured a large house near Topeka, Kansas, where he established the "College of Bethel," attracting a student body composed of a small group of ministers and community workers whom he challenged to search the scriptures for insights into experiencing the power of the Holy Ghost. With particular attention to the Pentecost texts in the second chapter of the book of Acts, the students concluded that Spirit baptism was manifested by and inseparable from speaking in tongues.

After weeks of prayer and study, the formative Pentecostal moment occurred on January 1, 1901. Parham reported on a student named Agnes Ozman, who

> asked that hands might be laid upon her to receive the Holy Spirit as she hoped to go to foreign fields [as a missionary]. At first I [Parham] refused not having the experience myself. Then being further pressed to do it humbly in the name of Jesus, I laid my hand upon her head and prayed. I had scarcely repeated three dozen sentences when a glory fell upon her, a halo seemed to surround her head and face, and she began speaking in the Chinese language, and was unable to speak English for three days.[55]

Some observers contended that they witnessed tongues of fire over the heads of other ministerial participants. The next day, after a lengthy period of prayer, Parham himself received the Spirit with the gift of tongues.[56]

Glossolalia was not new in the history of the church. What was new was the insistence that it was a normative sign of the experience of the second blessing, a practice soon institutionalized into numerous Pentecostal groups. Parham viewed the experience as a reassertion of "the Apostolic Faith," concluding in an article from 1902:

> Christ did not leave his believing children without signs of distinction to follow them that the world might know who were Christians and who were not. Neither did he send forth his servants to preach vague speculative theories of a world to come, but…feeding the hungry, clothing the naked, healing the sick, casting out devils; speaking with new tongues; confirming the word of inward benefit—wrought in Jesus Christ—by these outward visible signs.[57]

Controversy over Ozman's experience and claims regarding glossolalia quickly descended on Parham and his supporters. The facility used by Bethel College was sold, forcing Parham to move the work from Topeka to Kansas City. When that location proved difficult, Parham and his wife, Sarah Thistlewaite Parham, took to the road espousing the truth of Spirit baptism, as evidenced in glossolalia, healing, and the gift of prophecy.[58] In 1905 they established another school in Houston, Texas, to which an African-American preacher named William Joseph Seymour (1870–1922) applied. With some trepidation about violating the strict racial boundaries of the day, Parham approved Seymour's admission, thus opening the door to another significant leader of early Pentecostalism.

In 1906, anticipating but lacking an experience of glossolalia, Seymour sensed a call to begin a new ministry in Los Angeles, writing:

> It was the divine call that brought me from Houston, Texas, to Los Angeles. The Lord put it in the heart of one of the saints in Los Angeles to write to me that she felt the Lord would have me come over here and do a work, and I came, for I felt it was the leading of the Lord. The Lord sent the means, and I came to take charge of a mission on Santa Fe Street, and one night they locked the door against me, and afterwards got Bro. Roberts, the president of the Holiness Association, to come down and settle the doctrine of the Baptism with the Holy Ghost, that it was simply sanctification. He came down and a good many holiness preachers with him, and they stated that sanctification was the baptism with the Holy Ghost. But yet they did not have the evidence of the second chapter of Acts, for when the disciples were all filled with the Holy Ghost, they spoke in tongues as the Spirit gave utterance. After the president heard me speak of what the true baptism of the Holy Ghost was, he said he wanted it too, and told me when I had received it to let him know. So I received it and let him know. The beginning of the Pentecost started in a cottage prayer meeting at 214 Bonnie Brae, [Los Angeles].[59]

Seymour first preached at the Santa Fe Holiness Mission, declaring without hesitation that the baptism of the Holy Ghost was inseparable from the outward sign of glossolalia. Members of the church agreed that the tongues experience could accompany Spirit baptism but disagreed over whether it was the normative requirement for the second blessing. Discord escalated into animosity when Seymour was literally locked out of the building upon returning for another service.[60] His rapidly expanding group of supporters moved their meetings to a warehouse on Azusa Street, establishing the Apostolic Faith Mission, a site that became the center of immediate Spirit baptism and historic Pentecostal identity. The Azusa Street revivals were characterized by Spirit-infused enthusiasms that caused congregants to shout, become slain in the Spirit, offer and receive healing, and speak in tongues. Seymour became the dynamic leader of the new movement, preaching, teaching, and healing. He soon established *The Apostolic Faith*, a periodical that attained a circulation of some fifty thousand people and documented continuing experiences of Spirit baptism.[61]

Frank Bartleman (1871–1936), another early participant in the Los Angeles revivals, described another ecstatic phenomenon known as the "new song," a peculiarly musical phenomenon "exercised, as the Spirit moved the possessors, either in solo fashion, or by the company. It was sometimes without words, other times in 'tongues.'... It seemed to still criticism and opposition, and was hard for even wicked men to gainsay or ridicule."[62] Bartleman labeled revival services at the Azusa Street mission as "continuous," a place where "people came to meet God." He concluded: "In that old building, with its low rafters and bare floors, God took strong men and women to pieces, and put them together again, for His glory. It was a tremendous overhauling process. Pride and self-assertion, self-importance and self-esteem, could not survive there. The religious ego preached its own funeral sermon quickly."[63]

Controversy over the nature and theology of Pentecostal religious experience developed almost immediately. One such division occurred when William Durham (1873–1912), a white man and former Baptist, filled with the Spirit at the Azusa Street Mission, began to exercise his considerable pulpit skills there. Bartleman commented that, "The fire began to fall at old Azusa as at the beginning."[64] Durham set himself against William Seymour, actions that led Seymour to have him locked out of the Mission. With a sizable portion of the Azusa congregation (including Frank Bartleman), Durham established a new Gospel Mission Church (North Avenue Mission) that soon drew large crowds to its ecstatic worship. Durham denied that the baptism of the Spirit required two to three dramatic spiritual crises, preferring instead a doctrine of the "Finished Work" of Christ by which justification and sanctification were united in the one initial experience of conversion.[65] Spirit baptism brought both unity and division as early Pentecostals sought to support ecstatic gifts with biblical orthodoxy.

Defining Sanctification and "Unknown Tongues"

From the beginning, Pentecostalism reflected a particular type of evangelical Restorationism. Like other revivalistic evangelicals, they affirmed belief in the inerrancy of scripture and the need for personal regeneration (conversion), along with Christ's virgin birth, sacrificial atonement, bodily resurrection, and premillennial second coming. From their holiness roots, Pentecostals insisted that a post-conversion second blessing (baptism of the Holy Spirit) was required of all who sought a deeper life of Christian discipleship and devotion, born of perfectionism, a continued cleansing from sin. Unlike many evangelicals, however, Pentecostals strongly believed that the gift of the Holy Spirit, made known in power on the day of Pentecost, had been restored to the church in these latter days, as evidenced in such signs as healing from disease and speaking in tongues.

Glossolalia was itself an overwhelming religious experience that confirmed Spirit baptism. The particulars of that gift were diverse and seemed to evolve with the Pentecostal movement itself. Agnes Ozman claimed to have been empowered by the Spirit to speak in the Chinese language (for at least three days), and both Charles Fox Parham and William Seymour apparently agreed that the fullest confirmation of glossolalia produced a foreign language in which to preach the gospel. Vinson Synan suggested that the early Pentecostals made "no distinction . . . between ecstatic utterances, known languages, or unknown tongues," but that they did differentiate between tongues as the necessary sign of the baptism of the Holy Spirit, and the "Gift of Tongues" that could engage believers throughout their lives.[66] The latter was a type of prayer language that denoted a specific encounter between God and the sanctified believer. Some might receive tongues that empowered a new linguistic ability; in others the gift might be an unknown tongue given only to a single believer. When prophecy was at hand, the Holy Spirit would inspire another person with the gift of interpretation (translation) for the edification of the entire congregation. Robert Mapes Anderson noted that, often, "messages in tongues and interpretations were at times used to introduce or legitimate controversial doctrines and practices."[67] Spirit-inspired prophecies delivered through glossolalia became one way of establishing or confirming the veracity of new revelations, ideas, and practices.

Scholars of Pentecostalism differ as to the centrality of glossolalia in the formation of the movement. Grant Wacker contended that while glossolalia remains a significant element of Pentecostal religious experience, there is evidence that "fewer than half of first-generation converts actually spoke in tongues."[68] Likewise, some early Pentecostal leaders placed glossolalia among various identifying marks of their new tradition, along with personal conversion, healing, and baptismal immersion. Wacker acknowledged that while these "qualifications" were present, there is no doubt that the gift of tongues became the defining outward sign of Pentecostal identity both inside and outside the movement.[69] Vinson Synan wrote that from the beginning of the Pentecostal movement, "tongues were the only initial evidence of the reception of the Holy Spirit," a fact that "gave Pentecostalism its greatest impetus."[70]

Allan Anderson insisted that for Charles Fox Parham, the movement originated in "a particular doctrine of a particular experience" (speaking in tongues as languages), while for William Seymour, its origins rested "in its oral, missionary nature and its ability to break down barriers, [all] emphases of the Azusa Street revival." Seymour apparently rejected Parham's idea that tongues were the absolute sign of Spirit baptism. Anderson and Walter Hollenweger agreed that, "Seymour and Azusa Street eclipsed" Parham with the insistence that the coming of the Spirit was a sign of God's intent to reconcile and equalize racial, class, and global divisions.[71]

Donald Dayton challenged the idea that glossolalia was the determining characteristic of the Pentecostal movement. He wrote, "The attention given to the practice of glossolalia has diverted interpreters from theological categories of analysis." This led many to believe that the gift of tongues was best understood as "an abnormal response to some form of 'deprivation,' whether sociological or psychological."[72] Amid these differences it is clear that glossolalia was and remains a major element in Pentecostal religious experience. As charismatic gifts spread to other non-Pentecostal communions, many Christians both Protestant and Catholic have claimed similar encounters with the Holy Spirit.

Healing and the Holy Spirit

The relationship between spiritual and physical healing is as old as the Christian church, beginning with the ministry of Jesus. Prayers for healing, often coupled with the chrism, or anointing with oil, are vital elements of Catholic and Protestant traditions alike. Yet the link between sanctification, perfection, and wholeness of spirit and body has been particularly significant within Holiness and Pentecostal communities.

For early holiness devotees, religious experience had implications for addressing and alleviating physical suffering. W. E. Boardman, a Presbyterian holiness leader, noted that some ten years following his conversion, "the Lord Jesus graciously revealed Himself to me... and brought me to accept Him and rest in Him each moment for present deliverance." This "new Light," Boardman said, brought with it "the office work of our gracious Lord as Healer."[73] In 1881 holiness writer Carrie Judd Montgomery founded the journal *Triumphs of Faith*, addressing a portion of her first editorial to "my dear invalid readers," admonishing them that "what is true of this precious spiritual healing is likewise true of physical healing by the 'Great Physician.'"[74] Montgomery and other holiness leaders believed that the atonement of Christ had significant implications for both spiritual and physical healing.[75]

Robert Mapes Anderson looked askance at many faith healing claims put forth by first-generation Pentecostals. He traced the use of external healing rituals, such as laying on hands, anointing with oil, and the utilization of "prayer handkerchiefs," and concluded that from the early days of the movement "every manner of disease and disability was alleged to have been cured." Anderson concluded that "in the intense emotional atmosphere of Pentecostal meetings, people suffering from functional disorders caused by psychic and nervous disturbance could no doubt experience 'cures' that are to be explained by the same causes."[76] Nonetheless, faith healing soon became a hallmark of Spirit possession among Pentecostals.

Pentecostalism in the American South: Revivals (and Race)

Tongues, healing, and other Spirit manifestations were not new to holiness groups in the American South. The 1906 Camp Creek holiness revival and similar meetings in North Carolina included glossolalia among many signs of the Spirit's presence. As news of events at Azusa Street circulated, a southern holiness preacher named G. B. Cashwell (18601916) traveled to Los Angeles to investigate. Stunned by the racially mixed Azusa Street congregation, Cashwell initially assumed that the emotional outbursts were more race-based than supernatural. Yet his own Spirit baptism occurred after he received the laying on of hands from an African-American, an act he described as making "chills to go down my spine," defying his deeply embedded racial bias.[77] Returning to the South as a Pentecostal preacher, Cashwell conducted a revival in Dunn, North Carolina, that may have marked the beginnings of Southern Pentecostalism. In the January 2, 1907, edition of *Apostolic Faith*, Cashwell observed that the "Spirit is being poured out here in Dunn as never before," noting:

> Many have come from South Carolina and Georgia and have received their Pentecost and gone back and there are some have received the baptism. . . . Nearly every service someone received their Pentecost and spoke in tongues. Some of our preachers have preached, sung and prayed in unknown tongues and without speaking a word of English, have awakened sinners. Several colored people have received their real Pentecost and speak in tongues. God has wonderfully blest some of the people with the gift of song.

Cashwell also reported that one "colored sister, a school teacher, received the Pentecost the other night and spoke in tongues for some time. She had manifested a call to foreign fields. All the people of God are one here."[78] Cashwell's early racial concerns had apparently taken a more positive turn, evidenced in various racially mixed revival meetings he led in North Carolina.

By 1908, Cashwell had convinced a majority in the Fire-Baptized Holiness Church to accept a Pentecostal interpretation of the baptism of the Holy Spirit. In 1911 the Pentecostal Holiness Church and the Fire-Baptized Holiness Church merged under the name Pentecostal Holiness Church. A group of Free-Will Holiness Baptists, drawn to Cashwell's theology of sanctification, formed the Pentecostal Free-Will Baptist Church, attracting numerous Southern Baptists to their number.[79] By 1907, Pentecostal views were accepted by Tennessean A. J. Tomlinson (1865–1943), who received Spirit baptism during one of Cashwell's sermons. Tomlinson, a founder of the Church of God, Cleveland, Tennessee, recalled that when the Spirit fell he was laid out "in a heap on the rostrum at... Cashwell's feet."[80]

In her study of *Appalachian Mountain Religion*, Deborah V. McCauley emphasized the unique role that mountain Baptist and Pentecostal traditions played in shaping indigenous religious identity in central Appalachia.[81] She insisted that those religious communities had often been overlooked or dismissed by the denominations that attempted to Christianize the region, as if they were devoid of religious community. McCauley concluded: "If anything, mountain religion has been a radical sign of contradiction within the broader religious culture."[82] Through interviews with mountain Pentecostals such as Brother Coy Miser, McCauley observed that Spirit-laden outbursts were beneficial for both the empowered individual and the worshiping community. She wrote that

> ecstatic religious experience or "blessings"... centering on the individual—were not simply a product of self-indulgence or total self-absorption fragmenting the worship service. Instead, such actions—individuals shouting, dancing, being slain in the Spirit, and so on—had the effect of being appreciated as "a blessing" also to those who witnessed them.[83]

Miser and other mountain preachers believed that these experiences "edify the church" because they were grounded in "the power of God through the Holy Spirit."[84] When McCauley asked Miser to describe "what it was like getting saved," he responded:

> I just got such a blessing, there was just something come down over me, you know, and I felt so good.... I was knocking the pots and pans off the wall. They run in to see what was the matter and it was me getting a blessing from the Lord.... I just had a good feeling because it's unspeakable, untalkable. You just can't tell it, but anyway that's when I changed and started living rightly.[85]

Appalachian Pentecostalism paralleled and distinguished itself from the larger Pentecostal context, particularly through independent mountain churches.

"Confirming the Word:" The Pentecostal Serpent-Handlers

Perhaps the most famous (or infamous) expression of Pentecostal religious experience in Appalachia is associated with the small group of serpent-handling churches and individuals that continue to exist in the region. The movement probably originated in the early days of Pentecostal presence in Appalachia, linked to a preacher named George Hensley, an illiterate Pentecostal evangelist influenced by the work of A. J. Tomlinson and the Church of God, Cleveland, Tennessee. Sometime in 1909, Hensley apparently introduced the practice at the Grasshopper Church of God in George Town, Tennessee, near Chattanooga.[86] Many believe that Hensley's first wife, Amanda, read and interpreted the scriptures to him, including insights into Mark 16:9-20, the so-called long ending of that Gospel.[87] The portion of that text cited most by serpent handlers includes verses 17-20 and reads:

> And these signs shall follow them that believe; In my name shall they cast out devils; they shall speak with new tongues; They shall take up serpents; and if they drink any deadly thing, it shall not hurt them; they shall lay hands on the sick, and they shall recover. So then after the Lord had spoken unto them, he was received up into heaven, and sat on the right hand of God. And they went forth, and preached every where, the Lord working with them, and confirming the word with signs following. (Mark 16:16-20 KJV)

Twenty-first century serpent-handler Jimmy Morrow concluded: "Serpent handling is a sign to confirm the Word. If a preacher is preaching the Word and feels the anointing to handle a serpent, Jesus Christ will give him victory over it. It takes the anointing of God to do the five signs."[88] A particular type of religious experience was required of those who felt "anointed" to act on the "signs" delineated in Mark's gospel.

The five signs identified in this passage include three that are accepted by most Pentecostal communions—casting out demons, speaking in tongues, and healing the sick. The other two signs impel serpent handlers to "take up" live poisonous reptiles and drink various types of poison when they feel the anointing of the Spirit to do so. They believe that their actions are both special encounters with the power of God and verification of biblical truth, "confirming the Word" for the rest of the church. They link biblical literalism with Spirit baptism. Serpent handling preacher Robert Grooms commented:

> The Word is spiritually understood. And without the Spirit of the Lord, nobody can understand it. You can read the Bible, and without the Spirit you can make many meanings out of it, many things. But with the Spirit of God, you get the true meaning. That's what's wrong with a lot of churches today. They don't have enough of the Spirit to understand what the Bible really means.[89]

Serpent-handling worship is often characterized by energetic preaching, pulsating music, shouting, speaking in tongues, dancing in the Spirit, and handling one or more of the poison-inducing reptiles. Persons who are bitten seldom seek medical care. Those who recover often suffer significant neurological damage to limbs or physical functions. At least a hundred people or more have died from snakebites or from drinking poison since the movement began. Much has been written about their peculiar expression of Pentecostal religious experience.[90] Their peculiar religious enthusiasm and biblical exegesis leads them to believe that they are confirming the word by exercising spiritual gifts that belonged to Jesus and the early apostles.

Sister Aimee: The Feminine and the Spirit

A well-known representative of Finished Work Pentecostalism was Aimee Semple McPherson (1890–1944), one of America's most prominent female preachers and founder of the International Church of the Foursquare Gospel (1927). Born in Canada to parents involved in the Canadian Salvation Army, McPherson claimed that her mother dedicated her to God when she was six months old, setting the stage for numerous supernatural childhood experiences.[91]

At the age of seventeen she was converted in a revival led by her future husband, Robert Semple, an occasion when she heard him speak in "other tongues." His sermons, delivered in tongues known and unknown, represented to her "the voice of God thundering into my soul awful words of conviction and condemnation."[92] McPherson recalled that after days of spiritual struggle with sin and her need for salvation, she cried out, "Oh, Lord God, be merciful to me, a sinner!" and received an immediate spiritual transformation, in which, "darkness passed away and light entered."[93] Soon she began to pray for an infilling of the Holy Spirit. In her memoir, *This Is That: Personal Experiences, Sermons and Writings of Aimee Semple McPherson*, she wrote: "Oh, how earnestly I sought the baptism of the Spirit. Sometimes when people come to the altar now and sit themselves down in a comfortable position, prop their heads up on one hand, and begin to ask God in a languid, indifferent way for the Spirit, it seems to me that they do not know what real seeking is."[94] At the age of eighteen she married Robert Semple and the two went as missionaries to China. Both contracted malaria almost on arrival, and Robert Semple died after only a few months. Aimee returned to the United States after giving birth to their only child, Roberta. Soon after, she met and married Harold McPherson at almost the same time she experienced a call to preach. She wrote that "the *Call of God* was on my soul and I could not get away from it. For this cause I had been brought into the world. With each throb of my heart I could hear a voice saying: "Preach the Word! Preach the Word! Will you go?…And I would throw myself on my knees tearfully sobbing."[95] Acquiescing to that call, she later recalled: "Oh, don't you ever tell me that a woman cannot be called to preach the Gospel! If any man ever went through one-hundredth part of the hell on earth that I lived in, those months when out of God's will and work, they would never say that again."[96]

She and Harold McPherson entered the Pentecostal preaching circuit, conducting revivals and tent meetings across the country. Sister Aimee, as she now called herself, reported that in one Florida tent meeting a Spirit-endued man "spoke in Hebrew and a Hebrew scholar who was present, heard and understood," and two men were said to have been healed, "one of a broken arm ... the other of a broken hand," and "one sister was healed instantly of cancer."[97] By 1918 Harold McPherson had had enough, abandoning the revival circuit and their marriage. A divorce was granted in 1921.

Returning to Los Angeles in 1918, Sister Aimee began raising funds for a new church that would become the center of her style of Pentecostalism. The Angelus Temple was dedicated in January 1923, a five-thousand-seat auditorium where she often preached to capacity crowds. The International Church of the Foursquare Gospel was founded in the Temple along with one of the first religious radio stations in the United States. McPherson's national reputation was not without controversy, evident in her various relationships with men, a strange "kidnapping" story, and her personal eccentricities. Nonetheless, she brought Pentecostal religious experience out into the public square, with a "foursquare gospel" that stressed salvation, baptism in the Holy Spirit, healing, and the immediacy of Christ's second coming.[98]

McPherson navigated the landscape of her time by working to avoid theological controversies associated with the Fundamentalist-Modernist debates that characterized much of the early twentieth century. Yet she did not hesitate to express her theological views regarding the nature of religious experience and the gifts of the Spirit. In a sermon entitled, "Covet Earnestly Spiritual Gifts," she delineated certain gospel empowerments available to those who were "recipients of full salvation, and the baptism of the Holy Ghost."[99] These gifts included the power to heal, with McPherson commenting that "cancers, tumors, tuberculosis, all manner of sickness has [*sic*] been healed instantaneously in answer to prayer right in our meetings." Full gospel believers could also witness such miracles as seeing "broken bones instantaneously and miraculously set and healed in answer to prayer."[100] The Spirit-anointed one could "discern the difference" between good and evil spirits, speak in languages they had never learned, and interpret "unknown tongues" as a word of instruction for the church.[101] McPherson fought racism and drug trafficking, founded a denomination, and insisted that women could be called to the pastorate. Allan Anderson wrote that McPherson "was the prototype of a new kind of US American Pentecostal that was able to use and adapt the prevailing popular culture of its day for its own purposes."[102] Her personal difficulties ultimately included a divorce from her third husband, David Hutton, and alienation from both her mother and her daughter. On September 27, 1944, she was found dead from a sleeping pill overdose that was declared accidental. Some fifty thousand people filed by her coffin as she lay in state at the Angelus Temple.[103] In the end, Sister Aimee Semple McPherson anticipated aspects of the healing revivals of the later twentieth century as well as the use of the media by a variety of Pentecostals who became radio and television personalities.

Faith Healing and Its Accompanying Evangelists

Religious experiences and faith healing did not begin with the Pentecostals. The seeds were sown in the Holiness movement of the nineteenth century. Multiple evangelicals in multiple denominations asserted the links between salvation and healing. Alexander Dowie (1847–1907) was a holiness preacher sometimes known as "the father of healing revivalism." He introduced the concept and practice of divine healing as early as 1882 in his native Scotland, before coming to the United States in 1888. He founded the Christian Catholic Church in 1896 and later claimed to be a reincarnation of the prophet Elijah. Dowie, a major force in the formation of the Divine Healing Association (1890), asserted that "entire sanctification" involved salvation, baptism in the Holy Spirit, and "healing through faith in Jesus."[104]

Episcopalian Carrie Judd Montgomery (1858–1946), inspired by an African-American holiness woman named Mrs. Mix, moved from Holiness to Pentecostalism through interaction with the Azusa Street mission. Her *Triumphs of Faith* magazine began with an editorial addressed to her readers that asserted, "Christ bore our sickness as well as our sins, and if we may reckon ourselves free from the one, why not from the other?"[105] For many devotees of the Holiness and Pentecostal movements, Christ's atonement was efficacious for the forgiveness of sin and promise of physical healing. Donald Dayton called attention to the work of R. Kelso Carter (1849–1928), a holiness writer, rancher, and physician, who wrote *The Atonement for Sin and Sickness* in 1884, emphasizing that "he who finds in Jesus the perfect cleansing of the soul and the keeping power against all sin, can be equally consistent in placing his body beneath the same wonderful salvation."[106]

Early Pentecostals often equated physical illness with demon possession and supported the belief that exorcism would bring healing of body and spirit for the "possessed" individual. Robert Mapes Anderson suggested that the terms "healing" and "casting out demons" were often used synonymously in early Pentecostalism when "all kinds of diseases were driven out of the bodies of men, women and children."[107] He contended that for Pentecostals the relationship between illness and healing centered in "an underlying animistic outlook so thoroughgoing that it came close at times to be a total explanation for human behavior," equating demons with all forms of sickness.[108]

This healing phenomenon became even more pronounced by the mid-twentieth century and the development of healing revivals and their representative evangelists. David Edwin Harrell wrote that 1947 marked a period when healing revivals erupted "with astonishing force" on the American scene. He cited John T. Nichol's comment that efforts aimed at curing the sick were "revived on a scale hitherto unknown."[109]

The initiator of the 1947 healing revivals was a remarkable log-cabin-born Kentucky preacher named William Branham (1909–1965). Ordained as an Independent Baptist and pastor of a small Baptist church in Jeffersonville, Indiana, Branham was by all accounts an unimpressive figure, who nonetheless "held audiences spellbound with tales of constant communication with God and angels." With uncanny sensitivity to hurting persons and a warm left hand anointed for healing, Branham "discerned the diseases of the sick and pronounced them healed."[110]

Branham's religious experience began with conversion, baptism in the Holy Spirit, and call to ministry. His first tent revival in Jeffersonville ended with a large baptismal service in the Ohio River. There on June 11, 1933, he claimed the first stage of a Spirit-induced anointing that endowed him with prophetic insights and healing skills. Branham recalled that in the midst of one of the baptisms a light shown just above him and, as "hundreds and hundreds of people on the bank" looked on, "a Voice" spoke from the light. It declared: "As John the Baptist was sent for the forerunner of the first coming of Christ, you've got a... Message that will bring forth the forerunning of the Second Coming of Christ." He reported: "And it liked to a-scared me to death."[111]

Branham moved more deeply into the Pentecostal movement, preaching revivals, baptizing, and proclaiming the imminent return of Christ. The definitive experience occurred in 1946 when Branham claimed to have been visited by an angel who "would weigh about two hundred pounds, clothed in a white robe." Admonishing him to "fear not," the angel acknowledged that he had been sent by God with the news that Branham's "peculiar life" had been ordained "to take a gift of divine healing to the people of the world. IF YOU WILL BE SINCERE, AND CAN GET THE PEOPLE TO BELIEVE YOU, NOTHING SHALL STAND BEFORE YOUR PRAYER, NOT EVEN CANCER."[112] This visitation marked Branham's own decision to embark on the healing ministry as his primary calling. It also exhibited the initial phase of what many called the "healing and charismatic revivals" of the twentieth century, a phenomenon that included preachers such as A. A. Allen, John Osteen, Jimmy Swaggart, and of course, Oral Roberts.[113]

Like others in the earlier holiness tradition, Branham believed that Christ's atonement opened the door to physical as well as spiritual healing and that demons were responsible for all illness. After experiencing the baptism of the Holy Spirit, he came to believe that the restoration of Pentecost was an empowering of the church with the gift of healing. Those who wished to be healed should first experience conversion through faith in Jesus Christ. Once salvation was secure, God was "obligated" to heal as promised in scripture.[114] God was the agent of healing, as confirmed by the testimony of the angel who brought word of his calling. Branham's gift of healing was evident in two powerful signs: his discernment of illness by means of "a vibration of his left hand" and a peculiar ability to know the "secrets of a person's heart."[115]

Branham's Pentecostal experientialism, distinguished by dreams, visions, revelations, and healings, led many to consider him a seer or prophet. He claimed to be able to foretell the pending death of audience members and to discern the specific sins that stifled healing in particular individuals. In one revival he called the exact name and birthplace of an audience member, and diagnosed her illness—two stomach tumors—on the spot. One observer noted that when that happened "pandemonium broke out among the great crowd. It seemed that everyone was weeping and sobbing and shouting all at once." The observer added: "Something happened to me inside, and I know that I shall never be the same again."[116]

William Branham died on December 29, 1965, from injuries sustained in an automobile accident near Abilene, Texas. His death stunned his national and international followers, some of whom apparently anticipated his resurrection from the dead. A delay in burial was less because of that possibility than that his spouse, also injured in the accident, might be able to attend the graveside service. Branham's body was buried shortly after Easter on April 11, 1966.[117] Harrell concluded that Branham was

> preeminently the visionary of the healing revival. He lived in a miraculous world. Simple almost to the point of transparency, Branham ministered to a generation of credulous people, a man of his times. To a Pentecostal world that craved marvels in the years immediately after World War II, he offered his sincerity and his fantastic array of personal spiritual experiences. To the modish charismatic movement of the 1960s, Branham was an outdated figure.[118]

Healing revivalists thrived in the post-war years, with services that included emotional and highly colorful preaching, dramatic conversions, and "Holy Ghost baptism," as well as a many outbursts of charismatic gifts. The latter events often caused participants to "fall out," throwing them to the floor in ecstatic states. Healing was in many respects the central experience of these meetings with the "healing line" as an organized way of bringing invalids to the evangelist. Harrell wrote that evidence of healing skills varied with the specific evangelist but often involved, "a feeling" in the hand, "an audible voice" of revelation, visions, "the presence of an angelic healer," or other evidences of the "miraculous."[119]

Pentecostals and the "Prosperity Gospel": Religious Experience as Entitlement

Pentecostalism shaped a phenomenon known as the "Prosperity Gospel," a religio-economic movement offering options for moving from spiritual sanctification to material success. Harrell, an early analyst of what some called the Health/Wealth Gospel, wrote:

> From the beginning the [Pentecostal] evangelists taught that prosperity was a blessing that belonged to God's people. Individual prosperity, however, could be expected only if one gave generously to God's work. As early as 1954 Oral Roberts was predicting a sevenfold return to those who supported his ministry: "And God impressed me to pray that our contributors will have their money multiplied to them a perfect number of times, putting back into their hands every dollar their needs require."[120]

He concluded: "By the 1960s, the promise of prosperity had come to rival healing as a major theme of the revival."[121] The Prosperity Gospel was underway. The grainy "healing lines" of the early Oral Roberts films are dramatic indications that the people who came for healing were, by and large, the individuals who lacked health insurance, had little money for medical care, and no hope for health, wealth, or salvation beyond the promises of the New Testament and the touch of Oral Roberts's warm right hand.

The Prosperity Gospel has many antecedents. First, it links salvation from sin with salvation from poverty, a response to American consumerism and economic disparity. Surveying "the ethics and aesthetics of black televangelism, Jonathan Walton observed: "A God-sanctioned message of financial liberation and prosperity resonates with many blacks who have seen their parents and grandparents stay at the bottom of American's capitalist economy because of this country's history of racial apartheid and who themselves desire a larger slice of America's economic pie."[122] Since Jesus tarried and the millennium appeared less immediate than previously perceived, then why not shake off poverty and live a little better in this world? The material success of certain preachers became a model for all who would live faithfully and thus reap a reward.[123]

Second, another cultural influence involved the power of positive thinking promoted by secularists the likes of Dale Carnegie (*How to Win Friends and Influence People*) and religionists such as Norman Vincent Peale (*The Power of Positive Thinking*) and Robert Schuller (*Possibility Thinking*). Positive attitudes, motivational encouragement, and self-sufficiency found its way into the evangelical mainstream when applied to Biblical teaching and pietistic/revivalistic language. American individualism and self-help emphases shaped the Prosperity Gospel movement significantly.

Third, evangelists, many struggling to support their own independent ministries, attempted to link healing and prosperity for those who would contribute funding to individual ministries. In his "seed faith" philosophy, Oral Roberts (1918–2009) introduced what became the time-honored method for gaining support and promising blessing. Harrell noted: "Roberts had pioneered the idea that giving would produce prosperity for the donor; by 1971 his book on seed-faith had been distributed to over a million followers. The key to prosperity, according to Roberts, was for a Christian to release faith by planting a seed, often by funding the evangelist's programs. In return, God would meet the desired need. *Abundant Life* magazine abounded in testimonies of successful seed-faith. A typical group of headings of personal testimonials in a 1970 issue read: 'A Raise, Plus a Bonus,' 'New Job as General Manager,' 'Sales have Tripled.'"[124]

Fourth, another important element of the Prosperity Gospel is found in the "Word of Faith movement," whose advocates insist that faith is the door to a salvation that "allows persons to exercise spiritual authority and walk in divine favor." The power of that Christian religious experience involves "the capacity to 'name' whatever one wants and 'claim possession of it by faith.'" Adherents suggest that the key to such spiritual success is found in the boldness of the believer to "name it and claim it," speaking one's desires to God in order to open God's desire to bestow all that Christians deserve in this world and not simply in the next.[125] Advocates of these views include prominent purveyors of media religion including Kenneth Hagin, Kenneth Copeland, Creflo Dollar, Benny Henn, Marilyn Hickey, Jan and Paul Crouch, and Mike Murdock, among others.

In the pamphlet, *How to Write Your Own Ticket with God,* Kenneth Hagin claimed that he was visited by Jesus himself who revealed this secret to him in four steps, including: 1) "Say it"—to speak one's desire is to receive that desire. 2) "Do it"—by acting on one's desire defeat is avoided and success assured. 3) "Receive it"—accept the power that is already waiting to be claimed. 4) "Tell it so others may believe"—let others in on the secret.[126] Copeland's approach includes acknowledging one's need or desire (physical or material); claiming scriptural promises for the desire; speaking it to make it happen.[127]

Prosperity preacher Mike Murdock delineates multiple "principles" for securing the desires of one's heart. Murdock combines biblical texts with pithy motivational points as a way of encouraging persons to live out their divinely appointed privilege, asserting that God promises benefits not otherwise available to disobedient (unsaved) people. He insists that "if you are living for Christ," then God's desire to give is equal to God's desire for the salvation of your soul. Indeed, the healing of both heart and body, Murdock says, "is what Calvary is all about."[128] Like others in the Word of Faith school, Murdock declares that, "What I say determines what God will do." He illustrates that with the story of the thief on the cross (Luke 23:39-43), noting that the "eternal plan of God was for that thief to be forever penalized, but one sentence from the mouth of the thief changed the plans of God forever."[129] He warns that "God only rewards 'overcomers'" and that "the size of your enemy determines the size of your reward." Murdock urges his listeners to choose the proper "mentor," the person whose advice they are following, asserting that "God puts something you need in someone you may not enjoy."[130]

Claiming the principle of "seed-faith," Murdock aggressively advises individuals to give specific amounts of money ranging from increments of $58 to $1000 that will serve as the foundation for spiritual and material blessings. While insisting that "nobody can buy a miracle from God," his telethons are filled with statements such as: "Every harvest requires a seed. God never opens His hand, opens His windows until we open our hands. But listen carefully, I don't know where you are going to get it. But if you can't even faith in a $1,000 seed to sow, how can you ever be debt free? If you can't even call in a seed, how could you call in a harvest?"[131]

A second and more subtle approach to the Prosperity Gospel is evident in popular preachers such as Joel Osteen, pastor of Lakewood Church, Houston, one of the largest Protestant congregations in the United States (50,000 members); and T. D. Jakes, pastor of Potter's House in Dallas, another mega-congregation. Distancing himself from the more crass approaches of prosperity faith, Jakes' reflects an attempt by certain Neo-Pentecostal African American clergy to preach the gospel, address issues of justice, and promote self-help and economic entrepreneurship among black churches and Christians. Walton wrote that "at least in print" Jakes has sought "to distinguish his theological perspective from that of the Faith movement." His written works reject both "classical Pentecostal asceticism that shun world goods and a Word of Faith doctrine that considers health and wealth to be signs of godliness."[132]

Jakes's website offers a variety of instructional options in discipleship and spirituality, including a $59.00 four-CD set called "Positioning Yourself to Prosper." His sense of spiritual empowerment, however, involves extending financial development in the black community. One recent study cites the Nehemiah Corporation of America as a particularly successful approach that offers "economic empowerment and wealth creation principally through homeownership and affordable housing." It reflects a belief that "sinners" have had the major wealth long enough, and it is time for the "righteous" to claim it for the future.[133]

Joel Osteen is his own entrepreneur, a blend of old-time religion born of his father's Baptist/Pentecostal roots, positive and possibility thinking techniques like those of Norman Vincent Peale and Robert Schuller, and a softer but consistent emphasis on seed-faith, all of which brings conversion, an improved attitude and self-image, and an expectation of material blessings.

Osteen himself seems made for the media, a new generation of televised, twittered preachers—razor thin, self-effacing, pragmatic and guileless to a fault. His sermons are folksy, positive, upbeat, and encouraging above all. Each begins with an affirmation of the authority of the Bible, clear assurance that neither Osteen nor his congregation have departed from the centrality of Holy Scripture as passed on to them by their elders including John Osteen, Joel's father, mentor, and founder of Lakewood Church. Once orthodoxy has been affirmed, Osteen then urges his sea of listeners in the former Compaq Basketball Arena to think well of themselves, to be happy, and to treat others with care and concern, traits that will inevitably lead to spiritual and material success. In some ways he seems to be a fascinating combination of old-time mass revivalism and new era self-help philosophy.

In other ways, however, Osteen seems a genuinely postmodern preacher, creating his own mini-denomination in one local congregation, asserting his own theological conservatism and ethical traditionalism, but hesitant to generalize regarding their global implications. Indeed, at times he seems hesitant to speak of theology at all, acknowledging that he has no undergraduate degree and no formal education in theological and biblical studies.[134]

In June 2005 Osteen showed up on "Larry King Live" with his spouse and copastor Victoria Osteen, to talk about his ministry, his public life, and his best-selling book *Your Best Life Now*. King, no stranger to American theological wars, asked Osteen, if "a Jew is not going to heaven?" Osteen responded:

> No. Here's my thing, Larry, is I can't judge somebody's heart. You know? Only God can look at somebody's heart, and so—I don't know. To me, it's not my business to say, you know, this one is or this one isn't. I just say, here's what the Bible teaches and I'm going to put my faith in Christ. And I just I think it's wrong when you go around saying, you're saying you're not going, you're not going, you're not going, because it's not exactly my way.[135]

Osteen's remarks created a firestorm from many evangelicals who charged him with undermining the uniqueness of the Christian message and the centrality of Jesus Christ as the only way to salvation for all humanity. The Houston pastor soon back-pedaled a bit, returning to "Larry King Live" in December 2006 to confirm his belief in the uniqueness of the Christian revelation as the only way to salvation. He continued to insist, however, that he did not know "the mind of God" in all eternal matters. He noted:

> I give a salvation call like Billy Graham every week, you know, for us to repent of our sins and—I mean it's the foundation of our faith, but I do feel like, as a pastor, I'm called to help teach people live their everyday lives and I feel like my greatest gift is in encouraging them, you know, helping them.[136]

Osteen is a second-generation charismatic, raised on Oral Roberts' "seed-faith" tradition, an early stage of the so-called health and wealth gospel in America. Osteen's father and theological mentor, John Osteen, left his Southern Baptist affiliation behind after receiving the baptism of the Holy Ghost through the influence of Oral Roberts, extending Lakewood Church's influence to a wider venue of charismatic-oriented Christians.[137] In *Your Best Life Now* Joel Osteen sets forth his own version of "seed-faith," writing:

> If you lost your job, don't sit around feeling sorry for yourself, go volunteer someplace. Sow a seed while you're waiting for that next door of opportunity to open. If you are believing for a better car, instead of complaining about the one you have, sow a seed by giving somebody a ride. If you are believing for your business to be blessed, help somebody else's business to grow. Do something to get some seed in the ground.... If you will sow an extraordinary seed, you will reap an extraordinary harvest.[138]

Given these dynamics, Joel Osteen is either the future of one powerful segment of American evangelicalism, or an illustration of the captivity of evangelicalism to a form of popular religion more akin to American enterprise than Christian theology—a motivational thinker for Jesus. Yet his influence is so widespread and his national reputation so significant that he and his church cannot be overlooked by students of contemporary American religion.

Joel Osteen and T. D. Jakes illustrate the changing nature of religion, especially Evangelicalism, in twenty-first century America. Osteen and Jakes are among a variety of technologically astute preachers who are shaping American public religion and pulpit prowess in multiple contexts. Like their homiletical predecessors, these twenty-first century preachers call persons to immediate faith in Christ, an evangelical conversion that changes their lives in this world and sets them on the road to eternal life in the next. Yet their methods often include intentional marketing techniques, motivational entrepreneurship, charismatic worship modes, and positive thinking strategies.

The Prosperity Gospel has antecedents in a variety of American religious and capitalistic influences including mass revivalism, the gospel of wealth, individualism, conversionism, entrepreneurship, motivational thinking, and the overarching American dream. That it should thrive primarily among certain types of American evangelicals is not surprising given the emphasis on free will, the possibility of conversion for all, the class-connections of early revivalism and Pentecostalism, and the implications of a certain kind of biblical inerrancy for those who need proof-texts to confirm their theology and their programs. Yet it is ironic that the Prosperity Gospel should arise in those religious traditions that, at least early on in their history, were adamantly opposed to worldliness, desiring separation from the principalities and powers of the evil age. In a sense, many of these traditions use the language of antiworldliness while promoting participation in worldly values and influences in their actions. Others, however, have completely eschewed the old separationist ideas in favor of a much more open affirmation of the possibilities of wealth, health, and immediate blessings with the "investment" of resources and the "make a wish list" approach to name it and claim it faith.

Nonetheless, the proliferation of Prosperity-preaching churches, websites and television ministries has blanketed the country with this theological and rhetorical approach to issues of spirituality, scripture, and personal financial possibilities. In fact, so widespread is the phenomenon that spiritual and material blessings are no longer thought to be occasional evidences of a mysterious divine intervention, but entitlements available for all who will boldly claim them and participate in a seed-faith program, "expecting a miracle." While preachers are often careful to include disclaimers that you cannot buy God's grace, their books and pamphlets suggest otherwise, spiritually signing God's name to promises not even God can fulfill.

Pentecostalism in the United States: From the Margins to the Middle

Pentecostalism began as a marginalized American sect, its members often caricatured as "holy rollers" who carried biblical literalism to "enthusiastical" extremes. Their identity was formed by a Restorationist reading of the book of Acts, a replication of Pentecost with its gifts of the Spirit for salvation, sanctification, "unknown tongues," healing, visions, and prophetic revelations. Revivalism and the earlier Holiness movement shaped Pentecostal theology of sanctification and ethical rigor. Never a monolithic movement, it is composed of varying communions and individuals across a wide spectrum of biblical interpretations and charismatic exercises. Pentecostalism's emphasis on the direct experience of the Holy Spirit and its resulting gifts has extended beyond the movement itself, influencing a charismatic spirituality evidenced in Spirit baptism, ecstatic worship practices, and a renewed concern for spiritual and physical healing throughout American Protestant communions.

★★ *9* ★★

Contemplation (and Controversy) in a World of Action: Roman Catholics and Religious Experience

A Sacramental Tradition

Religious experience in American Roman Catholicism often seems as complex as it is obvious, anchored in a global church with historic sacraments that chart a clear path toward encounter with the Divine, nuanced in multiple spiritualties liberal and conservative, mystical and pragmatic, populist and esoteric, monastic and diocesan. From the earliest colonial explorations, the Church in the New World reflected the enduring doctrinal, ecclesial, liturgical, and sacramental lineage of traditional Catholicism, but the unique environment of the American Republic carried them into diverse approaches to the theology and practice of the spiritual life.

Early on, Catholic clergy followed the *conquistadores* and explorers, establishing mission outposts spread from Mexico in the south to Canada in the north, committed to evangelizing native peoples and introducing the sacraments, while often serving as mediators in the inevitable conflicts between indigenous and colonial populations. Religious experience was closely linked to the sacraments of the church—baptism, confirmation, penance, Eucharist, holy orders, marriage, and extreme unction—each a means of grace offered within the one body of Christ to transport individuals through this world and prepare them for the next. These outward and visible signs of inward and spiritual grace were tangible verification of a mystical and internal transformation. Through the doctrine of transubstantiation, Roman Catholics affirmed that the Real Presence of Jesus Christ came into them as they literally ate his flesh and drank his blood, transformed from bread and wine through the consecration of the Mass. In its perpetual sacrifice, Christ was offered anew on every altar for the sins of the world. Salvation itself was a lifelong pilgrimage intersected along the way by God's presence in the physical and spiritual elements of the sacramental. The sacraments were central to the liturgical life of the Church, offered through timeless ritual in a universal language (Latin) and uniting all Catholics regardless of race, ethnicity, or social location. Catholic historian Jay P. Dolan noted that unlike private devotions, the Mass and the other sacraments "were the official public worship of the church and the principal way that people gained access to the supernatural."[1]

For the Catholic faithful, clergy and laity alike, liturgy was inseparable from orthodoxy, right doctrine as passed on by the Church from Christ through the apostles, creeds, councils, and popes. Apostolic succession meant that the authority of Christ extended to bishops and priests, enabling them to mediate God's grace through the sacraments. The "Dogmatic Constitution on the Church," approved by Vatican Council II in 1965, confirms that linkage, noting,

> They are fully incorporated into the society of the Church who, possessing the Spirit of Christ, accept her entire system and all the means of salvation given to her, and through union with her visible structure are joined to Christ, who rules her through the Supreme Pontiff and the bishops. This

> joining is effected by the bonds of professed faith, of the sacraments, of ecclesiastical government, and of communion.[2]

The conciliar document adds that an individual "is not saved," who, although a "part of the body of the church, does not persevere in charity." Such a person remains in the "bosom of the Church," but "only in a 'bodily' manner and not 'in his heart.'"[3]

Catholics and Conversion

Catholic religious experience incorporated, but did not require, a dramatic conversion or immediately transforming supernatural experiences. William James understood such sacramentalism as weighted toward the "once-born" rather than the "twice-born" approach to salvation. He cited Francis W. Newman's description of the "once-born" as those who "see God, not as a strict Judge, not as a Glorious Potentate; but as the animating Spirit of a beautiful harmonious world Beneficent and Kind, Merciful as well as Pure. The same characters generally have no metaphysical tendencies: they do not look back into themselves."[4] James added that "in the Romish Church such characters find a more congenial soil to grow in than in Protestantism, whose fashions of feeling have been set by minds of a decidedly pessimistic order."[5] Sacramental grace and doctrinal orthodoxy carried the faithful into relationship with God in Christ, a lifelong process of conversion that involved faith and works, experience and action. These beliefs and practices distinguished Catholicism from the highly individualistic approach of Protestants (justification by faith alone) and shaped "the sense of corporate responsibility that was the hallmark of the Catholic Middle Ages."[6]

For those entering the church from birth, regeneration was inseparable from the sacramental grace of baptism and confirmation, yet mystical encounter was also a distinct possibility, as mirrored in the lives of the saints and the blessed whose stories and personal writings represented an important literary corpus of spiritual insight and guidance. Experientialism had a long history in the piety of the medieval church, through a variety of devotional rituals, icons, prayers, and exercises aimed at intensifying faith within and alongside the church's sacramental life. At the same time, church leaders were often quick to respond to individuals and movements whose religious experiences and theological emphases threatened episcopal authority or doctrinal orthodoxy. Today's mystic could become tomorrow's heretic.

Conversion was an important concept and image for those adults who moved from Protestantism, faulty Christianity at best, false Christianity at worst, involving a break with past religious identity for a new, truer faith. Moving toward such a conversion, Orestes Brownson wrote that in passing "from Protestantism to Catholicity" converts "break with the whole world in which we have hitherto lived; we enter into what is to us a new and untried region, and we fear the discoveries we may make there, when it is too late to draw back." Himself a convert, Brownson concluded that to enter the "old Catholic Church" was "to leave no bridge over which we may return. It is a committal for life, for eternity."[7]

In his study of Catholic liberalism, Robert D. Cross suggested that for Catholics, "conversion means the profession of faith, by a former nonbeliever, in the supernatural authority of the Church as authorized representative in all matters concerning salvation." Catholics, particularly conservatives, were convinced that conversion offered a clear choice in securing salvation beyond both secularism and Protestantism. Cross wrote that individuals converted to Catholicism "because it offered unity instead of pluralism, absolute dogma instead of an unqualified liberty of opinion, a deep devotionalism instead of an arid rationalism."[8] This was not simply moving from one ecclesial organization to another, but a decision to receive the sacramental grace of God as manifested in the one true Church.

Colonial Catholicism

The links between sacrament and dogma were evident in the initial efforts at evangelization in the Americas. Commenting on the early Spanish explorations, Theodore Maynard contended that "from the beginning the

Spanish enterprise, however much it may have had as its object the extension of Spanish dominions and the obtaining of private gain, never lost sight of the much grander object of making the New World Catholic."[9] Maynard claimed that the first Mass celebrated in what would become US territory occurred in 1526 in the region where English Protestants would later establish Jamestown, Virginia.[10] For the Catholic missionaries in colonial America, native peoples were to receive both the sacraments and the catechism, as Jay P. Dolan commented: "To reinforce the teachings of the catechism, the missionaries, following the old adage of *lex orandi, lex credendi* (the law of prayer establishes the rule of faith), relied on the elaborate ritual of the Catholic liturgy."[11] Thus liturgy, catechism, and "a fear of universal damnation," became for many the primary tools of colonial evangelization.[12] While numerous individuals and entire tribes turned to Catholic Christianity, Dolan concluded that overall, for both Spanish and French missionaries, "to convert and civilize the Indians was a monumental task which ultimately ended up in frustration and failure."[13] Much of this was due not only to the clash of cultures, but also to the logistical difficulties of language, translation, and Native American susceptibility to European-manifested disease.[14]

As the original thirteen colonies took shape, Catholics were a decided minority, often suspect by Protestant dissenters, many of whom had experienced various forms of persecution from the Church in Europe. Maryland, the "Catholic colony," received a royal charter in 1632 and the country's first archbishop, John Carroll (1735–1815), was based there, consecrated to the office in 1790. Dolan described numerous prospects and challenges confronting the Church in a democratic society. In the Protestant-privileged culture, the question "Can a Catholic be an American?" was raised by Catholics and non-Catholics alike, becoming more controversial as "Romanist" immigrants poured into the country in the nineteenth century. Fear of Catholics as a new religious majority whose eternal destiny depended on loyalty to an Italian pope became a source of anti-Catholic nativism that endured well into the twentieth century. Immigration and Americanization brought great challenges as American Catholics moved from minority status to become the largest religious communion in North and South America. In 1815 there were some one hundred thousand Catholics in the US, but by 1865 that number had burgeoned to more than 3.5 million, a reality that contributed to a time of great transition in the American Church.[15]

Catholic immigrants divided over their own ethnic-oriented Catholicism shaped in German, Irish, Italian, and Latino contexts, contributing to assorted theological debates and ecclesial power struggles. The Holy See and the global Catholic hierarchy often labored to retain authority in a church increasingly impacted by American democratic ideals, individualism, and capitalism.[16] John Hughes (1797–1864), archbishop of New York, 1842–1864, reasserted the importance of episcopal authority in the face of "lay trustee" governance in Catholic parishes, noting, "Episcopal authority came from above and not from below and Catholics did their duty when they obeyed their bishop."[17] Yet for all his autocratic style, Hughes stressed the importance of Catholic social engagement, often contrasting it with Protestant individualism. He declared that "the grace of Christ is the capital renovating the power of the soul, and enabling her to enter into the commerce of charity, with God and the neighbor for its objects, and by which treasures, in the language of Scripture, may be laid up in heaven."[18] Hughes insisted that in contrast to Protestantism, Catholicism had within it the ability to "bring temporal interests into harmony with spiritual—infuse some portion of the attributes of God, justice and mercy into the minds and hearts of princes, of legislators, of nobles, of landlords, yea, if possible of capitalists."[19] As Hughes and others saw it, Catholic religious experience was inseparable from appropriate Christian action.

Jay Dolan insisted that seventeenth century colonial Catholics were essentially "second-class citizens" discriminated against politically, professionally, and socially." With the Revolution, however, Catholics were given "religious and political freedom" that, along with Enlightenment ideals, would significantly impact their identity as Americans and Catholics.[20]

Dolan noted that in both seventeenth- and eighteenth-century America, the "religion of the people" was very similar, with personal and communal spirituality nurtured through the Mass and "the ever-present manual of prayers." These books offered daily devotions for the year with "various litanies and psalms as well as devotions for Mass, confession, and Communion."

Dolan illustrated the renewal of Catholic devotional practices as evident in the contribution of Protestant-become-Catholic priest John Gother (d. 1704) who produced some sixteen volumes of prayers, litanies, and spiritual direction. He concluded that the piety encouraged by these books might be characterized "as personal and interior" in their emphasis on spiritual experience.[21] Gother was mentor to Richard Challoner (b. 1691), whose 1740 collection of prayers and litanies, entitled *The Garden of the Soul,* became so popular that "Garden of the Soul Catholic" became descriptive of a particular type of personal piety. It stressed the need for "external rituals" to nurture an "interior, personal piety" within the Catholic practitioner, through appropriate fasting and prayer along with consistent confession and participation in Communion.[22] These pious practices promoted religious experiences characterized by "personalism, discipline, and sobriety" among American Catholics in the eighteenth century and beyond. Joseph Chinnici labeled the Catholicism of this period "baroque devotionalism," reflected in "a penitential system" emphasizing basic human "sinfulness," and piety centered in "relics, indulgences, pious practices and saints' lives."[23]

Catholic Devotions as Religious Experience

This "devotional Catholicism" flourished with nineteenth-century immigrant culture, among clergy and laity alike. Since the Mass was in Latin, the literature of devotion was in the vernacular, published for use alongside liturgical traditions. Devotion was nothing new in the Church, but became a tool for renewing Catholic identity in a new, Protestant-based culture.[24]

Orestes Brownson, sometime Transcendentalist turned Catholic, was a leading advocate of the devotional life in post–Civil War American Catholicism. Brownson, whom Chinnici labeled "the leading Catholic intellectual of the time," called for a renewal of Catholic devotion amid the dramatic numerical expansion of the church in a democratic environment. Addressing this American "autonomy of the temporal," Brownson urged Catholics to pursue "robust virtues," what Chinnici characterized as "self-reliance, courage, individual initiative, and intellectual development." This spiritual renovation would involve "loyalty to the hierarchy," along with devotional exercises pursued through pilgrimages, liturgies, prayers, readings, and spiritual reflection, centered in "interior dispositions and an awareness of the mystery of Christ."[25] Amanda Porterfield insisted that Brownson was convinced that in America, Catholic, not Protestant, spirituality would ultimately fulfill Christianity's "mission to build God's kingdom on earth." Catholic spirituality and action had the potential to actualize "Protestant post-millennial dreams."[26] Many Catholic converts were drawn to the Church by what Porterfield called "the spiritual realism of Catholic metaphysics and the transformative power of Catholic ritual." Those like Orestes Brownson and Isaac Hecker who had lingered a bit with Transcendentalism may also have appreciated Catholicism's ability to extend "the esthetic and mystical side of New England Puritanism" within the context of "Romantic idealism."[27] Their approach reflected an eclecticism that would come to characterize many expressions of spirituality in American life.

Another convert, Thomas Scott Preston, pastor of St. Ann's Church, New York City, urged similar devotions, especially to the Sacred Heart of Jesus, as a way of renewing waning faith, resisting doctrinal compromise, and reaffirming allegiance to clerical authority. These conservative principles would aid the Church reclaiming its place at the center of the "social order."[28] Brownson and Preston were among numerous clergy (many of whom were converts from Protestantism) who viewed devotional renewal as "a significant component of Catholic self-definition," creating "new models for holiness" in the American Church. Writing in 1888, Otto Zardetti, Bishop of Saint Cloud, Minnesota, summed up the contribution that devotion could make to Catholic identity, noting, "Devotion, as well as Religion, is at first something internal, spiritual, and as such is the universal source or origin of all external worship." Yet "every internal religious event soon becomes externally perceptible," creating "a spiritual bond of common feelings and views the minds of pious people already impressed and influenced alike by the same internal devotion."[29]

In her study of Catholic devotion, Ann Taves suggested that personal and communal piety, long a part of Catholic spirituality, received renewed impetus from nineteenth-century church leaders through publications that linked laity to "various religious figures, including God, Jesus Christ, the Sacred Heart of Jesus, and the Virgin Mary."[30] These printed materials served as doctrinally approved devotional guides to be utilized within and alongside the formal liturgical life of the Church. Donald Attwater described these "popular devotions" as "spontaneous movements of the Christian body toward this or that aspect of the faith, sanctified individual, or historical event, approved by authority and usually expressed in authorized vernacular formulas and observances."[31] Attwater located these practices within the broader context of Catholic liturgy with particular attention to eucharistic spirituality. Taves added her own qualification to Attwater's definitions, suggesting two distinct "categories" of devotion, one that involved "prayers in the vernacular to be used by the laity" and focused on eucharistic observances, and a second category evident in what Attwater called "sanctified individual, or historical event." The latter classification Taves labeled "generalized devotions," as utilized by organizations such as the Confraternity of the Blessed Sacrament, the Sodality of the Immaculate Conception, the Society of the Holy Rosary, and the Confraternity and Sisterhood of the Scapular.[32] Devotional prayers and readings were often promoted by numerous orders, including Franciscans, Dominicans, Jesuits, and Carmelites. Most of these devotions carried papal indulgences and were validated through the use of approved rubrics, and the appropriate spiritual internalization. As Taves observed, these devotions were often thought to "be supernaturally, as well as ecclesiastically, sanctioned." They were usually "focused and specialized," directing the practitioner to a specific prayer, saint, and devotional action.[33]

At the center of these devotional practices was special reverence toward the Blessed Sacrament at communion or "reserved" in each parish church as the object of "adoration or veneration of Jesus' presence in the consecrated host."[34] Devotional responses to the person and work of Jesus required meditation on his life and ministry, particularly his passion and crucifixion. Devotion to the Sacred Heart of Jesus, a tradition long present in the Church and widespread in the United States by the late nineteenth century, was an abiding symbol of and participation in the love and sacrifice of the savior who offered himself for the sins of the world.[35] In iconic paintings and prints, the Sacred Heart of the suffering Christ is wrapped with thorns as evidence of the depth of his love and his sacrifice for humanity. Liturgically, Sacred Heart devotion was recommended as a weekly observance involving prayers, readings, and contemplation of Christ's sufferings observed each Thursday from 11 p.m. until midnight. It concluded with Holy Communion received each first Friday for nine straight months as "reparation for the indignities inflicted upon the sacrament by those indifferent and ungrateful," an act that was believed to have salvific implications.[36]

Devotion to the Blessed Virgin Mary, also an abiding tradition in Catholicism, became increasingly important in nineteenth-century America, and included the recitation of the rosary with its affirmation, "Hail, Mary, full of grace, blessed art thou among women, and blessed is the fruit of thy womb, Jesus. Holy Mary, Mother of God, pray for us sinners now and in the hour of our death."[37] Originating in the thirteenth century, "saying the rosary" involved a set of beads that aid the faithful in prayers and meditation that invoked the "Our Father," the "Hail, Mary," and the "Gloria Patri." Marian devotion became a hallmark of Catholic piety in nineteenth- and twentieth-century America, particularly after Mary's Immaculate Conception was declared an article of church dogma by Pope Pius IX in 1854.[38] Nor was the rosary the only source of Marian devotion. Prayers addressed to Mary were a prominent part of devotional literature. One benediction favored by the ex-Protestant and monastic founder Mother Elizabeth Ann Seton (1774–1821) reads,

> Mary Queen & Virgin pure! As poor unfledged birds uncovered in our cold and hard nests on Earth we cry to her for her sheltering outspread wings—little hearts not yet knowing sorrow—but poor tired and older ones pressed with pains and [hungry for] peace & rest—O our Mother!—and find it in thee.[39]

Devotion to the Holy Spirit

Devotional practices could be intensified. Novenas are periods of specific intercessory prayer and devotion in response to spiritual quests or struggles in the face of life's harsh realities. They are utilized in devotions both public and private, calling the faithful to extended and intense experience of the presence of God, opening the possibility of God's miraculous intervention in the lives of those in need, or offering spiritual strength for coping with life's uncertainties. Sally Cunneen called the novena "an objective reminder that Christ is present here and now," inside and outside the life of the Christian.[40] Novenas were an extended way of cultivating the presence of the Holy Spirit in the individual life.

Joseph P. Chinnici documented the intensification of devotion to the Holy Spirit as an overarching theme of post–Civil War religious experience in American Catholicism. He traced this particular type of spiritual renewal to a body of literature that addressed the meaning of and relationship with the Holy Spirit in both the Church and the individual. Chinnici viewed British Cardinal Henry Edward Manning (1802–1892) as a major proponent of and influence for devotion to the Holy Spirit in nineteenth-century Catholicism. Manning, a convert from Anglicanism, wrote *The Temporal Mission of the Holy Ghost*, a volume printed in some seven American editions, 1865–1890, and *The Internal Mission of the Holy Ghost*, published in five US editions, 1875–1890.[41] Manning, a thoroughgoing ultramontanist in his support for papal authority, understood the Holy Spirit to be the antidote to "denial of the [revealed] truth," "infidelity," and sinfulness in the life of the Christian. Episcopal authority was for him confirmed and nurtured by the role of the Holy Spirit in both church and state. With the experience of faith in Christ, Manning believed that the work of the Holy Spirit began by "illuminating the reason, moving the will, and kindling in the heart a love of the truth."[42]

Chinnici called Isaac Thomas Hecker (1819–1888), another convert from Protestantism and founder of the Missionary Society of St. Paul the Apostle (Paulist Fathers), "the most important indigenous source for devotion to the Holy Ghost in the United States," a person preoccupied "with the inner life." In Hecker's ever-developing journey through Methodism, Transcendentalism, and Romanticism, his concern for the work of the Holy Spirit, known within a Catholic context, came to represent "the fullness of Christian perfection, union, and communion" he had long sought.[43] He understood such devotion to be a powerful tool for developing a distinctly Catholic spirituality amid the dominant Protestant environment of nineteenth-century America. In 1843, the year before he was formally received into the Church, Hecker wrote in his diary,

> The Catholic Church alone seems to satisfy my wants my faith life soul... I may be laboring under a delusion; any thing you please. Yet my soul is catholic and that faith answers responds to my soul in its religious aspirations and its longings. I have not wished to make myself catholic but it answers to the wants of my soul. It answers on all sides.[44]

Strongly committed to evangelizing Protestant Americans and presenting a Catholicism compatible with democracy, Hecker never really challenged Church dogma or episcopal authority once he made his commitment to Rome. He seems to have understood the Holy Spirit as represented in Catholic "institutional structures, intellectual tradition, and mystical sacramentalism."[45] The gift of the Holy Spirit was inseparable from its mediation through the Catholic Church. He wrote, "The Church embraces in its cultus the absolute Holy in all its forms of expression as consequences not as causes. It is the generator; It is not regenerated by them. We hold that Poetry Philosophy the Arts and Sciences are the immediate consequences of the inspiration given to Men by Jesus Christ through medium of the Catholic Church."[46]

For Hecker, the experience of the Spirit made it possible to fulfill what he called the "longing of every soul to be united with God." The result would be a new era of the Holy Spirit, renewing the individual and the community of faith. In an 1875 essay entitled *An Exposition of the Church in View of Recent Difficulties and Controversies, and the Present Needs of the Age*, Hecker offered a summary of what lay ahead:

> The renewal of the age depends on the renewal of religion. The renewal of religion depends upon the greater effusion of the creative and renewing power of the Holy Spirit. The greater effusion of the Holy Spirit depends on the giving of increased attention to His movements and inspirations in the soul. The radical and adequate remedy for all the evils of our age, and the source of all true progress, consist in increased attention and fidelity to the action of the Holy Spirit in the soul.[47]

In Hecker's view, devotion to the Holy Spirit was a gift of grace that offered American Catholics spiritual renewal, progress, and a new humanitarianism for responding to the social needs of the country and the world. He insisted that "once born of the spirit we shall be led by it in all reforms to do and to abstain from all things which are an hindrance an obstruction to the full and complete harmonious life of the spirit in us."[48]

John Farina saw Hecker as an illustration of the varying impact of the nineteenth-century Romanticism on the devotional movement in Catholic life. He concluded that the religious experiences fostered through dedication to the Virgin Mary, the Sacred Heart, and the Infant Jesus, as promoted by Catholic devotional literature, placed renewed emphasis on "sentimental, subjective feelings of piety." Devotional publications contributed to an increasing "concern for personal salvation," as well as "sentiment, ritual, and 'feminine' traits of docility and submissiveness." Ann Taves suggested that Catholic women understood these models of piety, since they evoked "feelings of dependence" that paralleled "the stereotypically 'feminine' role'" required of nineteenth-century marriage.[49] Farina commented that Catholic devotion, like Romanticism, sought "to unite the mystical and the concrete, the ideal and the real," nurturing a spirituality that promoted individual piety within the boundaries of hierarchical supervision. Taves noted that these "devotional practices" were utilized by the church hierarchy "to standardize" piety under priestly oversight, creating a set of distinctively Catholic pietistic observances that united the faithful against potential threats to orthodoxy and authority. She concluded the devotions "directly and indirectly enhanced the hierarchy's control over the laity, while fostering a distinctively Catholic identity" with more international rather than local or national "overtones."[50]

Farina extended the critique with his assertion that in shaping its devotional movement the Church removed from its piety the most effective elements of the Romantic movement—"the self-reliance, the rebellion, the reliance on intuition." He concluded, "Thus stripped of its soul, sentiment became sentimentality, passion became bathos, self-reliance became personalism, and loyalty to the intuitive perception of truth became submission to the church's hierarchy." Spiritual renewal did occur, "but only within a tightly controlled system"[51] Thus devotion deepened piety even as it fostered uniformity.

Parish Mission Movement

The parish mission was a particular style of preaching and liturgy conducted in local Catholic congregations, dating from the sixteenth century when certain religious orders sought to "bring help to so large number of souls who, by ignorance of the things necessary for their salvation, live in a state of sin and are exposed to eternal damnation."[52] By the seventeenth century it had become a frequent tool among European Catholics for renewing Catholic piety and converting non-Catholics to the faith. With the growth of eighteenth-century republicanism, however, many Europeans resisted its association with the Catholic hierarchy, papal authority, and "the exaggerated piety" of the Baroque era.[53] As Catholic immigration increased in nineteenth-century America, the parish mission became a valuable tool for reviving the lapsed, renewing the faithful, and converting non-Catholics, many of whom were familiar with revivalistic practices. These missions, or "Catholic revivals," became by 1829 "an accepted feature of Catholic evangelization."[54] To accomplish these ends, clergy, including bishops, often visited Catholic parishes, preaching in churches or other public venues for extended periods of time. Experiential religion was central to these endeavors. After Kentucky's first bishop, Benedict J. Flaget (1763–1850), conducted an eight-day preaching mission in the Cathedral at Bardstown, a local priest observed, "All hearts appeared to be truly moved. This was seen in the vividness of the sorrow and in the abundance of tears which accompanied the confession of their sins."[55] Revival sermons warned of the dangers of hell, unconfessed mortal sins, and the justice of a righteous God. They ended with a call to accept God's abiding mercy and return to the life of Christian devotion pledged at baptism.[56] A leaflet utilized in a nineteenth-century New York preaching mission described the salvific intentions of the event:

> A mission is a time when God calls with a more earnest voice than at other times all persons, but sinners especially to work out their salvation with fear and trembling.... It is a time when priests from early morning till night wait in the confessionals for you, to absolve you from your sins, and restore you to God's favor. It is a time for you to remember that you have a soul to save, and to try to save it.[57]

Parish missions also occurred among Catholics in the South, transmitting what Randall Miller called "an individualistic piety" aimed at quickening a "religious intensity and devotion" that "strengthened the institutional Church." Southern missions promoted "religious awakening" as well as a specific "moral discipline" that included "temperance, frugality, and self-denial." These gatherings drew Catholics of various ethical and economic backgrounds "in a common religious experience."[58]

In many ways Catholic revivalism paralleled that of Protestant revivalism—dynamic preachers offering dramatic homiletical imagery of judgment and grace, heaven and hell, sin and repentance—all within a call to conversion and perseverance in Christian commitment. Yet it was also distinct in its assertion that through the sacrament of baptism and the grace of confirmation the seeds of new life were already present in every Catholic, and needed only to be reawakened, engendering a new life of sacramental devotion. Jay Dolan noted that for the Catholic revivalists,

> Conversion was a personal experience, but one that could only be fulfilled through the sacramental life of the institution. This dimension of the

> conversion experience complemented the individualistic quality of Catholic revivalism. Ideally a conversion experience was but the first step of a renewed process of growth which would be nurtured by the sacramental life of the church. Catholic evangelicalism blended nurture with conversion by its insistence on the sacraments as both the fulfillment of conversion and the means to preserve and perfect this religious experience.[59]

Parish missions often concluded with a time for renewing baptismal vows, a reminder that baptism as an infant marked the beginning of a covenantal relationship with God. Thus conversion was personal and individual but "sustained only through the church."[60] Once conversion and baptismal renewal had been made, revival participants were encouraged to persevere, utilizing the many devotional pathways available to them to continue in moral living and Catholic spirituality.

The literature, ritual, and prayer life of the devotional movement offered spiritual resources for nurturing the life of the Spirit, through participation in "frequent communion, devotion to Mary, and the cult of the sacred heart."[61] Scapulars, rosaries, holy medals, and personal crucifixes, all available for purchase at the parish missions, were the outward signs of an inner spirituality that enhanced the faith and the faithful. Parish missions were a significant effort to renew the Catholic community, deepening piety and participation in the sacraments while promoting conversion for Catholic and Protestant alike.

Twentieth-Century Catholicism: Liturgy, Spirituality, and Identity

The twentieth century generated innumerable changes for Roman Catholics, particularly in the American Church. Two world wars and the extended Cold War that followed brought the Church into conflict and controversy with both fascism and communism. A discernible progressivism, long present in the Church, made itself increasingly known, particularly on issues of theology, world religions, church-state relationships, and other religiocultural dynamics. Vatican Council II (1962–1965) presented the Church with new responses to modernity, opening the door to a variety of changes, if not in terms of dogma, certainly in relation to liturgy, ecumenical cooperation, interfaith dialogue, and overall Catholic identity. In her study of *The Transformation of American Religion*, Amanda Porterfield observed that Vatican II expanded (for some) the idea of "the Church as the people of God," broadening personal and communal devotion to the "living presence of Christ to include the people of God," in the Church or in other faith traditions where spiritual faithfulness was evident.[62]

As American Catholics grew into the country's largest religious communion, they confronted internal debates over the nature of Catholicism, itself increasingly impacted by pluralism in its various religious and secular expressions.[63] Internally, doctrinal divisions between liberals and conservatives were not unrelated to questions of religious experience. One of the early responses to these twentieth-century challenges came from a movement known as the Catholic Revival.

The Catholic (Literary) Revival

Peter A. Huff called the Catholic Revival "a distinctive chapter in modern Catholic intellectual history," extending from the death of British Cardinal John Henry Newman (1801–1890) to the period shortly before Pope John XXIII (1881–1963) convened Vatican II in 1959. Huff dubbed it "an extraordinary 'Catholic moment'" evidenced in "a resurgence of Catholic literary activity" and hope for "a revitalization of Catholic intellectual life."[64] Instigated by a minority group of "intellectual elites," both clergy and laity, the participants sought to unite Catholic tradition with Christian humanism in responding to new realities of the "modern world."[65] The intellectual and spiritual breadth of the movement was delineated in a 1931 article in the American Catholic periodical *Commonweal* labeling it an attempt to renew "Scholastic philosophy," promote Catholic higher education, expand concern for "art and letters and science," and bring Catholic insights to bear on "modern economic problems." The movement addressed "the tremendous growth of missionary activities, [and] the outpouring of new manifestations of mysticism and spiritual devotions, particularly among the laity."[66] In that way, the Catholic (literary) Revival had implications for a renewal of religious experience in the American Church.

In Europe, this "literary resurgence" was promulgated by such Catholic converts as John Henry Newman, Graham Greene, Evelyn Waugh, and G. K. Chesterton. American writers included converts/luminaries such as Dorothy Day, Thomas Merton, Robert Lowell, Tennessee Williams, and Walker Percy. The considerable works of lifelong Catholic Flannery O'Connor reflected significant interaction with the varied religious experiences evident in Southern evangelicalism.[67] For these and other writers, historic Catholicism remained a storehouse of traditional sources found in reason (Scholasticism), sacramentalism, and mystery, each offering powerful antidotes to the materialism, hedonism, secularism, and cynicism present throughout modern society. Peter Huff noted that while few of these writers challenged Catholic orthodoxy head on, they often showed "impatience with the Catholic ghetto's rejection of modern art and literature."[68]

Peter Hawkins called Flannery O'Connor (1925–1964) a writer who sought "to portray the transforming action of the divine within human life" in response to those modern skeptics who had lost "a powerful sense of God," in themselves and their society. For Hawkins, O'Connor discovered "a new language of grace in order to confront the reader with the experience of God," in a culture where an appreciation for God's "mysterious presence" could no longer be taken for granted.[69] Hawkins cites O'Connor's comments in an essay entitled *Mystery and Manners*, in which she suggested,

> For the last few centuries we have lived in a world which has been increasingly convinced that the reaches of reality are very close to the surface, that there is no ultimate divine source, that the things of the world do not pour forth from God.... For nearly two centuries the popular spirit of each succeeding generation had tended more and more to the view that the mysteries of life will eventually fall before [the] modern.[70]

Paradoxically, O'Connor brought her own Catholicism into novels that vividly describe the transformational, even bizarre nature of religious experience in the Protestant-dominated South. In a story called "The River," a boy named Bevel is evangelized and immersed by a Pentecostal revivalist, an event so sacramental and comforting that the boy sees it as a way to escape his abusive family life.

> "If I baptize you," the preacher said, "you'll be able to go to the Kingdom of Christ. You'll be washed in the river of suffering, son, and you'll go by the deep river of life. Do you want that?" "Yes," the child said, and thought, "I won't go back to the apartment then, I'll go under the river."[71]

In the end, Protestant conversion and immersion baptism become mysterious sacraments that foster both peace and suicide in the innocent, abused child:

> He intended not to fool with preachers any more but to Baptize himself and to keep on going this time until he found the Kingdom of Christ in the river. He didn't mean to waste any more time. He put his head under the water at once and pushed forward.... He plunged under once and this time, the waiting current caught him like a long gentle hand and pulled him swiftly forward and down. For an instant he was overcome with surprise: then since he was moving quickly and knew that he was getting somewhere, all his fury and fear left him.[72]

"The River" confirms Peter Hawkins's observation that O'Connor's stories reveal "the sense of an encounter with reality too real for humans to bear for very long, but an encounter which nonetheless changes those who were there."[73]

In America, significant elements of the Catholic Revival reflected an emerging liberalism concerned to reconnect the Church with its ancient spirituality, intellectual rigor, and liturgical vitality. Garry Wills suggested that for liberals, "real Catholicism is the very basis of beauty and of truth; its ideals are unconsciously sustained by people who have escaped the cultural limitations of the institutional church."[74] The religious experience these Catholics sought placed great emphasis on the spiritual transcendence and immanence of the Mass, the impact of monastic devotions and disciplines, and an appreciation for the historic order and authority of the Church's hierarchy. Wills noted that this "intense religiosity, far from inhibiting freedom in the secular sphere, encouraged it."[75] It was a religious experience that exulted in the monastic separatism of Thomas Merton (1915–1968), who urged Catholics to "untether yourself from the world and set yourself free," and the social activism of Catholic Worker Movement founder Dorothy Day (1897–1980) who advised engagement in and with community as "the social answer to the long loneliness."[76] Day's description of her conversion to Catholicism offered a personal assessment of the dynamics of Catholic spirituality, liturgy, and mystery. In her autobiography, *The Long Loneliness,* Day confessed that when she first articulated the story of her conversion,

> I left out all my sins but told of all the things which had brought me to God, all the beautiful things, all the remembrances of God that had haunted me, pursued me over the years so that when my daughter [Tamara] was born, in grateful joy I turned to God and became a Catholic. I could worship, adore, praise and thank Him in the company of others. It is difficult to do that without a ritual, without a body with which to live and move, love and praise. I found faith, I became a member of the Mystical Body of Christ.[77]

Day's social activism was grounded in a profound sense of mysticism nurtured by the Jesuit tradition of Ignatian spirituality by which Catholicism would become a source for redeeming and transforming American culture and religion.[78] Converted to Catholicism after years of a bohemian lifestyle in New York, Day acquiesced to Catholic dogma even as she challenged Catholic social conscience. Her religious experience became inseparable from her commitment to the poor, directed through the Catholic Worker Movement. She wrote,

> We felt a respect for the poor and destitute as those nearest to God, as those chosen by Christ for His compassion, Christ lived among men. The great mystery of the Incarnation, which meant that God became a man that man might become God, was a joy that made us want to kiss the earth in worship, because his feet once trod the same earth. It was a mystery that we as Catholics accepted.[79]

As a specific movement, the Catholic Revival did not long endure. By the 1950s, its "gradual dissolution" had begun for reasons related to the Catholic "sense of apartness" from the larger culture, the remaining effects of immigrant Catholic experience, and the difficulties inherent in sustaining a creative indigenous literary tradition. Peter Huff concluded that while the Catholic Revival fostered "a rather bleak portrait of the modern world," the work of Vatican Council II was the Church's "official, though belated, reconciliation with modernity."[80]

Merton, Day, and O'Connor, among others, became primary sources of influence in the renewal of interest in spirituality, a broad approach to contemplation, reflection, and action that encompassed individuals inside and outside the Church in the late twentieth and early twenty-first century. While it was not an exclusively Catholic movement, Catholic writers and thinkers, ancient and modern, contributed significantly to its development.

These women and other classical Catholic mystics have been discovered by Protestants across America who read them, cite their works, and use their insights to shape their own spiritual pilgrimages. Nonetheless, contemporary analysts warn modern readers about the dangers of reading ancient mystics in light of current culture. Mark Gibbard suggested that "the desert Fathers can still speak to us today, as Henri Nouwen has shown in his *Way of the Heart*, but only if we discard their excessive otherworldliness and their crude demonology." Gibbard cautioned against the cultural "escapism" evident, indeed encouraged, by works such as *The Cloud of Unknowing* and Julian of Norwich's *Revelations of Divine Love*, both of which "imply that anyone who is going to be deep in prayer must turn from the world." He urged modern readers to "distinguish between the heart of an author's teaching and the superficial conditioning of his or her own era."[81]

Few twentieth-century Catholics have had greater impact on the shape of spirituality in America than the Trappist monk Thomas Merton (1915–1968). Merton, his person, writings, and insights into the spiritual life, exerts a profound effect on a wide variety of seekers. Merton's extensive literary corpus, itself evidence of an evolving spirituality, is surveyed avidly by persons within and without the Church. His spiritual autobiography, *The Seven Storey Mountain* (1946), remains a literary bridge between Catholics and non-Catholics, even as it reflects the most Catholic phase of Merton's own religious pilgrimage.

As the title of one of his books suggests, *Contemplation in a World of Action* was perhaps the hallmark Merton's approach to the spiritual life. His concern for spiritual discipline was linked to his consistent, sometimes outspoken, support for the Civil Rights and anti-war movements, as well as his long time connection to the Catholic Worker and other socially oriented organizations. His conversion to Catholic faith was a long time coming, but once discovered, it set in motion a dramatic personal transformation and an ever-expanding spiritual journey. In 1942, his first Christmas in the Abbey of Gethsemani, Merton wrote, "I seemed to be the same person, and I was the same person, I was still myself, I was more myself than I had ever been, and yet I was nothing. It was as if the floor had fallen out of my soul and I was free to go in and out of infinity."[82]

Merton's spirituality involved a direct encounter with the Divine, a concern to penetrate the "cloud of unknowing" in search of grace and salvation. In the *Sign of Jonas* he wrote,

> God, my God, God whom I meet in darkness, with You it is always the same thing! Always the same question that nobody knows how to answer! I have prayed to You in the daytime with thoughts and reasons, and in the nighttime You have confronted me, scattering thought and reason. I have come to You in the morning with light and with desire, and You have descended upon me, with great gentleness, with most forbearing silence, in this inexplicable night, dispersing light, defeating all desire. I have explained to You a hundred times my motives for entering the monastery and you have listened and said nothing, and I have turned away and wept with shame. Is it true that all my motives have meant nothing? Is it true that all my desires were an illusion? While I am asking questions which You do not answer, You ask me a question which is so simple that I cannot answer. I do not even understand the question.[83]

For Merton, the experience of spiritual darkness was inseparable from the experience of God; "joy and peace and fulfillment" were "to be found somewhere in this lonely night of aridity and faith."[84] In his study of Merton and mysticism, Raymond Bailey concluded that the Trappist writer understood religious experience as beginning and ending "with the self." Like many of the great Catholic mystics, Merton insisted that the center of the spiritual life was "not knowledge, but love." Love was the ultimate sign of human regeneration.[85] Merton's spiritual pilgrimage took him into dialogue with various Eastern religions, particularly apparent in Buddhist and Christian monastic spirituality. His accidental death in Bangkok in 1968 occurred at a conference on such spiritual traditions. He noted that "far from being suspicious of the Oriental mystical traditions, Catholic contemplatives since the Second Vatican Council should be in a position to appreciate the wealth of experience that has accumulated in those traditions."[86]

Thomas Merton remains an anomaly in American Catholic life. On one hand he is perhaps America's best-known representative of monastic vocation, an immensely popular spiritual guide, grounded in Catholic theology and Trappist identity. Yet many view him as the harbinger of a new spiritual pluralism, freely exploring complementary and contradictory traditions. Jewish writer Shaul Magid observed,

> Thomas Merton's popularity in America remains peculiar. . . . Many of his avid readers are not sure whether he was a voice from the past or from the future, a voice to return or a call to renew. In many ways Merton served as the spiritual conscience of late twentieth-century America, gently teaching with his life and letters the substantive difference between religion and spirituality.[87]

Perhaps Merton both initiated and anticipated a type of religious experience that pursues the inner life but with elements of social responsibility, interfaith dialogue, and religious identity in an increasingly pluralistic global environment. In both substance and symbol he remains both guide and exemplar for multiple elements of American religious life. First, his experience as both Trappist monk and popular writer coincided with an era of unprecedented social and religious acceptability for American Catholics, enriched by a certain ecumenical optimism following Vatican II and John F. Kennedy's election as the nation's first Catholic president. By century's end, however, these successes were compromised by clergy shortages, declining church attendance, financial difficulties, and ethics scandals.[88] Second, Merton's person and publications became significant resources in the rise of the "spirituality movement" in American religious life. His evolving dialogue with non-Catholic religious communities anticipated and shaped ecumenical and interfaith conversations that continue to this day. Third, Merton's own religious experience, grounded in a monastic vocation, linked solitude and contemplation with a profound social imperative that addressed many of the great public upheavals of the times. In a sense he personified the dilemma of many American religionists—how to retain a specific religious identity while pursuing conversation, instruction, and spiritual exploration with those whose traditions are distinct, even contradictory.[89]

Catholic Religious Experience: Spirituality and Sacrament

Merton's approach to religious experience, his links to Asian religions, and the popularity of his literary corpus for persons inside and outside the Church illustrated the influence of Catholicism in the developing spirituality movement in the latter twentieth and early twenty-first century. Amanda Porterfield assessed that contribution to American spirituality, concluding,

> Thus Catholic spirituality served as an important vehicle for the dissemination of Asian ideas within American Protestant churches. Through a process of liturgical renewal that swept through many American churches in the sixties, Protestant and Catholic spiritualities drew closer together, and new developments in Catholic spirituality influenced American Protestants as well as Catholics.[90]

For Catholics themselves, however, religious experience remains inseparable from the liturgy and the sacraments. The "Constitution on the Sacred Liturgy," approved by Vatican Council II, makes sanctification inseparable from liturgy, noting,

> In the liturgy the sanctification of [humanity] is manifested by signs perceptible to the senses, and is effected in a way which is proper to each of these signs; in the liturgy full public worship is performed by the Mystical Body of Jesus Christ, that is, by the Head and His members. From this it follows that every liturgical celebration, because it is an action of Christ the priest and of His Body the Church, is a sacred action surpassing all others. No other action of the Church can match its claim to efficacy, nor equal the degree of it.[91]

Yet Porterfield was quick to assert that the reemphasis and renewal of the sacramental "was split open and spilled out into the larger culture of the late sixties and seventies," energizing many dissenting movements for civil rights and against war. She concluded, "For Catholics, the meanings and expressions of sacramentalism were expanding as a result of the new expansiveness and openness to innovation associated with Vatican II." While this openness may have had limited impact on Catholic conversions, it provided "a more diffuse attunement to sacramentalism wherever it could be found or invented."[92]

As the twenty-first century took shape, the institutional Roman Church (particularly in the West) was sent reeling by issues related to dramatic declines in the number of priests, monks, nuns, the drop in attendance at Mass (especially among "Anglo-Catholics"), and the enduring controversy regarding pedophile priests and the bishops who shielded them from formal prosecution. Even then, the literature of Catholic spirituality continued to inspire not only Catholics, but also a growing number of Protestants and secularists who sought clues to the great *Cloud of Unknowing.* That spirituality continued to give the faithful assurance that Christ could literally be taken into the soul and body of the sinful individual, tangible experience of the eternal grace of God.

★★ *10* ★★

The Christ of Many Experiences: Some Latter-Day Voices

The history of religious experience in the United States is inseparable from the pluralism of its religious communities. A study of Christian religious experience in context reveals multiple "senses" of many hearts. From the colonial period onward, diverse morphologies shaped Catholic and Protestant understanding of the nature of faith and the means of entering into God's grace. A variety of religious affections were evident, in the sobs of four-year old Phoebe Bartlet in her Northampton closet, the "the falling exercise" of the camp meetings, the séances of the Fox sisters, the glossolalia of Azusa, and the "call and response" of African-American congregations. Religious experience drove persons into and away from community, sometimes extending sexual boundaries; sometimes eliminating sex all together. Catholics maintained devotion to the Blessed Sacrament and the Blessed Virgin Mary, convinced that the risen Christ literally came into them spiritually and physically, his very body and blood miraculously reconstituted in the Mass. Protestants, promoting religious experiences aplenty, continued to struggle with whether or not Christ had actually entered into their hearts and if he had, how to keep him there.

From the late nineteenth to the early twenty-first centuries religious experientialism continued unabated, encompassing new debates over old dogmas represented in movements related to premillennialism, fundamentalism/modernism, and Evangelicalism, as well as in renewed pursuits of mysticism and spirituality. Revivalism as a mechanism for drawing multitudes of persons into Protestant conversion reached its peak in the late nineteenth and early twentieth centuries, only to experience precipitous decline a hundred years later. Fundamentalism, born of rationalism, revivalism, and premillennial fervor, questioned the validity of religious experience apart from confessional orthodoxy, particularly the nature of Christ's atoning sacrifice on the cross. Christocentric liberals attempted to locate the spiritual life in the context of modern science and timeless experientialism. Amid these doctrinal controversies, a renewed concern for Christian mysticism offered classic and contemporary resources for direct encounter with the Sacred. Neo-Evangelicalism distinguished itself from fundamentalist caricatures while reasserting conservative approaches to the possibility of salvation, the nature of conversion, and the encounter with culture. By the late twentieth century a sustained interest in spirituality signaled varying experiential possibilities, often drawn from diverse sources of devotional literature, conversion morphologies, and contemplative techniques, practiced inside, outside, or alongside traditional religious settings. These modern and even postmodern approaches represent varying alternatives to spiritual experience from the late nineteenth to the early twenty-first century.

Christ's Premillennial Return: An Imperative for Conversion

D. L. Moody, R. A. Torrey, Billy Sunday, and Billy Graham were premillennialists, convinced that Jesus Christ would soon return to establish his millennial (thousand-year) reign on earth, a spiritual transformation that would lead to the ultimate defeat of Satan and the fullness of the kingdom of God. While not a new idea, premillennialism gained particular prominence in the nineteenth century to become one of the hallmarks of the burgeoning fundamentalist movement and its challenge to theological liberalism. Nineteenth-century premillennial speculation gained renewed impetus through the Millerite movement, whose founder William Miller (1782–1849) predicted Christ's second advent "about the year 1843."[1] Miller, a Baptist preacher from the Burned-Over District, produced intricate biblical and chronological calculations regarding the second coming with particular attention to the books of Daniel and Revelation. His views were published in a best seller entitled *Evidence from Scripture and History of the Second Coming of Christ* (1842). The Millerite movement drew followers from multiple denominations, spawning numerous millennial publications and public meetings, where Miller's calculations were intended to encourage nonbelievers to receive conversion before it was too late. *Evidence from Scripture and History* ended with the following admonition:

> And to you, impenitent friend, God has at all times given you warning of his approaching judgments. If you repent, believe his word, and break off your sins by righteousness, he is faithful and just to forgive you your sins. Why not take warning by the past? Is there no example for you? . . . "Can ye not discern the signs of the times?" . . . Why not listen, then, to the warnings and admonitions, to the calls and invitations, to the examples and precepts contained therein? "Can ye not discern the signs of the times?" Will God cut off the unbelieving Pharisee for not discerning the signs of the times, and let you, with twofold more light, go free? No: how can ye escape, if you neglect this great salvation? Watch, then, "the signs of the times." I say, Watch.[2]

The signs of the times mandated a salvific religious experience for all who would escape judgment at the pending day of the Lord.

The Great Disappointment that resulted from the failure of Miller's calculations terminated his movement and hastened his death in 1849, but did not end premillennial speculations, some of which were taken up in various Millerite-related Adventist groups, including the Advent Christian Church and Seventh Day Adventism. The latter denomination was shaped by the visionary experiences of the prophet Ellen Harmon White (1827–1915), whose revelations confirmed speculations that Christ had "cleansed" the heavenly sanctuary in preparation for his full return. White's preaching campaigns produced enthusiastical outbursts characteristic of earlier revivals, and her biblicism called believers to direct encounter with God and reappropriation of certain biblical mandates—sabbatarianism and biblically based dietary practices—a new Restorationism in preparation for Christ's second advent. The gift of prophecy was verification of her own experiential insights.[3]

White's visions served other purposes as well. Jonathan Butler suggested that the Adventist doctrine of "conditional mortality," the belief that the dead remained "asleep" until the final resurrection when only the redeemed would rise, "represented not only the anti-Calvinist rejection of eternal punishment... but an effort to obliterate Spiritualism" as a valid spiritual enterprise. It also differentiated Ellen White's visionary revelations from those of certain "female spiritualist mediums" whose work appeared "sociologically identical to Mrs. White."[4]

Millerites and Adventists were not the only premillennialists among nineteenth- and twentieth-century Protestants. As the "signs of the times" appeared more ominous following the Civil War and later the Great War, many Christians came to believe that Christ's return was both imminent and essential. A dispensational premillennialism, advocated by John Nelson Darby and Cyrus Scofield, divided human history into eras (dispensations) by which God dealt with creation, leading ultimately to Christ's premillennial return and the rapture of the saints from the earth.[5] Once again, millennial expectations were grounds for immediate religious conversion before the end came and the fate of the "lost" was set for eternity.

American Fundamentalism and Religious Experience

Fundamentalism, a reassertion of classic Christian doctrines in response to developments in theological liberalism, affirmed an orthodoxy that included, among other things, the infallibility (inerrancy) of scripture, the substitutionary atonement of Christ, his virgin birth, and bodily resurrection. Many, but not all fundamentalists added Christ's premillennial return to that list of nonnegotiable dogmas. Where religious experience was concerned, fundamentalists questioned whether a valid encounter with Divine grace was possible apart from recognition of those unchanging dogmas that defined forever what made Christianity truly Christian. Princeton professor J. Gresham Machen (1881–1937) published *Christianity and Liberalism* (1925) in an effort to distinguish Christian truth from liberal fiction. The modern church was in trouble, Machen believed, for admitting into membership "great companies of persons who have never made any really credible confession of faith at all and whose entire attitude toward the gospel is the very reverse of the Christian attitude."[6] Theological liberalism was not simply a heresy within the realm of Christian thought and praxis. Rather, "it proceeds from a totally different root, and it constitutes, in essentials, a unitary system of its own." For Machen, liberalism differed from Christianity "in its view of God, of man, of the seat of authority *and the way of salvation.* And it differs from Christianity not only in theology but in the whole life."[7] Thus claims to a valid Christian experience were invalid when the source of those claims failed to affirm the necessary orthodox, biblical doctrines and values long held within traditional Christianity.

Machen repudiated the liberal assertion that the veracity of Christian faith rested primarily in Christian experience. "The Christian movement," he said, "was based, not upon mere feeling, not upon a mere program of work, but upon an account of facts. In other words it was based upon doctrine."[8] As William Hutchison observed, in Machen's view religious experience (conversion) began by accepting "the primacy of doctrine itself."[9] Salvation was predicated on the "facts" of redemption—Christ's atoning sacrifice on the cross, his physical resurrection, and victory over death, along with the faith that rested in those salvific divine actions.[10]

Martin Marty noted that while fundamentalists were unable to agree on various doctrines, specifically the nature of the sacraments, "their selected dogmas served better for the defining of causes." Thus, "fundamentalists especially resisted what they called the impulse of liberals to spiritualize or symbolize what they thought they must take literally." This was illustrated in their insistence that salvation was predicated on "a literal substitutionary blood atonement" to describe Jesus's salvific action on the cross.[11] Machen concluded that liberals believed "that applied Christianity is all there is of Christianity, Christianity being merely a way of life." True Christians, however, believed "that applied Christianity is the result of an initial act of God."[12] In contrast to liberal optimism regarding human nature, the Christian had but one salvific message: "Human goodness will avail nothing for lost souls; you must be born again."[13]

Machen, along with other Reformed theologians, insisted that the veracity of Christian doctrine was grounded in the historic creeds and confessions of the church. These unchanging truths were nonnegotiable affirmations of the essential elements of Christianity. To reject them in response to Enlightenment rationalism or an idolatrous approach to new science or biblical criticism was to question the veracity of scripture and destroy the essence of faith. Fundamentalist leaders were clearly conversionists, insisting that a personal experience with Jesus Christ was essential for those who would claim a salvific encounter with a just and merciful God.

Yet, as C. Allyn Russell concluded, "Religion for them was an objective, divine 'given' from a transcendent God, rooted not in human aspiration, exhortation or mediation, but in the historical facts of the birth, life, death and resurrection of Jesus." Beyond that collective sense of supernaturalism, they were united around a shared commitment regarding the "inerrancy of the Scriptures in their original documents."[14] This objective approach was brought to bear on religious experience. Writing in *The Fundamentals* (1917), H. M. Sydenstricker outlined the "science of conversion," the insistence that "the conversion of the human soul" could be "accomplished by scientific methods" set forth in God's infallible word."[15] The writer set out the ordered "proposition" whereby conversion was secured, a way grounded in God's redemptive activity in Christ, the work of the Holy Spirit, and "an absolute faith on the part of the human agent" that God would work through these specific means.[16] He concluded that "the whole process of conversion" revealed "the fundamental principle that like begets like, and means produce results according to purely scientific laws, and if the results are not scientific they are spurious, external and temporary."[17] For this Mississippi fundamentalist pastor and others like him, conversion was a powerful experience by which sinners were "washed in the blood of the lamb" and transformed by the Holy Spirit into new creations. But that divinely appointed plan of salvation was not a mere superstition from a religiously primitive era. It was a timeless "scientific" procedure set forth by God in an infallible record.[18]

Fundamentalist theologians such as Machen warned that liberals were using the language of Christianity but robbing it of its doctrinal veracity. The liberal emphasis on Divine benevolence ignored a sense of God's judgment and holiness; their optimism regarding the human condition undermined the reality of original sin; their concern for subjective religious experience weakened the factual authority of scripture; and their stress on Christ as example and moral influence dismissed the meaning of his death and resurrection as the substitutionary sacrifice for human sin.[19]

The Centrality of "Experience": A Christocentric Liberal Approach

The "Christocentric liberal" tradition whose theology Machen and other fundamentalists found wanting offered a different vision of Christianity. As the editors of the sourcebook *American Christianity* described it, "Christian liberalism undertook to re-think the character of God in the light of Christ." The nature of God was most evident in the life and work of Jesus Christ. This led them to embrace the ultimate benevolence of God's nature, and the unity of the human race in love and compassion.[20] Christocentric liberals urged the church "to come to terms with all aspects of modern knowledge," reflected in new truths found in evolution, psychology, democratic idealism, and the historical-critical approach to scripture. At the center of such theological liberalism was the idea of experience, the timeless link between Jesus Christ and his continuing presence in the church and in the world. Nancey Murphy suggested that "early-twentieth-century modernists offered experiential accounts of Christian theology." She noted that University of Chicago professor Shailer Mathews (1863–1942) "emphasized the priority of religion over doctrine. Religion itself is a matter of experience, attitudes and moral convictions." Christian doctrines, however, were "to be judged on the basis of their effectiveness in inspiring religious convictions and loyalties."[21] Friedrich Schleiermacher's insistence that "doctrine is to be evaluated in light of experience, never the reverse" provided a philosophical rationale for liberals' approach to dogma. Murphy concluded, "So God-consciousness is the foundation of all religion." Religious language, confessions of faith, and theological affirmations "are all built up from this experience."[22] Dogma without experience was a dead letter.

William Adams Brown (1865–1943), whose *Christian Theology in Outline* provided a systematic approach to christocentric liberalism, linked God's benevolence with experience, writing,

> In the divine Fatherhood Christian faith finds included the power and authority for which absoluteness stands, the kinship which is involved in personality, and the holy and loving character which Christ has revealed. This conception, gained from personal experience of God's redemptive love in Christ, Christian faith carries over to mankind at large.[23]

Brown defined conversion as a "turning from selfishness to service through penitence and faith," but noted "two different concepts" of its meaning. The first involved "a distinct crisis in the religious experience, involving a radical alternation in the prevailing tendencies of life," an experience evident in "the revival meeting and the inquiry room."[24] The other type commenced "with the beginnings of conscious experience," often without a "definite moment" for recognizing grace. "True proof" of such a conversion rested in the "character" of one's "present choices" and a "growing experience of dependence upon God and love."[25] Here Brown clearly echoed William James' distinguishing between once-born and twice-born religious experiences.

Brown's contemporary, William Newton Clarke (1841–1912), also produced a systematic theological text that delineated the nature of experience as understood in the christocentric liberal context. In *An Outline of Christian Theology*, he defined Christian experience as "the life, individual and collective, that consists in fellowship with God as Christ reveals him, and in the fruits of that fellowship." So essential was that experience that it was "the actual life of Christianity itself; in it Christianity lives and has its being." Without that experience, the Bible would have been a mere record "of an ancient and forgotten life, powerless to preserve Christianity in the world."[26] In fact, Christianity could have survived without the Bible, but not without "the experience of salvation," which was "the living proof and testimonial of Christianity."[27]

Clarke and others liberals understood Christian experience to be the timeless link between the many eras of Christian life and thought. He concluded, "If the theology of a [particular] time is various and changing, it is because the life of the time is various, growing, transitional." The engagement of Christian experience was essential in spite of critics who claimed it was "too subjective and variable to be trusted."[28] The continued dynamic of Christian experience was evidence of "a perpetual movement of the Spirit of God, . . . a divinely guided progress" that produced "an ever growing Church" as well as "an ever growing theology."[29] As William Hutchison suggested, this "new theology held a more interior and spiritual idea of the presence and agency of God."[30]

Clarke's student, Harry Emerson Fosdick (1878–1969), became one of the most famous christocentric liberals of his generation, as pastor of Riverside Church, New York City. In defense of Clarke and his perspectives, Fosdick wrote, "As for men such as Dr. Clarke, their revolt, like that of Jesus against the orthodoxy of his time, was in the interest of a deeper, more vital, more transforming Christian experience than literalism, legalism and authoritarianism could supply. The result for many of us was not alone a new theology but a new spiritual life."[31] Fosdick acknowledged his own "struggle for a convinced faith" involved an "emphasis on direct, immediate personal experience as the solid ground of assurance." He noted that "organized religions" reflected two basic approaches, both evident in New Testament: "Stress on the objective authority of church, Scripture and creed"; and "Stress on 'the divine-human encounter' within the soul, on personal experience of God's transforming and sustaining grace." He concluded, "There seems to me no doubt that the latter is primary."[32] While Christian theology was profoundly important, "Christian experience is the abiding continuum underlying vital faith."[33]

In a sermon entitled "The Christ of History and the Christ of Experience," Fosdick summarized the liberals' idea of christocentric experience. He declared,

> They call us modernists. Very well, let us be modernists! But remember that our modernism is not what modernism too often tends to become: a set of abstract hypotheses, a system of theoretical propositions. Our religion is impersonated. Christianity is Christ. And to know him and love him until his spirit is reproduced in us and the Christ of history becomes the Christ of experience—that is vital Christianity.[34]

Fundamentalism and modernism created major confrontations and schisms in Protestant communions in twentieth-century America. Battle lines were drawn in what seemed a life-and-death struggle for the soul of Christian identity. As the debates intensified fundamentalism became its own divisive movement within conservative, Evangelical communions. J. Gresham Machen was forced to leave his position at Princeton, founding Westminster Theological Seminary as a bastion of Reformed theology and fundamentalist philosophy. Other schisms within the conservative camp also occurred. By the end of World War II the founding of the National Association of Evangelicals and the development of a movement that came to be known as Neo-Evangelicalism, suggested that new approaches to religious experience were taking shape in the US among those who sought to make conversion normative.

American Evangelicals: Varieties of Religious Conversion

George Marsden and Grant Wacker suggested that Evangelicalism "refers to that broad movement, found especially in British and American Protestantism, that insisted that 'the sole authority in religion is the Bible and the sole means of salvation is a life-transforming experience wrought by the Holy Spirit through faith in Jesus Christ.'"[35] In its most basic sense, evangelical conversion involves a turning from one way of life to another, specifically from non-Christian to Christian life. Theologically, the process of conversion is the way to justification by faith in Christ. This idea is endemic to Evangelicalism. Evangelical theologian Donald Bloesch noted that justification by faith alone (*sola fide*) "is not only belief or intellectual assent; rather, it signifies whole-hearted trust and commitment. It is a faith that is grounded in the work of Christ and fulfilled in loving obedience."[36] Bloesch insisted, "The key to evangelical unity lies in a common commitment to Jesus Christ as the divine savior from sin, a common purpose to fulfill the great commission and a common acknowledgment of the absolute normativeness of Holy Scripture."[37] He speculated that these basic concerns might make Evangelicalism the "ecumenical movement of the future" because of its capacity to unite persons around biblical and conversionist truths across denominational boundaries. While such unity is present, more recent developments suggest that Evangelicals themselves may differ considerably, less over the need for salvation, than the processes for securing it. Evangelicals speak and write extensively and provocatively of the need for redemption in Christ. Across the late twentieth and early twenty-first centuries, however, discovering the means to that salvation has become something of a dilemma. The question remains, how does one secure such a spiritual benefit? How does the objective idea of an encounter with Christ translate into a subjective experience with God? Indeed, while acknowledging that an experience with Christ is essential for salvation, American Evangelicals have never fully agreed on the process whereby such salvation was secured.

James Davison Hunter surveyed the "coming generation" of Evangelicals and concluded that Evangelical Protestantism may "be *incapable* of adequately reinforcing" the traditional theological boundaries that previously provided the identity of the movement.[38] Thus he suggested that "from all indications the pluralism of opinion over theological, moral, familial, and political issues in Evangelicalism (already wide-ranging) is expanding and not coalescing into a new consensus."[39] That pluralism is particularly evident in the diversity of conversion morphologies present within the American Evangelical community.

The idea that a personal experience of divine grace is essential for those who claim Christian identity is a hallmark of Evangelical theology. Most Evangelical groups use traditional conversionist language in detailing the way of salvation. Closer examination, however, reveals considerable diversity of emphasis, intent, and theology of the nature and process of religious experience itself. Certain representative approaches involve processes that might be called 1) **Plan conversionism**, 2) **Lordship conversionism**, 3) **Positive-Thinking conversionism**, 4) **Marketing conversionism**, and 5) **Propositional conversionism**.

Plan conversionism is one of the best known and most popularly identifiable methods practiced among traditional Evangelicals. Traced through the revivalistic traditions of Charles G. Finney, D. L. Moody, Billy Sunday, and Billy Graham, by the late twentieth century it was popularized in James Kennedy's book *Evangelism Explosion* and in conversion rubrics like the "Four Spiritual Laws" associated with Campus Crusade for Christ, or "the Romans Road to Salvation" used in many Baptist contexts. Through a step-by-step process sinners acknowledged their sinfulness and invited Jesus into their hearts, praying a short prayer by which conversion was secured.

Plan salvation involved a "sinners' prayer" similar to that used by Moody and other urban evangelists. Seekers were asked to pray or repeat the following:

> Dear heavenly father, I know that I am a sinner. Thank you for sending your son, Jesus Christ, to die on the cross for my sins. I confess my sins to you and turn from those sins. I open the door of my life and ask Jesus to come in as my savior and Lord. I give everything that I am and everything that I ever will be to you. Take control of my life and help me to be the kind of person you want me to be. In Jesus name, Amen.

Theologically, Plan salvation reflected a highly individualized, largely Arminian approach to conversion with a strong emphasis on the immediacy of salvation through the exercise of individual free will. Through the plan, salvation is secured on demand, a potentially rapid strategy for entering into religious experience. Critics suggested that it is too easy, creating occasion for cheap grace and superficial faith.

The debate over plan conversionism is often related to another morphology, that of so-called **Lordship conversionism**. Lordship conversion has often been identified with the polemical writings of John MacArthur (1939–), pastor of Grace Community Church, Sun Valley, California, since 1969. MacArthur not only promotes a particular conversionist morphology, but also does not hesitate to criticize those plans and programs that he feels inappropriate, unbiblical, and heretical. In *The Gospel according to Jesus*, MacArthur insisted that confusion over the nature of salvation exists among people in the pews because they have "heard two conflicting messages from the same conservative, fundamentalist and evangelical camp."[40] These two views involved the relatively simple idea of receiving Christ as Savior versus the more intensive call to receive him as both Savior and Lord, the latter approach reflected in MacArthur's writings. As MacArthur understood it, much of contemporary Evangelicalism promoted an "easy-believism" that welcomed all comers but failed to confront them with the moral and spiritual imperatives of the gospel. He noted, "The Gospel in vogue today holds forth a false hope to sinners. It promises them they can have eternal life yet continue to live in rebellion against God. Indeed, it encourages people to claim Jesus as Savior yet defer until later the commitment to obey Him as Lord."[41] For MacArthur, the failure of Evangelicals to articulate the demands of the Gospel "spawned a generation of professing Christians whose behavior often is indistinguishable from the rebellion of the unregenerate."[42] He called those desiring conversion to receive Christ as both Savior and Lord, accepting the grace to enter into Christian faith and the responsibility to live according to the spiritual and ethical teachings of the scripture.

MacArthur did not hesitate to challenge prevailing morphologies used by Evangelicals for guiding sinners to conversion. He wrote,

> Listen to the typical gospel presentation nowadays. You'll hear sinners entreated with words like, "accept Jesus Christ as personal Savior"; "ask

> Jesus into your heart"; "invite Christ into your life"; or "make a decision for Christ." You may be so accustomed to hearing those phrases that it will surprise you to learn none of them is based on biblical terminology. They are the products of a diluted gospel. It is not the gospel according to Jesus.[43]

MacArthur insisted that the religion of Jesus involves "a call to discipleship, a call to follow Him in submissive obedience, not just a plea to make a decision or pray a prayer."[44] Those who do not link salvation and submission, MacArthur believed, were promoting an intellectualized gospel in which faith is "merely intellectual assent to a set of biblical facts. . . . Believing those facts constitutes saving faith."[45] All else is secondary. Instead, MacArthur described genuine conversion as "a divine miracle, and there are no formulas which can bring it about or explain it. There is no four-step plan of salvation, or any prefabricated prayer that can guarantee the salvation of a soul."[46] MacArthur's Reformed theology shaped his understanding of grace as infused into the heart and life of the elected sinner.

At a "Strange Fire" conference at his church in 2013, MacArthur charged the modern Pentecostal movement with falsely co-opting the doctrine of the Holy Spirit and turning it into a frenzied movement that promotes signs and wonders, miracles, and prophecy, spiritual gifts that ended with the apostolic era. He contended that the movement was satanic and destructive to the church, their religious experience unrelated to genuine Christianity.[47]

While John MacArthur is pastor of a mega-church, he has not hesitated to criticize those mega-churches that reflect a religious experience connected to what might be termed **Marketing conversion**. Mega-churches may be defined as congregations of several thousand members that provide specialized services to special-interest subgroups, led by charismatic, authority-figure pastors, and are organized around intentional marketing techniques. Bruce and Marshall Shelley suggested that these churches are not "tradition bound," but are "market driven."[48] Most are mini-denominations, providing services—education, publication, mission, and identity—in one congregation that were previously available through denominational networks or parachurch agencies. While these congregations tend toward a conservative-evangelical orientation, "distinctive doctrine does not seem to be the primary force behind their growth."[49]

Mega-churches use the language of Evangelicalism, their ministers claim an abiding "passion for souls," and their methods are aimed at bringing persons to faith in Christ. Yet their critics ask whether their commitment to marketing principles obscures, even transforms, their message. The literature of the movement often couches evangelism in business terminology. In *Marketing the Church*, George Barna observed, "Think about your experience for a minute. When you share your faith with a nonbeliever, you are actually marketing the church."[50] Barna insisted that because of its failure to address the marketplace adequately, "the evangelical church in America is losing the battle to effectively bring Jesus Christ into the lives of the unsaved population."[51] Marketing techniques were the means for gaining a hearing for the gospel. Barna even articulated the gospel in the language of the market. He wrote that "the key to leading people to accept our core product—salvation through a personal relationship with Jesus Christ—is by establishing nurturing relationships with other people, with the goal of leading them to explore what the Church has to offer."[52] Christians were to be "marketing agents of the Church," with Jesus as the model in both "ministry and in marketing."[53] He concluded, "as we look at Jesus the marketer, we also have to realize that He paid a price for His marketing activities."[54] For Barna, "Any church growth strategy that is geared to increasing the number of people without emphasizing the necessity of commitment to Jesus Christ is working in opposition to scriptural command."[55] He warned churches not to become so obsessed with method that they offered "cheap grace" or lost sight of their Evangelical mission.

Critics fretted that the medium might instead overpower the message. In *Selling Jesus, What's Wrong with Marketing the Church*, Douglas Webster distinguished between conversion to "popular cultural religion" and conversion to Christianity. He observed that the church "is not an audience positively inclined toward Jesus, but a company of committed individuals whose lives depend upon the truth that Jesus Christ is Lord. The church must not obscure this truth by transforming a congregation into an audience...proclamation into performance or... worship into entertainment."[56]

An Evangelical, Webster expressed concern that marketing conversion promotes techniques that obscure the nature of conversion. Citing Stanley Hauerwas and William Willimon, Webster noted, "The church becomes one more consumer-oriented organization, existing to encourage individual fulfillment rather than being a crucible to engender individual conversion into the Body."[57] Although marketers utilize Evangelical language in calling persons to accept a traditional plan of salvation, the method often overpowers the message. Webster concluded, "Unconsciously the evangelical church has slid toward New Age thinking, catering to the self as god, by offering an impressive range of what we call 'necessities' rather than 'sacrifices.'"[58]

Critics of marketing conversionism have frequently linked it to **Positive-Thinking conversionism**, an approach frequently associated with the twentieth-century theology/philosophy of Norman Vincent Peale (1898–1993) and Robert Schuller (1926–), and in the twenty-first century with Joel Osteen and other mega-church leaders. Long debated inside and outside American Evangelism, Positive Thinking conversionism remains a significant influence in popular religious life. Norman Vincent Peale's *Power of Positive Thinking* elicited both positive and negative responses when it first appeared in the 1950s. Peale related Christianity and religious experience less to sin and repentance than a more positive way of viewing the self. He called persons to recognize the goodness and potential that were essentially inherent in each individual. Salvation began as one learned to think positively about self, God, family, nation, and future. Conversion through positive thinking invited persons to "picturize" certain goals, carry that image to God in prayer, and with God's almost inevitable blessing, create necessary steps to achieve the goal.[59]

In her biography of Peale, Carol George linked the preacher's understanding of conversion and Christian living to the New Thought movement of the late nineteenth and early twentieth centuries. She described New Thought as "that branch of the harmonial metaphysical tradition which traced back to Ralph Waldo Trine, Charles Fillmore, Julius and Anetta Dresser, and even the pioneering Phineas Quimby."[60] In *The Power of Positive Thinking*, and other works, Peale joined New Thought metaphysics with his own brand of Methodist Evangelicalism, Calvinist terminology, and conservative political activism. George noted, "Eclectic, synthetic, obviously uncreedal and unsystematic, his particular theological blend combined aspect of evangelical Protestantism, metaphysical spirituality, and the American Dream, a distinctly American form of popular evangelism."[61] While many American Evangelicals rejected "Pealism" as an appropriate morphology for salvation, it secured a place within popular Evangelicalism as one of several broad options for discovering divine grace.

Television preacher Robert Schuller made no secret of Peale's influence on his philosophy of Possibility Thinking, the central theme of his Evangelical ministry. He believed that his way of articulating religious experience was geared to secularized Americans who no longer heard or understood traditional theological appeals. Possibility thinking was simply a "communication strategy" for telling the old, old story of Jesus.[62] Indeed, Schuller considered himself primarily an evangelist, seeking to bring the Christian gospel to a highly secularized California (and American) environment.[63] Like Peale, Schuller combined the language of traditional Evangelicalism with that of psychology and personal therapy. He insisted that his evangelism was based on "a 'human-need' approach rather than a theological attack."[64] As he saw it, the gospel offered the restoration of self-esteem, a sense of self-worth that empowers persons to think and dream in light of the possibilities ahead of them. For Schuller, sin was "a terribly weak and insecure ego," a poor self-image.[65] Genuine religious experience brought a new sense of self, overcoming not original sin, but original insecurity. Such a restoration allowed the individual to serve God in self-sacrificing ways.

Schuller's version of the sinner's prayer includes the following:

> Jesus Christ, I accept You as my forgiving savior. I don't understand what Your death on the cross means. But I know that in some way You died for me.... You have by Your suffering and death on the cross accepted the responsibility of my sins. You have fulfilled the justice that demands that

> wrong be punished. And you mercifully promise to extend this forgiving credit to my account. By your death justice and mercy are both fulfilled. Thank You, Jesus Christ. Amen.[66]

William Dyrness wrote sympathetically of Schuller's intentions but criticized his basic premise as encouraging "a deep-seated American tendency to evade and ignore negative aspects of life, aspects that cannot be addressed in a fallen world without suffering, defeat, and sometimes even death."[67] Many of Schuller's critics contended that his evangelism was based primarily on psychology and pragmatism, a departure from christocentric Evangelicalism. John MacArthur attacked Schuller's "pragmatist manifesto," an essentially person-centered approach rather than a "theocentric attitude" based on tradition and platitudes. Schuller declared that "the unconverted will, I submit, take notice when I demonstrate genuine concern about their needs and honestly care about their human hurts."[68] MacArthur responded that such an approach is "an overt appeal for the church to proclaim a man-centered, not a God-centered, message." For MacArthur, Schuller's idea that the gospel satisfied human beings' deepest need, the "spiritual hunger for glory," actually constituted a false gospel. MacArthur concluded that Schuller's person-centered gospel "couldn't be more wrong. The gospel is about God's glory, not man's."[69]

Schuller unapologetically defended his approach to religious experience and the effort to use modern psychology and technology to awaken the broken egos of contemporary Americans. In his later years, controversy struck the Garden Grove Community Church, leading to bankruptcy and the sale of the church to the Orange County Catholic diocese.[70]

The tension between modernity and conversionism is evident in **Propositional conversionism**, a continuing emphasis of certain fundamentalist Evangelicals. This approach to conversion entailed the role of reason and the affirmation of certain basic doctrinal propositions regarding Christianity. Donald Bloesch called such Evangelical propositionalism a type of "faith-moralism" which includes "assent to (certain) propositional truths" in which an experience with Christ is inseparable from nonnegotiable dogmas related to who he was and what he accomplished salvifically in the world. As noted earlier, this was a major contention of early 20th century fundamentalists such as J. Gresham Machen.[71]

Propositional approaches to conversion raise numerous questions about the nature of religious experience. What nonnegotiable doctrines about Jesus are essential to salvation? Does one believe in Jesus and then discover essential doctrines or are certain dogmas so intricate to Christian faith that they cannot be separated from genuine conversion? Evangelicals have generally affirmed that persons need only know that Christ is the way to salvation. Yet they also have insisted on certain immutable dogmas that described the meaning of Jesus Christ and his mission to humanity—virgin birth, substitutionary atonement, bodily resurrection, and the nature of divine revelation. From an Evangelical perspective, can one reject any or all of those doctrines and still have a genuinely Christian religious experience?

Adrian Rogers (1931–2005), longtime pastor of Belleview Baptist Church, Memphis, Tennessee, introduced a powerful argument for relating personal faith to orthodox doctrine, as illustrated in belief in an affirmation of the virgin birth of Christ. A well-known evangelist among Southern Baptists, Rogers asserted that belief in the virgin birth was essential to salvation. He declared, "If you don't believe in the virgin birth of Christ, not only do you have difficulty with the character of Mary... the character of Jesus... the character of God, but you've got a big difficulty in your own character. And I'm going tell you something else; I would not give you half a hallelujah for your chance of heaven if you don't believe in the virgin birth of Jesus."[72] Rogers concluded, "No virgin birth, no deity; no deity, no sinlessness; no sinlessness, no atonement; no atonement, no hope."[73] For Rogers and others, orthodox dogmas regarding Jesus' life and work were inseparable from a salvific encounter with him.

"Intimate Consciousness:" Mysticism in Twentieth-Century America

The publication of William James's *Varieties of Religious Experience* (1902) sparked a renewed interest in mysticism and the long history of religious exploration inside and outside the Christian church.[74] In the early twentieth century, mysticism offered yet another spiritual option amid the doctrinal debates raging between fundamentalists and liberals. While the religious enthusiasms of earlier periods were sometimes thought to have certain mystical overtones, they were less apt to be connected to the broader mystical tradition inherent in segments of Christian history. Yet many twentieth-century seekers were explicit in their search for and experience of mystical encounters. They drew on the history of Christian mysticism, even as they affirmed that such experiences were available to all who would truly seek them. Writing in 1912, A. S. Martin commented,

> There has been no similar movement of mystical thought so widespread and original in impulse since before the Reformation, a fact which at once proclaims its own intrinsic importance, and its high interest for that revival of religion and re-statement of theology which are generally felt to be a chief need of the day.[75]

In *American Mysticism*, Hal Bridges proposed certain issues that influenced early twentieth century interest in mysticism. First, American mystics traced their lineage to Jonathan Edwards, Ralph Waldo Emerson, and other religionists who explored the spirituality of the transcendental. Second, American mystics were drawn to philosophical idealism, which emphasized "the spiritual and monistic view of reality." Third, evolutionary concepts aided mystics in their appeal to the evolving consciousness of human life. Modernist emphasis on divine immanence increased speculation as to the presence of God in each life. Fourth, Eastern religions also contributed to the literature and practice of mysticism, offering alternative techniques for contemplation and reflection.[76]

In *The Varieties of Religious Experience*, William James identified mysticism by means of four specific "marks." These included "ineffability," "a Noetic quality," "transiency," and "passivity."[77] *Ineffability* meant that the experience "defies expression, that no adequate report of its contents can be given in words." A *Noetic quality* suggests that mystical experiences "are states of insight into depths of truth unplumbed by the discursive intellect," evident in "illuminations" and "revelations," often carrying "a curious sense of authority."[78] *Transiency* meant that these "mystical states cannot be sustained for long." Indeed, James proposed that most lasted no more than half an hour, or at most a rare two hours. They were simply too intense to be sustained for extended periods of time.[79] While persons may move toward mystical encounters with intentionality, using certain manuals or spiritual guides, *passivity* sets in when the mystic's will seems "in abeyance... grasped and held by a superior power." This passivity may be revealed in "prophetic speech, automatic writing, or the mediumistic trance."[80]

James went to great lengths to illustrate the intensity and diversity of mystical encounters through multiple case studies from those who claimed to have experienced them. He then admonished skeptical readers, "Even the least mystical of you must by this time be convinced of the existence of mystical moments as states of consciousness of an entirely specific quality and of the deep impression which they make on those who have them."[81] He acknowledged the lengthy mystical tradition evident in Christian, primarily Catholic, history while noting that "apart from what prayer may lead to, Protestant mystical experience [particularly for Evangelicals] appears to have been almost exclusively sporadic."[82]

Perhaps no twentieth century individual personified the renewed interest in mysticism more than Rufus Jones (1863–1948), Quaker writer and professor at Haverford College. Jones was once called "the most eminent American mystic of recent times, if, in fact, he is not the American mystic *par excellence*."[83] He was a prolific author with multiple volumes dealing with mystics, mysticism, and experientialism, books written for a twentieth-century audience seeking to understand if not pursue the topic. Jones described mysticism as "the type of religion which puts the emphasis on immediate awareness of relation with God, on direct and intimate consciousness of the Divine presence. It is religion in its most acute, intense and living stage."[84] Jones testified to his own mystical encounters, beginning in his twenties, but cautioned against "crystallizing" such personal experiences into institutional formulations or marginalizing mystics outside the larger Christian community.[85]

Jones's approach to mysticism was increasingly democratic. After years of reflection, he acknowledged that an "undeveloped, and uncultivated form of mystical consciousness" was inherent in all human beings.[86] He divided classic mystics into two distinct classes: "negation mystics" and "affirmation mystics." Negation mystics sought to lose themselves through some means of absorption into the Godhead, a type of mysticism Jones believed to end "in contradiction and confusion or at least would so end if the persons were faithful to their principles."[87] Affirmation mystics understood the mystical vision, not as an end, but a beginning, a continuous desire for an immediate sense of the presence of God. These mystics sought both the spiritual experience and ways to act in obedience to that vision.[88] He acknowledged common threads in the mystical pursuits, but hesitated to identify a concrete "path" that would ensure mystical encounter, preferring instead to speak of an unpredictable "way of surprise and wonder."[89] For Jones, mystical progress enabled individuals to overcome selfishness, and to give themselves to personal reflection, love of beauty, and the continued contemplation guided by the classics of Christian devotion. Through it all, the mystical center remained a "unification of the inner powers of the self."[90]

Rufus Jones's Quaker commitments were evident in his concern for a mystical experience that produced significant ethical manifestations. He classified as mystical experience any "immediate consciousness of personal relationship with the Divine," a "mystical aspect" known in "our highest moral moments." These encounters are never without a sense "that the 'call' of duty comes from beyond our isolated self." The sheer "augustness of conscience" is so profound that untold individuals have named "it the voice of God." Such "high moments of obedience" are "essentially mystical—an experience which cannot be analysed and reduced to 'explanation' in terms of anything else."[91] Often mystical encounters with the Sacred confront individuals and groups at worship, those "times when the soul feels its real powers and when the possibilities of life are discovered, and they make ordinary performances of religious service seem, in comparison, poor and dry." These moments Jones, declared, "are beyond explanation, but they are not abnormal."[92]

Rufus Jones was among the first of a community of individuals from multiple faith traditions who pursued the study and practice of mystical experience in the early to mid -twentieth century. Others include Jones's Quaker counterparts Thomas Kelly (1893–1941) and Douglas Steere (1901–1995), Universalist turned Episcopal priest Joseph Fort Newton (1876–1950), African-American Howard Thurman (1899–1981), Catholics Thomas Merton (1915–1968), Sister Joan Chittister (1936–), and writer/teacher Henri Nouwen (1932–1996), as well as Baptist E. Glenn Hinson, and writers Flannery O'Connor and Kathleen Norris (1947–). Thomas Kelly's approach to the mystical life parallels that of Rufus Jones, his Haverford College colleague. His classic work, *A Testament of Devotion* (1941), begins with an affirmation that all human beings can know mystical encounter, asserting, "Deep within us all there is an amazing inner sanctuary of the soul, a holy place, a Divine Center, a speaking Voice, to which we may continuously return."[93] Kelly echoes Jones's view of the mystic as in the world but not of it, noting that the inner life takes persons "in two opposing directions." One relinquishes "earthly attachments and ambitions—*contemptus mundi*," while the other demands "a divine but painful concern for the world—*amor mundi*." Thus God "plucks the world out of our hearts," while also hurling "the world into our hearts," where individuals and God "carry it in infinitely tender love."[94] Hal Bridges contended that Kelly's "solution to the problem of evil appears to be the mystical self-naughting which joyfully surrenders to God all worldly desire, even the desire to escape suffering." His mysticism reflected an expansive concern to alleviate suffering, but an insistence that individuals could only attempt to respond to specific needs, "*my* [particular] responsibility...in a world too vast and a lifetime too short for me to carry all responsibilities."[95]

Douglas Steere, another Haverford professor, also linked mystical encounter and worldly action. "The redemptive process," Steere suggested, "sprang out of the heart of the Creator of nature; it is a kind of second creation...directed to free souls who, in spite of belonging to God and owing all to God, are yet free to reject and repulse his costly advances." These "faithful souls" "join with Christ and the Father in laying siege to the heart of the world."[96]

Hal Bridges noted that while Howard Thurman's approach to mysticism had "much in common" with that of Rufus Jones, it differed in that Thurman was an African-American born into Southern segregationist culture and the liberationist context of the black church.[97] Thurman achieved notoriety not only for his work in founding the Church for the Fellowship of All Peoples, San Francisco, and as Dean of Marsh Chapel and professor at Boston University, but also as a result of his many writings that charted elements of the mystical life. Bridges cites passages from Thurman's 1961 address at the Baltimore Friends School entitled "Mysticism and the Experience of Love." In it Thurman asserted that individuals could "become at home *within*" by making their own inner spirit "the trysting place" where they meet the Divine. He confessed that "the cruel vicissitudes of the social situation" in which "American society" forced him to live required him to seek "resources or a resource" for sustaining his life. So in mysticism Thurman found "the equilibrium and tranquility of peace" to "live under siege" in American society.[98] American Christians, he believed, had "betrayed the religion of Jesus" by permitting racial segregation.[99]

Thurman identified himself as an "affirmation mystic," one who chose not to "escape in mere asceticism" but must "embrace the social whole and seek to achieve empirically the good" that had taken position of his life. This meant bringing one's "own spirit, those stubborn and recalcitrant aspects of it, under the domination of the God" with whom one has found "mystical union."[100] Affirmation mystics "must be as charitable toward the weaknesses of others" as they are to the weaknesses in themselves. They must recognize that "consciously or unconsciously" they "share in the collective guilt" of the age in which they live and find ways to "work out an atonement for this guilt in ways that would be redemptive and not make this action the goal of life." Finally, affirmation mystics can in no way approve of "violent coercion." Rather, affirmation mystics understand "that working and waiting are two separate activities of the human spirit" and recognizing that violent spiritual reality means waiting for "the new day... which can be achieved by God and God, alone."[101]

The Church for the Fellowship of All Peoples, which he helped to found, linked something of Thurman's mystical insights with his pluralistic vision of faith. He declared of the church, "We believe that in the presence of God with His dream of order there is neither male nor female, white nor black, Gentile nor Jew, Protestant nor Catholic, Hindu, Buddhist, nor Moslem, but a human spirit stripped to the literal substance of itself."[102] At the same time, Thurman's was a thoroughly christocentric mysticism, not simply a nebulous or generic spirituality. He wrote, "In Jesus Christ as symbol, temporary or permanent, the Christian mystic sees the meaning of the triumph of spirit over the body; the transcending and triumphant power of God over the most relentless pressure and persistence of things that divide and destroy."[103]

In the late twentieth and early twenty-first century, discussions of mystical elements of religious experience often linked to the so-called spirituality movement, in which Christian mysticism was one category of a broader approach to the meditative and experiential techniques of varying writers from multiple faith perspectives. This is not only true of the use of Howard Thurman's writings and insights, but also the works of Merton, Nouwen, Chittister, and others.[104]

"The Totality of the World": Defining Spirituality

By the twenty-first century, few observers of American culture would deny that there was an increasing curiosity about, if not participation in, varying dimensions of the spiritual life. Precise definitions of such spirituality are often difficult to formulate. For Christians, the term *spirituality* covers a wide spectrum that includes a recovery of early Christian literature, monastic writings, and disciplines, the "classics of Christian devotion," and various methodologies for securing "sanctification." Others who have little or no commitment to a particular religious tradition may choose to explore spiritual dynamics that draw on insights from various world religions, native folk traditions, or the occult. While much spirituality is anchored in specific religious traditions and practices, many contemporary individuals seem to prefer a more eclectic or blended approach that draws on multiple ideas and texts.

In its broadest sense, a concern for spirituality involves ways of cultivating or "practicing the Presence" of God, the Sacred, or the Other through innumerable, sometimes highly symbiotic, means. In describing spirituality, Peter H. Van Ness uses what he calls "a more dramatic idiom": *Toti se inserens mundo* ("Plunging oneself into the totality of the world"). It is, he says "an outer and an inner complexion, . . . the quest for attaining an optimal relationship between what one truly is and everything that is; . . . a quest that can be furthered by adopting appropriate spiritual practices and by participating in relevant communal rituals."[105] In this way, spiritual explorers may seek to encounter transcendence—a force or idea beyond themselves—or immanence—a sense of the Other or otherness present in themselves or in the world around them.

Roger Gottlieb echoed this idea when he wrote that "'spirituality' is a way to be fully at home in our lives and on this earth." It "can be expressed in the vocabularies of many different traditional faiths—or can be part of an agnostic stance which has no particular belief in God."[106] Such an eclectic or open-ended spirituality often seems rampant in twenty-first-century America as seekers pursue traditional and nontraditional approaches to spiritual exploration. Karen Smith suggested that spirituality involves "both intellectual knowledge and [religious] experience," a search for the knowledge of God and "an awareness of the transcendent." She called for a "dialogue between doctrine and experience" in the pursuit of a broad spirituality.[107] Smith cited Philip Sheldranke's assertion that "desire is at the heart of all spirituality. It is an energy that powers spirituality but, conversely, spirituality is concerned with how people focus desire. Christian spirituality embodies the sense that humanity has a longing that can only be satisfied in God."[108]

Gottlieb cautioned about interpreting spirituality as a purely personal exercise, insisting that it should also lead individuals "toward outer examination, outer transformation, and the pursuit of justice in the world." For "a spirituality of resistance, the costs of living a purely 'inner,' purely 'personal' spiritual life are too high." Rather, "spiritual progress" requires persons "to live on *this* earth," ever conscious of what is transpiring the larger culture and "resisting" what is evil or destructive.[109]

While interest in spirituality is certainly not new, many Americans continue to explore an assortment of paths to the spiritual life manifested inside and outside traditional religious institutions. In short, many Americans seem concerned about spiritual fulfillment and, like good American consumers, are willing to shop around until they find what they are looking for. In the quest for spiritual experience, the lines between Catholic and Protestant, liturgical and nonliturgical, Christian and non-Christian practices may become increasingly blurred. While many draw on multiple religious traditions, methodologies, and texts, the ancient history and traditions of Catholic spirituality make the Church a valuable resource for those who cultivate the pursuit of the spiritual life.

Many seekers utilize Roman Catholic approaches to spiritual formation, devotional literature, and monastic spirituality, yet have no personal or institutional connection to historical Catholicism at all. Catholic retreat centers, many located within monastic environments, report a burgeoning community of persons who desire such contemplative environments for their own spiritual pursuits. Such monastic retreat centers are often booked solid for up to a year in advance as believers and nonbelievers seek solitude and common prayer in those sacred environs. Few who utilize such sacred space have any intention of entering Catholic religious vocations or even engaging in the sacramental life of the Church. One Benedictine commented, "In twenty-first century America, everyone wants to take a retreat at a monastery but almost no one wants to become a monk!"

Catholic devotional literature provides spiritual direction for innumerable individuals, many of whom have no official relationship to the Roman Catholic Church. Although a Protestant, Kathleen Norris has written extensively about the benefits of her sojourns into monastic settings. *The Cloister*

Walk provides accounts from her stays at St. John's Abbey in Minnesota and extols blessings she received there. Norris described the ways in which the Rule of St. Benedict became transformative for her at a very difficult time of her life, noting, "I met the Rule by happy accident, *when I found myself staying in a small Benedictine convent* during a North Dakota Council on the Arts residency at a Catholic school."[110] Then she confessed,

> Quite simply, the Rule spoke to me. Like so many, I am put off by religious language as it's manipulated by television evangelists, used to preach to the converted, the "saved." Benedict's language and imagery come from the Bible, but he was someone who read the psalms every day—as Benedictines still do—and something of the psalms' emotional honesty, their grounding in the physical, rubbed off on him.[111]

By implication, the Rule "rubbed off" on Kathleen Norris fifteen hundred years later.

One need only traverse the shelves of the trade bookstores across the nation to find evidence of the popularity of the classics of Catholic devotion as religionists and secularists alike discover the strange and powerful writings of assorted mystics. Many women, Protestants and Catholics, are drawn to the writings of Julian of Norwich, Hildegard of Bingen, Teresa of Avila, and Sor Juana de la Cruz, to name only a few. Julian, Hildegard, and Teresa were given to visions and ecstatic encounters with the Divine, experiences that seem to captivate contemporary readers. From her German monastery, Hildegard (1098–1179) wrote of such a cataclysmic event,

> It happened that in the eleven hundred and forty-first year of the Incarnation of the Son of God, Jesus Christ, when I was forty-two years and seven months old, Heaven was opened and a fiery light of exceeding brilliance came and permeated my whole brain and inflamed my whole heart and my whole breast, not like a burning but like a warming flame, as the sun warms anything its rays touch.[112]

More recently, however, the Pentecostal/Charismatic vision of enthusiastic religion has found its way into numerous faith communities. By the

1970s students of American religion were documenting a "Neo-Pentecostal" or Charismatic movement evident in the counter culture of the Jesus Movement with its antidrug programs ("getting high on Jesus"), its contemporary worship practices, and its emphasis on Spirit baptism outside the norms of traditional Protestantism. Soon many non-Pentecostals attested to encounters with the Spirit as confirmed by particular charismatic enthusiasms. Charismatic Lutherans, Catholics, Episcopalians, Baptists, and nondenominationalists now lift their hands in common and personal prayer, dance, sing, and shout in the Spirit, and anoint the sick with oil. Some even speak in tongues, in public worship or as a type of private "prayer language." Preaching conferences, syndicated television broadcasts, or mass rallies such as those of the Promise Keepers organization are often distinguished by numerous charismatic manifestations. In fact, one of the most amazing religious phenomena of the twenty-first century is the extensive proliferation of charismatic experiences among a wide variety of Christian communions and individuals. The move toward "contemporary" worship services is sometimes an open door to certain charismatic practices in some of the most staid Protestant denominational-based churches.

Many Evangelical college students also reflect the influence of a more charismatic approach to spirituality. In public and private colleges and universities across the country, student-led, student-organized worship services are characterized by contemporary Christian music, "praise choruses" (brief hymns with catchy lyrics and words posted on a screen above the congregation), small-group prayer time, and informal, exuberant preaching.

These types of religious experience might be described as "charismatic lite," observances distinguished by "hands, no tongues," in which participants willingly raise their hands in song and prayer as a charismatic sign of their praise to God, but most do not practice glossolalia. They are Charismatic but not necessarily Pentecostal. Charismatic influence on worship in a wide variety of Christian communions illustrates yet another blurring of the lines of between many religious groups. Others manifest speaking in tongues through private "prayer language" of secret devotions, not in public expression.

Elements of Catholic, charismatic, globalist, and nonconformist spirituality may be fused in the practices of some religious Americans. There are communions that claim the name "Charismatic Episcopalians," mingling prayer book liturgy with Spirit-filled enthusiasms. Likewise, certain Buddhist and Christian monastics now provide retreats for persons interested in exploring the shared spiritual legacies of those two traditions. In many communities, public religious occasions, once labeled "ecumenical," are now designated "inter-faith," bringing together representatives of Christian, Jewish, Muslim, Buddhist, and other communions.

What does this extensive concern for spirituality suggest about the American religious future? On one hand, the phenomenon may simply be another great American self-help fad and a further indication of the rabid individualism that lies at the heart of the American psyche. Obsession with personal spirituality may be an attempt by American materialists to fill yet another void in their unending search for fulfillment. On the other hand, interest in spirituality may imply that even in a highly secular environment, some religious and nonreligious Americans continue to search for signs of spiritual immanence and transcendence, a sense of the "Presence" that is at once beyond and within themselves.

Toward the future, the quest for spiritual experience no doubt will be influenced by an abiding religious and cultural pluralism that challenges Protestant, perhaps even Christian, hegemony over religious insights and institutions. Religious liberty, a freedom that Americans always seem to grant grudgingly to immigrant or indigenous religious communities, must be extended in ways that foster dialogue and learning. It may also contribute to a new tribalism as old fears create new bigotry. Leaders of Evangelical Christian groups, many of whose members draw spiritual sustenance from Catholic or charismatic practices, currently fret that this eclecticism will undermine doctrinal orthodoxy and foster a worrisome "universalism" among the faithful. Many wonder how best to respond hospitably to other spiritual traditions, while asserting the uniqueness of their own faith, all without appearing to be intolerant.

Other religious communions may be forced to determine how much of their spiritual tradition can be bartered in a pluralistic environment and how much can only be properly appropriated only within a specific context of faith and practice. Many classic Pentecostals, for example, worry that charismatic Christians have co-opted the outward manifestations of spiritual experience while avoiding the "hard sayings" of the gospel regarding holiness of life and the daily struggle for "Christian perfection." Some Catholic leaders fear that many who visit monasteries today will move on to Cherokee sweat lodges or New Age pyramids tomorrow. Cherokee religious leaders disagree over whether to admit persons with no Native heritage to sweat lodges and other sacred rites. An eclectic pluralism may foster a kind of generic spirituality without context, community, or specificity.

Whatever else it may mean, the concern for spirituality is yet another indication of a state of permanent transition that has descended upon American religious institutions. Many Americans interested in spiritual renewal are not seeking it in institutional religion. They are sometimes identified as "believers but not belongers," individuals who pursue spiritual fulfillment, but not as participants in established denominations, churches, and programs. Even those inside conventional communions seem to wear their affiliations loosely. Many seem willing to jettison previous affiliations if more fruitful spiritual experiences may be secured elsewhere. That trend seems certain to continue.

"Believers but not Belongers": Religious Experience and the Future

If nothing else, the rise of the spirituality movement in the late twentieth and early twenty-first centuries illustrated the real presence of religious pluralism in the United States, not simply in Judeo-Christian groups, but in multiple religious traditions and practices evident throughout the country. Amanda Porterfield observed that in spite of "remarkable similarities in the transformations of religion in the mid-eighteenth and late twentieth centuries," the "changes that occurred in American religious life since the 1960s were unprecedented." While the religious landscape remained predominately Christian, it was "deeply altered" by varying religious ideologies, including numerous "Buddhist ideas" that "filtered" into diverse elements of the culture.[113] Likewise, an expanding number of Americans seemed to have disengaged entirely from formal religious institutions.

Few individuals have illustrated the impact of religious pluralism, particularly among Christians and Buddhists more than than the Vietnamese Zen Buddhist Thich Nhat Hanh (1926–), monastery founder, peace activist, and writer. Nominated for the Nobel Peace Prize by Martin Luther King Jr. in 1967 (no prize was given that year), Thich Nhat Hanh's effort to link elements of Buddhist and Christian spirituality are evident in his best-selling work, *Living Buddha, Living Christ*, published in 1995. He wrote, "On the altar in my hermitage in France are images of Buddha and Jesus, and every time I light incense, I touch both of them as my spiritual ancestors."[114] As he saw it, dialogue between the religious communities identified by those two inspired individuals was essential for deepening the spiritual experience of both groups. Such discourse offered "the possibility of making a change within ourselves, that we can become deeper. Dialogue is not a means for assimilation in the sense that one side expands and incorporates the other into its 'self.'" Rather, the conversation partners "have to allow what is good, beautiful and meaningful in the other's tradition to transform us."[115] Linking Buddhist "mindfulness" with the presence of the Holy Spirit, Thich Nhat Hanh insisted that living faith must transcend "rigid beliefs and notions," an ever-evolving pilgrimage toward "joy, peace, freedom, and love." He concluded that "our actions must be modeled after those of the living Buddha or the living Christ. If we live as they did, we will have deep understanding and pure actions, and we will do our share to help create a more peaceful world for our children and all of the children of God."[116] He freely acknowledged differences between the two groups while challenging the idea "that Christianity provides the only way of salvation and all other religious traditions are of no use. This attitude excludes dialogue and fosters religious intolerance and discrimination. It does not help."[117]

Thich Nhat Hanh's approach to religious experience parallels that of his friend, Trappist Thomas Merton, who likewise encouraged Buddhist/Christian pursuit of shared spiritual quests while acknowledging realistic differences. In *Mystics and Zen Masters* Merton wrote,

> Zen enlightenment is an insight into being in all its existential reality and actualization. It is a full alert and superconscious act of being which transcends time and space. Such is the attainment of the "Buddha mind," or "Buddhahood." (Compare the Christian expressions "having the mind of Christ" [1 Cor. 2:16, being "of one Spirit with Christ," "He who is united to the Lord is one spirit" [1 Cor. 6:17], though the Buddhist idea takes no account of any "supernatural order" in the Thomistic sense.)[118]

Merton's investigations of Zen Buddhism, Sufi mysticism, and Taoist contemplation grew out of his own quest for common threads of shared religious experiences. He noted,

> It is in surrendering a false and illusory liberty on the superficial level that man unites himself with the inner ground of reality and freedom in himself which is the will of God, of Krishna, of Providence, of Tao. These concepts do not all exactly coincide, but they have much in common. It is by remaining open to an infinite number of unexpected possibilities which transcend his own imagination and capacity to plan that man really fulfills his own need for freedom. The *Gita*, like the Gospels, teaches us to live in awareness of an inner truth that exceeds the grasp of our thought and cannot be subject to our own control. In following mere appetite for power we are slaves of appetite. In obedience to that truth we are at last free.[119]

Merton's untimely death in Bangkok, Thailand in 1968 occurred at a monastic gathering where discussion of Buddhist/Catholic spirituality was an important topic.

Amanda Porterfield concluded that Merton

> gathered Hindu, Buddhist, and Native American mythologies together within the framework of Christian mythology and Catholic monasticism. At the same time, he loosened the connection between monastic mysticism

> and the Catholic Church and set it free for anyone to use as a base for uniting the mystical and mythological aspects of various religious traditions in various forms of personal spirituality.[120]

Diana Butler Bass suggests that while "religious people" often view "spirituality" as a "vacuous or vague" concept, it is neither. She writes, "Despite a certain linguistic fuzziness, the word 'spiritual' is both a critique of institutional religion and a longing for meaningful connection." Instead it may well describe "a search for new gods" in a world where older forms of religion "and the institutions that preached, preserved, and protected" them "lose credibility."[121] Thus spirituality may represent "an important stage of awakening."[122]

Bass's observations regarding the loss of credibility by traditional religious communities seemed to be confirmed for organized religion in general, and Protestants in particular, by cultural transitions evident the early twenty-first century. In *American Grace: How Religion Divides and Unites Us* (2010), sociologists Robert D. Putnam and David E. Campbell surveyed decades of religious polling in what they called the "malleable nature of American religion," a "fluid" environment in which religious pluralism and polarization seem to coexist.[123] They documented long-term declines among Protestant "mainline" denominations at 13 percent of the population, plateauing among American Evangelicals, a drop from 28 percent in the 1990s to 24 percent in the early 2000s, with Catholicism, the largest religious communion in the US, claiming 18 percent of the population but with dramatic declines among "Anglo-Catholics." At the same time, their data suggested a dramatic rise in the "nones," those who when polled indicate that they have no formal religious affiliation. This group, long numbered at around 7 percent, jumped to between 15 percent and 20 percent by 2010.[124] Yet in the multiple choices of American religious and experiential pluralism, many of these "nones" simply consider themselves "believers but not belongers," or "spiritual but not religious."[125]

In discussing these cultural and religious transitions, David Lyon noted that where Peter Berger linked modernity with "homeless minds," postmodernity might well produce "homeless hearts," shaped by individualism, "personal freedom, and creativity."[126] Rooted in the 1960s, this "romantically inspired expressive individualism... came home to roost in the 1990s." Lyon cited Robert Wuthnow's contention that such individualism involves elements of "the autonomous subject" in which "religious expression is becoming increasingly the product of individual biographies."[127] While certain persons may "believe without belonging" to traditional religious communities, what is the basis of their belief and practice and "what sorts of attachments and connection do persist" after they have set aside participation in particular religious communions and experiences?[128] Lyon suggested that although "grand narratives" of religious life and practice might be "fading," that did not mean that all communal narratives were absent from or outside aspects of the sacred. Nonetheless, these postmodern stories were "much more fluid, malleable, and personalized" than those of an earlier, more modern, orientation.[129]

Other writers are quite optimistic about these postmodern transitions in spirituality and experientialism. Diana Butler Bass contended that "conventional religion is failing and a new form of faith, which some call 'spirituality' and can also be called *religio*, is being born."[130] She called this phenomenon "a new spiritual awakening,... being performed in a networked world, where the border between sacred and secular has eroded and where the love of God and neighbor—and the new vision of belonging, behaving, and believing—is being staged far beyond conventional religious communities."[131] This "interfaith awakening" does not promote one global or "imperialistic religion" but requires an ability to affirm a particular religious identity, while recognizing the multiplicity of spiritualities that honor "the wisdom of others in a mutual, spiritual quest toward 'full human existence.'"[132] Bass joined Harvey Cox, Phyllis Tickle, and other twenty-first century religionists in anticipating what Cox called "the Age of the Spirit," an era that Bass described as "an effusive, experiential, practice-centered impulse of faith sweeping across the globe," and present in segments of the world's great religions.[133] Cox labeled this spiritual renewal "the rediscovery of the sacred *in* the immanent, the spiritual *within* the secular."[134] He connected religious experience with "awe and mystery," writing, "Faith begins with awe in the face of mystery. But awe becomes faith only when it takes the next step."[135] Cox concluded that a renewed movement of the Spirit was evident across the postmodern globe, contributing to the "shaking and renewing" of traditional Christianity. He wrote, "Faith, rather than beliefs, is once again becoming its defining quality, and this reclaims what faith meant during its earliest years. By the twenty-first century the old church/state alliances dating from the Constantinian era are finally disappearing." Instead, "a newly global Christianity, enlivened by a multiplicity of cultures and yearning for the realization of God's reign of *shalom*, is finding its soul again."[136]

Phyllis Tickle called this transitional movement "the Great Emergence," "a monumental phenomenon" that impacts all aspects of individual and communal life, spiritually, politically, economically, and socially. Like Bass and Cox, she is optimistic about the promise of this new era, a time that she believes will produce a "more vital form of Christianity, . . . reconstituted into a more pure and less ossified expression of its former self." As in other periods of awakening and renewal, the "Great Emergence" promises to increase "exponentially the range and depth of Christianity's reach."[137]

Noting the benefits and challenges of social media from radio to Internet, Tickle commented that "we cannot ignore the passing of much religious experience, instruction, and formal worship from sacred space to secular space and perhaps even more significantly into electronic space." She noted that "millions of Americans" receive pastoral care, religious instruction and, one might add, the path to spiritual experience through multiple websites across the Internet.[138] Tickle observed that computers extend the idea of the priesthood of all believers "in ways the Reformation could never have envisioned."[139] She concluded, "To the extent that faith can be formed or dissuaded by the contents of the mind as well as those of the heart, then such license has huge implications for the Great Emergence and for what it will decide to do about factuality in a wiki world."[140]

In many ways, the United States has often seemed a "Christ haunted" environment, as Flannery O'Connor called the South. From the colonial era to the twenty-first century, religious experience was shaped by and within multiple religious communities from the "once-born" experiences of Catholic and Protestant sacramentalism, to the "second birth" required by revivalistic conversionists, to certain mystical or experiential elements variously evident among Transcendentalists, Quakers, Spiritualists, and Social Gospel Liberals. Millennialism and the possibility of the coming kingdom heightened religious experiences from communitarian Shakers and Oneidaites to Mormons, Pentecostals, and premillennialist fundamentalists and postmillennial Social Gospelers. New eclectic spiritualities took shape that produced other options for encounter with the Sacred, at least in those who still found it a worthy pursuit.

Some twentieth-century analysts offered valuable assessments, even anticipating the transition that lay ahead. In an essay called "The Night Spirit and the Dawn Air" Merton wrote, "The religious genius of the Protestant Reformation, as I see it, lies in its struggle with the problem of justification in all its depth." He suggested that in its "simplest form" justification involves the conversion of "the wicked and the sinful to Christ." Merton insisted that Protestants expanded such justification in its "*most radical form*" to the more "problematic" call for the conversion "of the pious and the good."[141] Catholics and Protestants alike could affirm that "conversion to Christ is not merely the conversion from bad habits to good habits, but *nova creatura*" transformation into a new creation "in Christ and in the Spirit." With their concern for good works, Catholics, Merton observed, sometimes "neglect the new being, life in Christ." Of Protestant conversionism, Merton concluded,

> And when Protestantism is unfaithful to its gift, it first lays down even the "new being" and the radical depth of conversion, in order to emphasize the pure grace and gift of Christ's pardon (hence we remain essentially wicked), or else, later, forgetting the seriousness of the need to convert the good, bogs down in the satisfied complacency of a rather superficial and suburban goodness—the folksy togetherness, the handshaking fellowship, the garrulous witness of moral platitudes. . . . Here is where *fides sola* may have proved to be dangerous. For the faith that justifies is not just any faith, or even the faith that, at revival time, *feels* itself justifies. In the end an insufficient faith

> is not belief in Christ and obedience to His word, but only a question of believing we believe because we are found acceptable in the eyes of other believers.[142]

Merton's comments on the vulnerability of spiritual experience in non-Catholic communions were offered cautiously, with more intense concern for dialogue than critique. He wrote,

> I will be a better Catholic, not if I can *refute* every shade of Protestantism, but if I can affirm the truth in it and still go further. So, too, with the Muslims, the Hindus, the Buddhists, etc. This does not mean syncretism, indifferentism, the vapid and careless friendliness that accepts everything by thinking of nothing. There is much that one cannot ""affirm" and "accept," but first must say "yes" where one really can. If I affirm myself as a Catholic merely by denying all that is Muslim, Jewish, Protestant, Hindu, Buddhist, etc., in the end I will find that there is not much left for me to affirm as a Catholic: and certainly no breath of the Spirit with which to affirm it.[143]

Porterfield goes even further in connecting religious pluralism and specificity with the heritage of New England Transcendentalism and Puritan experientialism. While recognizing that the "new religious world" of late twentieth-century America was "post-Protestant," she insisted that "the identification of spiritual life with recognition of the beauty of being," evident in the work of Jonathan Edwards, "would be endorsed by many recent proponents of spirituality."[144] Whether Edwards would appreciate manifold "*senses* of the heart" remains an issue for continued discussion.

Notes

Preface

1. William James, *Varieties of Religious Experience* (New York: The Modern Library, 1902), 8.

2. Horace Bushnell, *Christian Nurture* (New York: Charles Scribner & Co., 1871), 10.

3. John Williamson Nevin, *The Anxious Bench* (Chambersburg, PA: Office of the German Ref. Church, 1844).

4. Isaac T. Hecker, *Isaac T. Hecker: The Diary*, ed. John Farina (New York: Paulist Press, 1988), 138.

5. James, *Varieties of Religious Experience*, 8.

6. Jonathan Edwards, "A Faithful Narrative of the Surprising Work of God," in *The Great Awakening*, The Works of Jonathan Edwards, vol. 4, ed. C. C. Goen (New Haven: Yale University Press, 1972), 200.

7. Barton W. Stone, *The Biography of Eld. Barton Warren Stone* (Cincinnati: J. A. & U. P. James, 1847), 34.

8. Matthew C. Bagger, *Religious Experience: Justification, and History* (Cambridge, UK: Cambridge University Press, 1999), 11.

9. Ibid., citing Jeffrey Stout, *The Flight from Authority* (Notre Dame: University of Notre Dame Press, 1981), 168.

10. William G. McLoughlin, *Revivals, Awakenings, and Reform* (Chicago: University of Chicago Press, 1978), 2.

11. John Calvin, *Institutes of the Christian Religion* (Edinburgh: T & T Clark, 1863), 513.

12. George Whitefield, "Repentance and Conversion," in *Sermons on Important Subjects* (London: Henry Fisher, Son, and P. Jackson, 1831), 665.

13. Wayne Proudfoot, *Religious Experience* (Berkley: University of California Press, 1985), 10.

14. James, *Varieties of Religious Experience*, 19.

15. Jacqueline Bernard, *Journey toward Freedom: The Story of Sojourner Truth* (New York: W. W. Norton & Company, 1967), 67.

16. Jonathan Edwards, *Religious Affections*, ed. John E. Smith (New Haven: Yale University Press, 1959), 272–75.

17. Bill J. Leonard, "Getting Saved in America: Conversion Event in a Pluralistic Culture," *Review and Expositor* 82 (Winter 1985): 111–12.

18. Ibid., 112.

1. A Sense of the Heart

1. Jonathan Edwards, *Religious Affections*, The Works of Jonathan Edwards, vol. 2, ed. John E. Smith (New Haven: Yale University Press, 1959), 272.

2. Ibid., 1.

3. Ibid., 2.

4. Ibid., 272.

5. Ibid.

6. Robert W. Jenson, *America's Theologian: A Recommendation of Jonathan Edwards* (New York: Oxford University Press, 1988), 66–67.

7. Ibid., 67.

8. Ibid., 68–69, citing Edwards's sermon, "A Divine and Supernatural Light."

9. Ibid., 69.

10. Wayne Proudfoot, *Religious Experience* (Berkley: University of California Press, 1985), xii.

11. Ninian Smart, *The Religious Experience*, 5th ed. (Upper Saddle River, NJ: Prentice Hall, 1996), 2–6.

12. Michael H. Barnes, *In the Presence of Mystery: An Introduction to the Story of Human Righteousness* (Mystic, CT: Twenty-Third Publications, 1987), 7.

13. Ibid., 12.

14. Ibid., 16–17.

15. Ibid., 19–22.

16. Ibid., 39–40.

17. A. D. Nock, *Conversion: The Old and the New Religion from Alexander the Great to Augustine of Hippo* (Baltimore: Johns Hopkins Press, 1933), 8–9.

18. Ibid., 7.

19. Ibid.

20. Luke Timothy Johnson, *Religious Experience in Earliest Christianity* (Minneapolis: Fortress Press, 1998), 53.

21. Ibid.

22. Proudfoot, *Religious Experience*, xiii.

23. Friedrich Schleiermacher, *On Religion: Addresses in Response to Its Cultured Critics*, trans. Terrence N. Tice (Richmond: John Knox Press, 1969), 207.

24. Ibid., 208

25. Proudfoot, *Religious Experience*, xiii, 6.

26. Terrence N. Tice, "Introduction," in Schleiermacher, *On Religion*, 10–11.

27. Proudfoot, *Religious Experience*, 10.

28. Ibid., 17. See also Schleiermacher, *On Religion*, 94.

29. Schleiermacher, *On Religion*, 78–79.

30. Ibid., 82.

31. Ibid., 85.

32. Ibid., 89–90.

33. Proudfoot, *Religious Experience*, 7.

34. Schleiermacher, *On Religion*, 140.

35. Ibid., 94. Schleiermacher is quick to suggest that "it is not necessary, however, to regard the deity as an object, individual and isolated." In the introduction to *On Religion* Tice notes Schleiermacher's limited use of the term *God*, since it carried "traditional connotations to the cultured critics of religion" he seeks to address. He also uses the term *Deity*, referencing a "supreme being as an active agent in history, but theologically neutral on the whole despite this fact." (Tice, "Introduction," in *On Religion*, 22–23.)

36. William James, *The Varieties of Religious Experience* (New York: The Modern Library, 1902, 1929), 6.

37. Ibid., 7.

38. Ibid., 8. See also Ann Taves, *Fits, Trances, & Visions: Experiencing Religion and Explaining Experience from Wesley to James* (Princeton, NJ: Princeton University Press, 1999). Taves offers a major study of both the history and phenomenology of various types of religious experience, with particular attention to certain psychophysical expressions of spirituality.

39. James, *The Varieties of Religious Experience*, 21.

40. Ibid., 29–30.

41. Ibid., 31–32, emphasis original. James acknowledges that the word *divine* can be problematic since the definitions as to what constitutes the nature of divinity vary from religion to religion, sect to sect. He illustrates that in the approach of Ralph Waldo Emerson who, James says, "seems to let God evaporate into abstract Ideality." James's study of religious experience is not limited to Judeo-Christian or traditionally theistic traditions.

42. Ibid., 39.

43. Proudfoot, *Religious Experience*, 76–77, 158–59.

44. Ibid., 158.

45. James, *The Varieties of Religious Experience*, 53.

46. Ibid., 55.

47. Ibid., 77.

48. Ibid., 79.

49. Ibid., 81–82.

50. Ibid., 89–90.

51. Ibid., 93.

52. Ibid., 128–29.

53. Ibid., 132.

54. Ibid., 142. James gives extensive attention to the life of Leo Tolstoy as illustrative of the struggles involved in securing the twice-born religious experience.

55. Ibid., 155.

56. Ibid., 160.

57. Ibid., 163.

58. Ibid., 184.

59. Ibid., 185.

60. Ibid., 186.

61. Ibid., 192–93.

62. Ibid., 200.

63. Ibid., 200–1.

64. Ibid., 204n2.

65. Ibid., 203–4.

66. Ibid., 205.

67. Ibid., 207. One of several case studies James uses to illustrate the self-surrender type of conversion is David Brainerd, whose conversion offers clear evidence of the struggle with sin and the continued struggle to relinquish the willfulness toward sin.

68. Ibid., 223.

69. Ibid., 224.

70. Ibid., 226.

71. Ibid., 233.

72. Ibid., 234–35. James quotes Emerson on distinctions and similarities between once- and twice-born individuals.

73. Ibid., 238–39.

74. Ibid., 240. He acknowledges that since the Reformation, Protestantism has

adapted that theology of the "sick soul" considerably, but that "the adequacy of his view of Christianity to the deeper parts of our human mental structure is shown by its wildfire contagiousness when it was a new and quickening thing."

75. Ibid., 242–46.

76. Ibid., 246.

77. Ibid., 475–76.

78. Ibid., 511.

79. Ibid., 498.

80. Taves, *Fits, Trances, & Visions*, 4–5.

81. Ibid., 3, 351–53.

82. Ibid., 351.

83. Ibid.

84. Ibid., 252.

85. Ibid.

86. Ibid., 361.

87. Lawrence S. Cunningham and John Kelsay, *The Sacred Quest: An Invitation to the Study of Religion*, 3rd ed. (Upper Saddle River, NJ: Prentice Hall, 2002), 39–41.

88. Rufus M. Jones, *The Testimony of the Soul* (New York: The MacMillan Company, 1936), 40–41.

89. Ann Taves, *Fits, Trances, & Visions*, 3.

90. Johnson, *Religious Experience in Earliest Christianity*, 60, citing "The Nature of Religious Experience," in J. Wach, *The Comparative Study of Religions*, ed. J. M. Kitagawa, Lectures on the History of Religions, n.s. 4 (New York: Columbia University Press, 1958), 27–58.

91. Taves, *Fits, Trances, & Visions*, 351.

92. Johnson, *Religious Experience in Earliest Christianity*, 62.

93. Ibid., 63.

94. Jones, *The Testimony of the Soul*, 41.

95. Ibid., 8.

96. Ibid.

97. William A. Clebsch, *American Religious Thought: A History* (Chicago: University of Chicago Press, 1973), 3–4.

98. Ibid., 4.

2. The Heart Prepared

1. Teresa of Avila, *The Life of Teresa of Jesus*, trans. E. Allison Peers (Garden City, New York: Image Books, 1960), 274–75.

2. Augustine, *The Confessions of St. Augustine*, trans. John K. Ryan (Garden City, New York: Image Books, 1960), 202.

3. Martin E. Marty, *Martin Luther* (New York: A Lipper/Viking Book, 2004), 64.

4. Ibid., 65.

5. John Calvin, *Institutes of the Christian Religion*, Vol. II, trans. Henry Beveridge (Edinburgh: T & T Clark, 1863), 244, Emphasis mine.

6. Edmund S. Morgan, *Visible Saints: The History of a Puritan Idea* (Ithaca: Cornell University Press, 1963), 67.

7. Calvin, *Institutes of the Christian Religion*, Vol. II, 242.

8. Ibid., 243.

9. Ibid.

10. Ibid., 245.

11. Ibid., 247.

12. John E. Smith, "Historical Introduction," in Jonathan Edwards, *Religious Affections*, The Works of Jonathan Edwards, vol. 2, ed. John E. Smith (New Haven: Yale University Press, 1959), 65.

13. Sydney E. Ahlstrom, *A Religious History of the American People* (New Haven: Yale University Press, 1972), 132. Ahlstrom noted that "after Cromwell's ascendancy these notions would also become widespread in England."

14. C. C. Goen, "Editorial Introduction," in Jonathan Edwards, *The Great Awakening*, The Works of Jonathan Edwards, vol. 4, ed. by C. C. Goen (New Haven: Yale University Press, 1972), 2.

15. Morgan, *Visible Saints*, 93.

16. Ibid., 66.

17. *The Waterland Confession (1580)*, in *Baptist Confessions of Faith*, ed. William L. Lumpkin and Bill J. Leonard, 2nd rev. ed. (Valley Forge: Judson Press, 2011), 54.

18. *A Declaration of Faith of English People Remaining in Amsterdam in Holland, 1611*, in Lumpkin and Leonard, *Baptist Confessions of Faith*, 111.

19. *A Confession of the Faith of Several Churches of Christ In the County of Somerset...*, in Lumpkin and Leonard, *Baptist Confessions of Faith*, 194.

20. *An Orthodox Creed, Or A Protestant Confession of Faith, being an Essay to Unite and Confirm all True Protestants*, in Lumpkin and Leonard, *Baptist Confessions of Faith*, 324.

21. *A Brief Confession or Declaration of Faith (1660)*, in Lumpkin and Leonard, *Baptist Confessions of Faith*, 208–9.

22. *The Confession of Faith, of those churches which are commonly (though falsely) called Anabaptist* (1644), in Lumpkin and Leonard, *Baptist Confessions of Faith*, 150–51.

23. Morgan, *Visible Saints*, 68.

24. Norman Pettit, "The Order of Salvation in Thomas Hooker's Thought," in

Thomas Hooker: Writings in England and Holland, 1626–1633, ed. George H. Williams, Norman Pettit, Winfried Herget, and Sargent Bush Jr., (Cambridge: Harvard University Press, 1975), 124, 127.

25. Thomas Hooker, "The Poor Doubting Christian Drawn Unto Christ," in Williams et al., *Thomas Hooker: Writings in England and Holland*, 176.

26. Ibid., 179, 181.

27. Ibid., 181.

28. Ibid., 182.

29. Ibid., 183, 184.

30. Norman Pettit, *The Heart Prepared: Grace and Conversion in Puritan Spiritual Life* (Middletown, CT: Wesleyan University Press, 1989), 100–1.

31. Edmund S. Morgan, *The Puritan Dilemma: The Story of John Winthrop* (Boston: Little, Brown and Company, 1958), 136–37.

32. John Cotton, *A Treatise of the Covenant of Grace*, (London, 1632), 35, cited in Williams et al., *Thomas Hooker: Writings in England and Holland*, 135.

33. Ibid., 121–23; see also John Cotton, *The Way of Life* (London, 1641), in Williams et al., *Thomas Hooker: Writings in England and Holland*, 134.

34. Pettit, "The Order of Salvation," in Williams et al., *Thomas Hooker: Writings in England and Holland*, 137.

35. Morgan, *The Puritan Dilemma*, 139.

36. Ibid., 140.

37. James K. Hosmer, ed., *Winthrop's Journal*, vol. 1 (New York: Charles Scribner's Sons, 1908), 195–96, cited in H. Shelton Smith, Robert T. Handy, Lefferts A. Loetscher, *American Christianity*, vol. 1, *1607–1820* (New York: Charles Scribner's Sons, 1960), 115.

38. Pettit, "The Order of Salvation," in Williams et al., *Thomas Hooker: Writings in England and Holland*, 136.

39. Ibid., 138.

40. Conrad Wright, *The Beginnings of Unitarianism in America* (Boston: Beacon Press, 1966), 16–17.

41. Ibid., 10.

42. Ibid., 15.

43. Calvin, *Institutes of the Christian Religion*, 2:531.

44. C. C. Goen, "Editorial Introduction," in Edwards, *The Great Awakening*, 12–13.

45. Ahlstrom, *A Religious History of the American People*, 159–60.

46. William G. McLoughlin, *Revivals, Awakenings, and Reform* (Chicago: University of Chicago Press, 1978), 25.

47. Ibid., 41.

48. Ibid.

49. George Fox, *The Journal of George Fox* (New York: Capricorn Books, 1963), 83.

50. Ibid., 82.

51. Smith, Handy, and Loetscher, *American Christianity*, 147–48.

52. Carla Gardina Pestana, *Quakers and Baptists in Colonial Massachusetts* (Cambridge, UK: Cambridge University Press, 1991), 12.

53. Smith, Handy, and Loetscher, *American Christianity*, 149.

54. Jon Butler, *Awash in a Sea of Faith* (Cambridge, MA: Harvard University Press, 1990), 23.

55. Pestana, *Quakers and Baptists in Colonial Massachusetts*, 13.

56. Ibid., 9.

57. Ibid., 23. The Midlands Baptist Confession of Faith reads, "Wee believe that there is one only true God which is one God who is eternall, almighty, unchaingable and incomprehensible, infinite; who is a spirit having his being of himself and giveth being to all creatures and doth what he will in heaven and earth moveing all things according to the cousell of his own will." (Lumpkin and Leonard, *Baptist Confessions of Faith*, 182.

58. McLoughlin, *Revivals, Awakenings, and Reform*, 35.

3. Colonial Awakenings

1. C. C. Goen, "Editorial Introduction," in Jonathan Edwards, *The Great Awakening*, The Works of Jonathan Edwards, vol. 4, ed. C. C. Goen (New Haven: Yale University Press, 1972), 2.

2. John Butler, *Awash in a Sea of Faith* (Cambridge, MA: Harvard University Press, 1990), 177. Butler cites Perry Miller, *The New England Mind: From Colony to Province* (Cambridge, MA: Harvard University Press, 1953), 105–18, along with other sources to confirm the claims of multiple awakenings during this period.

3. William G. McLoughlin, *Revivals, Awakenings, and Reform* (Chicago: University of Chicago Press, 1978), 25.

4. Conrad Cherry, *God's New Israel* (Chapel Hill: University of North Carolina Press, 1998); and Ernest Lee Tuveson, *Redeemer Nation* (Chicago: University of Chicago Press, 1974).

5. The literature surrounding the interpretation of the Great Awakening is extensive. Diverse views are evident in Alan Heimert, *Religion and the American Mind* (Cambridge, MA: Harvard University Press, 1966); Edwin S. Gaustad, *The Great Awakening in New England* (New York: Harper & Row, 1957); C. C. Goen, *Revivalism and Separatism in New England* (New Haven: Yale University Press, 1962); John Butler, *Awash in a Sea of Faith*; Frank Lambert, *Inventing the "Great Awakening"*

(Princeton, NJ: Princeton University Press, 1999); and Robert Brockway, *A Wonderful Work of God: Puritanism and the Great Awakening* (Bethlehem, PA: Lehigh University Press, 2003).

6. Lambert, *Inventing the "Great Awakening,"* 174.

7. Ibid., 176.

8. William James, *The Varieties of Religious Experience* (New York: The Modern Library, 1929), 223.

9. Goen, "Editorial Introduction," in Edwards, *The Great Awakening*, 3.

10. Edwin S. Gaustad, *The Great Awakening in New England* (Chicago: Quadrangle Books, 1957), 17.

11. Norman Pettit, *The Heart Prepared: Grace and Conversion in Puritan Spiritual Life*, 2nd ed. (Middletown, CT: Wesleyan University Press, 1989), 207.

12. Ibid.

13. Jonathan Edwards, *A Faithful Narrative of the Surprising Work of God*, in Edwards, *The Great Awakening*, 146.

14. Ibid., 148–49.

15. Ibid., 150.

16. Ibid., 177–78. For a discussion of the multiple editions of the treatise see Edwards, *The Great Awakening*, 99–142.

17. Ibid., 175.

18. Edwards, *A Faithful Narrative of the Surprising Work of God*, 160–77; see also Edmund S. Morgan, *Visible Saints: The History of a Puritan Idea* (Ithaca: Cornell University Press, 1963), 91; and Bill J. Leonard, "Getting Saved in America: Conversion Event in a Pluralistic Culture," *Review and Expositor* (Winter 1985): 116.

19. Edwards, *A Faithful Narrative of the Surprising Work of God*, 148.

20. Ibid., 182.

21. Edwards, *A Faithful Narrative of the Surprising Work of God*, 192.

22. Ibid., 194.

23. Ibid., 198.

24. Ibid., 200.

25. Ibid., 202–4.

26. Ibid., 206.

27. George M. Marsden, *Jonathan Edwards: A Life* (New Haven: Yale University Press, 2003), 167.

28. Samuel Blair, *A Short and Faithful Narrative, Of the late Remarkable Revival of Religion In the Congregation of New-Londonderry* (Philadelphia, 1744), in *The Great Awakening: Documents on the Revival of Religion, 1740–1745*, ed. Richard L. Bushman (New York: Atheneum, 1970), 73.

29. Ibid.

30. Ibid.

31. Ibid., 76.

32. Alexander Garden, *Regeneration, and The Testimony of the Spirit. Being the Substance of Two Sermons Occasioned by some erroneous Notions of certain Men who call themselves Methodists* (Charleston, S.D., 1740; reprinted Boston, 1741), in *The Great Awakening: Documents Illustrating the Crisis and Its Consequences*, ed. Alan Heimert and Perry Miller (New York: The Bobbs-Merrill Company, Inc., 1967), 50.

33. Ibid., 55–56.

34. Ibid., 60.

35. Charles Chauncy, *Enthusiasm described and caution'd against* (Boston, 1742), in Heimert and Miller, *The Great Awakening*, 231–32.

36. Ibid., 232–33.

37. Ibid., 236–37.

38. Ibid., 239–41.

39. Ibid., 253–54.

40. Charles Chauncy, *Seasonable Thoughts on the State of Religion in New England* (Boston, 1743), in Heimert and Miller, *The Great Awakening*, 300.

41. Ibid., 301. Italics are from the printed text of the sermon.

42. John E. Smith, "Historical Introduction," in Edwards, *Religious Affections*, 11, 12.

43. Ibid., 16.

44. Edwards, *Religious Affections*, 96.

45. Ibid., 197.

46. Ibid., 102.

47. Ibid., 147.

48. Smith, "Historical Introduction," 20–21.

49. Edwards, *Religious Affections*, 152.

50. Ibid., 157.

51. Ibid., 160.

52. Ibid.

53. Ibid., 161

54. Edwards, *Religious Affections*, 193.

55. Ibid.

56. Ibid., 209.

57. Ibid., 212.

58. Ibid., 221.

59. Ibid., 222–23.

60. Ibid., 272. Bold print added for emphasis.

61. Ibid.

62. Ibid., 273–74.

63. Ibid., 311.

64. Ibid., 316. Edwards would witness this evangelical humiliation carried to great extreme in the spiritual life of David Brainerd, whose diary he published even as he cautioned against its ascetical excesses.

65. Ibid., 412.

66. William A. Clebsch, *American Religious Thought: A History* (Chicago: University of Chicago Press, 197), 17.

67. Ibid., 17–18.

68. Charles Lippy, *Seasonable Revolutionary: The Mind of Charles Chauncy* (Chicago: Nelson-Hall, 1981), 25. Among others, Lippy cites the following works as illustrating such treatment of Chauncy: Conrad Wright, *The Beginnings of Unitarianism in America* (Boston: Beacon Press, 1955); and Alan Heimert, *Religion and the American Mind* (Cambridge, MA: Harvard University Press, 1966).

69. Ibid., 26.

70. Ibid., 27.

71. Ibid., 31.

72. Ibid.

73. Charles Lippy, *Seasonable Revolutionary*, 35.

74. Sarah Pierpont to Eleazar Wheelock (New Haven, Conn.), May 30, 1743, cited in Bushman, *The Great Awakening*, 53.

75. James Davenport, *The Reverend Mr. James Davenport's Confession and Retractions* (Boston, 1744), cited in Bushman, *The Great Awakening*, 53–55. Emphasis original.

76. Lambert, *Inventing the "Great Awakening,"* 60.

77. Ibid.

78. Ibid.

79. Gilbert Tennent, *The Danger of an Unconverted Ministry, Considered in a Sermon* (2nd ed., Boston, 1742) cited in H. Shelton Smith, Robert T. Handy, Lefferts A. Loetscher, *American Christianity*, vol. 1, *1607–1820* (New York: Charles Scribner's Sons, 1960), 312–13.

80. Ibid., 324. Emphasis mine.

81. Ibid., 325.

82. Ibid., 326.

83. Ibid., 328.

84. Ibid., 322.

85. Jonathan Edwards, *The Life of David Brainerd*, ed. Norman Pettit (New Haven: Yale University Press, 1985), 43.

86. Norman Pettit, "Editor's Introduction," in Edwards, *The Life of David Brainerd*, 22.

87. Jonathan Edwards, "Author's Preface" in Edwards, *The Life of David Brainerd*, 91.

88. Ibid., 93.

89. Edwards, *The Life of David Brainerd*, 194.

90. Ibid., 195–96.

91. Ibid., 183.

92. Edwards, *The Life of David Brainerd*, 31.

93. Joseph A. Conforti, *Samuel Hopkins and the New Divinity Movement* (Grand Rapids: Christian University Press, 1981), 2.

94. Ibid., 3.

95. Ibid., 3– 4.

96. Ibid., 27.

97. Ibid., 60–61.

98. Ibid., 69.

99. Ibid., 70.

4. New Measures

1. Sidney E. Mead, *The Lively Experiment* (New York: Harper & Row, Publishers, 1963), 104.

2. Christopher H. Evans, *Histories of American Christianity: An Introduction* (Waco: Baylor University Press, 2013), 115.

3. Prof. (Chauncey) Goodrich, "Narrative of Revivals of Religion in Yale College," *Journal of the American Education Society* (February 1838), republished in *The American Quarterly Register* 10 (1838): 294.

4. Ibid., 295.

5. Ibid., 298.

6. Ibid., 298–99.

7. Ibid., 310.

8. Theophilus Arminius, "Introductory remarks to Short Sketches of Revivals of Religion, among the Methodists in the Western Country, *The Methodist Magazine* vol. 2 (1819): 395.

9. Ibid.

10. John B. Boles, *The Great Revival, 1787–1805* (Lexington: The University Press of Kentucky, 1972), 113–14.

11. Ibid., 132.

12. Ibid., 128–29.

13. Ibid., 125, 139.

14. James McGready, "Letter," October 23, 1801, in F.R. Cossitt, *The Life and Tmes of Rev. Finis Ewing* (Louisville: Woods, 1853), 494; and Paul K. Conkin, *Cane Ridge: America's Pentecost* (Madison: University of Wisconsin Press, 1990), 56–57.

15. Richard M'Nemar, *The Kentucky Revival, or, A Short History* (Cincinnati, OH: Art Guild Reprints, Inc., 1808), 19. M'Nemar is also spelled as McNemar in some sources.

16. Ellen Eslinger, *Citizens of Zion: The Social Origins of Camp Meeting Revivalism* (Knoxville: The University of Tennessee Press, 1999), 194.

17. M'Nemar, *The Kentucky Revival*, 20.

18. Ibid., 23.

19. Eslinger, *Citizens of Zion*, 190–91.

20. Ibid., 194.

21. Conkin, *Cane Ridge: America's Pentecost*, 61–62.

22. Ibid., 71–72.

23. Barton W. Stone, *The Biography of Eld. Barton Warren Stone, written by himself* (Cincinnati: J. A. & U. P. James, 1847), 9.

24. Ibid., 11.

25. Ibid., 9.

26. "The Last Will and Testament of the Springfield Presbytery," 1804, in *A Documentary History of Religion in America To the Civil War*, ed. Edwin S. Gaustad (Grand Rapids: William B. Eerdmans Publishing Company, 1993), 364–65.

27. Richard M'Nemar, *Observations on Church Government by the Springfield Presbytery* (Cincinnati: Art Reprints, 1808), 10. Emphasis original.

28. Ibid., 11, 16.

29. Conkin, *Cane Ridge: America's Pentecost*, 94.

30. Eslinger, *Citizens of Zion*, 195.

31. Conkin, *Cane Ridge: America's Pentecost*, 93–94, citing a letter from a Kentucky minister included in a letter from Moses Hoge to Dr. Ashbel Green, September 10, 1801.

32. Stone, *The Biography of Eld. Barton W. Stone*, 39.

33. Ibid., 40.

34. Ibid.

35. Ibid., 41.

36. Ibid.

37. Ibid., 42.

38. Ibid., 41.

39. Ibid., 42.

40. D. Newell Williams, "The Social and Ecclesiastical Impact of Barton W. Stone's Theology," in *Explorations in the Stone-Campbell Traditions: Essays in Honor of Herman A. Norton*, ed. Anthony L. Dunnavant and Richard L. Harrison Jr. (Nashville: Disciples of Christ Historical Society, 1995), 14.

41. Peter Cartwright, *Autobiography of Peter Cartwright* (New York: Carlton & Lanahan, 1856), 3–25.

42. Ibid., 34–35.

43. Ibid., 37

44. Ibid.

45. Ibid., 38.

46. Ibid., 63–64.

47. Ibid., 75.

48. Ibid.

49. Ibid., 48.

50. Ibid., 46–51.

51. Ibid.

52. Ibid., 51–52.

53. Cartwright, *Autobiography of Peter Cartwright*, 46.

54. Ibid., 47.

55. Stone, *The Biography of Eld. Barton W. Stone*, 45.

56. Ibid.

57. The Stone-Campbell Restorationist Movement shaped various traditions including the Christian Church, the Christian Church (Disciples of Christ), and the Churches of Christ. An excellent historiographical survey of these traditions and views of their origins may be found in Michael W. Casey and Douglas A. Foster, "The Renaissance of Stone-Campbell Studies: An Assessment and New Directions," in *The Stone-Campbell Movement: An International Religious Tradition*, ed. Michael W. Casey and Douglas A. Foster (Knoxville: The University of Tennessee Press, 2002), 1–65.

58. Richard M. Tristano, *The Origins of the Restoration Movement: An Intellectual History* (Atlanta: Glenmary Home Missioners, 1985), 44.

59. Ibid., 52.

60. Stone, *The Biography of Eld. Barton Warren Stone*, 203.

61. Tristano, *The Origins of the Restoration Movement*, 46.

62. Ibid., 43.

63. Stone, *The Biography of Eld. Barton Warren Stone*, 206. The italics are Stone's.

64. Williams, "The Social and Ecclesiastical Impact of Barton W. Stone's Theology," 14.

65. Ibid.

66. Tristano, *The Origins of the Restoration Movement*, 44.

67. Ibid., 87–88.

68. Ibid., 88–89; and Alexander Campbell, *The Christian System* (Cincinnati: The Standard Publishing Company, 1835), 93.

69. Campbell, *The Christian System*, 94.

70. John L. Morrison, "A Radical Voice Crying in an Emotional Wilderness," in Casey and Foster, *The Stone-Campbell Movement*, 170.

71. Ibid.

72. Campbell, *The Christian System*, 45. Emphasis original.

73. Ibid., 250.

74. Tristano, *The Origins of the Restoration Movement*, 91.

75. Ibid.

76. Nathan O. Hatch, "The Christian Movement and the Demand for a Theology of the People," in Casey and Foster, *The Stone-Campbell Movement*, 131, citing Alexander Campbell, "An Oration in Honor of the Fourth of July, 1830," *Popular Lectures and Addresses* (Philadelphia, 1863), 374.

77. Ibid., 133.

78. Whitney R. Cross, *The Burned-Over District: The Social and Intellectual History of Enthusiastic Religion in Western New York, 1800–1850* (New York: Harper Torchbooks, 1950), ix.

79. Charles G. Finney, *Memoirs of Charles G. Finney* (New York: Fleming H. Revell, 1876), 4.

80. Ibid.

81. Ibid., 7.

82. Ibid., 9.

83. Ibid., 12.

84. Ibid., 19–20.

85. Ibid., 23.

86. Ibid., 45–47.

87. Ibid., 55. In the *Memoir* Finney goes to great length to distinguish his theological position on conversion, atonement, and other issues from that of Gale, the proponent of Princeton Theology; see 55–60.

88. Ibid., 77.

89. Charles G. Finney, *Lectures on Revival of Religion* (Oberlin, OH: E. J. Goodeich, 1868), 9.

90. Ibid., 9–10.

91. Ibid., 10–11. Emphasis original.

92. Ibid., 12.

93. Ibid. Emphasis original.

94. Ibid., 15

95. Finney, *Memoir*, 189.

96. Ibid., 190.

97. Ephraim Perkins, "A 'Bunker Hill' Contest, A. D. 1826..." (Utica, 1826), n.p. cited in "The Oneida and Troy Revivals," *Christian Examiner and Theological Review* 4, no. 3 (May/June 1827): 256.

98. Ibid., 181–82.

99. Ibid., 182.

100. Finney, *Memoir*, 288.

101. Ibid., 289.

102. Perkins, "A 'Bunker Hill' Contest," 257.

103. Ibid.

104. Ibid., 258.

105. "Dr. Beecher and Mr. Beman's Convention on Revivals," *Christian Examiner and Theological Review* 4 (July–August 1827): 360.

106. Ibid.

107. Ibid., 366.

108. Ibid., 367.

109. John Williamson Nevin, *The Anxious Bench* (Chambersburg, PA: Publication Office, 1844), 67.

110. Ibid., 68.

111. Ibid., 70–71.

112. Ibid., 73–75.

113. Ibid., 76.

114. Ibid., 77. Emphasis original.

115. Ibid., 83.

116. Ibid., 84.

117. Albert Barnes, "Revivals of Religion in Cities and Large Towns," in *The American National Preacher* 15 (January 1841): 4.

118. Ibid., 4. Emphasis original.

119. Ibid. Emphasis original.

120. Ibid., 5.

121. Ibid., 6.

122. Catherine L. Albanese, ed., *American Spiritualities: A Reader* (Bloomington, IN: Indiana University Press, 2001), 183.

123. Curtis D. Johnson, *Redeeming America: Evangelicals and the Road to the Civil War* (Chicago: Ivan R. Dee, 1993), cited in Albanese, *American Spiritualities,*184. See book citation materials.

124. Horace Bushnell, "Living to God in Small Things," in *Sermons for the New Life* (New York: Scribner, Armstrong & Co., 1873), 292–93, cited in Horace Bushnell *Sermons*, ed. Conrad Cherry (New York: Paulist Press, 1985), 4.

125. Cherry, "Introduction," in Bushnell, *Sermons*, 2–3.

126. Ibid., 10.

127. Ibid., 10–13.

128. Bushnell, "Christ the Form of the Soul," in *Sermons*, 54–55.

129. Horace Bushnell, *Christian Nurture* (New York: Charles Scribner & Co., 1871), 10.

130. Ibid., 22.

131. Ibid., 29.

132. Ibid.

133. Jacob Knapp, *Autobiography of Elder Jacob Knapp, With an Introductory Essay by R. Jeffery* (New York: Sheldon and Company, 1868), 42.

134. Andrew Norwood, *Pilgrimage of a Pilgrim for Forty Years* (Boston: By the Pilgrim, 1852), 50.

135. Ibid., 52–53. Emphasis original.

136. Richard Carwardine, *Trans-Atlantic Revivalism: Popular Evangelicalism in Britain and America 1790–1865* (Westport, CT: Greenwood Press, 1978), 18.

137. Albert Barnes, "Vindication of Revivals, and their Influence on this Country," *The American National Preacher*, vol. XV (January 1841), 45.

138. Barnes, "Revivals of Religion in Cities and Large Towns," 52.

139. Ibid., 52–53.

140. Ibid., 72.

141. Calvin Colton, *The History and Character of American Revivals of Religion* (London: Frederick Westley and A. H. Davis, 1832), 14–15.

142. Carwardine, *Trans-Atlantic Revivalism*, 18–19.

143. Ibid., 19.

144. Ibid.

145. Ibid., 25.

146. Robert Mapes Anderson, *Vision of the Disinherited: The Making of American Pentecostalism* (New York: Oxford University Press, 1979), 38.

147. Carwardine, *Trans-Atlantic Revivalism*, 20–21.

148. Anderson, *Vision of the Disinherited*, 38.

149. H. Richard Niebuhr, *The Kingdom of God in America* (New York: Harper Torchbooks, 1959), 179–80.

150. William G. McLoughlin, *Revivals, Awakenings, and Reform* (Chicago: University of Chicago Press, 1978), 141.

151. Jerald C. Brauer, "Conversion: From Puritanism to Revivalism," *The Journal of Religion* 58 (July 1978): 241.

152. Ibid.

153. Ibid., 242.

154. Ibid., 242–43.

155. C. C. Goen, "Ecclesiology Without Ecclesiology: Denominational Life in America," *Religion in Life* 48 (Spring 1979): 24.

156. James W. Alexander, "The Holy Flock," in *The New York Pulpit in the Revival of 1858, Sermons* (New York: Sheldon & Company, 1860), 27–28.

157. Ibid., 28–29.

158. William Ives Budington, "What Shall I Do To Be Saved?" in *The New York Pulpit in the Revival of 1858, Sermons*, 200.

159. Ibid., 204.

160. Ibid., 205–6.

161. Theodore L. Cuyler, "Past Feeling," in *The New York Pulpit in the Revival of 1858*, 57. Emphasis original.

162. Ibid., 58–59.

163. William G. McLoughlin Jr., *Modern Revivalism: From Charles Grandison Finney to Billy Graham* (New York: The Ronald Press, 1959), 172.

164. Ibid., 174–75.

165. Ibid., 175.

166. Ibid., 244–46.

167. Ibid., 182.

168. Ibid., 167.

169. Ibid., 220–40. McLoughlin offers extensive detail of Moody's revival organization and method.

170. Dwight L. Moody, "Sinners Seeking Christ," in *Select Sermons* (Chicago: The Moody Press, n.d.), 76. Emphasis original.

171. Moody, "On Being Born Again," in *New Sermons, Addresses, and Prayers* (New York: Henry S. Goodspeed & Co., 1877), 123.

172. Moody, "Regeneration is Instantaneous," in *New Sermons, Addresses, and Prayers*, 362.

173. Ibid.

174. Moody, "There Is No Difference," in *Select Sermons*, 40. Emphasis original.

175. Moody, "Regeneration," in *Moody: His Words, Work and Workers*, ed. W. H. Daniels (New York: Nelson & Phillips, 1887), 386.

176. Ibid.

177. Moody, "Baptism of the Holy Spirit for Service," in *Moody: His Words, Work and Workers*, 399.

178. Moody, "Farewell Sermon: God Able To Keep," in *New Sermons, Addresses, and Prayers*, 534–35.

179. Moody, "Baptism of the Holy Spirit for Service, 400–1.

180. R. A. Torrey, "The Way of Salvation," *Revival Addresses* (New York: Fleming H. Revell, 1903), 131–32. Emphasis original.

181. Ibid., 132–33.

182. Ibid., 141. Emphasis original.

183. Ibid., 142.

184. Torrey, "What Are You Waiting For?" in *Revival Addresses*, 214.

185. Torrey, "Heroes and Cowards," in *Revival Addresses*, 247. Emphasis original.

186. Ibid.

187. Torrey, "The Way of Salvation," in *Revival Addresses*, 137–38. In praying for a specific individual who had difficulties with alcohol, Torrey added, "Lord Jesus, set me free from the power of drink and the power of sin."

188. T. T. Martin, *Hell and Other Sermons* (Nashville: Southern Baptist Convention Sunday School Board, 1923), 220.

189. Billy Sunday, "Why Delay Your Real Conversion?" in www.biblebelievers.com/billy_sunday.

190. McLoughlin, 433.

191. Ibid., 434.

192. Carl Sandburg, "To a Contemporary Bunkshooter," *Chicago Poems*, http://carl-sandburg.com/to_a_contemporary_bunkshooter.htm.

5. Over-Souls and Spirits

1. Ralph Waldo Emerson, *Nature* (chapter 6, "Idealism"), http://oregonstate.edu/instruct/phl302/texts/emerson/nature–emerson–b.html#Chapter VI.

2. Sydney Ahlstrom, *A Religious History of the American People* (New Haven: Yale University Press, 1972), 600.

3. Ibid., 598.

4. Catherine L. Albanese, *Corresponding Motion: Transcendental Religion and the New America* (Philadelphia: Temple University Press, 1977), 72.

5. James Freeman Clarke, *Repentance toward God* (Boston: Office of the Christian World, 1844), 10–19; cited in Albanese, *Corresponding Motion*, 80.

6. James Freeman Clarke, *Manual of Unitarian Belief*, "Conversion," http://www.americanunitarian.org/manual.htm.

7. Clarke, "Comparative Theology of Heathen Religions," *Christian Examiner*, 62 (1857): 185–87; in *American Christianity*, vol. 2, *1820–1930*, ed. H. Shelton Smith, Robert T. Handy, and Lefferts A. Loetscher (New York: Charles Scribner's Sons, 1963), 163.

8. Albanese, *Corresponding Motion*, 173.

9. *The Early Works of Orestes Brownson*, vol. 3, *The Transcendentalist Years, 1836–1838*, ed. Patrick W. Carey (Milwaukee: Marquette University Press, 2002), 11.

10. Ibid., 14.

11. Octavius Brooks Frothingham, *Transcendentalism in New England: A History* (New York: G. P. Putnam's Sons, 1876; Harper Torchbook edition, 1959), 199. Emphasis original.

12. William Ellery Channing, "Unitarian Christianity," (1819), in *William Ellery Channing: Selected Writings*, ed. David Robinson (New York: Paulist Press, 1985), 71–95.

13. Channing, "Likeness to God," in *William Ellery Channing: Selected Writings*, 150.

14. Channing, "Spiritual Freedom," in *William Ellery Changing: Selected Writings*, 201.

15. Ibid., 203.

16. Ibid, 198–99.

17. Ibid., 198–99.

18. In Smith, Handy, and Loetscher, *American Christianity*, vol. 2, 123. Emphasis original.

19. Ibid., 124.

20. *The Early Works of Orestes A. Brownson*, vol. III, 6.

21. Mark Lilla, *The Stillborn God: Religion, Politics and the Modern West* (New York: Alfred A. Knopf, 2007), 135–36.

22. Frederick Ives Carpenter, "Transcendentalism," in *American Transcendentalism: An Anthology of Criticism*, ed. Brian M. Barbour (Notre Dame: University of Notre Dame Press, 1973), 24, citing *The Complete Works of Ralph Waldo Emerson* (Boston, 1903–4), 1:339–40.

23. Smith, Handy, and Loetscher, *American Christianity*, vol. 2, 121.

24. Frederick Ives Carpenter, "Transcendentalism," 24.

25. Ibid., 25. Carpenter reminds readers that Emerson ultimately equated "intuition with 'instinct'" creating "a Pandora's box of primitivistic and romantic delusions," questionable efforts worthy of serious critique.

26. Ralph Waldo Emerson, *The Transcendentalist*, 1842, http://www.emersoncentral.com/Transcendentalist.htm.

27. Ibid.

28. Carpenter, "Transcendentalism," 25.

29. William A. Clebsch, *American Religious Thought: A History* (Chicago: University of Chicago Press, 1973), 79.

30. Albanese, *Corresponding Motion*, xii–xiii.

31. Clebsch, *American Religious Thought*, 77.

32. Ibid., 27.

33. H. C. Goddard, "Unitarianism and Transcendentalism," in *Studies in New England Transcendentalism* (New York: Columbia University Press, 1908); republished in Barbour, *American Transcendentalism: An Anthology of Criticism*, 161.

34. Ibid.

35. Frothingham, *Transcendentalism in New England: A History*, 108.

36. Ibid.

37. Ralph Waldo Emerson, *Nature*, http://oregonstate.edu/instruct/phl302/texts/emerson/nature-contents.htmlBLT54906_MP011.docx; see also Ahlstrom, *A Religious History of the American People*, 601.

38. Emerson, *Nature*.

39. Ibid., n.p.

40. Ibid., n.p.

41. Albanese, *Corresponding Motion*, 6.

42. Goddard, "Unitarianism and Transcendentalism," 161.

43. Emerson, *Nature*, chapter 6.

44. Albanese, *Corresponding Motion*, 6–7.

45. Clebsch, *American Religious Thought*, 77.

46. Emerson, *An address Delivered Before the Senior Class in Divinity College, Cambridge, Sunday Evening, July 15, 1838*, in http://www.emersoncentral.com/divaddr.htm. Emphasis original.

47. Ibid.

48. Ibid.

49. Ibid.

50. Ralph Waldo Emerson, "The Over-Soul," in *Essays by Ralph Waldo Emerson* (Boston: Houghton, Mifflin and Company, 1865), 252–53.

51. Ibid., 255.

52. Ibid., 274.

53. Ibid 276.

54. Ibid., 277.

55. Ibid., 278.

56. Sacvan Bercovitch, *The Puritan Origins of the American Self* (New Haven: Yale University Press, 1975), 157–86; Perry Miller, "From Edwards to Emerson," *The New England Quarterly* 13 (1940): 589–617, reprinted in Barbour, *American Transcendentalism: An Anthology of Criticism*, 63–81; and Clebsch, *American Religious Thought: A History*, 11–111.

57. Bercovitch, *The Puritan Origins of the American Self*, 154.

58. Ibid., 157.

59. Ibid., 157–58. Bercovitch cites several of Emerson's sources, including "Young American," "Divinity School Address," and "Fortune of the Republic," in Emerson, *Works*, 1:391, 364–70, 150; 11:537, 540.

60. Ibid., 157.

61. Perry Miller, "From Edwards to Emerson," 78.

62. Ibid., 73.

63. Ibid., 76.

64. Ibid., 79.

65. Bercovitch, *The Puritan Origins of the American Self*, 160.

66. Norman Pettit, *The Heart Prepared: Grace and Conversion in Puritan Spiritual Life*, 2nd ed. (Middletown, CT: Wesleyan University Press, 1989), 214–15.

67. "(Sarah) Margaret Fuller (Ossoli) 1810–1850," http://www.alcott.net/alcott/home/champions/Fuller.html?index=1.

68. "(Sarah) Margaret Fuller (Ossoli) 1810–1850," http://www.alcott.net/alcott/home/champions/Fuller.html?index=1. Emphasis original.

69. Bernard Rosenthal, "Introduction," in Margaret Fuller, *Woman in the Nineteenth Century* (1845) (New York: W. W. Norton & Company, Inc., 1971), viii.

70. Fuller, *Woman in the Nineteenth Century*, 102. Jacob Behmen (Bohme) (1575–1624) was a seventeenth century German mystic and writer on Christian spirituality, a strong proponent of the inner life of spiritual experience and reflection; Claude Henre de Rouvroy, comte de Saint Simon (1760–1825), was a utopian socialist whose book *The New Christianity* sought to move beyond dogma in order to reduce Christianity to its most basic premises and practices, encourage greater egalitarianism, and work to alleviate poverty.

71. Ibid., 115–16.

72. Cynthia J. Davis, "Margaret Fuller, Body and Soul" *American Literature* 71, no. 1 (March 1999): 34; and Fuller, *Woman in the Nineteenth Century*, 63–64.

73. Davis, "Margaret Fuller," ibid.

74. Fuller, *Woman in the Nineteenth Century*, 112.

75. Ibid., 122.

76. Ibid., 123.

77. Ibid.

78. Albanese, *Corresponding Motion*, 152.

79. Ibid., 154–55.

80. Smith, Handy, and Loetscher, *American Christianity*, vol. 2, 128–29.

81. Ibid., 129.

82. Ralph Waldo Emerson, *Nature*, chapter 6; see also Albanese, *Corresponding Motion*, 20.

83. Catherine L. Albanese, *America: Religions & Religion*, 5th ed. (Boston: Wadsworth, 2013), 24.

84. Ibid., 26.

85. Ibid., 28.

86. Jon Butler, *Awash in a Sea of Faith: Christianizing the American People* (Cambridge: Harvard University Press, 1990), 75.

87. Ibid., 77.

88. Ibid., 92.

89. Ibid., 228–29.

90. Albanese, *America: Religions & Religion*, 184.

91. Ibid.

92. Ibid., 185–86.

93. Robert C. Fuller, *Mesmerism and the American Cure of Souls* (Philadelphia: University of Pennsylvania Press, 1982), 3.

94. Ibid., 8–9.

95. Ibid., 73–74.

96. Charles G. Finney, *Lectures on Revivals of Religion* (Oberlin, Ohio: E. J. Goddeich, 1868), 12.

97. Whitney R. Cross, *The Burned-Over District: The Social and Intellectual History of Enthusiastic Religion in Western New York, 1800–1850* (New York: Harper Torchbook, 1950), 342; see also Fuller, *Mesmerism and the American Cure of Souls*, 77–78.

98. Butler, *Awash in a Sea of Faith*, 235.

99. Fuller, *Mesmerism and the American Cure of Souls*, 81.

100. Ann Taves, *Fits, Trances, & Visions: Experiencing Religion and Explaining Experience from Wesley to James* (Princeton, NJ: Princeton University Press, 1999), 128.

101. Ibid., 131.

102. Frank Podmore, *Modern Spiritualism: A History and a Criticism*, vol. 1 (New York: Charles Scribner's Sons, 1902), 157; and Taves, *Fits, Trances, & Visions*, 131–35.

103. Taves, *Fits, Trances, & and Visions*, 134–35.

104. Fuller, *Mesmerism and the American Cure of Souls*, 89.

105. Cross, *The Burned-Over District*, 342.

106. John Humphrey Noyes, *The Putney Community*, compiled and ed. George Wallingford Noyes (Oneida, New York, 1931), 170.

107. Ibid., 170–71.

108. Ahlstrom, *A Religious History of the American People*, 483; and Fuller, *Mesmerism and the American Cure of Souls*, 88.

109. Cyriel Odhner Sigstedt, *The Swedenborg Epic* (New York: Bookman Associates/AMS Press, 1952), 184.

110. Catherine L. Albanese, *A Republic of Mind and Spirit: A Cultural History of American Metaphysical Religion* (New Haven: Yale University Press, 2007), 141.

111. Fuller, *Mesmerism and the American Cure of Souls*, 90–91; and Ahlstrom, *A Religious History of the American People*, 484–85.

112. Emanuel Swedenborg, Spiritual Diary, (1758), vol. 2, trans. George Bush and John H. Smithson, 1883. http://www.sacred-texts.com/swd/sd/sd02.htm.

113. Emanuel Swedenborg, *Arcana Celestia, 1882–1885*, cited in George Bush, *Mesmer and Swedenborg: or, The Relation of the Developments of Mesmerism to the Doctrines and disclosures of Swedenborg* (New York: Joshua Allen, 1847), 24.

114. Emanuel Swedenborg, *Hobart's Life of Swedenborg*, 42, cited in Bush, *Mesmer and Swedenborg*, 25.

115. Sigstedt, *The Swedenborg Epic*, 232–33.

116. Emanuel Swedenborg, *True Christian Religion*, 851, cited in Bush, *Mesmer and Swedenborg*, 26.

117. Sigstedt, *The Swedenborg Epic*, 314.

118. Andrew Jackson Davis, *The Magic Staff: An Autobiography of Andrew Jackson Davis* (Boston: Colby & Rich, 1885), 42. Emphasis original.

119. Ibid., 204. This phrase is actually the title of chapter 32 of the autobiography; see 204–12.

120. Ibid., 211.

121. Ibid., 215. Emphasis original.

122. Ibid., 221

123. Ibid., 249.

124. Ibid., 263.

125. Catherine L. Albanese, "On the Matter of Spirit: Andrew Jackson Davis and the Marriage of God and Nature," *Journal of the American Academy of Religion* 60 (Spring, 1992): 5.

126. R. Laurence Moore, *In Search of White Crows: Spiritualism, Parapsychology, and American Culture* (New York: Oxford University Press, 1977), 12–13.

127. Andrew Jackson Davis, *The Magic Staff*, 311. Italics are from Davis.

128. Ibid., 320.

129. Ibid., 333. Swedenborg offered the entranced Davis multiple spiritual in-

sights, including dictating a letter that Davis was ordered to send to George Bush, author of the book, *Swedenborg and Mesmer*. Bush later criticized Davis for exhibiting ideas that revealed "a mixture of truth and falsity on the grand doctrines of Christianity." See p. 338.

130. Andrew Jackson Davis, *Great Harmonia*, vol. 1, (1851), 266, cited in Albanese, "On the Matter of Spirit: Andrew Jackson Davis and the Marriage of God and Nature," 1.

131. *Great Harmonia*, 367. This insight Davis called the height of "intuition."

132. Ibid., 382–83.

133. "The Rationalism of the Day: Andrew Jackson Davis—Spiritual Manifestations," *The United States Review*, 1853–1856 (March 1853): 3.

134. Ibid. Emphasis original.

135. Ibid., 486.

136. Ibid., *The Arabula, or the Divine Guest* (Boston: Colby & Rich, 1881), 82–83. Emphasis original.

137. Ibid., 88.

138. Frank Podmore, *Modern Spiritualism*, 164.

139. Ibid., 152.

140. Ibid., 156–68, 200–4.

141. Ibid., 303–61.

142. Robert W. Delp, "A Spiritualist in Connecticut: Andrew Jackson Davis, the Hartford Years, 1850–1854," *New England Quarterly* 53 (September 1980): 345.

143. Albanese, "On the Matter of Spirit: Andrew Jackson Davis and the Marriage of God and Nature," 3.

144. Ann Braude, *Radical Spirits: Spiritualism and Women's Rights in Nineteenth-Century America*, 2nd ed. (Bloomington, IN: Indiana University Press, 2001), 4.

145. Ibid., 6.

146. Ibid., 41.

147. Moore, *In Search of White Crows*, 19.

148. Podmore, *Modern Spiritualism*, 179–82.

149. Barbara Weisberg, *Talking to the Dead: Katie and Maggie Fox and the Rise of Spiritualism* (San Francisco: HarperSanFrancisco, 2004), 68.

150. Moore, *In Search of White Crows*, 7–8. The rappings did not sound for Leah Fox, only for Kate and Margaret. Rather, spirits confronted her when she was in a mesmerized state. See Weisberg, *Talking to the Dead*, 68.

151. Podmore, *Modern Spiritualism*, 183.

152. Todd Jay Leonard, *Talking to the Other Side: A History of Modern Spiritualism and Mediumship* (New York: Universe, Inc., 2005), 28.

153. Ibid., 29.

154. Moore, *In Search of White Crows*, 15.

155. Ibid., 25. Such camps included Lilly Dale, New York; Cassadaga, Florida; and Chesterfield, Indiana. See 25n.

156. Ibid., citing Moncure Conway, *Autobiography, Memories, and Experiences of Moncure Daniel Conway* (Boston: Houghton Mifflin, 1904), 1:149.

157. Braude, *Radical Spirits*, 19.

158. Ibid., 27.

159. Braude, *Radical Spirits*, 192–202. See also Weisberg, *Talking to the Dead*, 145–48.

160. Leonard, *Talking to the Other Side*, 73, 92.

161. Weisberg, *Talking to the Dead*, 260.

162. Ibid., 261.

163. Braude, *Radical Spirits*, 200.

164. Weisberg, *Talking to the Dead*, 262.

6. At the Marriage Supper of the Lamb

1. John McKelvie Whitworth, *God's Blueprints: A Sociological Study of Three Utopian Sects* (London: Routledge & Kegan Paul, 1975), 1.

2. Edward Deming Andrews, *The People Called Shakers* (New York: Dover Publications, Inc., 1953), 5.

3. Whitworth, *God's Blueprints: A Sociological Study of Three Utopian Sects*, 13–14.

4. Ibid., 14.

5. Stephen J. Stein, *The Shaker Experience in America: A History of the United Society of Believers* (New Haven: Yale University Press, 1992), 6.

6. Ibid.

7. Andrews, *The People Called Shakers*, 7–8.

8. Ibid., 8.

9. Stein, *The Shaker Experience in America*, 4–5; and Andrews, *The People Called Shakers*, 9.

10. Andrews, *The People Called Shakers*, 11.

11. Ibid., 12–13.

12. Stein, *The Shaker Experience in America*, 13–14.

13. Ibid., 18–25. Little was written down in those years regarding the message or messages given by these missionaries. In fact, Shaker historiography is often shaped by accounts such as the *Testimonies*, recollections written much later than they actually occurred and thus of uncertain accuracy in detailing the details of the early Shaker message and practice. See Stein, *The Shaker Experience in America*, 25–31.

14. Ibid., 15; and Andrews, *The People Called Shakers*, 27–28.

15. Ibid., 28.

16. Andrews, *The People Called Shakers*, 12. See Rev. 12:1.

17. Ibid., n. p.; see section entitled "The Office of the Spiritual Mother of the New Creation."

18. John Dunlavy, *The Manifesto, Or a Declaration of the Doctrine and Practice of the Church of Christ* (USA: Nebu Public Domain Reprints, 1847), 482.

19. Ibid.

20. Paulina Bates, instrument, *The Divine Book of Holy and Eternal Wisdom*, vol. 1, (arranged and prepared for the Press at New Lebanon, NY, 1849), n. p.; section entitled "All Must be Forsaken by Christ; The Manner of Christ's Coming. . . ."; see also www.passtheword.org/shakermanuscripts.

21. Ibid., n. p.; see section entitled "The True Meaning of 'Woe to them that are with child'. . . ."

22. "The Gospel Preached to Departed Spirits," *Testimonies of Mother Ann Lee and the Elders*, chapter 27, in http://www.passtheword.org/shakermanuscripts/Testimonies/tstmonys.htm.

23. Julia Neal, *The Kentucky Shakers* (Lexington: The University Press of Kentucky, 1977), 49.

24. Ibid.

25. Whitworth, *God's Blueprints*, 50.

26. Ibid., 53–54.

27. Gerard C. Wertkin, *The Four Seasons of Shaker Life: An Intimate Portrait of the Community at Sabbathday Lake* (New York: Simon and Schuster, 1986), 40. See also Abigail Pratt, "The Redemption and Reinterpretation of Women through Shaker Religious Experience" (unpublished Master of Divinity paper, School of Divinity, Wake Forest University, November 2012), 7.

28. Charles Nordhoff, *The Communistic Societies of the United States from Personal Visit and Observation* (New York: Dover Publications, Inc., 1966), 232. Emphasis original.

29. Ibid., 233.

30. Ibid., 233.

31. Ibid., 240.

32. Ibid., 242.

33. Ibid., 229.

34. Edward D. Andrews, *The Gift to Be Simple* (New York: Dover Publications, 1940), 116.

35. Bates, instrument, "All Must be Forsaken by Christ; The Manner of Christ's

Coming. . . . ,"in *The Divine Book of Holy and Eternal Wisdom*, vol. 1; see section entitled "Wisdom Speaks on the Role of the woman in Regeneration."

36. Ibid., n. p.; see section entitled "The True Meaning of 'Woe to them that are with child'. . . ."

37. George Wallingford Noyes, *Religious Experience of John Humphrey Noyes* (New York: McMillan Company, 1923), 39, in http://library.syr.edu/digital/collections/r/ReligiousExperienceOfJohnHumphreyNoyes.

38. Whitworth, *God's Blueprints*, 89–90.

39. Lawrence Foster, *Religion and Sexuality* (New York: Oxford Press, 1981), 78.

40. Whitworth, *God's Blueprints*, 92.

41. Ibid., 95.

42. John Humphrey Noyes, "Bible Communism," 1849, reproduced in Katherine Anne Heim, "Oneida's Utopia: A Religious and Scientific Experiment," appendix B (unpublished Master of Arts Thesis, California State University, Fall, 2009).

43. Nordhoff, *The Communistic Societies of the United States*, 269–70. Emphasis original.

44. Ibid., 270.

45. Noyes, *Religious Experience of John Humphrey Noyes*, 96.

46. John Humphrey Noyes, "The Battle-Axe and Weapons of War Letter," August 1837, published in *The Witness* (January 23, 1839), reproduced in Heim, "Oneida's Utopia: A Religious and Scientific Experiment," appendix C.

47. Noyes, "Bible Communism."

48. George Wallingford Noyes, compiler, *Free Love in Utopia: John Humphrey Noyes and the Origin of the Oneida Community*, ed. and intro. Lawrence Foster (Urbana: University of Illinois Press, 2001), xx.

49. Sydney Ahlstrom, *A Religious History of the American People* (New Haven: Yale University Press, 1972), 499.

50. Whitworth, *God's Blueprints*, 161–62; and George Wallingford Noyes, *Free Love in Utopia*, xiii–xv. After the sexual situation changed at Putney, Noyes was charged with two counts of adultery. Fearing that he might be lynched or sent to prison, he jumped bail and retreated from Vermont.

51. Richard L. Bushman, *Joseph Smith and the Beginnings of Mormonism* (Urbana: University of Illinois Press, 1984), 54.

52. Ibid., 55.

53. Ibid., 56.

54. Ibid., 57.

55. Jan Shipps, *Mormonism: The Story of a New Religious Tradition* (Urbana: University of Illinois Press, 1985), 3

56. Bushman, *Joseph Smith and the Beginnings of Mormonism*, 61.

57. Ibid., 62.

58. Shipps, *Mormonism: The Story of a New Religious Tradition*, 10.

59. Ibid.

60. Lawrence Foster, *Religion and Sexuality: Three American Communal Experiments of the Nineteenth Century* (New York: Oxford University Press, 1981), 130–39.

61. Ibid., 133, citing *Saints Herald* 21(October 1, 1874): 584. Briggs was a nineteenth-century leader of the Reorganized Latter Days Saints (RLDS).

62. Whitney R. Cross, *The Burned-Over District: The Social and Intellectual History of Enthusiastic Religion in Western New York, 1800–1850* (New York: Harper Torchbooks, 1950), 145, citing Alexander Campbell, *Delusions: An Analysis of the Book of Mormon, etc.* (Boston: 1832), 13.

63. Ibid.

64. Bushman, *Joseph Smith and the Beginnings of Mormonism*, 149–50.

65. Shipps, *Mormonism: The Story of a New Religious Tradition*, 2–3.

66. Ibid., 3.

67. Ibid., 3–4.

68. Bushman, *Joseph Smith and the Beginnings of Mormonism*, 6.

69. Harold Bloom, *The American Religion: The Emergence of the Post-Christian Nation* (New York: Simon & Schuster, 1992), 90.

70. Ibid., 94.

71. Ibid., 95.

72. Catherine L. Albanese, *A Republic of Mind and Spirit: A Cultural History of American Metaphysical Religion* (New Haven: Yale University Press, 2007), 142.

73. Ibid., 146.

7. The Yoke of Jesus

1. Thomas Wentworth Higginson, *Black Rebellion* (New York: Arno Press, 1969 [1889]), 188–89; see also Katharine L. Dvorak, *An African-American Exodus: The Segregation of the Southern Churches* (New York: Carlson Publishing Inc., 1919), 42.

2. Gerald LamontThomas, *African American Preaching: The Contribution of Dr. Gardner C. Taylor* (New York: Peter Lang, 2004), 18.

3. "Records of the Forks of Elkhorn Baptist Church, Kentucky, 1800–1820," in William Warren Sweet, *Religion on the American Frontier: The Baptists 1783–1830* (Chicago: University of Chicago Press, 1931), 328–29. Emphasis mine.

4. Ibid., 330.

5. Cecil Wayne Cone, *The Identity Crisis in Black Theology* (Nashville: AMEC, 1975), 49; see also Dvorak, *An African-American Exodus*, 41.

6. Dvorak, *An African-American Exodus*, 42.

7. Albert J. Raboteau, *Slave Religion: The "Invisible Institution" in the Antebellum South* (New York: Oxford University Press, 1978), 42.

8. Ibid., 47; see also Henry H. Mitchell, *Black Church Beginnings* (Grand Rapids: William B. Eerdmans Publishing Company, 2004), 2.

9. Raboteau, *Slave Religion*, 48.

10. Ibid., 47.

11. Mitchell, *Black Church Beginnings*, 3. In this assertion Mitchell cites the work of W.E.B. DuBois, Herskovits, George P. Rawick, John W. Blassingame, and Mechal Sobel.

12. Ibid., citing W.E.B. DuBois, *The Negro* (New York: Oxford University Press, [1915] 1970), xiii, 113–14.

13. Mitchell, *Black Church Beginnings*, 2, citing Albert Raboteau, *"Canaan Land": A Religious History of African Americans* (New York: Oxford University Press, 2001), ix.

14. Christine Leigh Heyrman, *Southern Cross: The Beginnings of the Bible Belt* (New York: Alfred A. Knopf, 1997), 51.

15. Anthony B. Pinn, *Varieties of African American Religious Experience* (Minneapolis: Fortress Press, 1998), 6–7.

16. Albert Raboteau, *Slave Religion*, 68, citing Daniel Alexander Payne, *Recollections of Seventy Years* (New York: Arno Press and the New York Times, 1969 [1886]), 54–55.

17. Mitchell, *Black Church Beginnings*, 14.

18. Ibid.

19. Ibid; and Albert Raboteau, *Slave Religion*, 57–58.

20. Albert Raboteau, *Slave Religion*, 58. Raboteau acknowledges that Herskovits pointed to various reasons for the success of Baptists among African-Americans including revivalism, powerful preaching, often by the "unlearned," and the relative ease of founding a Baptist congregation.

21. Charles Colcock Jones, *The Religious Instruction of the Negroes in the United States* (Savannah, GA: 1842; New York: Kraus Reprint Co., 1969), 125–27; cited in Harry V. Richardson, *Dark Salvation: The Story of Methodism as It Developed among Blacks in America* (Garden City, NY: Anchor Press/Doubleday, 1976), 27.

22. Brad R. Braxton, "Lifting the Veil: The *Shoah* and the *Maafa* in Conversation," *Perspectives in Religious Studies* 38 (Summer 2011): 190.

23. C. Eric Lincoln, "The Black Heritage in Religion in the South," in *Religion in the South*, ed. Charles Reagan Wilson (Jackson: University Press of Mississippi, 1985), 25, cited in Gerald Lamont Thomas, *African American Preaching: The Contribution of Dr. Gardner C. Taylor* (New York: Peter Lang, 2004), 12.

24. Cotton Mather, "Sermon 179 [August 24, 1703]," in *A Compleat Body of Divinity in Two Hundred and Fifty Expository Lectures on the Assembly's Catechism*

(Boston, 1726; reprint ed., New York, 1969), 616, cited in H. Shelton Smith, *In His Image, But... Racism in Southern Religion, 1780–1910* (Durham: Duke University Press, 1972), 5. Emphasis original.

25. H. Shelton Smith, *In His Image, But...*, 9. Fleetwood was bishop of Asaph. Emphasis original.

26. Ibid., 11.

27. Ibid., 153.

28. L. V. Stennis, *Why Sit Here Until We Die?* (Seattle: Chi-Mik Publishing Company, 1981), 17, cited in Thomas, *African American Preaching*, 15.

29. Raboteau, *Slave Religion*, 61; see also Heyrman, *Southern Cross*, 49

30. Richardson, *Dark Salvation*, 25.

31. Heyrman, *Southern Cross*, 49–50.

32. Clifton H. Johnson, ed., *God Struck Me Dead: Religious Conversion Experiences and Autobiographies of Ex-Slaves* (Philadelphia: Pilgrim Press, 1969), iii–iv.

33. Ibid., viii.

34. Ibid., ix.

35. Ibid., xi.

36. Ibid., 15.

37. Mechal Sobel, *Trabelin' On: The Slave Journey to an Afro-Baptist Faith* (Princeton, NJ: Princeton University Press, 1979), 108.

38. Johnson, *God Struck Me Dead*, 15.

39. Ibid., 109–10.

40. Sobel, *Trabelin' On*, 109.

41. Ibid. Emphasis original.

42. Ibid., 113.

43. Ibid., 118–19.

44. James H. Cone, "Black Theology as Liberation Theology," in *Down By the Riverside: Readings in African American Religion*, ed. Larry G. Murphy (New York: New York University Press, 2000), 395.

45. Albert J. Raboteau, *Slave Religion*, 215–16. The origin of this practice is uncertain; it may have also represented the presence of the Spirit or spirits at the secret gatherings.

46. Ibid., 217; see also Sobel, *Trabelin' On*, 171.

47. Sobel, *Trabelin' On*, 171–72.

48. Raboteau, *Slave Religion*, 219.

49. W.E.B. DuBois, *The Negro Church* (Atlanta: Atlanta University Press, 1898), 5, cited in Thomas, *African American Preaching*, 20.

50. Raboteau, *Slave Religion*, 232; see also Thomas, *African American Preaching*, 20.

51. Allen Dwight Callahan, *The Talking Book: African Americans and the Bible* (New Haven: Yale University Press, 2006), 11.

52. Ibid., 14.

53. Ibid., 16.

54. Ibid., 19.

55. Luke A. Powery, "Steelman Lecture," School of Divinity, Wake Forest University, September 23, 2013.

56. Ibid. See also Luke A. Powery, *Dem Dry Bones: Preaching, Death and Hope* (Minneapolis: Fortress Press, 2012).

57. Johnson, *God Struck Me Dead*, 21.

58. William H. Myers, *God's Yes Was Louder Than My No: Rethinking the African-American Call to Ministry* (Grand Rapids: William B. Eerdmans Publishing Company, 1994), 24–35.

59. Ibid., 36.

60. Richardson, *Dark Salvation*, 68.

61. Ibid.

62. Ibid., 70.

63. Jarena Lee, *The Life and Religious Experience of Jarena Lee, a Coloured Lady, Giving an Account of her call to Preach the Gospel*, in *Sisters of the Spirit: Three Black Women's Autobiographies of the Nineteenth Century*, ed. William L. Andrews (Bloomington, IN: Indiana University Press, 1986), 29. Emphasis original.

64. Ibid., 33–34.

65. Ibid., 35.

66. Ibid., 36.

67. Ibid., 5–6.

68. Ibid., 37.

69. Thomas, *African American Preaching*, 22.

70. Richardson, *Dark Salvation*, 180.

71. Quoted in Thomas, *African American Preaching*, 41.

72. Ibid.

73. W. E. B. DuBois, "Of the Faith of the Fathers," in *The Souls of the Black Folk* (Greenwich, CT: Fawcett Publications, Inc., 1961), 141.

74. Ibid., 181.

75. Ibid., 183.

76. Ibid., 141.

77. Ibid., 141–42.

78. C. Eric Lincoln and Lawrence H. Mamiya, "The Black Sacred Cosmos," in *Down by the Riverside: Readings in African American Religion*, ed. Larry G. Murphy (New York: New York University Press, 2000), 33.

79. Ibid., 34.

80. Ibid.

81. Ibid., 35.

82. Leon F. Litwack, "The Gospel and the Primer," in Murphy, *Down by the Riverside*, 113.

83. Mitchell, *Black Belief: Folk Beliefs of Blacks in America and West Africa* (New York: Harper & Row, Publishers, 1975), 127.

84. Ibid., 132, 135.

85. James H. Cone, *A Black Theology of Liberation* (New York: J. B. Lippincott Company, 1970), 55.

86. Ibid., 54.

87. James H. Cone, "Black Theology as Liberation Theology," 398.

88. "Deconstructing Constructionism," http://noteasybeingred.tumblr.com/post/206038114/alice–walkers–definition–of–a–womanist–from–in.

89. Ibid. Emphasis original.

90. Toinette M. Eugene, "Lifting as We Climb": Womanist Theorizing about Religion and the Family," in Murphy, *Down by the Riverside*, 442.

91. Stephanie Y. Mitchem, *Introducing Womanist Theology* (Maryknoll, NY: Orbis Books, 2002), ix.

92. Ibid., 23, 46.

93. Ibid., 47.

94. Ibid., 49.

95. Linda E. Thomas, "Womanist Theological, Epistemological, and a New Anthropological Paradigm," *Cross Currents*, www.crosscurrents.org/thomas.htm.

96. Emilie M. Townes, "Á Womanist Perspective on Spirituality in Leadership," *Theological Education* 37 (Autumn 2001): 83.

97. Ibid., 82–83.

98. Kelly Brown Douglas, *Sexuality and the Black Church: A Womanist Perspective* ((Maryknoll, NY: Orbis Books, 1999), 84, citing Toinette Eugene, "While Love is Unfashionable: Ethical Implications of Black Spirituality and Sexuality," in *Sexuality and the Sacred: Sources for Theological Reflection* (Louisville: Westminster John Knox Press, 1994), 106.

99. Townes, "A Womanist Perspective on Spirituality in Leadership", 100.

100. James Marsh, *God's Long Summer: Stories of Faith and Civil Rights* (Princeton, NJ: Princeton University Press, 1997), 46–47.

101. Ibid., 21–22.

102. Ibid., 24.

103. Ibid., 28.

104. Martin Luther King Jr., *Stride toward Freedom: The Montgomery Story* (New York: Harper & Row, 1958), 114–15.

105. James Baldwin, *The Fire Next Time* (New York: A Dell Book, 1962), 48.

106. Ibid., 44–45.

107. Ibid., 46–47.

108. Ibid., 57–58.

109. Ibid., 59–60.

110. James Melvin Washington, *Frustrated Fellowship: The Black Baptist Quest for Social Power* (Macon, GA: Mercer University Press, 1986), 204–5. Washington's conclusions were originally directed at black Baptist traditions, but they have implications for the larger movement of African-American religious experience.

8. Experiencing the Full Gospel

1. John Wesley, *The Principles of a Methodist* (1742), in *The Works of John Wesley* 9, ed. Rupert E. Davies (Nashville: Abingdon Press, 1989), 64.

2. Ibid., 64–65. Wesley himself added a parenthetical note regarding the possibility of multiple "degrees of justification." See note 12, page 64. Emphasis original.

3. Ibid., 54. See 1 Thess. 5:23; 1 John 1:7; and 1 John 1:5, 7.

4. Ibid., 55.

5. Donald W. Dayton, "Pneumatological Issues in the Holiness Movement," *Greek Theological Review* 31, nos. 3–4, (1986): 373.

6. John Wesley, "Christian Perfection," in John Wesley, *Sermons on Several Occasions* (London: Wesleyan Methodist Book Room, n. d.), 579.

7. Charles G. Finney, *Lectures on Revivals of Religion* (Oberlin, OH: E. J. Goodeich, 1868), 428.

8. Ibid., 430.

9. Donald Dayton, *Discovering an Evangelical Heritage* (Grand Rapids: Baker Academic, 1988).

10. Ann Taves, *Fits, Trances, and Visions: Experiencing Religion and Explaining Experience from Wesley to James* (Princeton: Princeton University Press, 1999), 232. Taves also cites A. McLean and J. W. Eaton, eds., *Penuel, or, Face to Face with God* (New York: W. C. Palmer, 1869; reprint ed., New York: Garland Pub. Co., 1984) 5–7.

11. Robert Mapes Anderson, *Vision of the Disinherited: The Making of American Pentecostalism* (New York: Oxford University Press, 1979), 30–34.

12. Ibid., 34.

13. Ibid.

14. Thomas Oden, "Introduction," in *Phoebe Palmer: Selected Writings* (New York: Paulist Press, 1988), 5–6.

15. Ibid., 6.

16. Ibid., 9–10, citing Charles Edward White, *The Beauty of Holiness: Phoebe Palmer as Theologian, Revivalist, Feminist, and Humanitarian* (Grand Rapids: Francis Asbury Press, Zondervan, 1986), 232. John Fletcher was an associate of John Wesley who was one of the early Methodists who spoke of the baptism of the Spirit. He believed that history had moved through three "dispensations" that mirrored the Trinity: the Father was reflected in the Old Testament era; the Son in the incarnation era; and the Spirit, a dispensation that ran from Pentecost to the return of Christ. Pentecost was the "moment of entire sanctification for the disciples." See Donald W. Dayton, "Pneumatological Issues in the Holiness Movement," 376–77.

17. Charles Edwin Jones, *Perfect Persuasion: The Holiness Movement and American Methodism, 1867–1936* (Metuchen, NJ: Scarecrow Press, Inc., 1974), 4.

18. Phoebe Palmer, "Entire Devotion to God," *Phoebe Palmer: Selected Writings*, 188.

19. Phoebe Palmer, "The Way of Holiness" (1843), *Phoebe Palmer: Selected Writings*, 178.

20. Phoebe Palmer, "Tongue of Fire on the Daughters of the Lord," *Phoebe Palmer: Selected Writings* (New York: Paulist Press, 1988), 34.

21. Ibid., 39.

22. Phoebe Palmer, "Entire Devotion to God" (1845), *Phoebe Palmer: Selected Writings*, 191.

23. Ibid., 196.

24. Phoebe Palmer, "Refining Processes" (1874), *Phoebe Palmer: Selected Writings*, 323. Emphasis original.

25. Ibid., 324.

26. Phoebe Palmer, ed., *Pioneer Experiences; Or, the Gift of Power Received By Faith* (New York: W. C. Palmer, 1868), reprint New York: Garland Publishing, Inc., 1984), v.

27. Hannah Whitall Smith, *The Unselfishness of God and How I Discovered It: A Spiritual Autobiography* (New York: Fleming H. Revell, 1903), in http://www.alampthatburns.net/smith/unselfishness.

28. Ibid., chapter 26, n.p.

29. Ibid. Emphasis original.

30. Ibid.

31. Hannah Whitall Smith, *The Christian's Secret of a Happy Life* (Published by Christian Witness Co.), 6., http://www.mtolivescog.org/uploads/4/9/6/8/4968655/the_christian_secret_of__happy_life.pdf.

32. Ibid., 21.

33. Ibid., 22.

34. Ibid., 28.

35. Hannah Whitall Smith, *The Unselfishness of God*, chapter 30, n.p. See also Melvin Easterday Dieter, *The Holiness Revival of the Nineteenth Century*, 161.

36. Melvin Easterday Dieter, *The Holiness Revival of the Nineteenth Century*, 163–64.

37. Ibid., 186. Dieter suggests that Robert Smith's "fall" was due to emotional collapse that came to be associated with moral compromise. Others continue to insist that he was guilty of certain sexually-related indiscretions. See G. Richard Fisher, "The Secret of a Christian Classic: The Unhappy Life of Hannah Whitall Smith," http://www.pro.org/hwsmith.htm.

38. Charles Edwin Jones, *Perfect Persuasion*, 8–9.

39. Ibid., 9.

40. Ibid., 10-11.

41. Melvin Easterday Dieter, *The Holiness Revival of the Nineteenth Century*, 106.

42. Ibid., 116–17. Dieter cites *Methodist* IX (August 4, 1897), 8–9, as quoted from the Waco, Texas, *Telegram*. See note 81.

43. Robert Mapes Anderson, *Vision of the Disinherited*, 39.

44. Ibid., 35.

45. Donald W. Dayton, "Pneumatological Issues in the Holiness Movement," 363. Founders included Daniel S. Warner, John P. Brooks, and B. A. Washburn. See Melvin Dieter, *The Holiness Revival of the Nineteenth Century*, 246–75.

46. Donald W. Dayton, *Theological Roots of Pentecostalism* (Grand Rapids: Francis Asbury Press, 1987), 15–17.

47. Ibid., 18. The "Statement of Truth" was taken from the "Statement of Faith" of the National Association of Evangelicals.

48. Robert Mapes Anderson, *Vision of the Disinherited*, 43.

49. Ibid. Founded in England in 1875 the Keswick Convention became an international organization of evangelicals committed to biblical inspiration, "the deity of our Lord and Saviour Jesus Christ," and "the Personality of the Holy Spirit" in experiencing the deeper life of Christian discipleship. See Charles Price and Ian Randall, *Transforming Keswick* (Carlisle, UK: OM Publishing, 2000), 13.

50. Grant Wacker, *Heaven Below: Early Pentecostals and American Culture* (Cambridge, UK: Cambridge University Press, 2001), 10.

51. Ibid., 10–11. Emphasis original.

52. Ibid., 13.

53. Robert Mapes Anderson, *Vision of the Disinherited*, 47.

54. Ibid., 49.

55. Charles F. Parham, "The Latter Rain" *Apostolic Faith* (December 1950–January 1951), 3, in William K. Kay and Anne E. Dyer, editors, *Pentecostal and Charismatic Studies, a Reader* (London: SCM Press, 2004), 11.

56. Grant Wacker, *Heaven Below: Early Pentecostals and American Culture*, 72.

57. Ibid., 24–25.

58. Robert Mapes Anderson, *Vision of the Disinherited*, 59–60.

59. "Pentecost Has Come," *The Apostolic Faith* (Los Angeles) I (September 1906), 1. Bonnie Brae Street was the first location of the group before they moved to 312 Azusa Street.

60. Robert Mapes Anderson, *Vision of the Disinherited*, 65.

61. Allan Anderson, *An Introduction to Pentecostalism* (Cambridge, UK: Cambridge University Press, 2004), 40–41. Allan Anderson reports that Charles Fox Parham was not permitted to become an "overseer" of the Azusa chapel and made certain racist remarks that included his assertion that he was sickened "to see white people imitating unintelligent, crude negroism of the Southland, and laying it on the Holy Ghost." Seymour also suffered rejection by other white Pentecostal leaders who set up competing and largely segregated ministries. (See page 40ff and Robert Mapes Anderson, *Vision of the Disinherited*, 190.)

62. Frank Bartlemann, *Azusa Street* (Plainfield, NJ: Bridge Publishing, 1925), cited in William K. Kay and Anne E. Dyer, editors, *Pentecostal and Charismatic Studies*, 15.

63. Ibid., 16.

64. "William H. Durham (1873–1912), www.revival-library.org/pensketches/am_pentecostals/durham.

65. Allan Anderson, *An Introduction to Pentecostalism*, 46–47. Anderson suggests that there were significant racial overtones to the "Finished Work" movement since the large majority of its devotees were white. Thus the controversy had both theological and racial implications for early Pentecostals. Anderson writes that "by 1914 some 60 per cent of all North American Pentecostals had embraced Durham's position."

66. Vinson Synan, *The Holiness Pentecostal Movement in the United States* (Grand Rapids: William B. Eerdmans Publishing Company, 1971), 118n.

67. Donald R. Wheelock, "Spirit Baptism in American Pentecostal Thought," (Ann Arbor: University Microfilms International, 1983), 111, citing Robert M. Anderson, "A Social History of the Early Twentieth Century Pentecostal Movement." (PhD dissertation, Columbia University, 1969), 265.

68. Grant Wacker, *Heaven Below*, 41.

69. Ibid., 41–42.

70. Vinson Synan, *The Holiness Pentecostal Movement*, 122.

71. Allan Anderson, *An Introduction to Pentecostalism*, 44–45.

72. Donald W. Dayton, *Theological Roots of Pentecostalism*, 16.

73. Ibid., 124.

74. Ibid., 126.

75. Ibid., 127–30; see also Robert Mapes Anderson, *Vision of the Disinherited,* 93.

76. Robert Mapes Anderson, *Vision of the Disinherited,* 93.

77. Ibid., 123.

78. G. B. Cashwell, "Pentecost in North Carolina," *The Apostolic Faith* (January 1907), 1.

79. Vinson Synan, *The Holiness Pentecostal Movement in the United States,* 129–33.

80. Ibid., 134.

81. Deborah Vansau McCauley, *Appalachian Mountain Religion* (Urbana: University of Illinois Press, 1995), 15–25.

82. Ibid., 8.

83. Ibid., 227.

84. Ibid.

85. Ibid., 315.

86. Jimmy Morrow with Ralph W. Hood, editor, *Handling Serpents, Pastor Jimmy Morrow's Narrative History of His Appalachian Jesus' Name Tradition* (Macon, GA: Mercer University Press, 2005), 16–18.

87. Mary Lee Daugherty, "Serpent Handlers: When the Sacrament Comes Alive," in Bill J. Leonard, ed., *Christianity in Appalachia: Profiles in Regional Pluralism* (Knoxville: University of Tennessee Press, 1999), 148–50. The passage from Mark's gospel around which serpent handlers base their unique religious experience is not found in the earliest extant manuscripts of the New Testament. Scholars refer to this passage as the "long ending," or the "false ending" of Mark, reflecting a later addition to the original gospel text.

88. Jimmy Morrow with Ralph W. Hood, *Handling Serpents,* 168.

89. Karen W. Carden and Robert W. Pelton, *Persecuted Prophets* (South Brunswick, NJ: A. S. Barnes, 1976), 155; see also Bill J. Leonard, "The Bible and Serpent-handling," in Peter W. Williams, e., *Perspectives in American Religion and Culture,* (Oxford, UK: Blackwell Publishers, 1999), 234.

90. Mary Lee Daugherty, "Serpent-handling as Sacrament," *Theology Today* (October 1976); David Kimbrough *Taking Up Serpents* (Chapel Hill: University of North Carolina Press, 1995); Ralph W. Hood Jr., and W. Paul Williamson, *Them That Believe: The Power and Meaning of the Christian Serpent-Handling Tradition* (Berkley: University of California Press, 2008).

91. Aimee Semple McPherson, *This Is That: Personal Experiences, Sermons and Writings of Aimee Semple McPherson* (New York: Garland Publishing, 1985—original in 1919), 18, 20–25.

92. Ibid., 39.

93. Ibid., 42.

94. Aimee Semple McPherson, *This Is That*, 47. Emphasis original.

95. Priscilla Pope-Levison, *Turn the Pulpit Loose: Two Centuries of American Women Evangelists* (New York: Palgrave Macmillan, 2004), 191. Emphasis original.

96. Ibid., 193.

97. Aimee Semple McPherson, *This Is That*, 133.

98. "Our Story: The History and Future of the Foursquare Church," www.foursquare.org/about/aimee_semple_mcpherson/p1-5.

99. Aimee Semple McPherson, "Covet Earnestly Spiritual Gifts," in *This Is That*, 578.

100. Ibid., 582.

101. Ibid., 584.

102. Allan Anderson, *An Introduction to Pentecostalism*, 57.

103. Priscilla Pope-Levison, *Turn the Pulpit Loose*, 200.

104. Donald Dayton, *Theological Roots of Pentecostalism*, 137; see also David Edwin Harrell, *All Things Are Possible: The Healing and Charismatic Revivals in Modern America* (Bloomington: Indiana University Press, 1975), 13–14.

105. Ibid., 126.

106. Ibid, 129–30.

107. Robert Mapes Anderson, *Vision of the Disinherited*, 95.

108. Ibid.

109. David Edwin Harrell, *All Things Are Possible*, 20.

110. Ibid., 25.

111. C. Douglas Weaver, *The Healer-Prophet, William Marrion Branham: A Study of the Prophetic in American Pentecostalism* (Macon, GA: Mercer University Press, 1987), 27.

112. David Edwin Harrell, *All Things Are Possible*, 27–28. Emphasis original.

113. Ibid., 53–83.

114. C. Douglas Weaver, *The Healer-Prophet*, 63.

115. Ibid.

116. David Edwin Harrell, *All Things Are Possible*, 38–39; and C. Douglas Weaver, *The Healer-Prophet*, 80–81.

117. C. Douglas Weaver, *The Healer-Prophet*, 152–53; and David Edwin Harrell, *All Things Are Possible*, 163–64.

118. David Edwin Harrell, *All Things Are Possible*, 165.

119. Ibid., 86. Harrell lists a number of healing evangelists who gained fame in various revival contexts in the mid-to- late twentieth century. These included A. A. Allen, W. V. Grant, Kenneth Hagen, David Nunn, Jack Coe, T. L. Osborn, and Oral Roberts.

120. Ibid., 105.

121. Ibid.

122. Jonathan L. Walton, *Watch This! The Ethics and Aesthetics of Black Televangelism* (New York: New York University Press, 2009), xiii.

123. Ibid., xi-xii.

124. Harrell, *All Things*, 158.

125. Walton, *Watch This!* 94.

126. Gary E. Gilley, "The Word-Faith Movement," in www.rapidnet.com/jbeard/bdm/Psychology/char/more/w-f.htm, 1.

127. Ibid.

128. Mike Murdock, "Seven Minutes of Wisdom," www.mikemurdock.com, June 13, 2007.

129. Ibid.

130. Ibid.

131. "Makin' Da Money... Anyway I Can," www.forgottenword.org/Murdock.html

132. Walton, *Watch This!* 109.

133. Milmon F. Harrison, "Prosperity Here and Now," www.beliefnet.com/story/25/story.

134. Osteen dropped out of undergraduate studies at Oral Roberts University after one semester. He notes that his fifteen years of work with his father, John Osteen, the founder and pastor of Lakewood Church, constituted his grassroots theological education. John Osteen founded Lakewood Church in 1959 after breaking with the Southern Baptists over issues related to charismatic gifts and the baptism of the Holy Spirit. The elder Osteen was greatly influenced by the Pentecostalism of Oral Roberts and his approach to church growth and "seed faith," an early stage of the so-called Prosperity Gospel.

135. "Osteen denies Christ on national TV," December 22, 2005, http://www.apostasywatch.com/Wolves/WolfReports/JoelOsteen/OsteendeniesChristonnationalTV/tabid/169/Default.aspx.

136. "CNN Larry King Live," December 22, 2006, http://transcripts.cnn.com/TRANSCRIPTS/0612/22/lkl.01.html.

137. David Edwin Harrell, Jr., *All Things are Possible: The Healing and Charismatic Revivals in Modern America* (Bloomington: Indiana University Press, 1975), 136, 187.

138. Joel Osteen, *Your Best Life Now* (New York: Warner Faith, 2004), 260.

9. Contemplation (and Controversy) in a World of Action

1. Jay P. Dolan, *The American Catholic Experience* (Notre Dame, IN: University of Notre Dame Press, 1992), 224.

2. "The Dogmatic Constitution on the Church," *Documents of Vatican II*, ed. Walter M. Abbott (New York: Guild Press, 1966), 33.

3. Ibid.

4. William James, *Varieties of Religious Experience* (New York: The Modern Library, 1929), 79–80.

5. Ibid., 80.

6. Joseph P. Chinnici, ed., *Devotion to the Holy Spirit in American Catholicism* (New York: Paulist Press, 1985), 46.

7. Jay P. Dolan, *In Search of an American Catholicism: A History of Religion and Culture in Tension* (New York: Oxford University Press, 2002), 62, citing O. A. Brownson, *The Convert or Leaves From My Experience* (New York: Edward Dunigan and Brother, 1857), 359–60.

8. Robert D. Cross, *The Emergence of Liberal Catholicism in America* (Chicago: Quadrangle Paperbacks, 1968), 59.

9. Theodore Maynard, *The Story of American Catholicism*, vol. 1 (Garden City, NY: Image Books, 1960), 29.

10. Ibid., 32.

11. Dolan, *The American Catholic Experience*, 48.

12. Ibid., 52.

13. Ibid., 55.

14. Ibid., 57–64.

15. John Farina, ed., *Isaac T. Hecker: The Diary, Romantic Religion in Ante-Bellum America* (New York: Paulist Press), 47.

16. Dolan, *In Search of an American Catholicism*, 6–9.

17. Ibid., 50. For a discussion of "lay trusteeship" in Catholic parishes, see Jay P. Dolan, *The American Catholic Experience*, 110–11, 165–68, 178–79.

18. Farina, ed., *Isaac T. Hecker: The Diary*, 46.

19. Ibid.

20. Dolan, *In Search of an American Catholicism*, 13.

21. Dolan, *The American Catholic Experience*, 91.

22. Ibid., 93.

23. Dolan, *In Search of an American Catholicism*, 24.

24. Ibid., 51–52.

25. Chinnici, *Devotion to the Holy Spirit in American Catholicism*, 8.

26. Amanda Porterfield, *The Transformation of American Religion* (New York: Oxford University Press, 2001), 63.

27. Ibid., 63–64.

28. Ibid., 10–11.

29. Ibid., 15, citing Otto Zardetti, *Special Devotion to the Holy Ghost, A Manual* (Milwaukee: Hoffman Brothers, 1888), 135–36.

30. Ann Taves, *The Household of Faith: Roman Catholic Devotions in Mid-Nineteenth-Century America* (Notre Dame, IN: University of Notre Dame Press, 1986), vii.

31. Donald Attwater, ed., *A Catholic Dictionary*, 3rd ed. (New York: MacMillan Co., 1961), s.v. "Devotions, Popular," cited in Taves, *The Household of Faith*, 22.

32. Taves, *The Household of Faith*, 14–15, 24. Scapulars were essentially "two small pieces of woolen cloth united with strings and worn over the shoulders" as a sign of devotion to the Virgin or her Son. See ibid., 37–38.

33. Ibid., 28–29.

34. Ibid., 31.

35. Ibid., 33–34.

36. Christopher J. Ruddy, "Contemporary Catholics on Traditional Options," in *America*, March 3, 2003, 8–9.

37. Taves, *The Household of Faith*, 36–37.

38. Sally Cunneen, "Contemporary Catholics on Traditional Options," in *America*, March 3, 2003, 9. The doctrine of the Immaculate Conception of the Blessed Virgin Mary means that Mary by a "singular act" of God was untainted from conception by the curse of original sin.

39. *Elizabeth Seton: Selected Writings*, ed. Ellin Kelly and Annabelle Melville (New York: Paulist Press, 1987), 57.

40. Taves, *The Household of Faith*, 41–42.

41. Chinnici, *Devotion to the Holy Spirit in American Catholicism*, 17. Chinnici lists additional devotional works that illustrate Holy Spirit devotion in the late 19th century, including: John Joseph Keane, *Pastoral Letter*; Keane, *Sodality Manual* (1879); Thomas Scott Preston, *Divine Paraclete* (1879); Otto Zardetti, *Devotion to the Holy Ghost* (1888); Thomas F. Hopkins, *Novena of Sermons on the Holy Ghost* (1901).

42. Ibid., 22, citing Henry Edward Manning, *The Internal Mission of the Holy Ghost*, 3rd ed. (New York: D. & J. Sadlier & Co., 1885), 26, 63, 74–75.

43. Ibid., 25. The Paulist Order was approved in 1858 with its first church and "foundation" in New York City. Its primary work involved evangelization, largely in the context of American culture and society. To extend that evangelization Hecker founded a publishing house known as Paulist Press in 1866.

44. Farina, *Isaac T. Hecker The Diary*, 97.

45. Chinnici, *Devotion to the Holy Spirit in American Catholicism*, 26.

46. Farina, *Isaac T. Hecker The Diary*, 221.

47. Chinnici, *Devotion to the Holy Spirit in American Catholicism*, 28–29.

48. Farina, *Isaac Hecker The Diary*, 145.

49. Ibid., 53–54; and Taves, *The Household of Faith*, 87. Taves notes that Protestants too during this period promoted a piety that connected images of the Divine parent with those of earthly and familial parents.

50. Taves, *The Household of Faith*, 111.

51. Farina, *Isaac T. Hecker The Diary*, 56.

52. Jay P. Dolan, *Catholic Revivalism: The American Experience 1830–1900* (Notre Dame, IN: University of Notre Dame Press, 1978), 13.

53. Ibid., 14.

54. Ibid., 19.

55. Ibid., 18.

56. Ibid., 77–78.

57. Ibid., 58.

58. Randall M. Miller, "A Church in Cultural Captivity: Some Speculations on Catholic Identity in the Old South," in *Catholics in the Old South*, ed. Randall M. Miller and Jon L. Wakelyn (Macon, GA: Mercer University Press, 1983), 43.

59. Dolan, *Catholic Revivalism*, 168.

60. Ibid., 170.

61. Ibid., 175.

62. Porterfield, *The Transformation of American Religion*, 61.

63. This study makes no attempt to provide the history of Catholicism globally or nationally during the twentieth century, except as it illustrates the nature of religious experience in the Church during this period. Summaries of the larger developments in Catholic history are found in such studies as: Jay P. Dolan, *The American Catholic Experience*; Jay P. Dolan, *In Search of an American Catholicism*; James Hennesey, *American Catholics* (New York: Oxford University Press, 1981); Robert D. Cross, *The Emergence of Liberal Catholicism in America*; Garry Wills, *Bare Ruined Choirs: Doubt, Prophecy, and Radical Religion* (New York: A Delta Book, 1972); Peter A. Huff, *Allen Tate and the Catholic Revival* (New York: Paulist Press, 1996); and Russell Shaw, *American Church: The Remarkable Rise, Meteoric Fall, and Uncertain Future of Catholicism in America* (San Francisco: Ignatius Press, 2013).

64. Huff, *Alan Tate and the Catholic Revival*, 11–12.

65. Ibid., 12.

66. Ibid., citing "The Catholic Revival, *Commonweal*, 4 March 1931, 478.

67. Ibid., 13–16.

68. Ibid., 17–18.

69. Peter S. Hawkins, *The Language of Grace* (New York: Cowley, 1983), 1–2.

70. Ibid., 9.

71. Flannery O'Connor, "The River," in *The Complete Stories* (New York: Farrar, Straus and Giroux, 1971), 168.

72. Ibid., 173–74.

73. Hawkins, *The Language of Grace*, 39.

74. Wills, *Bare Ruined Choirs: Doubt, Prophecy, and Radical Religion*, 45.

75. Ibid., 48.

76. Ibid., 48–49; and Dorothy Day, *The Long Loneliness: An Autobiography* (San Francisco: Harper & Row, 1952), 224.

77. Day, *The Long Loneliness*, 10.

78. Porterfield, *The Transformation of American Religion*, 76.

79. Day, *The Long Loneliness*, 204.

80. Huff, *Alan Tate and the Catholic Revival*, 21–25.

81. Mark Gibbard, "The Adaptation of Historic Spirituality for Today," in *The Study of Spirituality*, ed. Cheslyn Jones, Geoffrey Wainwright, and Edward Yarnold, SJ (New York: Oxford University Press, 1986), 577.

82. Thomas Merton, "Unpublished, from the Original Manuscript of *The Seven Storey Mountain*," in *A Thomas Merton Reader*, ed. Thomas P. McDonnell, rev. ed. (Garden City, NY: Image Books, 1974), 156.

83. Thomas Merton, *The Sign of Jonas* (Garden City, NY: Image Books, 1956), 342–43.

84. Raymond Bailey, *Thomas Merton on Mysticism* (Garden City, NY: Image Books, 1975), 114, citing Thomas Merton, *What is Contemplation?* (London: Burns, Oates & Washbourne, 1950), 20.

85. Ibid., 115.

86. Thomas Merton, *Mystics and Zen Masters*, (New York: Farrar, Straus and Giroux, 1961), viii.

87. Shaul Magid, "Monastic Liberation as Counter-Cultural Critique in the Life and Thought of Thomas Merton," *Cross Currents* 49 (Winter 1999/2000): 447.

88. Robert D. Putnam and David E. Campbell, *American Grace: How Religion Divides and Unites Us* (New York: Simon & Schuster, 2010), 140–48, 296–307.

89. Portions of this paragraph are taken from Bill J. Leonard, "Thomas Merton, Spiritual Identity, and Religious Dialogue: The Walls of New Freedom," in *Perspectives in Religious Studies* 38, no. 2 (2011): 197.

90. Porterfield, *The Transformation of American Religion*, 87.

91. Abbott, *The Documents of Vatican II*, 141.

92. Porterfield, *The Transformation of American Religion*, 108, 110.

10. The Christ of Many Experiences

1. Miller's early predictions encompassed a broad date from March 1843 to March 1844; when the "Great Disappointment" occurred, Miller set a specific date of October 1844. That date passed as the "Second Great Disappointment." See Wayne

R. Judd, "William Miller: Disappointed Prophet," in *The Disappointed: Millerism and Millenarianism in the Nineteenth Century*, ed. Ronald L. Numbers and Jonathan M. Butler (Bloomington: Indiana University Press, 1987), 17–35.

2. William Miller, *Evidence from Scripture and History of the Second Coming of Christ* (1842), http://www.sacred-texts.com/chr/esc/esc21.htm.

3. Jonathan M. Butler, "The Making of a New Order: Millerism and the Origins of Seventh-day Adventism," in Numbers and Butler, *The Disappointed*, 202–3.

4. Ibid., 203.

5. George M. Marsden, *Fundamentalism and American Culture* (New York: Oxford University Press, 1980), 43–71; and Timothy P. Weber, *Living in the Shadow of the Second Coming: American Premillennialism 1875–1925* (Chicago: University of Chicago Press, 1979), 17–42.

6. J. Gresham Machen, *Christianity and Liberalism* (New York: The MacMillan Company, 1923), 159.

7. Ibid., 172. Emphasis mine.

8. Machen, *Christianity and Liberalism*, 21.

9. William R. Hutchison, *The Modernist Impulse in American Protestantism* (New York: Oxford University Press, 1976), 264.

10. Machen, *Christianity and Liberalism*, 122–38.

11. Martin E. Marty, *Modern American Religion*, vol. 2: *The Noise of Conflict, 1919–1941* (Chicago: University of Chicago Press, 1991), 163.

12. Machen, *Christianity and Liberalism*, 155.

13. Ibid., 156.

14. C. Allyn Russell, *Voices of American Fundamentalism* (Philadelphia: Westminster Press, 1976), 213.

15. H. M. Sydenstricker, "The Science of Conversion," in *The Fundamentals*, vol. 4, ed. R. A. Torrey, A. C. Dixon et al. (Grand Rapids: Baker Book House, [1917] 1972), 49, 52.

16. Ibid., 53.

17. Ibid., 58.

18. Joel A. Carpenter, *Revive Us Again: The Reawakening of American Fundamentalism* (New York: Oxford University Press, 1997), 76–77.

19. Russell, *Voices of American Fundamentalism*, 144; and Machen, *Christianity and Liberalism*, 7.

20. H. Shelton Smith, Robert T. Handy, and Lefferts A. Loetscher, eds., *American Christianity: An Historical Interpretation with Representative Documents*, vol. 2 (New York: Charles Scribner's Sons, 1963), 257. The early advocates of this christocentric liberal approach often spoke of "the Fatherhood of God and the Brotherhood of Man," a phrase that was later re-formed to be more gender inclusive.

21. Nancey Murphy, *Beyond Liberalism & Fundamentalism: How Modern and*

Postmodern Philosophy Set the Theological Agenda (Valley Forge: Trinity Press International, 1996), 23.

22. Ibid.

23. William Adams Brown, *Christian Theology in Outline* (New York: Charles Scribner's Sons, 1907), 100; and Smith, Handy, and Loetscher, *American Christianity*, vol. 2, 257.

24. Ibid., 408.

25. Ibid., 409.

26. William Newton Clarke, *An Outline of Christian Theology* (New York: Charles Scribner's sons, 1914), 18.

27. Ibid.

28. Ibid., 19.

29. Ibid., 20.

30. Hutchison, *The Modernist Impulse in American Protestantism*, 119.

31. Harry Emerson Fosdick, *The Living of These Days: An Autobiography* (New York: Harper & Row, Publishers, 1956), 66–67.

32. Ibid., 234.

33. Ibid., 235.

34. Harry Emerson Fosdick, *What Is Vital in Religion* (New York: Harper & Brothers, 1955), 43.

35. Grant Wacker, *Augustus Strong and the Dilemma of Historical Consciousness* (Macon: Mercer University Press, 1985), 17; and George Marsden, *Understanding Fundamentalism and Evangelicalism* (Grand Rapids: William B. Eerdmans Publishing Co., 1991), 125.

36. Donald Bloesch, *The Christian Life and Salvation* (Colorado Springs: Helmers and Howard, 1991), 138.

37. Donald Bloesch, *The Future of Evangelical Christianity* (Colorado Springs: Helmers and Howard, 1988), 5.

38. James Davison Hunter, *Evangelicals, The Coming Generation* (Chicago: University of Chicago Press, 1987), 183. Emphasis original.

39. Ibid., 185.

40. John MacArthur, *The Gospel according to Jesus* (Grand Rapids: Zondervan, 1988), xiv.

41. Ibid., 15

42. Ibid., 16.

43. Ibid., 21.

44. Ibid.

45. Ibid., 67.

46. Ibid., 94.

47. Alex Murashko, "After John MacArthur's Strange Fire," *Christian Post*, Oct. 23, 2013, http://www.redletterchristians.org/john-macarthur-attacks-charismatic-movement-strange-fire-conference/.

48. Bruce and Marshall Shelley, *The Consumer Church* (Downers Grove, IL: InterVarsity Press, 1993), 204.

49. Ibid., 205.

50. George Barna, *Marketing the Church* (Colorado Springs: Navpress, 1988), 16.

51. Ibid. 21.

52. Ibid., 53.

53. Ibid., 150.

54. Ibid., 151.

55. Ibid., 17.

56. Douglas Webster, *Selling Jesus: What's Wrong with Marketing the Church* (Downers Grove, IL: InterVarsity Press, 1992), 16.

57. Ibid., 92, citing Stanley Hauerwas and William Willimon, *Resident Aliens* (Nashville: Abingdon Press, 1989), 33.

58. Ibid.

59. Carol George, *God's Salesman: A Life of Norman Vincent Peale* (New York: Oxford University Press, 1992), 139.

60. Ibid., 134.

61. Ibid., 135.

62. William Dyrness, *How Does America Hear the Gospel?* (Grand Rapids: William B. Eerdmans Publishing Co., 1989), 123.

63. Bruce and Marshall Shelley, *The Consumer Church*, 196.

64. Ibid., 197, citing Robert Schuller, *Self-Esteem: The New Reformation* (Waco, TX: Word Books, 1982).

65. Dyrness, *How Does America Hear The Gospel?*,124.

66. Ibid., 125.

67. Ibid., 129.

68. John MacArthur, *Our Sufficiency in Christ* (Dallas: Word, 1991), 153–54.

69. Ibid., 154.

70. Adelle Banks, "Crystal Cathedral: Robert A. Schuller Says Sibling Rivalry Fueled Downfall," Religious News Service, March 22, 2012, http://www.huffingtonpost.com/2012/03/22/crystal-cathedral-robert-schuller-downfall_n_1368321.html.

71. Bloesch, *The Christian Life and Salvation*, 139.

72. Adrian Rogers, "The Virgin Birth," (audio tape recording, Pastors' Conference, SBC, June 8, 1986).

73. Ibid.

74. John Wright Buckham, *Mysticism and Modern Life* (New York: Abingdon Press, 1915), 21; W. R. Inge, *Mysticism in Religion* (Chicago: University of Chicago Press, 1948), 151.

75. A. S. Martin, "Survey of Recent Literature on Mysticism," *Review of Theology and Philosophy* 8 (August 1912): 69n.

76. Hal L. Bridges, *American Mysticism: From William James to Zen* (New York: Harper & Row, 1970), 9.

77. William James, *The Varieties of Religious Experience* (New York: The Modern Library, 1902), 371–72.

78. Ibid., 371.

79. Ibid., 372.

80. Ibid.

81. Ibid., 388.

82. Ibid., 399.

83. Henry N. Wieman and Bernard E. Meland, *American Philosophies of Religion* (Chicago: Willett, Clarke and Co., 1936), 120–21.

84. Rufus Jones, *Studies in Mystical Religion* (London: MacMillan Co., 1909), xv; and Rufus Jones, *Some Exponents of Mystical Religion* (New York: Abingdon, 1930), 15.

85. Rufus Jones, *The Inner Life* (New York: The MacMillan Co., 1919), 24–25.

86. Ibid., 179; and Rufus Jones, *A Call to What is Vital* (New York: The MacMillan Co., 1948), 64–65.

87. Rufus Jones, *Social Law in the Spiritual World* (New York: George H. Doran, 1923), 134–35.

88. Ibid., 136–37.

89. Elizabeth Gray Vining, *Friend of Life: The Biography of Rufus Jones* (New York: J. B. Lippincott Co., 1958), 260.

90. Rufus Jones, *Pathways to the Reality of God* (New York: The MacMillan Co., 1931), 26.

91. Jones, *Studies in Mystical Religion,* xviii.

92. Ibid., xx.

93. Thomas R. Kelly, *A Testament of Devotion* (New York: Harper & Row, Publishers, 1941), 29.

94. Ibid., 47.

95. Bridges, *American Mysticism*, 47. Emphasis original.

96. Douglas V. Steere, *Dimensions of Prayer* (New York: Woman's Division of Christian Service, the Methodist Church, 1962), 15.

97. Bridges, *American Mysticism*, 51.

98. Ibid., 52. Emphasis original.

99. Ibid., 57.

100. Howard Thurman, *A Strange Freedom: The Best of Howard Thurman on Religious Experience and Public Life*, ed. Walter Earl Fluker and Catherine Tumber (Boston: Beacon Press, 1998), 121–22.

101. Ibid., 123.

102. Bridges, *American Mysticism*, 58.

103. Thurman, *A Strange Freedom*, 13–14, 113–14.

104. Works that bridge those perspectives of mysticism and spirituality include the following: Raymond Bailey, *Thomas Merton on Mysticism* (Garden City, NY: Image Books, 1976); George Kilcourse, *Ace of Freedoms: Thomas Merton's Christ* (Notre Dame: University of Notre Dame Press, 1993); Thomas Merton, *Mystics and Zen Masters* (New York: Farrar; Straus and Giroux, 1961); Henri J. M. Nouwen, *Pray to Live* (Notre Dame: Fides/Claretian, 1972); Henri J. M. Nouwen, *Adam: God's Beloved* (Maryknoll, NY: Orbis Books, 1997); Henri J. M. Nouwen, *The Genesee Diary: Report from a Trappist Monastery* (Garden City, NY: Doubleday, 1976); Henry J. M. Nouwen, *Making All Things New: An Invitation to the Spiritual Life* (San Francisco: Harper and Row, 1981); Kathleen Norris, *The Cloister Walk* (New York: Riverhead Books, 1987); Joan D. Chittister, OSB, *Called to Question: A Spiritual Memoir* (New York: Sheed & Ward, 2004).; E. Glenn Hinson, *A Serious Call to a Contemplative Life-Style* (Philadelphia: Westminster Press, 1974); E. Glenn Hinson, *A Reaffirmation of Prayer* (Nashville: Broadman Press, 1979); E. Glenn Hinson, *A Miracle of Grace: An Autobiography* (Macon, GA: Mercer University Press, 2012).

105. Peter H. Van Ness, ed., *Spirituality and the Secular Quest* (New York: The Crossroad Publishing Company, 1996), 5.

106. Roger S. Gottlieb, *A Spirituality of Resistance* (New York: The Crossroad Publishing Company, 1999), 9.

107. Karen E. Smith, *Christian Spirituality* (London: SCM Press, 2007), 8, 10.

108. Karen E. Smith, *Christian Spirituality*, citing Philip Sheldrake, ed., *The New SCM Dictionary of Christian Spirituality* (London: SCM Press, n.d.), 231.

109. Gottlieb, *The Spirituality of Resistance*, 13. Emphasis original.

110. Norris, *The Cloister Walk*, 5. Emphasis mine.

111. Ibid., 6.

112. Fiona Maddocks, *Hildegard of Bingen: The Woman of Her Age* (New York: Doubleday, 2001), 61.

113. Amanda Porterfield, *The Transformation of American Religion* (New York: Oxford University Press, 2001), 229.

114. Thich Nhat Hanh, *Living Buddha, Living Christ* (New York: Riverhead Books, 1995), 6; see also Porterfield, *The Transformation of American Religion*, 125–58.

115. Ibid., 9.

116. Ibid., 136.

117. Ibid., xxi.

118. Thomas Merton, *Mystics and Zen Masters* (NY: Farrar, Straus and Giroux, 1961), 17.

119. Thomas Merton, "The Significance of the Bhagavad-Gita" in *The Asian Journal of Thomas Merton* (New York; New Directions Publishing Corp., 1973), 353.

120. Porterfield, *The Transformation of American Religion*, 83.

121. Diana Butler Bass, *Christianity after Religion: The End of Church and the Beginning of a New Spiritual Awakening* (San Francisco: HarperOne, 2012), 68.

122. Ibid.

123. Robert D. Putnam and David E. Campbell, *American Grace: How Religion Divides and Unites Us* (New York Simon & Schuster, 2010), 4–5.

124. Ibid., 103–16; 134–60.

125. David Lyon, *Jesus in Disneyland: Religion in Postmodern Times* (Cambridge, UK: Polity Press, 2000), 35, 88. See also Robert Wuthnow, *After Heaven: Spirituality in America since the 1950s* (Berkeley: University of California Press, 1998).

126. Ibid., 50–51.

127. Ibid., 51, citing Robert Withnow, *The Struggle for America's Soul* (Grand Rapids: William B. Eerdmans Publishing Co., 1989), 116.

128. Ibid., 81.

129. Ibid., 84–85.

130. Butler Bass, *Christianity after Religion*, 259.

131. Ibid., 258.

132. Ibid., 244.

133. Ibid., 245; and Harvey Cox, *The Future of Faith* (San Francisco: HarperOne, 2009), 1–20.

134. Cox, *The Future of Faith*, 2. Emphasis original.

135. Ibid., 37.

136. Ibid., 223–24.

137. Phyllis Tickle, *The Great Emergence: How Christianity Is Changing and Why* (Grand Rapids: Baker Books, 2008), 13–17.

138. Ibid., 106.

139. Ibid., 107.

140. Ibid.

141. Thomas Merton, "The Night Spirit and the Dawn Air," in *Conjectures of a Guilty Bystander* (Garden City, NY: Image Books, 1968), 168–69. Emphasis original.

142. Ibid., 169.

143. Ibid., 144; see also Allan M. McMillan, "Seven Lessons for Inter-faith Dialogue and Thomas Merton," *Merton Annual* 15 (November 2002): 205.

144. Porterfield, *The Transformation of American Religion*, 230–31.

Index

CPSIA information can be obtained at www.ICGtesting.com
Printed in the USA
LVOW12*1043271214

420205LV00005B/85/P

9 781630 885854